PILLARS OF FAITH

Nancy Tatom
Ammerman   ·   PILLARS OF FAITH

*American Congregations
and Their Partners*

University of California Press

Berkeley   Los Angeles   London

University of California Press
Berkeley and Los Angeles, California

University of California Press, Ltd.
London, England

©2005 by the Regents of the University of California

Library of Congress Cataloging-in-Publication Data

Ammerman, Nancy Tatom, 1950–
Pillars of faith : American congregations and their
partners / Nancy Tatom Ammerman.
p. cm.
Includes bibliographical references and index.
ISBN 0-520-24311-0 (hardcover : alk. paper)—
ISBN 0-520-24312-9 (pbk. : alk. paper)
1. United States—Religion. 2. Religious institutions—
United States. 3. Religion and sociology—United States.
I. Title.
BL2525.A563   2005
206'.5'0973—dc22   2004017991

Manufactured in the United States of America
14 13 12 11 10 09 08 07 06 05
10 9 8 7 6 5 4 3 2 1

Printed on Ecobook 50 containing a minimum 50%
post-consumer waste, processed chlorine free.
The balance contains virgin pulp, including 25%
Forest Stewardship Council Certified for no old
growth tree cutting, processed either TCF or ECF.
The sheet is acid-free and meets the minimum requirements
of ANSI/NISO Z39.48-1992 (R 1997) (Permanence
of Paper).

CONTENTS

ILLUSTRATIONS

ACKNOWLEDGMENTS

The project that stands behind this book required exactly the sort of network of resources and partnership that the book itself attempts to document. It required the generous financial support of the Lilly Endowment, but also the generous intellectual and moral support of Craig Dykstra and Christopher Coble, our program officers there. It also required the experience and skill of the staff at the Hartford Institute for Religion Research at Hartford Seminary, where the project was headquartered. My colleagues David Roozen and Adair Lummis were consistently challenging and helpful partners, while Mary Jane Ross and Sheryl Wiggins worked their magic in managing everything from mailings to transcripts and data entry. Many of the final details of producing this book were made easier by the able assistance of Karen Rucks at Boston University. From 1997 through 1999 Scott Thumma served as the day-to-day manager of the massive data-gathering enterprise, and he undertook the initial cataloging and sorting of the "partner organization" data as well. His insights and care have helped to make this book possible. Scott is also responsible for creating the Hartford Institute Web site, where background details and research reports on the project can be found.

Our data-gathering partners were located in the communities we studied. Leslie Irvine worked with us in Hartford. Sally Smith Holt and Darren McDaniel worked with Professor Darren Sherkat in Nashville. Annette Prosterman, Sharon Bjorkman, Jon Wiggins, and Debra Washington Mubashir worked with Professors Fred Kniss and Mark Shibley in Chicago. Zoey Heyer Gray worked with Professor

Mary Jo Neitz in Missouri. Daryl Healea worked with Professor Penny Long Marler in Alabama. Sandra Woerle and Doreen Neely worked with the late Professor Patrick McNamara in Albuquerque, and Jill Gill worked with Professor Avery Guest in Seattle. They were a formidable team without whose eyes and ears my window on American congregational life would have been much smaller.

Jill Gill and Daryl Healea also read the first draft of this book and provided the sort of helpful feedback possible only from someone who has "been there." As always, my colleagues on the Congregational Studies Project Team (Jackson Carroll, Carl Dudley, Penny Edgell, Nancy Eiesland, Larry Mamiya, Bill McKinney, Robert Schreiter, Stephen Warner, and Jack Wertheimer) read working chapter drafts and brought their considerable disciplinary expertise and breadth of religious knowledge to helping me sharpen and clarify what I was trying to say.

The arguments made in Chapter 8 were enriched by opportunities to present early versions as part of the 2003 Earl Lectures at Pacific School of Religion and the 2003 Scott Lectures at Brite Divinity School. That chapter was also sharpened by the comments of Stephen Warner. My thinking about the role of congregations in public life, reflected in that chapter, also owes a great deal to the conversations of the "Intellectual Foundations" project sponsored by the Hauser Center at Harvard University.

Another extraordinarily important contribution to this book came from a gathering organized by my colleagues at the Louisville Institute. Associate Director Bill Brosend invited Rev. John Roper, Rev. Peg Nowling, Rev. Dominic Nigrelli, Rabbi Stanley Miles, Rev. Michael Singletary, and Sister Sheryl White to spend a day talking with me about the book. This talented and diverse group of clergy reflected back to me what they heard in the draft they read, and their responses helped to shape the book.

I have also been privileged to have received the careful critique of my fellow sociologists Michael Emerson and Arthur Farnsley. Mark Chaves's contributions went beyond even his helpful reading of my first draft. Throughout the project we have compared data and tried out analyses with each other. His willingness to share the fruits of his National Congregations Study has been a generous scholarly gift for which I am grateful. I am also indebted to Andrew Walsh for reviewing what I had to say about Eastern Orthodoxy and Bryan Froehle for doing the same on Roman Catholicism. Bryan was especially meticulous in reminding me of all the ways my Protestant assumptions were showing. Finally, theologian Ian Markham and historian James Wind each helped me to sharpen the focus and argument of the book. None of these readers, of course, should be blamed for any inaccuracies or lack of clarity that remains.

But the bigger picture is this: over seven hundred people were willing to sit down with us to talk about the organizations they work with; and the passion and vision of those conversations kept me going in the long months of analyzing data and crafting chapters. These are people who are investing their lives in doing "religious work," and it is their story I want to tell. I am grateful for the welcome they gave and for the work they are doing.

CHAPTER ONE · Common Patterns
and Diverse Streams

America's Communities of Faith

At the close of the twentieth century, the United States was, by all accounts, among the most religious of modern Western nations. In spite of high levels of education, technology, and mobility—long assumed to be harbingers of religious decline—almost all Americans said they believed in God, the vast majority identified with a particular religious tradition, well over half actually belonged to a local congregation, and somewhere between 25 and 40 percent of the population (depending on which surveys you believe) showed up for services on any given weekend.[1] Even if we take the more modest estimate that a quarter of the U.S. population regularly attends religious services, that means tens of millions of American adults weekly make their way to the gathering place of a community of faith. This is a book about what they are doing there.

For several decades no one thought much about that question. People studying religion either wrote about the great theological and cultural trends of the day or asked individuals what they believed. Because "church" was officially separate from "state," secular students of American public life usually ignored institutional religion entirely. Ironically, many theologians were no more interested in local congregational life than were most social scientists. Arguing that the true task of God's children was to change the world, they wrote off staid organizations like local congregations as irrelevant at best. Congregations seemed equally irrelevant in a society full of people who proclaimed themselves "not religious, but spiritual." Best not to be too influenced by churches and synagogues, they said.[2] Better to seek out your own spiritual and moral path. American religion, by these accounts, seemed to be carried either in the hearts of individual seekers or in the great theological ideas that have shaped our culture as Judeo-Christian.

While individuals in the United States are indeed free to pursue their own spiritual path, they are also free to gather with like-minded others, to establish religious organizations, and to pursue religious goals. Whether called a parish or an Islamic Center or a synagogue or any of a dozen other names, people in the United States have historically gathered into local religious communities (Holifield 1994). Even though many Americans choose to express their religious longings privately, congregations persist as sites of voluntary collective religious activity. When crisis strikes, even the most autonomous seeker is likely to look for the comforting presence of the gathered faithful; and when persons and families pass significant milestones, the witness of a community still seems important.[3]

In fact, both the great theological traditions and America's spiritual seekers are likely to be anchored in the practices of local congregations. American religion has thrived not because it has freed each individual to pursue his or her own spiritual quest or because uniquely viable theological ideas have taken root here, but because American law and society have created a space for voluntary religious communities.[4] Those local congregations stand at the heart of the pragmatic religious life that flourishes here. People gather to sustain spiritual life and accomplish valuable work. What they experience in congregations may shape their families, vocations, politics, and leisure in new ways. Even religious communities that are not visibly active may indirectly affect the larger world.

Because religious organizations do not enjoy state subsidies (except in the form of certain tax benefits and exemptions), they must depend on their own adherents for institutional survival. The lack of official support for religion, far from dooming it, has produced a proliferation of religious groups unparalleled elsewhere in the world. Groups vary, from venerable Episcopalians to upstart sects and new immigrant religions, and so do the organizations they set up—from local congregations to national publishers to religious social service organizations. People in this country assume that if there is religious work to be done, they can organize voluntarily to do it.

Collectively, these gatherings of religious people have an enormous impact. Congregations combine and channel those individual religious energies into more than the sum of their parts. Their collective material and moral resources are then refined and multiplied by the vast network of suppliers and service agencies, publishers and mission boards—a thriving "religion industry" that makes their own work possible (Wuthnow 1994a). This book is about that collective religious activity, both as it shapes the individuals who participate in it and as it enters the wider social world. If congregations are at the heart of the distinctive religious experience of the United States, it seems advisable to know something about just what it is they are doing and how it is possible for them to do it.

AMERICAN DIVERSITY: IDENTIFYING THE STREAMS

Not all congregations are alike, of course. People set free to create their own local religious gatherings have established some three to four hundred thousand organizations, each with its own history, its own ways of worshiping, and its own ideas about how people ought to live.[5] But there are common patterns in how people have chosen to gather. Some of those patterns seem to come from the contingencies of being a congregation in the American cultural context. Sociologists call this "institutional isomorphism"—organizations that occupy the same "field" (or category) come to look like each other, both in function and in structure. We can recognize that a group is a congregation and not a supermarket, both because of what they do and because they have different kinds of departments and different ways of relating to the public.[6] A congregation might send out an advertising flyer complete with coupons, but we would recognize that as "out of character." Even when an organization differs from others in its field, there is a pattern against which those differences are measured. So, if a congregation does not have a clergyperson or does not worship weekly, everyone recognizes that these are differences to be explained.

The pattern that shapes American congregational life is essentially Protestant in form, but, as Stephen Warner has observed, groups from Catholic to Muslim have adapted their religious practices to the "de facto congregationalism" of the American system (Warner 1993). They build buildings, designate leaders, undertake projects, elect boards of trustees, and schedule weekly worship and religious education. Members voluntarily join and leave and just as voluntarily choose which religious authorities they will honor. Both what they do together and how they do it result in part from a peculiarly American way of organizing religion. The dimensions of those organizational constraints are a primary focus of this book.

But the life of a congregation also results from the particular religious tradition to which it belongs. In spite of the proliferation of self-made religious gurus and one-of-a-kind spiritual cells, most American religious groups can be recognized as part of a relatively few streams of tradition. A little more than a generation ago Will Herberg (1960) named them "Protestant, Catholic, Jew," but today American

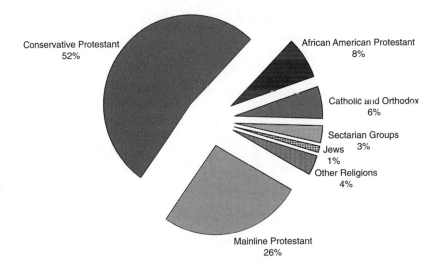

Conservative Protestant
52%

African American Protestant
8%

Catholic and Orthodox
6%

Sectarian Groups 3%

Jews 1%

Other Religions
4%

Mainline Protestant
26%

FIGURE I
American Congregations in Seven Streams of Religious Tradition

religious life presents a more variegated picture—seven broad traditions embracing the enormous diversity of American religious communities. Each is larger than a single denomination or faith tradition, constituting a cluster of groups with a common history and common ways of organizing. Figure 1 provides a picture of the size of each tradition, based on the number of its *congregations* (not adherents).

Protestants (collectively) remain the most numerous among us and in many ways still dominate, despite the erosion of that position over the last century. But Protestantism itself has diverse streams.

These include the liberal and moderate Protestants we will call *"Mainline."*[7] I have long resisted that designation and the assumptions that seem to go with it, but in the historic picture of American religion, it has a certain descriptive value. It does describe the kind of privileged position these groups occupy even today.[8] They are still a force to contend with even though they are outnumbered two-to-one by Conservative congregations and have lost adherents and closed congregations over the last three decades.

Mainline influence dates to the beginning of European settlement in the seventeenth century. Episcopal (then Church of England) and Congregationalist (then Separatist or Puritan) groups were among the first to arrive here; Presbyterians and Quakers soon followed. That founding generation of Protestants also included some influential Baptists, especially those who fought to establish the freedoms of the First Amendment (McBeth 1987; Pestana 1991). In the nineteenth and early twentieth centuries, the Mainline expanded enormously as various immigrant Lutheran and Reformed groups slowly assimilated into American society, and Methodists largely left their revivalist frontier roots and settled into middle-class parishes in towns and cities (Finke and Stark 1992; Hatch 1989).[9]

Roughly a quarter of all U.S. congregations identify with one of these moderate-to-liberal Christian traditions, and our research team interviewed in 193 of them.[10] What makes up this stream? Certainly not a single theology or liturgy or even mode of church government. Some are "high church," others "low church." Some have bishops and others do not. Some denominations have serious internal divisions between their more liberal majorities (with which denominational leaders usually identify) and less liberal members and congregations. But the average congregation within the Mainline *is* more liberal than its typical Pentecostal and Southern Baptist neighbors. No single theology predominates, but there is a certain tolerant, practically oriented, Mainline theological style.[11]

More important, the Mainline is distinctive for its very acceptability. Congregationalist and Presbyterian and Episcopal and Methodist and Lutheran remain among the most recognizable and respectable religious "labels" in American society. They are respectable, in part, because their members have been disproportionately middle class for several generations, and they expect their clergy to be well educated, reflecting their expectation that both clergy and laity will take an active role in the world. They are "church-like," to use Troeltsch's designation for groups that think of themselves as responsible for the spiritual lives of a whole population (Troeltsch 1931).

Mainline congregations and denominations form the backbone of most interfaith and ecumenical activity, and some schemes for categorizing American religion simply call these the "ecumenical Protestants." This is not entirely fair, however, since at least some in the other two streams of Protestantism also share ecumenical goals and also hold membership in the National Council of Churches (NCC), historically the nation's leading ecumenical body. While almost all the congregations included in the Mainline category belong to the NCC, so do almost all the second group of Protestant congregations—the *African American Protestants*. (The Church of God in Christ is the one exception among the historically black denominations.) Too many treatments of American religion have overlooked the African American family of denominations, a uniquely American set of religious traditions.

The roughly fifty thousand churches of the seven largest historic African American denominations have developed and sustained their own forms of congregational life and have been critically important to the individuals and communities that have depended on them. Commonly included in this family are the giant National Baptist Convention, USA, Inc., with its two smaller sisters the National Baptist Convention of America and the Progressive National Baptist Convention. But also included are three groups in the Methodist tradition—African Methodist Episcopal (AME), African Methodist Episcopal Zion (AMEZ), and Christian Methodist Episcopal (CME). All these groups trace their beginnings to the eighteenth century, as fugitive and freed slaves in the North and plantation slaves in the South. After the Civil War, these separate congregations and new denominations grew in numbers and importance.[12]

At the turn of the twentieth century, both black and white Protestant churches were reshaped by the emerging Pentecostal movement, a movement that is present today in all the streams of Christian tradition, indeed, around the world. The first Pentecostal denomination, founded in 1907, was the African American Church of God in Christ, which joined the black Baptists and black Methodists (along with many smaller groups) to constitute what is commonly called "the Black Church," comprising about 8 percent of American congregations (fifty-three of the ones in which we interviewed).[13] In black churches, life is deeply shaped by a God who can change lives, both individually and corporately. The experience of slavery and the symbolic importance of the Exodus story, along with a passion for freedom and equality, shape the African American religious experience (Paris 1985).

The Black Church tradition is more than a set of ideas, however. It often includes styles of music and preaching and participatory worship that are not found elsewhere. The contrast between the Black Church experience and typical white Protestantism was especially vivid to me one Sunday when I visited several different congregations around Chicago. After a three-hour service in a black Baptist church, I attended the evening service of a conservative Dutch Reformed (Reformed Church in America, or RCA) congregation. About to utter a vigorous "Amen," I realized how shocked my pew-mates would have been to hear it. Their quiet worship style does not call for audible response from the listeners.

The RCA church's Sunday night service was the first hint that it identified with *Conservative Protestantism*, the third stream of Protestant tradition. Unlike some of its more liberal East Coast sisters in the RCA, this congregation emphasizes personal piety and exhorts its members to evangelize their neighbors. Its subdued style sets it apart from the African American church I had just attended, but neither would it be mistaken for the equally sedate, liberal Episcopal church where I had started my day of Sunday visits.

Conservative Protestant denominations are more likely to join the National Association of Evangelicals than the National Council of Churches (although the RCA belongs to both). Southern Baptists are the best known and largest Conservative Protestant group, but traditional evangelicals like the Southern Baptists are joined by charismatic and Pentecostal churches, a few "confessional" churches (like the Wisconsin and Missouri Synods of the Lutheran Church), and a growing number of "nondenominational" churches.

Many of these churches would call themselves "evangelical," using that word in a distinctly twentieth-century way. Before the 1920s, most American Protestants— whatever their denomination—would have claimed to be evangelical. They would have embraced a commonsense biblicism, an emphasis on individual piety, and a commitment to preaching the Christian gospel around the world. But in the early decades of the twentieth century those emphases became more clearly the distinct property of Conservative Protestants; and by the middle of the century the vast pandenominational evangelical movement would begin to forge the religious culture now shared by diverse Conservative traditions.[14] Across those traditions, the piety and the evangelism remain, and a personal, life-transforming relationship with Jesus is at the center of their religious life.

Those who see evangelicals as outsiders misread both American history and American culture.[15] Some groups among them are nearly as old as the American republic, and in the "Bible Belt" of the South and Midwest a revivalist piety has long dominated the religious culture (Shibley 1991). Presidents since Jimmy Carter have claimed either membership in or an affinity with evangelicalism. Roughly half of American congregations—226 of the ones in which we interviewed—are located in the Conservative Protestant stream. Numerical dominance notwithstanding, Conservative Protestants themselves often retain a sense of "outsiderness" that mirrors the dismissive response they sometimes get from liberals. They do not assume that the leaders of the culture will be their allies (C. Smith 2000).

These three Protestant streams include the majority of American members and the majority of American congregations, but well over a quarter of all religious adherents in the United States are *Roman Catholic* or *Eastern Orthodox*, who make up the fourth stream. In many cities they are a dominant and visible majority. There are some two thousand Eastern Orthodox congregations and almost twenty thousand Roman Catholic parishes in the United States.[16] The number of *parishes* is deceptively small, because most parishes have very large memberships.

Catholic and Orthodox churches constitute about 6 percent of all U.S. congregations, including forty-five of those in our sample.

The large size of the typical parish is a distinctive feature of these congregations. The National Congregations Study reported, for instance, that 18 percent of Roman Catholic parishes had more than twenty-five hundred persons associated with the congregation; less than 1 percent of all other congregations were that big (Chaves 2000). They are not just bigger than average. They are also more likely to be defined by ethnicity and place in ways uncommon among American Protestant churches. When the prospective husband in the movie *My Big Fat Greek Wedding* is baptized into the Greek Orthodox faith of his intended bride, his new family exclaims, "Now you're Greek!" Ethnicity and religious affiliation are one. Similarly, to be Italian or Spanish implies being Roman Catholic, even for people who do not consider themselves especially religious.

I group Catholic and Orthodox traditions together here, even though these two international Churches—Eastern and Western—have officially been divided by schism for over a thousand years.[17] Common patterns of organization and practice in this country justify this categorization. Both churches have explicitly recognized non-U.S. ethnic and national origins, while maintaining allegiance to a universal Church that transcends local parishes. Both have also been bastions of highly formalized and sacramental liturgies that stand in contrast to Protestant simplicity.

Neither Catholicism nor Orthodoxy is new to the United States; both arrived with early pioneers and conquerors, often long before the territory became part of the United States. Catholic and Orthodox populations grew throughout the nineteenth century, but especially as new immigrants arrived from 1870 to 1920. Hundreds of distinctive church buildings took their place in American cities and neighborhoods. Both traditions struggled to organize themselves in the breach between American voluntarism and their own religious authorities based in other lands.[18] Even as they preserved their native religious traditions, they established institutions in this country that were *organized* along American lines, with boards of trustees and more lay involvement than might have been common elsewhere.[19]

The long-standing mutual suspicion between American Protestant culture and these immigrant traditions began to erode in the 1950s and 1960s. That move was signaled and facilitated by the theological work of John Courtney Murray, who laid a foundation for Catholic acceptance of church-state separation and democracy; the Second Vatican Council and its call for greater openness in the Church; the election of John Kennedy; and the move of vast numbers of American Catholics into higher education, suburbia, and the middle class. All these factors brought greater acceptance of Catholic parishes alongside their Protestant neighbors.[20] Many Orthodox churches have become equally middle class and at home in a pluralist democracy. Some have adapted worship to more American patterns; others remain as mysterious to Americans today as veiled Catholic sisters were to their parents in the 1950s. They often represent small, obscure countries, and they sometimes enshrine political divisions that reflect the conflicts from which immigrant members long ago fled, resulting in a bewildering array of names on Orthodox churches in the United States (Albanese 1992, 291). Orthodoxy and Catholicism, however, are similar in that more recent cohorts of immigrants are remaking an otherwise assimilated Church.

Those four streams—Catholic and Orthodox parishes and three broad groups of Protestant congregations—still account for the vast majority of local religious gatherings. The dominantly Christian character of the U.S. population is changing, but the Christian patterns are still the water in which everyone else swims.

No one knows that Christian dominance better than *American Jews*. Almost from the beginning of European colonization of North America, a few of those who came were Jewish. Today roughly 2 percent of the U.S. population is Jewish, and just under 1 percent of the nation's congregations are synagogues and temples.[21] Nor is this population evenly spread throughout the country. In the Northeast, Florida, California, and a few other states, concentrations are much higher than the overall average, while in many other places (such as the rural southern and midwestern communities where we surveyed) synagogues are not a part of the religious mix at all. Not everyone who identifies as Jewish affiliates with Jewish religious institutions, but synagogues remain important to Jewish identity and tradition (Cohen 2000) and give Jews an organized place in the interfaith religious landscape. Together, the three dominant strands of Jewish religious practice are important far beyond their small numbers in defining the shape of American religion. We talked with people in ten Jewish congregations, not enough to draw grand generalizations, but enough to hear something of how Jewish congregational life is a distinctive strand in the American religious experience. We will use these conversations, along with research done by others, to examine how Jewish congregations have made a place for themselves.

Now surpassing the Jewish presence in combined numbers and breadth of distribution are the dozens of *Other Religions*, a category too broad to designate any other way. From Hindus to Muslims to Buddhists and Jains, post-1965 immigration has brought a new religious pluralism to American society.[22] We talked to people in eleven such groups, present in all the communities in which we worked, save one.

We will supplement what we heard and the patterns we saw in this small sampling of cases with insight from the growing body of literature that examines this new pluralism. Other authors will provide the detailed and deep descriptions our study will not allow. What we can do, as we survey the whole of the American congregational scene, is note indications of how these newer traditions may be shaping their organizational lives.

Combined, these mosques and temples and other religious centers probably number twice the roughly thirty-five hundred Jewish synagogues. What justifies treating them as a single category is not commonality of belief or practice, but rather their newness and relative marginality to the American religious scene. The largest and most visible contingent among them are American Muslims, encompassing both a large and growing immigrant population from all over the world and a rapidly growing African American membership (Ahmed 1991; J. Smith 1999). Whether Muslims now outnumber Jews in the American population is a subject of debate, but no one doubts—especially after September 11, 2001—that local mosques have become a part of the American religious scene.

Like Muslims, Hindus and Buddhists have actually been in the United States for over a century (Eck 2001; Mann, Numrich, and Williams 2001). Thousands of Chinese workers came to the American West after 1849 and brought Buddhist traditions with them. By the 1960s, Buddhist and Hindu teachings had found their way into the more experimental side of American religion in Transcendental Meditation, Yoga, Krishna Consciousness, and the like; but the real growth in both Buddhism and Hinduism came with the post-1965 influx of immigrants from India, China, Japan, and the rest of Asia. As new groups in each tradition have found each other in American cities, they have established temples where they can practice native traditions and teach them to the next generation (Kurien 1998; R. B. Williams 1994). As a minority in American society, practitioners must create institutions for which their own culture and tradition may have few patterns.

These ancient Asian traditions are joined in America's "new pluralism" by the oldest American religious traditions, the Native American ones. Long assumed to have been extinguished by Christian missionaries, these ancient American traditions are reasserting their presence and place in U.S. society.[23] All these diverse and sometimes fragile "Other Religions" are fundamentally altering how Americans think about themselves.

Fitting none of these categories are three of America's homegrown "new religions"—the Christian Scientists, Latter-day Saints, and Jehovah's Witnesses. Each grew out of Christianity but also celebrates new religious revelations and sacred texts that most Christians do not accept. Those doctrinal innovations are one of the reasons we label them *Sectarian Groups*. This label, implying tension between dominant and dissenting groups, is especially apt here. These groups have often stood at odds with American society, and their practices have sometimes set the legal precedents that define "free exercise" for the rest of us.[24] But their position at the margins should not be confused with unimportance. The historian Laurence Moore argues that such "outsiders" are the hallmark of American religion, exemplifying the religious inventiveness that characterizes our history (Moore 1986). Nor is their marginality to be equated with numerical weakness. There are nearly as many local (Jehovah's Witness) "kingdom halls" and (Mormon) "wards" as Roman Catholic parishes. They were often especially resistant to our interviewers, so our sample underrepresents the population, but we did talk with representatives of thirteen congregations from these traditions, and we will supplement what we heard there with the historical and ethnographic work others have done.

Latter-day Saints (often known as Mormons) are the oldest among these groups, emerging in the middle of the nineteenth century from Joseph Smith's visions. As his followers made their way west, they were persecuted at nearly every turn, and Smith himself was killed before they reached Utah and set up their kingdom of Deseret. Famously inventive and self-sufficient, they survived and even thrived in that arid land. Today Mormons have spread far from that western home, becoming one of the most rapidly growing movements in the world (Ostling and Ostling 1999; Shipps 1985). They have entered the American middle-class mainstream, but the Sectarian differences remain—in commitments to strict dietary and behavioral standards, in high levels of involvement in church life, and in esoteric rituals and clothing.[25]

Christian Science followed Mormons onto the scene in the last quarter of the nineteenth century, proclaiming new possibilities for divine healing. Mary Baker Eddy first published her ideas in *Science and Health* in 1875 and founded the Church of Christ, Scientist, four years later. The movement's first decade was very difficult, but by the end of the century the church was established and growing.[26] Eddy's personal charisma and formidable organizing skills built a movement whose Reading Rooms and internationally known newspaper make it a recognizable cultural presence. Although the Church does not release membership numbers, there are reasons to suspect that membership has been declining. Their Sectarian insistence on resisting modern medicine continues to mark the movement as outside the American mainstream and often has made recruitment difficult.

Jehovah's Witnesses resist mainstream medical regimes as well, especially blood transfusions. Interpreting biblical injunctions about "taking" blood literally, they have gone to court rather than allow themselves or their children to be given blood. Their children are routinely set apart from their peers in other ways as well, since Witnesses also refuse to salute the flag or to celebrate birthdays or other holidays. While Latter-day Saints supplement the Christian Bible with the *Book of Mormon* and Christian Scientists read *Science and Health,* Jehovah's Witnesses have their own translation of the Bible and always read it through the official interpretations provided by publications from the Watchtower Society.

The Jehovah's Witness movement dates to the 1880s, when Charles Taze Russell began publishing the journals now familiar as *The Watchtower* and *Awake!* He eventually predicted that Jesus would return in 1914 and gather up 144,000 followers as a signal of the end of time. When the date came and went—and the movement grew far beyond 144,000—the theology evolved, but the emphasis on "end times" and an imminent cleansing of the earth remains. Every adult member becomes a "publisher" of this news, going door to door with movement literature.[27] With over six million members in 235 countries, Witnesses join Latter-day Saints among the ranks of fast-growing world religious movements (Stark and Iannaccone 1997; Wah 2001). In their distinctive beliefs, high levels of religious commitment, and willingness to be separate from society, these Sectarian groups have created their own mode of participation in the American religious system, and together they constitute as much as 7 percent of the whole.[28]

Seven streams, rather than three—Mainline Protestant, Conservative Protestant, black churches, Catholic and Orthodox, Jewish, Sectarian, and Other Religions—are shown in Figure 1. No single catchy title can describe American religion today. There are enormous differences even within each stream, but each is defined by internal characteristics and a history that this book will explore. Each has adapted to America's peculiar ways of organizing religion, recognizing the right of each individual to join or not join and accommodating to the existence of dozens of different religious neighbors. Both the common work of congregations and the variations defined by these seven religious streams are at the heart of what makes American religion unique.

LOCATING AMERICA'S RELIGIOUS DIVERSITY

Describing that mixture of common work and diverse streams took us to research sites from coast to coast. We selected seven locations where we could spend time getting to know the religious landscape, talk with people in local congregations, and find out about the other local and regional organizations through which they do their work. These seven, taken together, represent the range of regions, demographics, religious traditions, and community size that constitute the larger American context.

In Hartford, Connecticut, we found some of the oldest congregations in the country, indeed, a plethora of the churches that claim the name "Congregationalist" for themselves, even if their official denomination is now the United Church of Christ (UCC). Hartford has more Protestant Mainline churches, as well as more Catholic parishes and Jewish synagogues, than is typical elsewhere in the country. In this community leading rabbis, the Catholic archbishop, the UCC conference minister, and sometimes the Episcopal bishop have historically spoken for the religious community. But African Americans and Hispanics (mostly, but not entirely, Puerto Ricans) have a significant presence in the metropolitan area's population of just under a million, and both have a growing voice on the religious scene as well. Hartford elected its first Hispanic mayor in 2001, and the city's black clergy today are often at the forefront of public initiatives. Diverse Catholic parishes, as well as large Hispanic Pentecostal churches, are found here, as is New England's largest Protestant church—a black Baptist "cathedral."

More than a day's journey by car to the south and west is territory that was settled in the nineteenth century rather than the seventeenth and has become the sprawling city of Nashville, Tennessee. The population of the Nashville metropolitan area, slightly larger than Hartford's, is growing rather than shrinking. While the United Church of Christ dominates Connecticut, with a "First Church" in the center of every town, in Nashville the very different "Churches of Christ" are around every other corner. More Nashville churches belong to this conservative, "nondenominational" denomination than to the South's traditional giants, the Southern Baptist Convention, the United Methodist Church, and the National Baptist Convention (each of which has its national denominational publishing house in town). As a booming New South city, nearly half of Nashville's congregations have been founded since 1970, and they are more likely than in most communities to have a healthy midsized membership roll (over one hundred regular attenders, that is). Many have highly mobile memberships who have recently moved to town and may have switched denominations in the process, and a growing number welcome a mixture of ethnic and immigrant populations. There is even a large and beautiful Hindu temple on the outskirts of town. While southern patterns are still visible in the culture, this is not simply a traditional southern town.

Traditional southern mores are far more prevalent in the rural counties we visited in Alabama. Situated an easy drive down I-65 from Nashville, between

Birmingham and Montgomery, about eighty thousand people—60 percent white and 40 percent black—live in the two counties we surveyed. Yet even here, a growing Hispanic population was evident, and a few churches had started holding Spanish-language services. The congregations here are overwhelmingly Protestant, with only two Roman Catholic parishes, one Jewish synagogue, and one African American mosque. Fully a third of all the area churches are Southern Baptist, and most of the rest belong to other evangelical and Pentecostal denominations. The churches in the small towns and countryside here are usually small (half have fewer than fifty regular attenders), historic (a quarter were founded before 1875), settled (only a third reported even "some" members who were new to the community), and disproportionately elderly (over a third said the majority of their members were over age sixty-five). Almost every church, moreover, reported its membership to be of a single ethnic group, and we found no women pastors.

In the eighteenth and nineteenth centuries, my pioneer ancestors were not content to cross the mountains into Tennessee. They kept going until they reached the fertile hills and fields of Missouri. The rural areas we visited in Missouri in the 1990s shared much of rural Alabama's church demography. Here, too, churches are small, historic, settled, and disproportionately elderly in membership. And here a small but growing number of Hispanics are taking up residence and beginning to change the flavor of the religious community. But this was never plantation country, and in five counties in the center of the state, 98 percent of the roughly sixty thousand inhabitants were Euro-American, and the German street signs and German town names reflected their dominant national heritage. The congregations those Germans founded—Catholic, Lutheran, and Reformed (now UCC)—worship across from the Baptists and Methodists in each small town. In this American rural heartland the full range of Mainline and Conservative Protestant churches is present, with a significant number of women pastors struggling to make a place for themselves. Down these country roads we found both the traditional churches of storied (and sung) memory and people sometimes willing to reinvent their traditions.

Halfway across the continent, Seattle, Washington, shares none of the nostalgia for nineteenth-century rural America. Reinventing traditions is what Seattle is all about, and often that means leaving organized religious life entirely. My pastor father used to joke, when he was laboring in southern California, that all that white stuff on the Rocky Mountains isn't snow. It's all the church membership papers people dropped on the way over! People in the Pacific region are twice as likely to report that they have no religious preference as are people in other parts of the country.[29] But many of them do join congregations, and often they start new ones. Seattle is too new to have many really old congregations. Indeed, well over half of today's groups have been created since World War II. Three-quarters of them told us that most of their members grew up in a different denomination, and most congregations described their members as mostly newcomers to the community. Very little about this city seems to be nailed down. It sits on the edge of the continent, facing west, and that means it has more Asian than African American or Hispanic residents. That is reflected in Asian Christian congregations, centers for Buddhists and Hindus, and congregations in which Asian, Hispanic, Anglo, and African American members mix in nearly equal numbers. There were also more female pastors here than in any other community we studied. But even with its reputation as a liberal and diverse enclave, Seattle has as many Conservative Protestant churches as any other part of the country, and several of them are booming megachurches with national television ministries.

Conservative megachurches are also booming in Albuquerque, New Mexico—not exactly the Bible Belt, but a rather typical western city, mixing rugged conservatism, ancient traditions, and a five-hundred-year Catholic history. This is a land of *mestizaje* (mixing).[30] Nearly a third of the congregations in this city of half a million draw a mix of the area's Hispanic and Anglo populations. A third of the city's population claims allegiance to its Roman Catholic churches, about forty huge parishes; the other two-thirds find a religious home (if any) in one of well over two hundred other congregations. While this southwestern city has abundant Catholic and Conservative Protestant churches, it has relatively few Mainline Protestant options and an astonishing array of choices beyond the Christian tradition. A small Jewish community has been present since early colonial days, but today they are joined by Muslims and other world religions, as well as by Native American groups and some offbeat new religious movements. This is also Mormon country. Like Seattle, Albuquerque lies within the western territory where the Church of Jesus Christ of Latter-day Saints has its greatest strength. In this city both the oldest American religious traditions (a Spanish Catholic cathedral and Native American ceremonies) rub shoulders with the newest.

In Chicago, Illinois, such jostling seems to take place on nearly every street corner. Rising from the ashes of its great 1871 fire, this city by the lake has become one of America's major gateways. Everybody is here—immigrant and native-born, Protestant, Catholic, Jew, and all the newcomers. Small and large, new and old, suburban and urban, the roughly five thousand congregations of Cook and DuPage counties mirror the nation as a whole. With nearly half the population claiming Catholic affiliation, Catholic and Orthodox parishes are nearly twice as prevalent as in the rest of the country. But all the other religious traditions are present as well.[31] Chicago's huge African American population has supplied important national leaders for National Baptists, for instance. Mainline Protestants have large and historic congregations like Fourth Presbyterian (Wellman 1999b) Moody Bible Institute established a wide circle of Conservative Protestant influence in the last century and remains a significant religious influence in the city. Willow Creek Community Church became the prototypical "seeker" megachurch at the end of the twentieth century with its sprawling campus in the northwest suburbs. Jehovah's Witnesses, Mormons, and Christian Scientists are present throughout the city, and every sort of Jewish congregation exists alongside every conceivable center of worship for people from religions throughout the world.

With a population over five million, Chicago and the surrounding counties is the largest and most complex place we studied. Many of its congregations are nearly invisible. They are small and transient, lacking phones, offices, paid staff, or denominational connections. We managed to talk with people from some of these elusive groups, but many remained out of our reach, sometimes because of language differences, which prevented conversations. But the stories of 183 diverse Chicago congregations join the stories of fifty-six from Hartford, seventy-four from Nashville, forty from Alabama, thirty-eight from Missouri, ninety-two from Seattle, and sixty-four from Albuquerque—549 in all—to paint a picture of American religion as it is practiced across traditions, histories, and landscapes.[32]

LISTENING TO THE STORIES

In each of these very different places, our team of researchers gathered stories. That team and I constitute the "we" who listened and observed and are reporting here what we saw. Each team was lead by a local faculty member, and I visited each site twice, accompanying team members on congregational visits, interviews, and meetings with church officials and service providers. Calling our research the Organizing Religious Work project, we spent just over a year gathering data. Working in 1997 and 1998, we began by compiling the most complete lists we could find of all the congregations in the areas we had chosen to study, and we generated a random sample from those lists. We were able to complete interviews with 70 percent of those we attempted to contact.[33] From the information we have on non-respondent congregations, we know that they were disproportionately small, had no church offices, and were not part of large mainstream denominations. Even with nearly a third not responding and an unknown number of congregations never appearing on a list from which we could draw samples, our resulting group of interviewees was remarkably broad and representative. Our seven geographic areas approximate in microcosm many of the religious and demographic characteristics of the United States as a whole. By randomly selecting a sizable sample in each area, we ensured that our interviews would give us as complete a picture as possible of congregational life.

In all, we talked with representatives of congregations from ninety-one different religious traditions in congregations ranging in size from four attenders to seventeen thousand. No significant segment of American religion was missing, but to make sure that the overall picture is not distorted in some way, we have weighted the descriptive statistics reported here to approximate the distribution of congregational size and denominational affiliation found in the National Congregations Study (NCS), a representative survey of the nation's congregations done at about the same time (Chaves et al. 1999). On most measures where the two surveys asked similar questions, our unweighted results were nearly identical,[34] but weighting makes us confident that when we talk about national averages or differences between one segment of American congregations and another, our numbers have not been skewed by having talked to too many Episcopalians or too few Baptists, too many big church pastors and not enough from the smallest congregations.

The stories in this book thus come from a broad and remarkably representative group of American congregations, but they are not anonymous numbers. The numbers and averages tell us something about the larger patterns we might not see in a single congregation, but the words of our local guides and our own experiences as visitors in these very particular places provide the human dimension that numbers sometimes miss. Recent large national surveys of congregations have given us a base for comparison, but our informants answered us in their own words. Out of the words and categories they used, I have sought to identify the contours of similarity and difference as they naturally occur. We have enough cases to see those contours and enough stories to glimpse what they may mean.

Our conversations with each congregational representative (usually the pastor or an equivalent leader) explored the history and weekly routines of that local community of faith. We asked about the theological and denominational traditions with which they identify, but we also asked what the congregation cares most about, what worries them about the world, which goals and activities command most attention and support. We wanted to capture both what congregations actually do and something of why they do it. How do they tell the story of what they are trying to accomplish in the world?

We also wanted to know about the partnerships and connections that make the work of congregations possible. If they were part of a denomination, we spent a good deal of time exploring just how active they are, what they receive in return, what they value about the connection, even whether they were alienated from the denomination and why. With each congregation, we gathered systematic information about the organizations it supports and the organizations, denominational and otherwise, that support it. Before we arrived, we had already asked the congregational representative to provide some written answers to questions about the congregation's size, budget, demographics, and the like. And before we left, we usually collected a pile of newsletters and weekly bulletins, brochures and annual reports, as well as our impressions of the building, its neighborhood, and what the bulletin boards and signs and the setting itself could tell us about the place.

All our interviewers worked with a common interview guide, but they often explored specific local stories in depth, leaving aside more general questions that were irrelevant to the group. No two interviews were exactly alike. While we identified key analytical categories both before the interviews and as we read the transcripts afterward, not every interview told us the answer to every question. We have categorized and counted responses, but there were almost always missing cases for any given question. From one table to the next, in the pages that follow, each category has different numbers of cases, reflecting that unevenness. There are common patterns across American congregational life but also significant variations that prevent a neat, uniform set of analyses.

We returned to thirty-two of the Christian churches from our original sample to find out more, especially to ask questions of individual members to supplement what we had learned from a single representative leader. Some of those individuals lend additional voices to the stories that unfold here. We observed worship services and committee meetings, convened focus groups and interviewed lay leaders. In addition, a total of 4,012 persons completed questionnaires during Sunday services, and we have weighted these individual responses to approximate the population of church attenders documented in the NCS (Chaves et al. 1999).

The questions that we asked in each phase of our study were an attempt to understand the intersection of the theological world of congregational life with the very earthly contours of the culture in which it exists and the resources it brings to its work.[35] Having more participants and more money may mean, for instance, that more work can be done. Traditions that allow local autonomy may shape congregational life differently from those in which a religious hierarchy controls local decisions. Congregations in cities may approach their tasks differently from those in the countryside, and well-educated and well-off congregations may organize differently from those with fewer worldly resources. Newly organized congregations may have different priorities from those established long ago. Because we talked to so many people, we can look for these basic organizational patterns, as well as for the ways different traditions shape religious life.[36]

As critical as congregations are to American religious life, they do not do their work alone. To understand congregations, we have to pay attention to the partnerships—often invisible to local worshipers—that make local religious gatherings possible. To learn about those partner organizations, we asked our informant to name all the suppliers and publishers, service agencies and community groups, ministerial associations and mission programs with which the congregation had a connection. For each connection, we noted whether they shared projects, donated money or volunteers, exchanged goods or services, or did some other form of resource sharing.[37] The resulting list ran to over five thousand entries, and from it we selected about two hundred organizations for follow-up interviews. We visited food pantries and shelters, called publishers and youth camps, talked with regional representatives of Alcoholics Anonymous and the Boy Scouts, and interviewed national and regional representatives of organizations from World Vision to Heifer International. We asked them about their work and about the role of congregations in it. We explored their own sources of support and sense of mission. In addition, we have consulted the Internet for details about some of the organizations that surround and enable the local work done by individual congregations.

Among the most important connections for many congregations are those with regional and national denominational organizations. Information about those groups came both from our interviews themselves and from the two sister projects to this one. As we were exploring local congregational life, Adair Lummis and David Roozen were directing projects aimed at better understanding how Protestant denominations do their work, focusing especially on eight diverse groups: the United Church of Christ, the United Methodist Church, the Episcopal Church, the Lutheran Church–Missouri Synod, the Reformed Church in America, the Assemblies of God, the National Baptist Convention, USA, Inc., and the Association of Vineyard Churches. Case studies of the national and regional units of these diverse religious groups allowed us to see some of the connections between congregations and denominations from the vantage point of regional and national headquarters.

PLOTLINES IN THE STORIES

From our conversations and observations and surveys, an account has emerged of what congregations seek to accomplish and what they do in pursuit of those goals. Throughout this book our focus is collective action, what a gathered community of faith *does* and the collective products that result from that action—its "work." Congregations create events and rituals, as well as buildings and newsletters. Some of their work is readily visible, while some is as elusive as a moment of transcendence. When we talked with people, we were as interested in activities as in beliefs, in contributions and task forces as in sermons.

Still, the story we heard about American congregational life is fundamentally a story about how people relate to God and to each other. We begin in the chapter that follows where most congregations begin—with their own religious traditions. Those who gather in local religious communities do so largely because an important spiritual dimension of human experience finds expression there. We need not argue (as the "functionalists" do)[38] that every human is inherently religious to recognize that many people seem able to respond to transcendence. As people reach toward that Something beyond, congregations provide an organized and recognized location for their quest.

But while congregations are doing spiritual work, they are also providing a place for *gathering*. Chapter 3 turns to the ties among those who pray together, study together, and worship together. They are at once creating a community and honoring their god. Whether in choirs or in Sunday school classes, altar guilds or worship services, even when people gather to focus attention on individual spiritual life, the presence of a community shapes the experience. We know that congregations are places where "social capital" (Putnam 2000) is generated, and here we look more closely at how they do it.

The spiritual and community building work of congregations is not done in a vacuum, however. Broad regularities shape congregational life, some coming from the culture and some from the various religious traditions to which congregations belong. Congregations do not choose to do what they do all on their own. As participants in a distinct "organizational field," they often structure their efforts around commonly accepted kinds of programs with commonly recognized kinds of personnel. Throughout this book we look for the interplay of institutional culture and religious tradition. Both are at work in shaping what congregations do and how they do it.

Nor do congregations stand alone in shaping the content of the programs they choose. Chapter 4 turns to the larger organizational network from which congregations draw ideas and materials. Whenever they gather for worship or fellowship or learning, their efforts are shaped by organizational resources that stretch far beyond their walls. Much of what each congregation does depends on the religious work done by others, work that has been preserved and carried on by organizational actors over the years. For about a century, the market for religious products has been segmented primarily into denominational niches. To be a denomination is to be, at least in part, a producer of resources that support the educational and worship life of constituent congregations. In recent years denominations have been joined by a long list of nondenominational religious publishers and suppliers, each vying for an expanding market share. At stake is not only the economic viability of various organizations, but also the shape of the religious landscape itself. Denominational religious suppliers have by no means disappeared—but neither can they be taken for granted. Chapter 4 examines that shifting balance in the support system that sustains the spiritual and fellowship work of congregations.

This internal world of religious life is not the only side of the story. For most— but not all—congregations, the circle of human caring reaches outside the membership. Communities of faith define their mission in terms of external impact as well as relationships with each other and with their god. They define this impact in different ways, but most claim an obligation to serve the world. This service to the world is the focus of Chapter 5. Some congregations try to serve the world by preaching a gospel they are convinced will change people's lives. Others try to serve the world by making sure that hungry and hurting people are cared for. A few try to do both. We look at who chooses which path and at which strategies are *possible*. As in all human organizations, size and resources shape what people do. Depending on its size, for instance, a congregation may mount a few outreach programs of its own; but in smaller congregations groups of members may simply organize a study group to keep issues and opportunities before the congregation as a whole.

Most often, when congregations want to reach beyond their own local community or want to do more than their own limited resources allow, they work through other organizational channels. Those outreach partnerships are the subject of Chapter 6. In local communities, serving the needy and enriching community life draw congregations into a range of public partnerships. Those partnerships often blur the presumed boundaries between "religious" and "secular" and offer us an opportunity to rethink how communities of faith participate in the work of building larger communities.

Whether they want to provide material aid and enrichment to needy people in the world or send a missionary to preach and teach, people in local congregations care about making a difference in the world, and they are likely to point to that pragmatic missional connection as the greatest value they derive from belonging to a denomination. Denominations, a major conduit for American religious energies for the past century and a half, remain important in outreach efforts that go beyond the local community. Alongside denomination-based efforts, there have long been independent "parachurch" mission agencies as well. Although liberal Protestants declared the missions era over nearly a century ago, in many ways missionary activity continues to be a focal point for collective religious work in American congregations.

Chapter 7 turns explicitly to how congregations embody larger religious traditions. With so many suppliers and partners, is there any order to the choice of congregational connection? Throughout the book I note the points where existing denominations structure the "markets" and where they do not. But here I focus on the larger question of what lies behind those markets. Denominations are not just suppliers of goods and services but communities that promulgate an identity.

A "denomination" is a peculiarly American religious communal structure. Denominations recognize the limits on their power (unlike legally established monopoly religions) but have the freedom to develop and practice their own religious ways. Is it possible to have a strong religious identity that is neither ascribed at birth nor divided from others by high boundaries? Can denominational traditions survive in a world of highly educated, mobile, denominational "switchers" who are perfectly free to choose whether and with whom to affiliate? Those questions are addressed in Chapter 7.

The final chapter brings the story back to what we have learned about the diversity and strengths of American religious life. We will note what makes congregations and denominations vulnerable at this moment in our history, looking for both the signs of hope and the signs of caution in the patterns we have seen. The architects of American political life dared to set religion free to survive or fail on its own. They created a social space for voluntary religious organizations, occupied today by at least three hundred thousand congregations, with thousands of religious charities and service agencies supplementing their work and at least that many businesses oriented to supplying their needs. It is time to journey into that thriving religious organizational world.

CHAPTER TWO · Building Traditions

Worshiping and Learning Together

Congregations are fundamentally *religious* organizations. That is such a common-sense assertion, but the perception of what congregations are about is often distorted by all the talk about them as deliverers of social services, builders of social capital, mobilizers of political constituencies, or even producers of culture. We will certainly return to their other roles in the world, but understanding American congregational life would be impossible if we did not begin by looking at the spiritual foundations.

Choosing to start the journey by examining the spiritual work of congregations is simply to follow the lead of the people we talked with. We asked the congregational leaders we interviewed, for instance, to rank a series of statements about "what really matters most" to their congregation. Two of those statements focused on the spiritual work they do: "having a worship service that fosters a close and spiritual connection to God" and "fostering members' spiritual growth." On a scale of 1 to 4, where 4 indicates "extremely important," spiritually enriching worship received an average rating across all American congregations of 3.74, and providing for members' spiritual growth was right behind at 3.67—the highest rated items on the list. Spiritual work, according to these local leaders, is central to what congregations should be doing.

Another set of numbers provides corroboration. The individual attenders who completed our Sunday morning survey were asked what attracted them to their congregation. The highest two items on their list (both rated at 3.27 on a similar four-point scale) were "the style and quality of worship" and "the preaching." Across all traditions, scores for these two items were higher than for questions about other aspects of congregational life and mission. When people arrive at the door, they may have many longings and expectations, but spiritually enriching preaching and worship are certainly among them.

Understanding what congregations do and why took us beyond these initial paper-and-pencil checklists, however. "What and why" are often addressed in formal mission statements that the congregations themselves produce, and our research team initially thought those statements might be helpful. But mission statements didn't prove to be very useful as a window on what congregations actually care about and do. When we asked if they had such a statement, a common response from our interviewees was "I know it must be here someplace." The pastor of a small Presbyterian church in Chicago said, "We have a mission statement that was written five or six years ago, and I don't think anyone could tell you what it is." What was contained in those elusive documents was indeed so general as to be nearly useless in describing the actual work each congregation currently seeks to accomplish.

Understanding the finer points of congregational life thus required more than a content analysis of mission statements or the answers to survey questions. It required a careful ear to the more open-ended stories we heard along the way. Over the course of the interviews, we asked leaders which congregational activities were most important to their members, what goals elicited the most energy and passion, what people worried most about, as well as how they would describe the congregation's mission in their own words. These conversations provide us with the signposts for the journey. No single answer, either on the survey or in the interview, was an especially reliable guide to the culture of the congregation; but when several responses were examined together, the patterns became clearer. Rather than a fixed set of categories for classifying and labeling congregations, these interview responses revealed some consistent themes that are present in multiple combinations across America's many religious traditions. These themes will help us begin to discern the contours of congregational life—contours whose most dominant lines are sketched by the way they approach these spiritual tasks.

FOCUSING SPIRITUAL ENERGIES

There are many ways to engage in the spiritual work of building faith. Both the style and content of congregational worship vary enormously across America's myriad local religious gatherings, and not every congregation places collective

TABLE I Spiritual Goals of Congregations in Different Religious Traditions

Goal	Mainline Protestant (193)	Conservative Protestant (226)	African American Protestant (53)	Catholic & Orthodox (45)	All Congregations (549)
	Congregations Naming Goal as One of Their Three Priorities (%)				
Corporate worship*	12	15	7	32	14
Develop individual spiritual lives*	37	18	21	23	26
Conversion*	12	75	57	6	50
Teach scripture & tradition*	1	20	11	3	12

NOTE: Number in parentheses indicates number of congregations in that group. All Congregations includes these four groups plus Sectarians, Jews, and Other Religions. For goals marked with an asterisk at least one of the differences among the groups is statistically significant at $p < .10$ (Oneway ANOVA, with Scheffe post-hoc comparisons).

worship events at the center of their service to their god. For some, teaching is as important as preaching, and for others both the teaching and the preaching are aimed at spiritually transformed lives. As we listened to congregational leaders talk about the spiritual work they try to do, four broad themes emerged. For some the central task is corporate worship, gathering people together to engage in the rituals of the faith. For others the primary task has as much to do with what people know and do. People need to be taught; ideas, traditions, and practices need to be preserved. For still others, the congregation's service of God finds its primary focus in the individual spiritual lives of those who come. What happens in the congregation is aimed at helping individual participants find comfort and direction for their lives. And for many others, that comfort and direction come only through an experience of conversion. The congregation's task is to prepare the way for conversion to happen.

As we listened to what people said about all the things their congregation tries to accomplish, we recorded and counted the three most dominant themes. Some of those themes concerned the work of service and fellowship, to which we will turn later. In other congregations more than one spiritual theme was dominant. The numbers in Table 1, then, are not intended to add up to 100 percent. They count just the spiritual tasks, showing how often these four themes were heard among the congregations in various Christian traditions.[1] While nearly every congregation places some kind of spiritual work high on its priority list, this table begins to show us how the shape of that effort is often molded by the particular stream of tradition within which the congregation stands. Each has distinctive ways of articulating *how* it seeks to help its members relate to the divine; each engages in particular ways of talking about how faith should be built.

WORSHIPING TOGETHER

Worship is so basic that some form of corporate ritual is universal across all the congregations in our sample. Even in communities of Hindus and Buddhists, where individual and familial celebrations are also religiously important, some occasions bring a significant portion of a community together for ritual events. An immigrant Buddhist reflected on why he and his family attend the temple: "Participating in religious services helps us grow spiritually. The Vihara provides a pious atmosphere that puts us into a spiritual trance in which all outward consciousness is forgotten . . . Our children are another important reason to attend the Vihara. We have a responsibility and a commitment to bring them up in the Buddhist way of life. . . . Attending the Vihara and participating in its activities is a proven way of getting that training" (Mann, Numrich, and Williams 2001, 54). Outside the context where these traditions are a natural part of the culture, maintaining religious practices as a minority calls for creative adaptation; and many of these new communities have even adopted the pattern of scheduling religious gatherings on Sunday. In the United States, from earliest Puritan settlements to modern American cities, commerce has remained relatively silent on Sunday mornings. Even if more young adults are worshiping at the "Church of the Holy Brunch" than in a local cathedral, the culture still provides at least minimal protection for this time, and congregations of all sorts fill that protected time with a worship service.

In some Christian churches, a distinct emphasis on worship is important to how the congregation understands its place in the world.[2] Those most likely to see corporate worship as the primary way to do their spiritual work are those in the "sacramental" Christian traditions—Catholicism, Orthodoxy, Lutheranism, and Anglicanism. Here theological imperatives, as well as individual expectations, demand that the Christian story be celebrated in "word and sacrament" each week. At an Antiochan Orthodox parish, the priest said simply, "Our mission is first of all to love God and to worship and adore Him. The activity of worship is very important to us." A third (32%) of the Catholic and Orthodox leaders we interviewed spoke in similar terms about what matters most (see Table 1).

Within Protestantism, the sacramental traditions cross the Mainline/Conservative line shown in Table 1. On both sides of that line people in sacramental traditions were almost twice as likely, compared to their nonsacramental Protestant neighbors, to prioritize corporate worship (21% vs. 12%). The pastor of a small Albuquerque Lutheran Church–Missouri Synod (LCMS, a group we classify as Conservative), sounded like he had read the results of our survey when he said, "I think that members expect a place that will provide some sort of consistency in terms of the quality of the worship experience." And at a medium-sized Hartford Episcopal parish (a denomination in the Mainline camp), the top priority was "worship, because . . . even if they are not here, they want to know that that is happening on Sunday morning. It takes on a life of its own."[3]

Placing corporate worship at the center of congregational life does not always mean celebrating the Christian sacraments. Churches in the Pentecostal and charismatic traditions emphasize worship as well (25 percent do, compared to 12 percent of non-Pentecostal Conservatives). Individual members may enjoy various "gifts of the Spirit" in private, but it is in the assembled congregation that prophecy, healing, and other ecstatic spiritual experiences are most likely to occur. The pastor of a small Alabama Assemblies of God church said, "I think our main purpose—our main reason for existence—is for the body to have a place to worship together." Speaking and praying in tongues, healing, and words of prophecy are regular features of congregational worship and provide the identifying marks of a religious movement that has spread across Protestant and Catholic groups and into all sorts of social and cultural locations around the world. Over the last three decades, for instance, the new movement called "The Vineyard" has updated the Pentecostal pattern for the baby boomer and post-boomer generations. Casual attire and soft-rock music define the Vineyard worship style, a style that epitomizes how Vineyard churches understand themselves. Like other new Pentecostal movements, the Vineyard thrives in the cities and suburbs of the north and west, not in the "back woods."[4] Whether Seattle young adults in jeans or Hispanic immigrants in Albuquerque, congregations in the charismatic and Pentecostal tradition are likely to see their distinctive form of worship as their most important collective task.

The work of creating opportunities for sacred worship is present, then, in virtually all congregations, each tradition shaping that work in its own way. Whether worship is part of the congregation's core mission is mostly a matter of the particular religious tradition of which it is a part—Catholic or Orthodox, Liturgical

Protestant, Pentecostal. But there are other social forces at work in shaping this priority as well. Even within a given tradition, a priority on collective worship is more likely to be present in larger congregations. Small congregations may recognize that elaborate rituals are beyond their means, and the people who choose those congregations likely do so for other reasons. In addition, even when we compare congregations of similar size and religious tradition, those that are urban and suburban, have younger members, and have more college-educated members are more likely to prioritize the collective worship experience. Beyond the shaping influence of religious traditions, each congregation is responding to the life experiences of its members and to the resources they can bring to producing collective worship experiences. Even this basic congregational work is an inextricable mixture of religious prescriptions and cultural patterns.

NURTURING INDIVIDUAL SPIRITUALITY

The second theme we encountered in the stories congregational leaders told about their work was a focus on the individual spiritual lives of the members. Many have a keen sense of the everyday challenges of living in American society, and they are convinced that the people who seek out congregations want to find spiritual guidance in the midst of those stresses and strains. Helping individuals find a spiritual focus in their lives was mentioned by over a third of all the leaders we interviewed (see Table 1), but it was an especially strong theme among the Mainline Protestants. At a Hartford Episcopal parish, we heard, "People want to be fed spiritually." In Nashville, at a small United Church of Christ, the pastor said that people want to know how they "can function in this world as Christians, how Christian faith informs them, gives them a sense of who they are in their lives and how they can live that out in the world."

Similar concerns were also heard, even if less commonly, among other Christian groups. The pastor of a very large Chicago Catholic parish said that the key concerns of his parishioners were "just to be fed spiritually . . . how to deal with issues in their lives because of the problems that we face in society." And the pastor of a Southern Baptist church in Seattle said that for his members "there is a lot of possibility for compromise. There's a lot of temptation to do a lot of things. And just that week-by-week encouragement, the focus on being connected with God, encountering God—we strive to do that."

Concern for individual spiritual development is also prevalent outside the mainstream Christian community. The spiritual side of Judaism has become more prevalent in recent years, alongside its emphasis on traditional learning and observance.[5] In Hartford a Conservative rabbi told us, "When we get together, there's a great hunger for basics and for kind of a spiritual dimension, the poetry behind the concrete action. We try to provide that whenever possible." At a small Christian Science church in Seattle, our informant said, "We're a very spiritual church. We believe the solution to every human problem is a spiritual one." Their goal, he said, is "healing, not just for ourselves, of course, but for the world. And our community."[6] Newer arrivals on the American religious scene are adding their own traditions as well. The leader of a small Sunni Muslim mosque in Alabama said, "We're not trying to escape to another world, but as the Prophet indicated, [there are] regular routine spiritual principles that we inject in our daily lives, which are called the pillars of the faith. We try to combine spiritual discipline with the material life." At a small Chicago Nichirin Buddhist temple, in spite of the barrier posed by our informant's limited English, it was clear that both Japanese and American practitioners come for spiritual reasons. "What do they gain?" we asked. "Maybe in their mind, peaceful," he responded. As Muslim, Hindu, and Buddhist gatherings take their place alongside Jewish and Christian ones, they bring their own spiritualities into the mix of American religious practice.

They share with other religious communities the basic work of creating opportunities for practitioners to encounter a presence beyond themselves, to place their everyday lives within a spiritual context. That individually centered spiritual focus is particularly characteristic of both the Other Religions and Mainline Protestants. No matter what size the congregation and no matter what its demographics, congregations in these religious streams are more likely to orient their spiritual work toward nurturing the everyday spiritual paths of their members.

CONVERSION

A much more common theme in American congregational identity (voiced in fully half the congregations where we interviewed) is the emphasis on evangelical Christian conversion—on being saved. For many churches the only legitimate goal is preaching that gospel. The success of each Sunday morning service is judged, like everything else about church life, by how consistently it points toward the need for conversion. The hymns, the sermon, and most of all the "invitation" at the end—all contain the essential elements of evangelical spirituality: all have sinned; God loves us in spite of our sin; Jesus' life, death, and resurrection paid the price for our sin; but each person must accept the pardon Christ's death offers. Each time a believer attends church, he or she is reminded that the spiritual life begins with a decision to follow Christ and continues in daily efforts to live by biblical guidelines.

The pastor of a large independent evangelical church in Hartford summed up the goal by saying, "We're here to exalt God—to evangelize the lost and edify the believers." Those two tasks—evangelizing and edifying—go together in how these churches think about their task. Even after having made an initial decision to be saved, each church gathering provides believers with reinforcement and reminders about why that decision was so important.[7]

This emphasis on evangelism is thus both an outreach goal (about which we will say more in Chapter 5) and a mode of spirituality for believers and their churches. To live as God desires is to witness to one's faith, as well as to help spread the gospel to the ends of the earth. To be a good church is to place evangelism and missions at the center of church life. When we asked individuals on our survey to rate various practices in terms of their importance to living a "good Christian life," the average Christian church member said that "bringing others to faith in Christ" is very important. But this sort of personal witnessing was considerably *more* important to members of Conservative Protestant and African American churches than to members of Mainline ones. In the former churches, 85 percent and 91 percent, respectively, said that sharing their faith was either very important or essential to living a good Christian life. In the Mainline churches only 54 percent said it was that important. Similar patterns were seen when we asked about the importance of a strong evangelism program at their churches. A slim majority of Mainline members (55%) want this in their churches, while the vast majority (86% and 95%) of Conservative and African American Protestants do.

In Catholic parishes this language about evangelism is less familiar. The importance of spreading the gospel is certainly preached, but the notion of personal "witnessing" is not the way most would describe that task. For Catholics, evangelism is a more holistic and corporate phenomenon, the witness of the Church itself to the power and presence of Christ in the world. Conservative and African American Protestant churches, on the other hand, almost always talked about personal evangelism and individual conversion as central to why they exist. Whether the church is big or small, rural or urban, old or young, in the Northeast or in the Bible Belt, the presence or absence of the conversion theme was a matter of religious tradition, not of demographics.

EDUCATING THE FAITHFUL

The religious work of congregations is often about worship and individual spiritual transformations, but it is just as often about the more routine and gradual process of teaching the practices and traditions of the faith. The fourth major spiritual theme in our congregational conversations was the theme of religious education, and nowhere was it more apparent than among Jewish leaders. All but one of the leaders we interviewed told us that Jewish education is the heart of what they do. The rabbi at a very large Reform temple in Seattle said his continuing goal is "to provide a solid base of Jewish education and identification," and his Orthodox counterpart at a small Seattle synagogue agreed. "I'm fanatical when it comes to Jewish education," he said. At a large Conservative synagogue in Hartford, the rabbi described a typical week this way: "You'll find a lot of activity focused on education. There would be ongoing classes on a weekly basis. . . . There would be family education for kids and parents." The rabbi at a large Chicago Reform temple echoed that assessment: "A major focus of our congregation is education." The goal, he said, is simply "to help our people live Jewish lives." Teaching the stories and customs, as well as the habits of religious observance, is a core task for the synagogues and temples of America. Both preserving tradition and teaching scripture are important to the work rabbis say they do.[8]

The Jewish emphasis on preserving and teaching religious traditions is different from the way most Christian congregations approach their task. A few Protestant congregations talked about preserving tradition, but they are mostly trying to prevent new innovations from diverting the faithful. As a Southern Baptist in Missouri put it, "I know one very important thing is that tradition is important. Being conservative and keeping that conservative church and not letting the church be swayed in effect . . . by what other churches are doing." The point in these tradition-oriented churches is not so much the teaching of a rich cultural heritage as protection from modern temptations.

More common among such Conservative Protestant churches is an emphasis on teaching members biblical principles for living. People need to know what the Bible teaches so they can live as God wants them to. Just as Jewish synagogues put a good deal of energy into Torah study, evangelical Protestants also want their members to know the Bible. For them the Bible defines and contains—indeed *is*— the tradition. The leader of a large Church of Christ congregation in Nashville said, "The basic belief behind the Churches of Christ is that the Bible is sufficient." A church is doing its job when the Bible is the touchstone for everything it does. As the pastor of a large Chinese evangelical church in Seattle said, "We use the Bible as our standard of measuring what is good and what is bad."[9]

The Bible is not just an abstract standard, however. These churches see teaching the Bible as the necessary corollary to preaching the gospel. Once people have been saved, they must become "disciples." When Conservative Protestants—including most African American churches—think about spiritual growth, they assume that

Bible study is the key. A Seattle pastor of a Wisconsin Synod Lutheran church said, "What people really need—they need the Word of God, and they need to grow spiritually." The Nashville Church of Christ pastor agreed: "Churches like ours should teach the Bible in an understandable and practical way." He, like most evangelicals, sees the Bible as the source for everyday wisdom about how to live.

This sort of talk about the Bible is remarkably absent from most liberal Protestant churches. In the notably conservative Episcopal diocese of Albuquerque, we did hear two parishes describe themselves as "Bible-believing Episcopal churches," but such descriptors were rare. Mainline Protestant churches do not describe "teaching the Bible" as central to their mission. Nor do most Roman Catholic churches, perhaps a legacy of former days when reading the Bible was not something ordinary members thought they could or should do. Even most African American churches do not *talk* about biblical tradition and instruction in the same way most white evangelicals do. The Bible is not absent in black churches—far from it. Biblical stories and language permeate all the tasks of the church, but the Bible seems less an end in itself.[10] Being "Bible believing" and placing biblical literacy high on the list of priorities is a particular mark of the churches in Conservative Protestantism.

Evangelical and Pentecostal churches are also distinctive in their emphasis on the particular beliefs and practices that constitute the tradition to be taught. Nearly half (47%) of the leaders in these groups mentioned particular distinctive religious beliefs or practices when they described their congregations—"We're the people who . . . " To be a good member or a good church entails learning and holding certain beliefs. In contrast, only 16 percent of Mainline Protestants, 11 percent of Catholic and Orthodox priests, and 16 percent of African American Protestant leaders talked about their churches in terms of particular beliefs that need to be taught. Preserving and teaching a doctrinal heritage is not their primary congregational goal.

In Sectarian groups, education is clearly important as well but is often subsumed in the process of proselytizing. A convert may go through months of study with a Jehovah's Witness or Latter-day Saint or Christian Science practitioner before ever joining the group. Members are unlikely to join until they have learned what the group is about, and they are unlikely to know unless they spend time being taught. Because these groups occupy a space at the margins of everyday American religious beliefs, introductory education is essential. After joining, intense study continues, as the convert learns how to defend and spread the faith. With so many new converts, there are also proportionately fewer second-generation members for whom childhood education is the primary means of entering the faith. For sectarian groups, education and conversion are intertwined goals.

Many Protestant congregations, on the other hand, may accept an inquirer straight off the street into full membership. Among Conservatives that initial acceptance is followed by the process of "discipleship" aimed at making converts biblically literate. Education is important but is likely to follow church membership, rather than precede it.

Expending congregational energy in religious education is a goal largely shaped by the religious tradition, but it is also a goal more likely pursued where education of other sorts is a commonplace in the congregation. Among Conservative Protestants, for instance, congregations full of people who have been to college are more likely to emphasize religious learning than are congregations where the average person is less well educated (27 percent of the former compared to 13 percent of the latter). Other demographic differences have no effect, but an emphasis on religious education is more likely where learning of all sorts is valued and available. Again, spiritual and worldly expectations meet in the way congregations think about their work.

Whether teaching or preaching, engaging in collective ritual or individual reflection and growth, congregations say that their primary focus is and should be spiritual. That should surprise no one. Yet in the rush to highlight the temporal benefits of congregational life, this more "otherworldly" side is sometimes downplayed. As we shall see, the spiritual and the temporal are by no means at odds with each other in most congregations; but beyond the good work that may be inspired by spiritual commitment, transcendence has its own logic. Those who gather in local religious communities do so in large measure because an important dimension of human experience finds expression there. If it is true that some significant portion of the human population has some spiritual sensibility, then we should not be surprised that social institutions—congregations in this case—have been organized to provide a recognized institutional location for spiritual activity. The work of relating humanity to the divine is, therefore, the core task that defines the resulting "organizational field."[11]

If those human spiritual sensibilities are not all alike, and people are free to organize groups to suit their own interests, we should not be surprised to find widely diverse congregations providing a necessarily broad array of opportunities for spiritual experiences, opportunities that a significant portion of the American population chooses to take.[12] Whether because of entrepreneurial "suppliers" (who have perhaps created a demand for diverse spiritual "goods") or because of inherently diverse market "demand," there is a dynamic interplay between the spiritual lives of individuals and the experiences offered and sometimes demanded by the gathered religious communities to which they belong. Worship, individual spiritual nurture, religious education, and conversion are the primary themes that give shape to that spiritual diversity, and they are themes largely given shape by particular religious traditions rather than by any local or demographic peculiarity of the congregation in question. At this most basic level, congregations are primarily sites for *religious* work, and that work is primarily defined by explicitly *religious* sources.

HOW DO THEY DO IT?

If congregations describe themselves as primarily organizations pursuing spiritual goals, what does that look like in practice? How do they deploy their resources to accomplish those goals? What would we see if we went for a visit? Over the course of our conversations with congregational leaders, we asked them about what happens in a "typical week," as well as what sorts of annual and other periodic events they hold. We probed for information on both formal and informal activities and organizations in the congregation, and we supplemented what they told us with a look at weekly bulletins and monthly newsletters (where those were available). We undoubtedly still missed getting a complete picture of the activities of many of these congregations. Congregations almost always do more than is readily apparent from even several sources of data.

In the description that follows, a congregation is counted as having a particular kind of activity if we have evidence that there is at least one group or event (an adult choir or children's Bible club, for instance) that regularly happens at least once a month. Our count underrepresents, therefore, the truly busy congregations where there are many different activities of any given type, meeting more than once a month. The church with a biweekly Thursday morning Bible Study is counted as having an adult spiritual activity but so is the (relatively rare) church that has a dozen such groups each week. This is a count of *types* of activities, not of the total *number* of activities. For each congregation, we recorded the eight most prevalent types of activities, *in addition to* their weekly worship event, their Sunday schools, and their choirs for children and adults. Eight types of additional activities were enough to capture the full range of work being done in 83 percent of the congregations. The relatively few congregations with more than eight kinds of activities also had many instances of those activities, and these very large and complex "outliers" are not fully accounted for in our counts. But the numbers in Table 2 give a fair indication of the sorts of activities found in the vast majority of congregations.

TABLE 2   Spiritual Activities of Congregations in Different Religious Traditions

Goal	Mainline Protestant (193)	Conservative Protestant (226)	African American Protestant (53)	Catholic & Orthodox (45)	All Congregations (549)
	Congregations with at Least One Regular Activity of This Type (%)				
Additional worship services*	8	45	39	51	33
Worship assistance groups*	7	2	7	50	6
Adult choir*	52	37	63	30	40
Children's choir*	21	11	50	9	16
Children's Sunday school	89	87	89	91	86
Weekday children's religious education*	7	20	9	33	16
Elementary and/or high school*	1	5	1	44	6
Adult Sunday school*	38	48	44	6	40
Adult spiritual group	72	73	86	73	74
Membership education*	9	12	30	44	16

NOTE: Number in parentheses indicates number of congregations in that group. All Congregations includes these four groups plus Sectarians, Jews, and Other Religions. For programs marked with an asterisk at least one of the differences among the groups is statistically significant at p < .10 (Oneway ANOVA, with Scheffe post-hoc comparisons).

Note that congregations do many things that are not "spiritual activities" and are thus not in this table. We will turn to other kinds of congregational work in later sections of the book. Table 2 enumerates the particular activities that support the various spiritual goals we heard described. Even this relatively long list of types of activities collapses an even longer list that emerged as we attempted to discern some order in the immensely varied activities found across the spectrum of U.S. congregations. Included in the "adult spiritual group" category, for instance, were weekday Bible and Torah studies, "spirituality" groups, prayer and healing groups, and a variety of other programs specifically aimed at the spiritual and religious lives of adult members.

Not shown in Table 2 is the single most common activity across all congregations. *Every* congregation we encountered had some form of regular gathering for worship. Not every congregation says that gathering for worship is central to its identity and mission, but they all do it. Not all these gatherings are weekly. Baha'is gather every nineteen days, for instance, and Hindus tend to gather for a variety of festivals and celebrations, unevenly spaced throughout the year. Muslims gather for Friday prayers. Jews gather on both Friday evening and Saturday morning. And most Christians gather on Sunday morning (Seventh-Day Adventists being the most visible exception). No matter when they do it, if they do nothing else, congregations spend organizational energy on worship.

What are people actually doing when they worship? It varies from the didactic to the ecstatic. Conservative Protestants include heartfelt singing and enthusiastic preaching in their pursuit of biblical education and evangelistic outreach. Mainline Protestants may use a thought-provoking sermon and awe-inspiring classical music as a path to individual insight and spiritual growth. Churches in the liturgical or sacramental traditions, both Catholic and Protestant, conservative and liberal, shape their worship around the celebration of divine presence in the Eucharist. Pentecostals and charismatics—white and black—encourage speaking in tongues, prophecy, being slain in the Spirit, or other ecstatic experiences. In many such churches rituals of healing occupy as central a place as a service of Eucharist does in other places. In many black churches there are also echoes of historic African religious rituals. Jewish worship, in contrast, is likely to be much more sedate. But collective prayer, spoken and sung, along with scripture and preaching, provides Jewish worshipers with opportunities for spiritual reflection and renewal. For Muslims at Friday prayers, there is a *khutbha* (or sermon) and chanted scripture, but also the experience of physically bowing in unison (and in close proximity) with fellow worshipers. As different as they appear at first, these many traditions each seek to use a range of ritual elements to elicit the spiritual formation they take as their primary task.[13]

Thanks to the detailed questions asked in the National Congregations Study, we know, for instance, that almost all Christian congregations have a sermon and at least some singing. In all traditions, pianos and organs are the most common instrumental accompaniment, but drums, electric guitars, and other instruments are also popular (Dudley and Roozen 2001). These surveys report that the majority of churches have choirs, and (as we will see) creating music for worship involves significant congregational energy. Listening to and participating in musical performances in worship services is the most common form of musical consumption and production in American society today (Chaves 2004, 188). The range and combination of activities that any given congregation includes may seem endlessly variable, but the template of preaching, praying, and singing shapes much of congregational worship. Each religious tradition may modify that template, but having a regular worship service is something they all do.

ADDITIONAL WORSHIP SERVICES

While regular worship is the baseline, most congregations do more. Fewer than 5 percent of congregations confine their activities to a single service of worship. Almost every congregation offers *something* else. Indeed, many congregations provide multiple opportunities each week just for worship. Sometimes doing so is a matter of accommodating a large congregation. Many large Catholic parishes, for instance, schedule multiple Masses spanning Saturday night and Sunday morning, expecting that the typical parishioner will choose the one most convenient or congenial to attend. But this sort of multiservice scheduling is not what is counted as "additional worship services" in Table 2. The count there reflects congregations that offer at least one opportunity for members to *return* to worship. In half of Catholic and Orthodox parishes, for instance, at least one weekday service is offered. In many parishes, daily early-morning Masses draw a core of the faithful to a time of prayer and contemplation before they begin their workday. Some Episcopal parishes follow a similar pattern, offering an early Eucharist at least one morning each week, while others offer a special healing or prayer service on a weekday evening.

In nearly half the Conservative Protestant churches, Sunday night and/or "midweek" services are the norm. These are often more casual than the Sunday morning equivalent, including favorite hymns, small-group prayer, and a participatory Bible study rather than a formal sermon. African American churches follow a similar worship pattern, although not in quite as many of their churches. Not nearly everyone comes to these evening services, but Sunday night and Wednesday night services are an evangelical cultural legacy. The smallest evangelical congregations are just as likely to have these services as are the largest. Offering this extra worship opportunity is not a matter of available resources or the pressures of size; it is rather a matter of identity, of being faithful to a tradition. Both Catholics and Conservative Protestants, different as they may be, organize around the expectation that one weekly worship experience is not enough.

For Mainline Protestants, worship is much more likely to be a once-a-week event. Similarly, in the Sectarian, Jewish, and Other Religions categories, there are only a few exceptions to the once-a-week (or less) pattern. About a third of Episcopal churches invite members back for worship at least once during the week, but almost none of the other Mainline congregations do. Sunday morning is not just their primary worship event: it is the only one.

CHOIRS

Across the Christian traditions, worship is almost always accompanied by music, often led by a choir (see Table 2). Very few (7%) outside the Christian tradition include a choir among their congregational activities,[14] but in almost half (43%) of the Protestant churches and nearly a third (30%) of Catholic and Orthodox ones, at least one volunteer adult choir participates in leading worship. Having choirs (for either adults or children) is more likely in some traditions than in others, but it is also more likely when a particular local congregation sees worship as a core task. At least in part, organizational energy spent on choral music is an extension of the priority placed on worship.

Neither religious tradition nor congregational priorities tell the whole story, however. That Mainliners are more likely to have choirs than are Conservatives, for instance, is also accounted for by size and location. Conservative congregations are somewhat disproportionately located in the rural areas where small churches without formally organized choirs are the norm. Other social forces are at work as well. Holding size and location constant, Mainline churches with choirs outnumber similarly situated Conservative ones about three to two. If an urban or suburban Mainline church also sees worship as central to its mission, it will nearly always (85%) have a choir. In a congregation with sufficient resources and a focus on worship, a choir is an expected part of the package. Religious mission and social resources combine to shape how congregations do their work.

The emphasis on choral music and worship in Mainline churches is also a reflection of their somewhat higher educational and income levels. Indeed, across all the religious traditions, choirs were more likely in congregations where a majority of participants have a college education and high family incomes. Knowledge, preferences, and habits established by higher education are often linked to the consumption of classical music (DiMaggio and Mohr 1985), and that larger cultural pattern finds its way into the organizational patterns of congregations. For Mainline Protestants these demographic and status realities also coincide with tradition. From the cantatas of Bach to contemporary settings by Rutter or Vaughan Williams, the overlap between classic choral repertoire and Christian church music is enormous. Having a choir is an organizational strategy that reflects a complicated mix of religious tradition, local priorities, resources, and cultural preferences.

Neither classical music nor formal choirs are absent from Conservative Protestant traditions, and classically oriented choirs are not the universal norm among Mainline ones, but the tendencies within the two traditions are in different directions. Conservatives have long had a tradition of keeping music accessible to the whole congregation. More recently that has often meant simple "praise choruses" anyone can sing, led by a small group of instrumentalists and singers who form a "praise team" rather than a choir.[15] Many Mainline churches, on the other hand, are housed in historic traditional sanctuaries and sponsor classical organ and choral performances that are open to the community at large. Investing in such musical offerings is part of the spiritual (and outreach) work done by these churches.

A tradition of choral and congregational singing is also strong within the African American churches. From field chants and work songs to spirituals to metered hymns to traditional and contemporary gospel music, black churches have carried on a vibrant array of musical traditions.[16] Nearly two-thirds of black churches told us that they have at least one adult choir, and in a third of those, there are multiple groups—often a men's choir, a women's choir, or a senior adult choir, in addition to the primary adult ensemble that often sings both in regular services and when pastor and congregants travel to fellowship with other churches. Church musician James Abbington claims that "in the African American church one typically will find at least five or six choirs, even if the church only has one hundred members" (Abbington 2001, 31). Arrayed in beautiful robes, these groups stand in the proud line of African American musicians who have given the United States many of its most renowned singers.

This is not something African American churches do just because they have the resources to do it. Rural churches and small churches are less likely to have this sort of organized music program; but in every size and location, black churches are more likely to have a singing group than are white churches. Indeed, the habit of sponsoring adult choirs is something African American congregations take with them into denominations that are historically white. Taking all other factors into account, congregations that are predominantly African American are more likely to have an adult choir, no matter what denomination they are in.

The very same pattern holds for children's musical activities. Black churches begin early to make the links among music, faith, and community, as, in their own way, do churches in the white Protestant Mainline. In both traditions congregations often invest organizational resources in music as a carrier of their religious culture. By contrast, we found no congregations outside the Catholic and Protestant traditions that included children's choirs in their round of activities. In addition, Catholics are much less likely to do so than are Protestants; and among white churches, children's choirs are less likely among Conservatives than among Mainliners.

Each stream of religious tradition shapes the musical investments of its congregations, but in all traditions, resources are a key factor as well. The bigger the church, the more likely they are to have a children's choir. The biggest churches may have multiple choirs designed for different age groups, in addition to bell choirs and even drama and liturgical dance ensembles. Religious traditions and congregational resources combine to explain why some congregations are more likely than others to pursue their spiritual goals through a children's choir.[17]

For many of those who sing, choirs pay both spiritual and social dividends. Many members find their closest friends among fellow singers and enjoy the camaraderie of rehearsal time, as well as the collective excitement of performing together. For most, this experience has a deep spiritual dimension as well. Both adults and children sing of their faith, expressing the joys and sorrows of life as only music can. Whether led by a fulltime professional musician or by a volunteer from their own ranks, a congregation's investment in a choir is an investment in the spiritual wellbeing of both singers and listeners.

WORSHIP HELPERS

The work of worship is supported by clergy and laity who plan and lead and participate. In addition to choirs and other musicians, there are also readers, ushers, servers, and sometimes even parking lot attendants. While most congregations mobilize ad hoc volunteers to do these tasks, in some traditions worship helpers form a more organized group. Over half of the Catholic parishes in which we interviewed, for instance, mentioned some sort of altar guild and/or liturgy planning group. Similarly, just over half of Episcopal parishes mentioned an altar guild. In most but not all churches where formal ritual is a central element in worship, special groups do the mundane work of washing linens and polishing brass, work that nevertheless takes on a sacred character because of its tie to worship. Joanna Gillespie (1993) argues that the Episcopal women she interviewed turn their service on the altar guild into "holy work." Said one, "You give this gift in a very secret way; that makes it so precious and so deep." As with choirs, these worship-assistance groups can also create opportunities for social bonding and interpersonal support. In planning and facilitating the congregation's most important sacred moments, these groups of parishioners (often mostly or exclusively women) strengthen both spiritual and social bonds.

African American churches have their own traditions of worship support in numbers not well reflected in Table 2.[18] Usher boards and other auxiliaries play visible roles in every traditional black Baptist service I have ever attended. One of my students explained to a class at Hartford Seminary, "About ushers? In the black church, it is BIG! Real BIG! There are junior usher boards, senior usher boards, men's usher boards. They have national conventions; they are uniformed; they are taught that they are the first and last person you see at church. They elect officers yearly; they are a vital ministry of any black congregation."[19] Ushers do far more than see members to their seats and hand out programs. Standing at white-gloved attention they occupy the church's aisles throughout the service, ready to assist with whatever is called for. In many churches white-capped nurses similarly occupy strategic seats throughout the sanctuary, ready to assist with both the spiritual and physical needs of the worshippers. Both groups have likely been to regional or national conventions at which they have honed and exhibited their skills. In addition, an elite group of women in the church may form a support group for the pastor, preparing the pulpit with as much care as an Episcopal altar guild would lavish on a communion table. Each tradition has created roles that allow some participants greater access to holy things, roles that invite them to assist their fellow parishioners in the spiritual experiences of worship.[20] Black Baptists, like Episcopalians and Roman Catholics—and unlike any of the other religious traditions—deploy some of their organizational energy in specialized support of corporate worship.

CHILDREN'S RELIGIOUS EDUCATION

In most congregations worship is a combination of multigenerational activity and adult-oriented experience. The work of addressing the spiritual needs of children falls more directly to each tradition's equivalent of Sunday school. Whether it substitutes for worship attendance or occurs before or after the congregation's primary worship service, some form of concentrated religious education for children is typically paired with the congregation's primary weekly worship gatherings. For many Jewish and Muslim groups, even though weekly worship happens on Friday or Saturday, or both, children's religious education occupies the traditional Christian time frame on Sunday morning. Jewish and Muslim children thus go to "Sunday school" just as do their Christian schoolmates. Indeed, synagogues in our study nearly matched churches in the prevalence of regular weekly children's religious classes. The new immigrant religions, on the other hand, were less consistent participants in this particular U.S. religious institution. The small Muslim masjid where we interviewed did not have a Sunday school, nor did the Zen Buddhist center, but the Hindu temple and one of the Nichiren Buddhist groups did.[21]

Within all the Christian traditions, however, regular weekly classes for children are expected. Those that do not have a Sunday school are likely to be very small (fewer than fifty regular participants) and report that they have few if any children for whom to form a Sunday school. Still, the threshold for providing children's classes is quite low. Christian and Jewish congregations with at least fifty regular attenders are very likely (93%) to have children's classes, no matter what their denominational tradition or the proportion of children among their attenders. Second only to a regular worship event, religious education for children forms the institutionalized backbone of congregational life. Different religious traditions may dictate what is taught, but organizing a weekly set of classes is a pattern set by larger cultural expectations.

For at least some congregations, Sunday school is just the beginning. Most Jewish congregations, for instance, have Hebrew schools that meet one or more days each week, offering both basic religious instruction and preparation for bar and bat mitzvahs. The priority on education we heard from rabbis is reflected in two-thirds of them reporting these weekday programs in their synagogues. Catholic parishes, similarly, are likely to have CCD (Confraternity of Christian Doctrine) classes, especially for youth preparing for confirmation. The 34 percent who reported such activities to us probably underrepresents the actual prevalence of weekday Catholic religious education. Among both Catholics and Jews, after-school religious education classes are a long-standing American tradition, while among Protestants they are much less common.[22]

The Protestant congregations most likely to gather their children during the week are Conservative churches, and the most common pattern among them is a

Wednesday night gathering involving adults and children alike. Sometimes there is a dinner, but even if not, the adults gather for Bible study and prayer, while children participate in programs rather like religious equivalents of scouting. As with other supplemental activities, these are rare among the smallest congregations, no matter what the tradition. Small congregations are unlikely to have the human and material resources necessary for supporting extensive children's programming. But weekday children's religious education is not just a luxury some congregations indulge in when they have plenty of money and members. They do it because their religious tradition and their own sense of mission encourage them to do so. Conservative Protestants are more likely than Mainliners to have programs, but even among Conservative Protestant churches, those that prioritize preaching and teaching the Bible are more likely to do weekday education, no matter what their resources or demographics. Similarly, among all congregations those that prioritize support for families are more likely to invest in these additional children's religious activities.

Tradition and mission are often embodied in and facilitated by denominational programs as well. Among Conservative Protestant churches that have at least fifty regular attenders, nearly a third (30%) have weekly children's programs (compared to 7 percent of comparable Mainline churches), but even within the Conservative world programs are most prevalent among denominations such as the Assemblies of God, Southern Baptists, and Nazarenes, where the denomination supplies a highly developed curriculum for an age-graded program. Assemblies of God youth, for instance, attend Royal Rangers and Missionettes, where they learn scripture, play games, do crafts, learn about and support missionaries, and work toward awards that are analogous to scout badges. The nondenominational program Awana provides a similar structure and was used in Southern Baptist, Evangelical Free Church, and National Baptist congregations, as well as in various of the independent churches we studied.[23]

The only Mainline Protestant denomination with anything like these youth mission and training organizations is the Reformed Church in America, and it sits squarely in the zone between the Conservative and Mainline traditions. This tiny denomination, with local groups of "Gems" and "Cadets," accounts for a third of all the Mainline weekday children's organizations we found. Other Mainline Protestant congregations are very unlikely to structure regular weekly religious education for their children beyond the Sunday school they almost all have.

They are also highly unlikely to create a whole separate religious school system. Historically, Protestant families could depend on public schools to reflect their values and even to include religious teaching in the school day (Brereton 1998). In many small towns the overlap between Sunday school and public school could be significant. (I was in fourth grade before I had a public school teacher who was not a member of the church I attended.) Catholics and Jews who wanted similar reinforcement of religious tradition, on the other hand, had to build their own schools. The residue of that history is that Catholics and Jews today are still far more likely than Protestants to invest the considerable resources necessary to build and maintain their own elementary and high schools. Nationally about one Roman Catholic parish in three has a school, and 52 percent of the Roman Catholic parishes we surveyed did.[24] Fewer Catholic children are in parish schools today than fifty years ago, but still about one in five get their elementary schooling within a Church context (Froehle and Gautier 2000, 72–73). Even with numerous and visible school closings, and with the increasing integration of Catholics into the American middle class, Catholic parishes are still more likely to have a school than are congregations in any other American religious tradition.[25]

Within Conservative Judaism, Solomon Schechter day schools are also prevalent, and both of the Conservative synagogues where we interviewed supported a school. Orthodox Jews educate their children in yeshivot, while Reform Jews have largely joined the public school system. Having previously moved into the public schools, Conservative Jews began to worry after World War II that supplemental after-school education was not sufficient. The growing Schechter school movement was their response.[26]

Only a few Protestant denominations have historically included schools in their ministry. Within Mainline Protestantism, the Episcopal Church is the most likely to support day (and boarding) schools. But unlike other parish schools, Episcopal ones pride themselves on religious diversity and tolerance and rarely have a majority of Episcopal students. Names like All Saints, Trinity, or St. Mark's are likely to be recognized in a local community as signaling the highest-quality private education. With famous elite boarding schools like Kent and Chatham Hall among their number, the link between Episcopal schools and the American upper class has a long history. Along with learning the rhythms of the Anglican liturgy and the layout of the Book of Common Prayer, Episcopal school students are shaped by the sensibilities and expectations of American's most well-off Protestants.

Lutherans, following their Catholic immigrant cousins, also established a strong system of schools in which youth learned their catechism alongside their multiplication tables. By the time we surveyed congregations in the late 1990s, those in the more liberal Evangelical Lutheran Church in America (ELCA) did not report any parish schools. They had joined other Mainline Protestants in dropping elementary and high schools as part of their efforts at religious education. On the Conservative side, however, more than a quarter (28%) of those in the Wisconsin and Missouri Synods reported schools. The Missouri Synod nationally reported just over a thousand elementary schools in 2001 (five times as many as the larger ELCA), with about half their student population coming from the LCMS parishes that run them.[27]

Seventh-Day Adventists (SDA) are the other Conservative denomination with a history of establishing schools (Knight 1984). Both their unique habit of worshiping on Saturday (unique at least for Protestants) and their strict dietary guidelines and health consciousness demanded protection from the cultural erosion secular public schools might threaten. One of the four SDA congregations we studied had a school, roughly equivalent to the one in five rate the North American Conference of the Church reports for the continent as a whole.[28] There are over one thousand Adventist schools here, but nearly another five thousand located elsewhere in the world. Like Catholics, Adventists are a multi-ethnic church body, and the non-Anglo members of these traditions have especially benefited from the education they have received in church schools. African Americans in both traditions, for instance, are twice as likely to be college graduates compared to their black Baptist peers (Kosmin and Lachman 1993, 272–73).

A new group of Conservative Protestants has entered the world of schooling more recently. Beginning especially in the 1960s, but accelerating in the 1980s, independent evangelical congregations have begun their own "Christian schools." Fourteen percent of the nondenominational and Independent Baptist churches in our sample were sponsoring schools. No less than earlier religious groups, these Conservative Christians perceive public schools as a threat to their way of life. No single denominational label identifies such schools, but the adjective "Christian" is widely recognized as a signal of their distinctive Conservative Protestant mission.[29]

So some but not all Protestant denominational traditions have established a pattern of sponsoring schools. In the Mainline there are Lutherans and Episcopalians. On the Conservative side, there are other Lutherans, Seventh-Day Adventists, and nondenominational churches. All these join the patterns set before them by Roman Catholics and Conservative Jews. Belonging to one of these schooling traditions is by far the most important factor in whether a local Protestant congregation will have its own school. Fourteen percent of those in groups where schools have been a tradition operate a school themselves, while only 1 percent of congregations in all the "non-school" religious traditions do. From Presbyterians to Southern Baptists and from Reform Jews to Methodists, almost no other congregations reported either an elementary or secondary school as a ministry. Without a denominational tradition of sponsoring schools, local congregations are extremely unlikely to do so. Congregations are making decisions about how they do religious education in part based on what "congregations like us" do.

Beyond those traditional precedents, demographics also make a difference, at least among Protestants. Catholic parishes seem to support schools regardless of their own resources and demographic constituency, but among Protestants institutionalized patterns combine with resources, demography, and the congregation's own sense of purpose to nudge some congregations more than others toward schools. As is so often the case, size matters. Where no schooling precedents exist, bigger congregations are more likely to be the ones that break the mold; but even within the traditions that have routinely supported schools, only 8 percent of small to midsized congregations (under three hundred) have schools, whereas half of larger ones do. In addition to having sufficient resources, it also helps to have a passion for serving families. Those that named family support as a specific local goal were most likely to have invested in maintaining a school. With no historic precedent and no specific sense of mission, almost no congregations have schools. With both precedent and a sense of mission, 42 percent do. Even relatively small congregations that see families as central to their mission—and have the support of traditions where schools are common—often devote some of their resources to the daily education of children.

The other factor at work here is race. Unlike the Catholic schools, non-Catholic schools are overwhelmingly found among white congregations. Controlling for everything else—the existence of a tradition of day schools, enough members to support one, and a congregational priority on supporting families—predominantly white congregations are twice as likely to have a school as are similar nonwhite congregations. We found only four congregations that broke this pattern: an African American Lutheran Church–Missouri Synod, in Chicago (where most LCMS churches have schools); one National Baptist Church, also in Chicago; and two mixed-ethnic nondenominational churches, one in Nashville and one in Seattle.

These last two are apparently too new to fall into the stereotype of southern Conservative "Christian schools" as "segregation academies." The Nashville church was founded in 1982, and its membership reflects the sort of prodiversity agenda for which there is now a niche in parts of the "New South." Its Seattle counterpart was founded only one year earlier, and its ethnic mix is not unusual in that Pacific Rim city. These new evangelical congregations have created schools to reflect their religious values, but with less of the racial baggage older congregations carry (Emerson and Smith 2000). But they are the exception. Whatever the reason, white Protestant congregations are more apt to spend the considerable resources to create a parish school than are their mixed and non-Anglo counterparts.

Still, the number of Protestant day schools is very small, and neither Mainline nor African American churches are very likely to offer *any* weekday religious education opportunities to their children and youth. The contrasts to Conservative, Catholic, and Jewish patterns are striking. While the typical Presbyterian or Congregationalist child may spend forty-five minutes in Sunday school (often while her parents attend worship), many evangelical children go to worship with their parents after already having been in Sunday school for an hour. They then return to church for at least another hour of religious activity midweek. Similarly, Jewish children may participate in a weekly Shabbat service, go to Sunday school, and attend after-school Hebrew classes. And whether or not their own congregation sponsors a school, Jews and Conservative Protestants are likely to know that there is a school nearby that might further deepen a child's religious knowledge and practice. The implicit message in these organizational patterns is that Jews and Conservative Christians (as well as Catholics) have a good deal of specialized religious knowledge to teach their children, while Mainline Protestants seem more confident that necessary religious knowledge can be gained (perhaps indirectly) from sources and experiences beyond the congregation.

ADULT RELIGIOUS EDUCATION

Educational activities for adults are not so prevalent as those for children. The norm for the spiritual support of adults—in all religious traditions—is some sort of activity during the week, a kind of optional continuing education. Three-quarters of all congregations provide at least one prayer or study group for the adults who choose to participate. Like offering children's Sunday school, this item on congregational calendars is more a matter of cultural expectations and resources than a matter dictated by any given religious tradition. There are no statistically significant differences between the various religious streams in the likelihood of offering weekday activities for the spiritual benefit of their adult members. As part of the institutional template for American congregational life, each tradition fills the expectation with its own spiritual content. It is a template, however, that is affected by size and location. Country churches are less likely to organize formal activities than city churches, and bigger churches do more than small ones. Size and location combine to multiply the likelihood of congregational programming for adults.

Scheduling weekend adult religious education that parallels weekend children's classes is, on the other hand, both less common and largely a matter shaped by religious tradition. Less than half (40%) of all congregations have adult classes that meet in conjunction with (usually before) the congregation's primary worship time, when most people are present. Conservative Protestant churches are the most likely to do this, while Catholics are the least likely to do so. In part, the Conservative response is a reflection of Conservative congregations' disproportionate emphasis on biblical learning and on conversion. But it is the tradition itself—not any given congregation's choice to emphasize these particular goals—that sets the pattern. The emphasis on continued learning in these evangelical traditions sets the baseline organizational pattern. But within the Conservative and African American churches, where adult Sunday school is more likely to be the norm, Bible Belt culture also reinforces that norm. Size and location multiply the likelihood that a given congregation will have an adult Sunday school. A good-sized southern church is nearly twice as likely to have such a program compared to a small nonsouthern one.

The absence of a tradition of adult Sunday school is especially noticeable among Catholic and Orthodox parishes. These groups pour exceptional energy into educating their young, but only a tiny proportion organize regular weekend study opportunities for adults, and only half as many Catholic adults (compared to Conservatives and African Americans) reported on our survey that they attend any kind of religious education even once a month. What Catholic parishes do offer in higher than average numbers, however, are membership education classes designed for those coming into the faith for the first time (see Table 2). Many Catholic parishes offer a Rite of Christian Initiation for Adults class for the increasing numbers of non-Catholics who are joining as seekers and spouses. A generation or more ago, intermarriage was rare, as were other conversions into what were then relatively insular religious enclaves. No more. A little over a third of the marriages officially recognized by the Catholic Church today are between a Catholic and a non-Catholic (Froehle and Gautier 2000, 13). In Reform Judaism the numbers are similar, and many synagogues offer a "Judaism 101" class for people who never learned the basics as children, either because they were brought up in nonobservant homes or because they were not born Jewish. While both Jewish and Catholic communities continue to worry about the effects of intermarriage, many synagogues and parishes are meeting the challenge by welcoming and teaching these newcomers.[30]

Members of newer immigrant traditions may not be "new members," but they are new to the task of living their traditions in the American context.

Congregations in Other Religions almost always reported having some sort of adult classes, since knowledge that might have been assumed in a home culture has to be taught here (Warner 2002a). Sectarian groups are similarly invested in gathering adults for religious education. Among Jehovah's Witnesses "studying" is sometimes a synonym for participation in the movement, and each of the two regular weekly meetings of the group involves study of the Bible, *The Watchtower*, and other official publications (Holden 2002, 64–67). These groups outside the historic mainstream of American religion know they must focus on providing adults with necessary instruction.

This attention to the education of converts and relative outsiders stands in contrast to the pattern among white Protestants. Even though 70 percent of white Protestant churches reported that half or more of their members grew up in some other denomination, most commonly that other denomination was another Protestant one, and the member was more of a "switcher" than a "convert." Even when most in the congregation are switchers, however, only 14 percent of these white Protestant congregations have regular classes for new members. African American churches, in contrast, are more likely to insist that all their new members spend several Sundays in a class taught by the pastor. There the basic teachings of the faith are reinforced, and pastors have a chance to establish strong personal connections with each entering member.

BLUEPRINTS FOR BUILDING FAITH

As institutions fundamentally organized around religious goals, American congregations are both immensely diverse and remarkably predictable. The spiritual work they do has come to be organized around three basic activities—worship, weekly religious education for children, and optional continuing education for adults. Those three are universal enough that they exist across religious traditions and with little in the way of variation that comes from the particular goals or resources of the local congregation.

Different streams of American religious tradition create very different communities of discourse about the proper spiritual mission for congregations, so that different themes are heard in the way different kinds of congregations talk about their work. Those locally articulated spiritual goals, however, mostly have indirect effects. That a given local leader emphasizes one priority over another—and thereby encourages one kind of activity over another—mostly results from the organizational templates provided by American culture and augmented by the particular religious stream of which that congregation is a part.

American culture expects its congregations to engage in worship, children's religious education, and some minimal educational opportunities for adults. Beyond those basics, however, a wide array of other spiritual opportunities exists in U.S. congregations. Which kind of activity one might find, from altar guilds to children's choirs and from adult Sunday school to a parish elementary school, depends on the particular religious tradition. The overall variety of offerings is highly dependent on the sheer size of the congregation and the organizational resources it can bring to the task of supporting its members' spiritual lives, but some patterns of activity persist even in the face of meager organizational resources. Conservative and African American Protestants are likely, for instance, to offer multiple worship opportunities and educational programs for both children and adults that similarly situated white Mainline Protestants and Catholics would not. Differences across religious tradition are strong and consistent. Congregations in some traditions simply expend more organizational energy on worship and religious education. The work of building faith is always a part of congregational life, but in some congregations other work gets equal or greater effort. The spiritual story cannot be told alone.

CHAPTER THREE · Building Communities

Food, Fun, and Fellowship

Participants in American congregations are in large measure there for the spiritual benefits they receive, and congregations claim the religious work of worship and education as their first priority. But congregations are also gathering places. They build and sustain relationships among their members, alongside relationships with the god who is the focus of their devotion. On our survey checklists both leaders and members said that this "fellowship" dimension was almost as important as the spiritual one. Leaders typically said that "creating a family-like" atmosphere and "providing fellowship activities" were very important. Members who completed the Sunday survey agreed that "a strong sense of fellowship" was a very important priority, and the congregation's friendliness and likeable pastor were very important to their choice to join.

Woven through all the spiritual work congregations do is the reality that it is being undertaken collectively. Alongside the "vertical" dimension of congregational life are the "horizontal" ties among those who gather. As we analyzed the goals and activities of congregations it was often impossible to disentangle the social from the spiritual. People pray together, study together, and worship together and are, at once, creating a community and honoring their god. Just as themes of spiritual priority emerged in our conversations, so did themes of fellowship and community building. In every religious tradition a substantial number of the leaders we interviewed talked about "belonging" as a key priority (see Table 3). Recall that we recorded and counted the three most dominant themes in our

TABLE 3   Fellowship Goals of Congregations in Different Religious Traditions

Goal	Mainline Protestant (193)	Conservative Protestant (226)	African American Protestant (53)	Catholic & Orthodox (45)	All Congregations (549)
			Congregations Naming Goal as One of Their Three Priorities (%)		
Provide a place to belong*	50	36	20	23	37
Support families*	16	16	35	39	18

NOTE: Number in parentheses indicates number of congregations in that group. All Congregations includes these four groups plus Sectarians, Jews, and Other Religions. For goals marked with an asterisk at least one of the differences among the groups is statistically significant at p < .10 (Oneway ANOVA, with Scheffe post-hoc comparisons).

informants' conversations about priorities. Some of those themes are not shown in Table 3 because they concern the spiritual work we have already examined or the work of service and missions to which we will turn later. In addition, some congregations emphasized more than one fellowship theme, so the numbers in Table 3 are not intended to add up to 100 percent. They count just the fellowship tasks, showing how often those themes were at the top of the list, and in 37 percent of all the congregations, we heard about a perceived need for community building as a primary concern. Part of what they understand themselves to be doing is providing a "home" for sometimes-rootless modern individuals.

Robert Putnam has warned that Americans are too prone to "bowling alone," that we are tending to our own needs and pleasures in ways that increasingly isolate us from others (Putnam 2000). As we asked congregational leaders about what issues and concerns most burdened their members, we often heard about the need for connection. In some cases it was loneliness, but more often they saw a desire to go deeper than everyday interaction allows and to invest in the lives of others. The rector of an Albuquerque Episcopal parish was especially eloquent: "The thing I hear about most is community . . . you know, having a place where you belong, where you can connect, where there is some depth that you share together." A member of an African American Methodist church in Chicago echoed that need for village and family. Church, she said, is "a place where you have family, and when you come to a big city from a small town, it's awfully nice to have someplace in that big city where people who don't live with you know where you are. Know who you are and what you're doing." Whether or not it is true that society is more fragmented today, many people believe it to be true, and congregations seem to be taking up both the concern and the challenge of responding.

The concern about fragmentation and community took a more poignant and specific form in the many worries we heard about families and children. This was the other significant way congregational leaders talked about their efforts to provide communal support (see Table 3). Almost one in five (18%) of the congregations we surveyed said that an important part of their mission is serving and supporting families. Drugs, education, and every kind of moral dilemma loom large in the minds of parents, and most of them hope that their congregations can help.

We heard concerns about families in all sorts of places, even where one might not expect people to be very worried. In rural Missouri a Catholic priest said his parishioners "want to know how to keep their kids from, you know, getting in trouble and that kind of stuff." Drunk driving by teens was a significant problem on the rural highways in that county, putting teens at risk of life and limb. In rural Alabama we found a small Beachy Amish community maintaining very traditional ways, but even there the leader said, "I would say that our family structure is probably the greatest thing on our minds—raising our families and training them, teaching them to be Christians." While the sense of threat may not be as great, the priority is still there. People want to belong to a community that will help them raise their children. Not nearly everyone who is a religious participant is also a parent, but local congregations recognize that one of their tasks is creating an environment where families can be supported in the difficult work of raising children.[1]

Few religious traditions in the United States are more focused on family life than the Latter-day Saints. A local leader in Albuquerque told us that "the ward [parish] is considered a resource to the family so that the family can accomplish and receive the kind of spiritual growth and nurture that it needs and the support that it needs." Similarly, a Jehovah's Witness leader in Nashville told us they were using their weekly book study meeting to cover "The Secret to Family Happiness." In these very distinct religious communities, the survival of the community and its traditions depends on the success of families in passing on their faith. We heard this in the Jewish emphasis on education as well. Congregations, especially those in minority communities, know that supporting family life is a critical part of their task.

Adults expect to find friendship and support for themselves, but they also see congregations as the sort of community that can be an extended family, filling in when their own efforts fall short. A member of an especially inclusive Episcopal parish in Albuquerque talked about what the church means for her. "One of the reasons I feel so comfortable here, especially as a single mom, is because I feel the kids are supported here. And I know if [my child] is out of line, somebody is going to say, 'You're out of line.' And that's really helpful for me." Not every congregation succeeds in providing effective support for families, but much of what members expect and leaders hope to supply is the sort of community where parents are not left on their own. Many want their congregations to be part of the "village" that raises the children.

The emphasis on community building for adults is present in substantial proportions of the congregations across every religious tradition, but it was stronger among the predominantly white Protestant groups, especially the Mainline (see Table 3). In the Mainline this theme was expressed in terms of welcome and hospitality. At a Chicago Lutheran church (ELCA) the simple goal was "to be a welcoming place." At a neighboring United Church of Christ church we heard, "If you wanted a one-word mission statement, it's 'welcome.'"

Evangelicals are no less convinced that human companionship is part of God's intention for congregations. They too talked about the importance of being friendly and welcoming newcomers into their fold. The pastor of a large independent evangelical church in Nashville said, "The church has taken on the vision of basically being very much, a very feeling, caring, loving, compassionate fellowship." Warmth and caring were words we heard often in these churches. In a devastated neighborhood in south Chicago, a small Assemblies of God mission church is "creating an environment where people can come, where it's safe and they have family. We try to create a family atmosphere." In surroundings where "community" is an especially endangered species, this congregation knows that caring relationships are a basic part of the task.

Noting the troubled context of this small church raises the question of whether the concern for community building is more important to some American congregations than to others. Are some people more worried than others? On closer inspection of our interviews, two interesting demographic differences appeared. First, congregations in the Northeast are considerably more likely to talk about the importance of community. The associate pastor at a midsized Hartford Congregationalist (UCC) church said, "There is a real hunger for community." Building relationships takes time and does not always come naturally, however, and a Hartford Episcopal rector noted with some pride, "This is a parish, I think, that breaks a lot of New England stereotypes of being cold and reserved. I think they are very warm." Perhaps that famous New England reserve helps to account for the concern about community so many leaders voiced, a concern these two Hartford churches were attempting to address.

The other demographic difference is the relative absence of concern for community among the rural congregations in our sample. Those most embedded in *gemeinschaft* (traditional face-to-face communities) do not think or talk about the need to repair fragmented relationships.[2] Community is not something they have to work to create or a problem to which congregations need to respond. To the extent that rural residents see each other in multiple contexts (church, school, business, civic groups) and have known each other over time, their relationships have a degree of depth that in other contexts must be intentionally constructed. Not all rural places are so settled, and some rural churches have to work at building community, but finding a place to belong is more salient in the cities and suburbs.

It is important to note that nearly half (47%) of urban and suburban congregations have fewer than one hundred regular weekly attenders, and some of those small to midsized congregations are strategic about the advantages of their size in the community-building task. In comparing his midsized Methodist church to the giant-sized Congregational church down the road, a Hartford pastor illustrated the difference this way: "When we do prayer concerns, . . . I call you by name. There are people that have just never seen that before. Because they've been one of a thousand." As we will see, larger congregations tend to build community by creating many small groups, activities, and programs. Small congregations, on the other hand, offer an intergenerational community-of-the-whole in which, like the bar on the television comedy *Cheers*, "everybody knows your name."

The emphasis on providing a place to belong is also strong among the Jewish congregations where we interviewed. They are well aware that a supportive community is necessary to sustaining a tradition and that people will not stay long for the learning if they do not like the people with whom they are studying. At a large Conservative synagogue in Hartford, the rabbi said, "There's a real strong sense of this as a place that means a lot to a lot of people. I like that. And people by and large are not only civil, but they genuinely like each other. . . . [They] really enjoy celebrating together."

Among people whose ethnic or religious identity is not supported by the larger culture, the congregation can become a special kind of home. The emphasis on belonging is especially acute among the many new immigrant groups making their way into American society. The pastor of a small Asian United Church of Christ congregation in Seattle struggled to explain how important people are for each other: "Providing a family is so important for us. . . . It is so precious for us because we believe we have to work together." The predominantly Asian congregations in our sample were especially insistent on the importance of establishing a welcoming community. Congregations are a safe space in an otherwise difficult cultural environment. Warner (1993; 1999) argues that because congregations are seen as a legitimate way for people to gather and organize, because religious practice is a protected right, people who otherwise have few cultural opportunities find in congregations places to celebrate and reinforce their sense of identity and solidarity as a group, a function repeatedly documented in research on a variety of immigrant groups in a variety of religious traditions.[3]

For mixed-ethnic congregations, the task of creating community is salient in a very different way. "Community" in general is not what must be built here, but the particular kind of community that bridges major cultural divides (Warner 1997). Some of these congregations are predominantly Anglo with more than a token 10 percent Hispanic, Asian, or African American population; but a few (outside the South, nearly one in six congregations) reported an even more thorough mix where no single group numbered more than 60 percent of the congregation. Leaders in these multi-ethnic congregations were more likely than most to talk about building community as their goal, a goal they know requires difficult and challenging work. As members bring divergent cultural experiences into a congregation, nothing can be taken for granted. Nothing else the congregation does will happen if it does not attend to the basic work of building relationships across these differences. A heavy dose of good will has to be combined with a steady diet of intentional opportunities for open communication.[4]

Building community presents a variety of challenges, depending on the context and the group attempting to form an ongoing set of human connections; but these are challenges many congregations see as central to their work. Some congregations foster more intimacy than others. Some have to be more intentional than others. And in any given congregation, some members are more deeply attached than others. Still, the work of building bonds of trust, caring, communication, and shared labor is part of what congregations do. Virtually no one said this was unimportant. Congregations differed only on how important it is in comparison to the other things they do.

While all voluntary organizations have the capacity to produce this sort of "bonding social capital," few have the sort of moral imperative to do so that congregations do. The Christian New Testament is replete with commands to "love one another, as I have loved you," to "bear one another's burdens," even to recognize one another as parts of one body. Likewise, the Hebrew prophets made clear that the love of God would be most in evidence when the people of Israel treated *each other* with justice and mercy. Islam enshrines the giving of alms as one of its "five pillars." Both theological traditions and American expectations have placed congregations in a strategic role. People who seek them out, no less than the leaders who articulate their goals, expect congregations to invest in building and sustaining human relationships.

HOW DO THEY DO IT?

If congregations describe themselves as organizations pursuing communal goals and supporting families, what does that look like in practice? How do they deploy their resources to accomplish those goals? How do they spend their time and energy? As our informants described their congregations' activities, their lists included a wide range of groups that seemed to us primarily aimed at providing opportunities for social interchange. Many, if not most, of these groups also include some religious (or community service) elements. A meeting might open with a devotional reading or include a time of prayer, for instance, while being primarily focused on playing basketball or planning a picnic. Or people might engage in Bible study while also spending time organizing disaster relief. Categorizing was often difficult, but the activities included in Table 4 seemed to place primary emphasis on building relationships and pursuing more this-worldly communal goals.

The types of activities listed here are summarized from a much longer list of things that congregations do when people get together to socialize—everything from excursions to the theater to craft guilds and parenting groups. Some activities gather the whole congregation to eat or play together. Others gather specialized groups. The most common of those groups are defined primarily by the "life stage" of the people involved. Others are defined by what the people do together. And still others are defined by a personal problem they are trying to solve.

While religious traditions help to shape the types of programs congregations plan, there are many other factors at work in organizing a monthly calendar of social activities. Spiritual activities are largely shaped by the particular religious tradition to which a congregation belongs, but fellowship work is shaped by a wider array of cultural and social forces as well. The most basic of these is the cultural template that puts social activities on the calendar at all. Across all the congregations we surveyed, 72 percent had at least one type of small social group or regular congregational social activity. Even in congregations with fewer than fifty participants, half organize social activities for their members. This is more than rationalized organizational necessity: it is not so much that members need to get to know one another as that social activities are something congregations are expected to do.

The institutionalized character of social activities can be seen both in overall prevalence and by contrasting the normative U.S. Christian and Jewish traditions with those who are (for different reasons) more marginal to those normative patterns.

TABLE 4   Social Activities of Congregations in Different Religious Traditions

Type of Program	Mainline Protestant (193)	Conservative Protestant (226)	African American Protestant (33)	Catholic & Orthodox (45)	All Congregations (549)
	Congregations with at Least One Regular Program Activity of This Type (%)				
Congregation-wide meals & events*	32	25	11	27	27
Life-stage groups*	60	58	60	71	57
Activity groups*	39	16	28	24	24
Problem assistance*	19	15	26	32	17
Average number of types of social activity groups*	2.33	1.80	1.87	2.45	1.95

NOTE: Number in parentheses indicates number of congregations in that group. All Congregations includes these four groups plus Sectarians, Jews, and Other Religions. For programs marked with an asterisk at least one of the differences among the groups is statistically significant at p < .10 (Oneway ANOVA, with Scheffe post-hoc comparisons).

Groups in the Other Religions have not yet fully assimilated, and groups in the Sectarian traditions often resist dominant cultural patterns, and neither are likely to have a full social calendar. While the average Christian or Jewish congregation has at least two kinds of fellowship activities, congregations in Other Religions have half that many; and fewer than one in three Sectarian congregations in our sample had any at all. The Jehovah's Witnesses we interviewed do not get together just for the fun of it (see also Holden 2002). Bonds are built through the work of evangelism, not for their own sake.

Buddhists and Hindus occasionally mentioned various arts and study groups to us, but other specialized social groupings were almost completely absent among groups from the Other Religions. Here the issue is more one of capacity than of prohibition. As struggling newcomers, many of these groups have more pressing concerns than organizing a softball team. The most common social activities among the new immigrants were communal meals designed to bring the whole group together (see also Ebaugh and Chafetz 1999). Entire Hindu, Muslim, Buddhist, and Baha'i communities gather for religious festivals that combine sacred tradition and communal celebration—and almost always involve food. Eating together enhances the work of teaching and the celebration of ritual for these immigrant religious communities.

CONGREGATION-WIDE EVENTS

When congregations of all sorts gather for communal events, they are likely to sit down to eat. One out of six (17%) reported gathering around food at least once a month. In the South, the number is one in four, as congregations carry on traditions of potlucks and covered dish and carry-in events. In some places congregations have transformed their eating together into elaborate coffee hours or catered dinners, but in all kinds of places and in all sorts of ways, congregations acknowledge the role of food in the work of building community (Sack 2000). A congregation's own sense of mission shapes this activity as well. Local congregations that say community building is one of their primary goals are half-again as likely to eat together as are congregations where that is a less central priority. Sharing food is thus both a widespread practice and, for some, an intentionally targeted strategy.

Shared food is supplemented in some places by other events undertaken just for the fun of it. In all, just over a quarter of congregations (27%) plan some sort of regular fellowship activity for the group as a whole. An annual church ski trip or caroling party in the winter may be complemented by a trip to a baseball game or participation in a parade in the summer. These congregation-wide social activities were reported least often in the African American churches where we interviewed. While these churches probably eat together more than we heard about (Dodson and Gilkes 1995), they also have a very particular definition of "fellowshipping." In their case the outing in question is not to a baseball game, but to a neighboring church. Choirs and delegations of church leaders often accompany their pastors to a sister church where the bonds of solidarity are celebrated and extended. These outings were not reported as social events, but are no less significant for building a sense of community.

LIFE-STAGE GROUPS

When congregations break down their members into smaller social groupings, the mode of organization is almost as institutionalized as the impulse itself. Most commonly, across all traditions, activities are defined by the gender, age, and/or marital status of the participants ("life-stage groups" in Table 4)—women's groups, singles groups, and the like. The most common life-stage group is a youth group. Nearly half (42%) of all Christian and Jewish congregations have them, and even a few of the Other Religions have formed this type of social group.[5] The youth in question may or may not also have a regular Sunday school class, but they are likely to gather on their own on a Friday night or Sunday night or a Saturday morning. Some religious content is often included, but the primary goal is to provide the congregation's youth with wholesome activities and relationships with coreligionists at a crucial time in their lives. In some congregations—most notably African American ones—these groups also provide opportunities for youth to learn leadership skills and try out their roles in the religious community. Such tasks are so universally recognized that youth groups are found without significant variation across all the Christian and Jewish traditions.

This is one of the ways congregations are responding to the pressures on family life we heard voiced from so many leaders. Across all the religious traditions, congregations that especially emphasize serving families are more likely to have youth groups. Among even the smallest congregations, those that highlight family support as part of their mission are twice as likely to have youth groups, compared to congregations that do not share that focus. But size and resources matter as well. Congregations that have at least one hundred participants are more likely to have youth groups, as are congregations that have more well-off members. Across religious traditions, local priorities and local resources are critical in establishing these groups.

The other most institutionalized form of life-stage group is the ubiquitous "ladies aid." Nearly a third of all congregations have some regular gathering that is defined just as a "women's group." This number does not include the countless additional congregations where the group really is a ladies *aid* (like an altar guild) or a women's religious education group (like a Bible study). The ones counted here place the accent on enjoying and caring for each other, even if they also occasionally learn and serve together.

Traditionally such groups met on a weekday morning, and many of them still do. Not surprisingly many are now struggling to survive, with fewer younger women joining to replace those who are aging and dying. In spite of these generational transitions, women's groups remain, especially within Mainline Protestantism. They are no more nor less likely in newer churches and synagogues than in older ones, nor where there are more older members than younger ones. In spite of shifting demographics, having a women's group remains part of the standard package of traditional congregational activities.

Men's groups are slightly less common, with just under a quarter of all congregations having some regular gathering of men. If 10:00 has been the women's designated meeting time, men have typically gathered at 7:00 A.M., before heading off for work. The most common men's group we found was the "prayer breakfast" (and most were clearly as much about the eating as the praying). Newer forms of men's groups have been appearing, however. Most famously, Promise Keepers (PK) has attempted to redefine male bonding for Christians. Seventeen percent of the Protestant churches we surveyed at least had taken a group of men to a PK event, but not nearly all of those had set up a local PK group for their own men.

A few congregations also organize "couples" groups, often for younger members who prefer to do their socializing together, rather than in single-sex groupings. A few more (but still only 4 percent) have a "singles fellowship." At the other end of the age spectrum, senior adults are about twice as likely as young adults to find a congregational group geared toward their interests. Sometimes given catchy names like "NTO" (never too old) or "golden agers," these groups gather for meals, entertainment, trips, mutual support, and sometimes a bit of late-in-life matchmaking of their own. This reflects the lively and engaged culture of today's retirement population and is most common in the best-educated congregations.

Singles and seniors, men, women, and youth—these constitute what Penny Edgell calls the "standard package" of life-stage groups from which congregations create a selection of possible gatherings for their members.[6] This is what most congregations mean when they say they "support families." Whether or not a specific congregation takes family ministry to be its special task, the larger culture expects the various members of families to find category-appropriate places in congregations. Until recently "women" and "men" translated into "wives" and "husbands," "single" meant not yet married, and "seniors" were disproportionately widows.

People whose life patterns fall outside the typical scenario are less likely to find congregational social gatherings to welcome them. Marler has demonstrated the degree to which congregational memberships, especially Mainline ones, still over-represent those who have followed a "traditional" family pattern of two parents and their biological children (Marler 1995). Wilcox notes that Mainline Protestant congregations actually have a smaller share of single parents and childless adults in church on any given Sunday than either Conservative Protestant churches or the population at large (Wilcox 2002). Edgell observed that many congregations have changed their rhetoric about family life, hoping to welcome nontraditional members; but the congregations most likely to talk about nontraditional families are actually the least likely to offer opportunities for such families to be acknowledged and gather. Our data confirm that finding. Groups for divorced people, for families who are adopting, or for families experiencing loss are far more common among Catholic, African American, and Conservative Protestant congregations than in the Protestant Mainline, where the new family rhetoric predominates. Non-traditional life-stage groups were found in about one in ten non-Mainline Christian churches, whereas only one in a hundred Mainline churches had such a group. Mainline Protestant churches are more likely than others to declare that they are open to gay and lesbian members, but still only a handful of the churches we studied had any regular gathering for gay and lesbian members.

While activities do not seem to follow rhetoric in support for nontraditional families, rhetoric does make a difference. Parenting groups occurred with about equal likelihood across religious traditions, but within each tradition congregations that especially emphasize a mission of serving families were almost five times as likely to have parenting groups (14%) as were congregations where that was not mentioned as a priority (3%). This seems to be a primary way they express their desire to be a family-friendly place. They provide more than just wholesome things for family members to do: they also offer parents a place to share concerns and learn from experts.

The presence and proliferation of life-stage groups in congregations is not a matter of ideology or religious tradition, at least within the mainstream. Organizing social activities—of all kinds—is more a product of context than confession. The culture expects congregations to organize *something*, and most of them do. Well over half (59%) of Christian and Jewish congregations (but almost none of the sectarian and Other Religions groups) have at least one such social gathering. But more than institutionalized cultural patterns are at work. Where social bonds can least be taken for granted, congregations are most intentional about organizing opportunities for connection to be made. Congregational size is, for instance, both a resource that makes social activities more possible and a reality that makes them more necessary. Nine out of ten large congregations (with over three hundred participants) have at least one kind of organized social activity, while only half of the smallest congregations do. Size is the single strongest factor in determining the extent of social programming in congregations.

In the middle range, however, a number of other factors come into play. In congregations big enough to do something, but not so big as to be able to do everything, spending energy on organizing social activities is most likely in places where social conditions have most disrupted traditional forms of community. In that middle range, two-thirds of rural churches and synagogues have social groups, while 83 percent of the urban and suburban congregations have at least one type of activity. "Small groups" and "fellowship" occur more naturally in rural communities and do not need to be created by a congregation. A Missouri UCC pastor told this story: "For example, we had a community parade under the direction of the parent teacher organization, but members in the church community were judges, myself included, you know. And then they had a service later, you know, where it was a fellowship hour. So it's under the heading of PTO, but the church is, you see—they just kind of integrate together."

Continuity of religious tradition makes a difference as well. No matter what size they are, congregations in which most people share a lifelong religious tradition form fewer small groups. The same pattern shows up when we compare different regions as well. The more mobile and restless west is also the place where congregations work hardest at organizing social activities. Differences based on size, location, and constituency hold across the various families of Christian and Jewish traditions. Nearly every church and synagogue organizes at least one kind of social group, but beyond that base the differences depend more on local culture, needs, and resources than on theological traditions.

Across the spectrum mainstream American congregations respond to the need for community by organizing social activities for their participants. Show up on Sunday morning, and you are likely to get an invitation for Friday night (or vice versa). While the occasion is most likely to be a group based on your age, gender, and/or family status, other groups exist as well; and it is here that differences among the traditions appear.

ACTIVITY GROUPS

Less common, but still present in a quarter (24%) of all American congregations, are groups defined by what people do, rather than who they are (see Table 4). These groups play baseball and basketball, do yoga and aerobics, put on dramas, and make quilts, among other things. No one type of group is found in more than a handful of places, but taken together, gatherings for shared activity routinely happen in a third of mainstream Christian and Jewish congregations that are big enough to support this sort of programming (fifty or more attenders). Sectarian congregations, on the other hand, are even less likely to have activity groups than they are to have men's, women's, or singles groups. None of the Mormon, Jehovah's Witness, or Christian Science groups where we interviewed reported any activity-based group. Getting together with fellow congregational members for sports, arts, and crafts is primarily characteristic of the Christian churches, most especially the Mainline Protestant ones.

One of the activities we found most often in Mainline churches was scouting. Ten percent of Mainline congregations sponsor their own scout troops (compared to 1 percent of all other congregations). Indeed, the bigger and more affluent the Mainline church, the more likely it was to have at least one scout troop, with almost a third (29%) of the highest income Mainline churches reporting troops. Given at least one hundred regular participants in a Mainline congregation, scout troops are twice as likely as any sort of weekday religious education for children (20 percent, as compared to 10 percent). This seems to reflect a Mainline desire for their children to become good citizens of the community. This is in dramatic contrast to the balance struck in Conservative Protestant and Catholic churches, where more than a third have weekday religious education, but less than 3 percent have scout troops.[7] As we will see, many additional churches of all sorts provide space and perhaps other support for *outside* scout troops, but the troops counted here are not just using church space. These are groups organized by church members primarily for their own children and led by church-related adults, even if also open to the community.

The activity of scouting is, then, a place where the boundaries between church and community are quite permeable, and those boundaries are also often permeable in sporting activities. Both children and adults hone the virtues of cooperation and citizenship on the playing field, and sometimes they do that as part of a congregational team. Church and synagogue teams are much more common among predominantly white congregations than among other ethnic groups. In both rural and urban areas, Tuesday night basketball leagues, summer softball teams, and even the occasional bowling league are found in about one in ten moderate-to-large-sized congregations.

Working out with congregational friends happens in fellowship halls as well as on the playing fields. Exercise groups, almost always women and (in our sample) overwhelmingly located in white Protestant churches, often combine concerns for spiritual and physical health with a chance to have fun together (Griffith 1997b). While some women are doing aerobics, others are making quilts. Craft groups are by no means universal, but 12 percent of Mainline Protestant congregations have them (more than in any other tradition), and the most common craft we encountered was the making of quilts. Sometimes given to needy people or sent overseas, these quilts are also likely to be sold to raise money for the congregation or for other good causes. In Missouri the annual "Festival of Sharing" includes a closely watched competition among quilt-makers from all over the state. Along with sales of other donated items, money from quilt sales goes to benefit a wide range of state charities.

An additional small number of congregations gather groups for other artistic activities.[8] Some enjoy playing musical instruments together. Others do drama or dance. The variety of arts being pursued crosscuts any tendency of more elite congregations to dominate the offerings. At the Seattle Vineyard, for instance, visual and musical arts are part of congregational life and important to many of the young adults who come. One of their regular home "cell groups" is devoted to "The Artist's Way," inviting members to connect their creative abilities with their spiritual life. As with other activity groups, arts groups are mostly found in bigger rather than smaller congregations, in urban and suburban rather than rural ones, and most often in the Protestant Mainline.

The list of activities being pursued by members of American congregations is nearly as long as the list of congregations. People who share an interest in reading novels or writing poetry, in riding motorcycles or folk dancing, are gathered by their congregations for the sake of personal and communal enrichment. They do things together that they enjoy, while getting to know each other and strengthening the congregation's communal networks. While the choice of activity may partly reflect the social location of the particular congregation, the choice to organize in this way is most common in the Protestant Mainline, where an activity group is as common as an adult Sunday school class. Mainliners are the ones most likely to voice concerns about the breakdown of community and the ones most likely to organize leisure activities for their members. And in the Mainline the investment in activity-based community building equals or exceeds investment in explicitly spiritual activities for either children or adults.

HELP WITH LIFE'S DIFFICULTIES

Most of congregational life is structured around the expectation of normalcy. Social activities and small groups gather to celebrate, support, and embellish the routines of daily life, providing places where men and women, artists and athletes can express and explore who they are in the company of fellow religionists. But not everything in life goes according to plan, and religious communities are places where such difficulties are acknowledged and supported.

When people in congregations talk about building relationships and creating community, they are talking about more than warm, fuzzy feelings. These relationships often take on a depth of mutual obligation that involves pain and sacrifice, as well as joy and celebration. Once having entered these communities, participants are challenged to care for each other, in good times and in bad, and most of this caring takes place informally, rather than through organized programs.[9] The church administrator at a Nashville Assembly of God church laughed when she said, "There's a lot of ministry that goes on person-to-person, a lot of what we call Pentecostal handshakes. It's not unusual for someone to come up and shake my hands and put a $10 bill or $20 bill or a $100 bill in them, because people who are praying and listening to the Lord know the needs even when they're not spoken." At a small Orthodox Presbyterian church in Albuquerque, the story was much the same: "If somebody needs something in the congregation, they're right there to help." These tangible forms of mutual support are another part of why congregations become so important to new immigrants. In Chicago we encountered a congregation whose religious roots are in Nigeria—the Holy Order of Cherubim and Seraphim. There we heard, "Our church has a lot of immigrants that are coming to this country. Some of them are very young families. . . . So, you have the church trying to be like a family structure. To be able to mend all of this together so they can have a life." Mending together a life often requires informal assistance, rituals of healing and mourning, and the timely visit of a pastor.

In addition to informal assistance, one in six American congregations has organized some sort of specialized response to life's difficulties (see Table 4). The smallest congregations are, not surprisingly, less involved, as are the congregations outside the mainstream Christian and Jewish traditions. But in a quarter (26%) of mid-to-large Christian churches (with a hundred or more participants), various forms of counseling and recovery have been formalized into programs and organizations.

Formal pastoral counseling is the strategy adapted by one in four of the congregations that has any program of care. Some of these congregations have the resources to put a specialized full-time pastoral counselor on staff, or someone who "hangs out a shingle" as a part-time family therapist or marriage counselor. In other cases the pastor merely "does a lot of counseling," as some of them told us. When problems arise, they are there to help. Some pastors and rabbis have received training in Clinical Pastoral Education, and others have been through official marriage and family therapy certification. They then offer these services to their members as well as to other community residents who may seek them out. This is a service more likely to be found where more of the members have been to college. College-educated members have higher expectations for professionalized and credentialed assistance, even from their congregations.

In a few cases (about 3 percent overall), the members themselves confront the problems they face by forming specialized support groups. Whether dealing with health issues or unemployment or family crises, a few congregations are able to muster enough internal interest and resources to form a regular support group.

As we will see in Chapter 6, these sorts of specialized support groups more often require resources beyond what one congregation can do. When a few members discover a mutual problem or concern, their congregation is usually a starting point, a base from which to reach out to other organizations in the community. But in a few cases the congregation itself is able to support their need. A similar pattern is present for addiction groups. Most of the AA and Narcotics Anonymous (NA) groups we found were joint ventures, drawing participants and resources from outside the congregation, even if they actually meet there. But in a small number of Christian congregations (about 3 percent), a group was started by members and still mostly functions as a ministry of the church.

A final way in which congregations help their members solve problems is by providing an organized network of lay caregivers. In many African American churches, for instance, "missionaries" have the special responsibility of tending to the spiritual and physical needs of members. These groups of women visit members who are sick or bereaved, providing prayers, companionship, and other assistance. Similarly, in many Mainline Protestant churches, members have received special training from Stephen Ministries for responding to the wide variety of needs that may arise. As with other forms of organized congregational activity, urban and suburban congregations, those with more members, and those whose members are better educated are more likely to have an organized program to help people with problems. Fifteen percent of urban and suburban, well-educated congregations had lay ministry groups, whereas none of the small, rural, less-educated congregations had such formalized routines. There the dense informal ties of the community provide what other congregations must intentionally organize. But in both formalized and unofficial ways, congregations are places where many people find assistance in times of need.

BLUEPRINTS FOR BUILDING
CONGREGATIONAL COMMUNITIES

The range of ways congregations gather is too broad for any one congregation to sponsor everything, but the vast majority of congregations sponsor something beyond their regular worship event. No two congregations are exactly alike, but the institutional expectations of American culture provide a template for organizing local religious life. Almost all congregations have at least one regular form of social activity. Whether—like most immigrant congregations in the new religious traditions—they sponsor only communal meals, or whether—like the most affluent, large, and well-educated Christian and Jewish congregations—they sponsor dozens of groups and activities, most congregations spend some of their organizational energy tending explicitly to the social needs of their members. This pattern is so institutionalized that it does not depend on the particular local mission priorities of each group. Those priorities and religious traditions may shape a congregation's unique array of groups, but the presence of social activities of some sort is nearly universal. Only in the most Sectarian groups are such activities absent. Jehovah's Witnesses, for instance, almost never have any organized social groups, and Conservative Protestants are less likely than others to sponsor activity groups. In these more evangelism-driven groups, social bonds are expected to arise out of shared religious work rather than being a direct focus of congregational energy themselves.

But beyond more insular traditions, the rhetorical emphasis on community building heard in America's congregations is clearly matched by a substantial investment in organized social gatherings in which people learn to care for each other and where they build up a store of shared experiences through which to interpret their lives. Congregations that face the greatest communal challenges—large, urban and suburban, religiously mobile—are also the most likely to make intentional investments in creating social bonds. They are voluntarily doing the pragmatic work of generating "social capital."

These social gatherings go hand-in-hand with the work congregations do to provide their participants with opportunities for relating to God. Whether in choirs or in Sunday school classes, altar guilds or worship services, even when people gather to focus attention on spiritual life, the presence of compatriots is integral to the experience. Similarly, when people gather to care for each other or to make a quilt, to share a meal or work on an addiction, the congregational context is likely to invoke the spiritual along with the social dimensions of the work they do together.

But even that spiritual and communal work is not done in a vacuum. As we have seen, there are broad regularities that shape congregational life, some coming from the external culture and some from the various religious traditions of which congregations are a part. There are cultural and material constraints as well. Congregations do not choose to do what they do all on their own. And they do not stand alone in shaping the content of the programs they choose. Denominations have a significant role in this process, but so do hundreds of other religious organizations. We now turn to this larger religious world.

CHAPTER FOUR

· Building Networks of Faith

Partners and Producers

When congregations gather to worship and educate each other in the faith, they draw on ideas and materials beyond what they themselves produce. Even when they gather for fellowship and care for each other in times of need, their efforts are shaped by cultural and organizational resources that stretch far beyond their four walls. Scriptures, hymns, images, and rituals have come down through decades, centuries, and even millennia. While each congregation may put its own unique stamp on these traditions, much of what it does depends on the religious work done by others, work that has been preserved and carried on by organizational actors. From the most spectacular sacred art to the most mundane supplies for registering guests or serving communion, congregations depend on stores and catalogs, publishers and Internet sites. They send leaders to workshops and seminars, call in consultants, and apply for grants. The more than three hundred thousand congregations in the United States form a major market for producers of everything from hymnals to religiously oriented children's toys, and what they consume is no less important to understanding them than is what they say and do.[1]

For about a century, the religious market has been segmented primarily into denominational niches. In the early twentieth century, Protestant denominations gathered the welter of nineteenth-century religious entrepreneurial activity into more "efficient" centralized bureaucracies (Primer 1978). As a result, part of what "denomination" came to mean was supplying the material (and ideological) resources constituent congregations would use to support their educational and worship life. Whether prescribed liturgical orders of service or the weekly bulletin template on which the local congregation could print its own worship guide, whether weekly Sunday school curricula or books and magazines for pastors, denominations have provided guidance and resources that have enriched congregational life while simultaneously binding those congregations to the traditions they share.

In recent years denominations have been joined by a long list of other religious publishers and suppliers, each vying for an expanding market share. Both denominational and nondenominational producers make their wares available through an expanding network of religious bookstores, so that clergy and members alike can browse aisles stocked with hundreds of books, tapes, teaching tools, liturgical supplies, and devotional objects. As denominational publishers have downsized and merged, the competition between them and the nondenominational producers has become a focus of keen interest. At stake is not only the economic viability of various organizations, but the shape of the religious landscape as well.

Cataloging what congregations use and who produces it was part of the task we undertook. The result was an enormous amount of detailed information, and the challenge was to see how the complicated inventory that emerged could amplify the story we had already heard and observed in the congregations themselves. Knowing where they buy their hymnals, for instance, does not seem as immediately important or interesting as observing the way music is woven into the lives of congregations. To get to the big picture, we had to invent categories for mapping terrain that has gone otherwise unsurveyed.

We began by asking our informants to record on their written survey the names of the publishers of their children's, youth, and adult religious education curricula. We also asked them to write in the name(s) of their hymnal(s) and of any prayer book or missalette they use. We then noted whether each of those publishers was associated with the respondent's denomination or not. The moment we began to look at the list, we should have known that this is not a simple story. Some people named no one; others named more than we had lines on the survey to accommodate. And just who are these publishers (over two hundred of them) and hymnal producers (over 125 of them)? What should count as denominationally related— only something like Cokesbury that is owned by the denomination, or something like Paluch that is clearly Roman Catholic, but not owned by the Church? Does it matter? Behind the categories and numbers in the pages that follow are hundreds of small decisions about how to describe an organizational field that is in the midst of significant change.

In the course of the interview we also asked people to expand on the written information they had given us by talking about any other study and program materials they use, including administrative and "how to" assistance. We asked them, for instance, where they go for architectural advice and religious supplies, such as candles, robes, and the like. Does it matter to them what the building and its religious decor look like? If so, who helps them do it right? We probed for who offers training and continuing education for both clergy and laity, asking especially about where they get worship ideas and evangelism assistance. We even asked whether and how they use the Internet. We wanted to know whose ideas and suggestions get into the hands of local leaders, whom they trust and why. We also asked, both on the survey and in the interview, about whether they receive any monetary assistance or have gotten grants for any of their programs.

Not everyone could think of anything very specific, so our counts probably underestimate actual resource use. What we did hear, however, constituted an almost overwhelming array of programs, organizations, and suppliers—over two thousand separate entries for the resources these 549 congregations use. The overall range of available religious resources is enormous; the following pages will attempt to trace a path through it.

SHAPING AND SUPPORTING CONGREGATIONAL WORSHIP

Some people who gather to celebrate religious rituals think of what they are doing as handed down through the ages nearly untouched by human hands. Others focus on the experience of the moment and assume that their worship is created out of their own spontaneous religious fervor. Both are partly right and partly wrong. Even those whose rituals are elaborately prescribed receive those prescriptions through human means, and even those whose praise is the most spontaneous are supported in their worship by mundane resources they take for granted. If worship is a key organizational activity in congregational life, there is good reason to expect that outside organizations will want to help them do it.

How congregations think about the nature and importance of worship does make a difference. One of the most important things to know about the resources supporting the worship life of a given congregation is whether or not its religious tradition prescribes a set of prayers and rituals that are to be performed when the congregation gathers. These "liturgical" traditions stand in contrast to other congregations that are freer to choose whether and what they will sing, how they will decorate their worship space, which scriptures (if any) will be the focus for reading or preaching (or both), and what order all of that will take. Congregations in liturgical traditions may have a good bit of freedom within the structure they have inherited, but the pattern itself has significant force. Catholic and Orthodox parishes are shaped by such liturgical traditions, but so are some Protestants. For that reason a new category appears in Table 5—"Liturgical Protestant." Episcopal and Anglican churches, along with three kinds of Lutherans (ELCA, LCMS, and Wisconsin Synod) have been grouped here. These denominations cut across the "Mainline" and "Conservative" groupings we have examined in earlier discussions; but in understanding their patterns of worship resource use, what they share in common as sacramental traditions overrides what separates them theologically. For instance, while only 10 percent of other Mainline Protestant churches, and almost no Conservative or African American churches, use a "book of worship" to structure their services, almost two-thirds of Liturgical Protestants do. The Episcopal Book of Common Prayer and the Lutheran Book of Worship are common fixtures in the pew racks of churches in these traditions. They are created and approved by official denominational governing bodies and published by the denomination's own press. While a few churches may experiment with variations on the prescribed structure and resources, denominational ritual patterns have a very strong presence.

Shared patterns of worship, drawing on common published sources, are equally strong in the Catholic, Eastern Orthodox, and Jewish traditions. Like the Liturgical Protestants, about two-thirds of these congregations named an official worship book as their guide,[2] and that stands in stark contrast to all the other religious traditions. Their pattern of resource consumption is shaped by religious tradition, not by how big or rich they are or where they are located. These three religious families— Jewish, Catholic and Orthodox, and Liturgical Protestant—share the habit of structuring worship around a book of prayers and readings, but they also share a higher overall emphasis on worship as central to their mission, a generally higher level of worship resource use, and (as we will see below) stronger ties to specifically denominational worship resources of all sorts. It takes more "stuff" to produce a worship service in these traditions, and that stuff is more likely to be distinctly shaped by a religious tradition, if not actually produced by the denomination.

Not every tradition encourages such elaborate ritual, but nearly all of them do encourage congregational singing. In some churches and synagogues the long-standing tradition has been for a music leader (such as the Jewish cantor) to set tunes orally for the participants to follow. But much more common are places were participants sing from a printed hymnal, a published collection of religious songs

TABLE 5   Worship Emphases and Worship Resources of Congregations in Different Religious Traditions

Emphasis or Resource	Mainline Protestant (144) (%)	Conservative Protestant (189) (%)	African American Protestant (53) (%)	Liturgical Protestant (86) (%)	Catholic & Orthodox (45) (%)	All Congregations (549) (%)
Emphasize worship as central to mission*	9	14	7	21	32	14
Use an official book of worship*	11	<1	0	68	72	13
Mentioned at least one external worship resource*	13	16	9	38	24	17

NOTE: Number in parentheses indicates number of congregations in that group. All Congregations includes these five groups plus Sectarians, Jews, and Other Religions. For emphases/resources marked with an asterisk at least one of the differences among the groups is statistically significant at p < .10 (Oneway ANOVA, with Scheffe post-hoc comparisons).

that express the stories and beliefs of their tradition. Six out of seven congregations in mainstream U.S. Christianity, along with Christian Scientists, Jehovah's Witnesses, and Mormons, say they use one. Within that dominant pattern, Catholics, who were historically less accustomed to singing (and can rely on songs printed in the back of the missalette), have lower rates than white Protestants, as do African American Protestants. But all those groups stand in marked contrast to the newer non-Christian groups, none of whom reported hymnal use. While Muslims and Buddhists do not have a tradition of collective singing, other new traditions in the United States may eventually follow the pattern of publishing and distributing religious music for participating congregations. Kurien (1998) found that the groups of Hindus she studied often spent time teaching each other *bajhans* (religious songs), extending and preserving the traditions they had brought with them. At the moment, however, that is still a local practice, rather than a regularized and published aid for preserving tradition.

Having a hymnal is the institutionalized dominant pattern. If a congregation is in one of the mainstream traditions that typically uses hymnals, no matter how small or poor, well educated or not, there will be hymnals in the pew racks. But which hymnal and how it is used varies enormously across American congregations (see Figure 2).[3] Denominations are the majority supplier to their constituent congregations, but they are by no means the only ones. Some traditions retain a long-standing reliance on sources other than hymnals. Many Catholic parishes use the songs printed in the back of the missalette. In African American churches (Protestant and Catholic), even when there is a hymnal available, much of the singing may be more spontaneous, picking up on well-loved gospel songs or following the choir in a rousing chorus. With a massive gospel music industry on which to draw, and a regular round of guest choir performances to provide inspiration, the musical well is never dry. Whether introducing the latest from CeCe Winans or leading a rendition of "Precious Lord" or "Take Me to the Water," music ministers in African American churches are integral to the entire worship experience. A line from a prayer or a sermon may lead to a few chords on the organ and the spontaneous participation of choir and congregation in a song they all know. While most black churches have hymnals, most black church singing today involves as much memory and collective improvisation as text-based performance.[4]

Among many Conservative Protestants, music has migrated from the printed page to the screen. Words for easily singable choruses and praise songs are placed on an overhead projector (or in more sophisticated congregations projected via computer),[5] leaving worshippers' hands free to clap along or extend into the air to

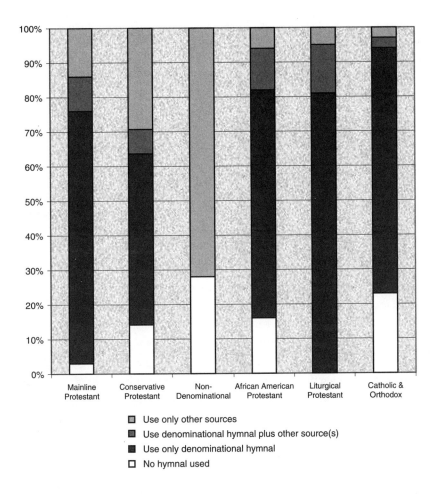

100% ─

90% ─

80% ─

70% ─

60% ─

50% ─

40% ─

30% ─

20% ─

10% ─

0% ─

Mainline Protestant   Conservative Protestant   Non-Denominational   African American Protestant   Liturgical Protestant   Catholic & Orthodox

☐ Use only other sources
■ Use denominational hymnal plus other source(s)
■ Use only denominational hymnal
☐ No hymnal used

FIGURE 2
Hymnal Use in Christian Congregations

express feelings of joy, supplication, or praise. Only a small minority of Conservative churches have given up entirely on hymnals (14 percent of those in a denomination, and about twice that many nondenominational ones), but that does not mean that they are denominational loyalists in their purchasing. Just under half of Conservative denominational churches reported that they exclusively use their own tradition's hymnal, while an additional 7 percent mix that hymnal with other sources, and more than a quarter buy music on the "open market."

What do they buy? Some use a hymnal from another denomination, but about half of those who reach outside their own denomination use one of the many offerings designed by evangelical publishing giants such as Word Music. Word's 1997 *Celebration Hymnal* was one of the most frequently named nondenominational worship resources we encountered. It includes traditional gospel favorites like "The Old Rugged Cross" and "How Great Thou Art," along with contemporary praise choruses. Like *Hymns for the Family of God* (Brentwood/Benson Music, 1976), also popular in the churches we surveyed, several million copies are in print, successfully spanning denominations across the evangelical spectrum and establishing a foothold within some Mainline quarters as well.

But buying an alternative hymnal is not the only possibility for today's congregations. Many now use a do-it-yourself selection of contemporary praise music from publishers such as Hosanna! (part of Integrity Music), Maranatha! Music, and Vineyard. With stables of popular recording artists and millions of CDs on the market, these companies have captured the new song-writing energies that emerged out of post-1960s evangelical megachurches—especially those aimed at young worshipers. In styles, depending on the generational target, that range from soft rock and folk to hip hop and R & B, young Christian musicians have been producing a new genre of church music.[6] Some of this music is very "homegrown," expressing the longings of the particular congregations and musicians that produce it. But some of it has quickly traveled through networks of church gatherings and made its way into print and onto recordings. Rick Founds's 1989 song "Lord I Lift Your Name on High" (Maranatha) and Graham Kendrick's 1987 "Shine Jesus Shine" (Hosanna) are among the most ubiquitous. I have sung one or both of those songs in settings as diverse as an inner city Assemblies of God mission, a suburban Seattle Reformed Church in America congregation, a Presbyterian youth ministry workshop, a California church growth conference, and at the seeker service of the famed Willow Creek Community Church. Along with more traditionally devotional sounds (e.g., Laurie Klein's 1978 "I Love You Lord" and Donna Adkins' 1976 "Glorify Thy Name"), these songs set the mood for worship in thousands of congregations—Conservative more than Mainline, but not entirely absent in the Mainline.

The ability of congregations to make overhead transparencies of these choruses and to pick and choose hymns from various sources has become possible both because of available reproduction technologies and because CCLI has made it legal. Christian Copyright Licensing International, begun in 1985 at a large Conservative church in Portland, Oregon, created the idea of a blanket "permission to use" agreement for music intended for congregational singing.[7] More than 129,000 churches around the world now use this service to cover their copying of music for worship, and a substantial number of the churches we surveyed reported that this sort of do-it-yourself strategy is how they put together their worship services.

This widespread experimentation with music stands in contrast to both the Liturgical denominations and the other Mainline Protestants. Every Liturgical congregation we surveyed reported using a hymnal, and more than three-quarters of them (81%) use only a hymnal produced by their own denomination. When they do venture beyond an in-house resource, they are as likely to choose a Catholic hymnal (such as *Gather*) as to draw from Maranatha or Integrity. In the liturgical churches singing is an integral part of worship, and songs carry the tradition. In one of the few studies of twentieth-century church music, Paul Westermeyer (1993, 187) writes, "As a general rule American denominations in the twentieth century did not deny their individual traditions. Instead, they continued to combine them with a cross section of other hymnic materials, adapted to their own idioms and confessional postures." Each Christian hymnal thus contains much in common with all the others, but the particular collections found in the ELCA's Lutheran Book of Worship or the Episcopal Church's 1982 Hymnal are part of what give those religious traditions their distinctive identity.

Not only the Liturgical traditions share this attachment to denominational hymnals, however. Throughout the Protestant Mainline, hymnals are nearly universal (97 percent use them) and very likely to be from the congregation's own denominational publisher (73%). A few, especially non-Anglo churches, borrow from other denominations, looking for songs that express their particular ethnic heritage. A few other Mainline churches experiment with choruses and the newer praise music, but in most of the Mainline, Sunday worship is built around traditional hymns of the faith sung from a book produced by the congregation's own denomination.

Where there is movement away from strictly denominational hymnal use, it is thus largely a matter of the religious traditions themselves: Conservative Protestant and African American congregations are much more likely to experiment than are Catholic or Mainline ones. But other forces, which can affect all types of churches, are at work as well. In rural locations, for instance, where religious traditions are perhaps most stable, denominational hymnal use is highest. Sixty percent of rural Protestant congregations use denominational hymnals, while 48 percent of urban and suburban ones do. Similarly, in congregations where most members grew up in the denomination, two-thirds use the traditional hymnal, while those hymnals are found in only half of congregations where the majority of members are switchers. Congregations founded since 1950 are much more likely to be eclectic in their musical choices than are congregations founded before that time. Only 41 percent of newer churches exclusively use denominational hymnals, while 61 percent of older churches do. The age of the members matters as well. Among "graying" congregations, where a majority of members are over sixty-five, nearly three-quarters stick to the denominational hymnal, while only 45 percent of younger congregations do. This picture is complicated since Conservative Protestant congregations are more likely to be newer and younger—and also more likely to experiment. But taking that into account, across every Protestant religious family, musical experimentation is more likely in urban and suburban areas, where more members are switchers, where fewer are aging, and in churches founded more recently. Where there is more of a stake in the status quo, congregations are more likely to retain their denominational hymnal; where traditions have a less firm hold, a wider variety of musical choices is likely to be present, necessitating a wider range of musical suppliers (see also Dudley and Roozen 2001).

Hymnals and prayer books are probably the most profound means by which outside suppliers shape what happens in congregational worship. More visually, however, worship in some congregations is accented by robes and vestments, candles and incense, banners and bulletin covers, visitor badges and decorative editions of sacred scripture. And behind the scenes worship leaders are reading books and Internet sites full of suggested service plans and stories to spice up a sermon or homily, while musicians are ordering music for choirs, organ, bells, and other instruments. The bigger the congregation, the more likely they were to name at least one supplier for such extra worship resources.

But far more important than size or any other factor was—again—religious tradition (see Table 5). Those who named specific suppliers of products that support their worship were disproportionately in the high-liturgy traditions. Compared to all other Christian congregations, they were more than twice as likely to name local religious bookstores, and specialty houses where they can find proper liturgical supplies. They are also likely to order from the catalogs of Almy, Robert Gaspard, and J. F. Morrow. These are all family-run companies that specialize in the clothing, implements, and decorative items associated with "high church" Christian worship, and many clergy get their first catalog before they graduate from seminary. All three of these companies describe their business as a ministry. They emphasize craftsmanship and the care with which items are made and the preciousness of the physical objects associated with worship. While one could buy candlesticks at Macy's, the candles to be placed on an altar seem to demand something more.

Material objects of all sorts can become visible links to the experience of divine presence,[8] so shopping the Almy catalog may be both a commercial transaction and a religious act.

While Christians are shopping for preaching robes and communion sets, Jews are likely shopping at the local Judaica store for kippot, Torah scroll crowns, and talits—created perhaps by a company such as Miriam Religious Manufacturing, equally devoted to the sacred quality of the items they make. African Americans join their more liturgical colleagues in seeking out robes—in this case robes for the several choirs many black churches sponsor. Theologian Robert Franklin recalls, "I grew up in a congregation whose impressive music ministry included a choir that moved to well-choreographed steps and was clad in magnificent robes" (Franklin 1994, 262). Color, fabric, design, and ornamentation embody, for many different kinds of worshipers, the sacred connections being made between a congregation and their god.

Catholics and white Protestants of all sorts sometimes seek out books and Internet sites to help them enhance what they do on Sunday. (African American church leaders reported less of this sort of resource use.) Most commonly the books our informants reported using were published by their own and other denominations, rather than by independent presses. Catholic church leaders can go to publishers such as J. S. Paluch to find routine supplies like missalettes, but also to find books of hints for creating effective homilies. Protestant publishers such as Abingdon, Augsburg Fortress, and Cokesbury produce books of sermons, theological reflections on worship, poems and artwork, dramas and children's messages for pastors in their own denominations and across the Protestant Mainline. Even here, those in the liturgical denominations are the most avid buyers. These traditions place worship at the top of the congregational priority list, and their patterns of resource use consistently reflect that priority.

Most nonliturgical Conservative churches have a Sunday gathering that stresses evangelism and teaching more than elaborate ritual, so both they and African American church leaders are less likely to browse catalogs and bookstores in search of material accoutrements for their Sunday services. Similarly, none of the congregations of Jehovah's Witnesses, Mormons, and Christian Scientists listed any external resources for worship, nor did the Hindu, Muslim, and Buddhist congregations we surveyed name any publishers, bookstores, or religious supply stores as resources for their work. Religious stores for these newer traditions clearly do exist, both in this country and in the sending countries from which migrants have come, but they have not yet become prevalent enough to show up in a survey like ours. A few mosques, for instance, have small stores attached, and occasional stores specialize in Hindu or Buddhist art, jewelry, clothing, and other religious items. The Internet, in turn, has made it possible for scattered adherents of migrant religious traditions to find everything from head coverings to electronic religious calendars that will remind them when to pray. Both individuals and communities can find products online that they might otherwise have to travel thousands of miles to obtain. When new worship centers are being built, however, experts from home are likely to be called here to provide the particular plans and crafts necessary. And when existing spaces are converted for make-do worship use, the prayer rugs or icons or altar are also likely to come from home.[9] At least for now, major sources for religious products and designs are still distant from the American communities where immigrants are making their homes.

This pattern stands in contrast to the readily available suppliers specializing in the building and furnishing of Christian and Jewish places of worship. There are U.S. companies specializing in the manufacture of church pews, pulpit furniture, baptisteries, and pipe organs, in addition to providing architectural advice and financing plans for American churches.[10] Even congregations that think of themselves as nonliturgical and spontaneous in their worship are likely to have a pulpit and pews, a communion table and choir robes; and if their own denomination does not have a source for those items, dozens of commercial firms will be happy to help them. As more and more mosques and temples are built, they are likely to join this market as well. Worship is central to the work done by all kinds of religious communities, and both official and unofficial suppliers help local congregations to create the sacred times and places where that work takes place.

SUSTAINING RELIGIOUS TRADITIONS

Worshipping together requires that a community of adherents has at least some minimal knowledge of the beliefs and practices of the tradition in which they are participating. Sustaining those beliefs and practices requires the work of religious education, and that work often rests on a foundation of programs and texts the congregation did not produce.

Earlier generations may have depended on oral tradition, passing religious wisdom from elders to youth, but at least for the last two centuries in the United States, that wisdom has been distilled into formal curricula and organized activities that were profoundly shaped by the invention of Sunday schools. At the beginning of the nineteenth century, the Sunday school movement began as an effort to provide both religious and basic literacy education to poor working children. Both in mission schools (for nonchurch-goers) and in church schools, children (girls as well as boys, black as well as white) learned to read and spell, recite scripture and behave well, often earning certificates for their accomplishments and taking home illustrated leaflets with Bible stories and inspirational tales. As Anne Boylan argues, the vehicles that bound the movement together were the press and the voluntary society. Missionaries traveled the land selling publications as they started new schools (Boylan 1988, 68–73). Soon both the program and the structure of the (nondenominational) American Sunday School Union were copied by Episcopal, Presbyterian, Methodist, Baptist, and other denominations, and by the end of the century denominations dominated the market.

Today religious books, magazines, videos, CDs, and Web sites are produced by an enormous array of organizations—some attached to denominations, but many created by religious (and secular) entrepreneurs. Sunday school is still a primary market, but so are youth groups, women's groups, and religious professionals, among others. Just as the religious voluntarism of the United States has made it possible for local believers to form their own congregations, it is also possible for any enterprising agent to produce and market the educational programs congregations will use. Navigating through the resulting array of available suppliers can be a significant challenge for local educators—not to mention for researchers who ask about them.

As we saw in Chapter 2, congregations put much of their organizational energy into religious education for their young. A weekly Sunday school (or some equivalent thereof) is still the most common way they do it, but there is certainly no single Sunday School Union producing all the books and magazines pupils will need. Across the Christian traditions, denominationally produced educational programs are the most common resource for educating children, but certainly not the only ones. Roughly half (52%) of Catholic, Orthodox, and denominationally affiliated Protestant congregations use only the materials provided by their own religious body. Another 10 percent supplement that material with resources from another publisher.

This lack of complete uniformity within Protestant denominations stands in contrast to the Sectarian groups, where *every* congregation that reported having a children's program also reported using official religious texts exclusively from their own in-house publishers. At the other end of the continuum are the Other Religions (as well as many Jewish leaders we talked with). They are somewhat less likely to report regular children's (or youth) programming and less likely to say that they use an officially published curriculum. They are not drawing on

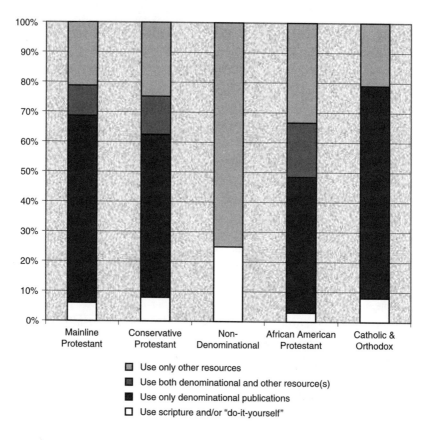

FIGURE 3
Educational Publications for Children in Christian Congregations

competing suppliers—rather, there are fewer institutionalized sources on which to draw.

In the Christian and Jewish traditions as well, not everyone buys a packaged curriculum of any sort. The pattern for some Jewish synagogues and a small segment of Christian churches is to create a locally improvised program of study. Some say that their primary text is just sacred scripture and/or a catechetical document. Several Church of Christ congregations said that they expect teachers to stand before their classes with only a Bible in hand, and nondenominational churches were also especially likely to choose this approach (see Figure 3). Part of the pattern of being "independent," for many, is eschewing mass-produced educational materials and sticking to the Bible.

Because most nondenominational churches are evangelical, and many describe themselves as "independent Baptists," when they do buy packages of educational materials, some turn to Conservative denominations like the Southern Baptist Convention or the General Association of Regular Baptists that they consider sufficiently evangelical and biblical to meet their needs. But the most common suppliers for nondenominational churches were independent publishers like Union Gospel Press or Standard Publishing.

Those same independent publishers supply many denominationally aligned churches as well (see Figure 3). Evangelical churches use Union Gospel and Standard, plus Gospel Light. Charismatic and Pentecostal churches often named Charisma Life as well. But the granddaddy of them all is David C. Cook. Begun in the late nineteenth century in Chicago, Cook was a pioneer in the production of printed resources for Sunday schools. Cook Communications Ministries now publishes books, Bibles, and Vacation Bible School curricula, in addition to Sunday school materials that are used in more than one hundred countries around the world.[11] Their continuing financial success made it possible for the company to buy out at least nine other evangelical publishers and resource suppliers in the 1980s and 1990s. They have also made inroads into the denominational market with lines tailored for Wesleyan, Reformed/Presbyterian, Episcopal/Anglican, and African American churches. Evangelical churches—both denominational and independent—were most likely to report using Cook publications, but at least a few African American, Mainline, and Catholic parishes did as well. Cook has earned a reputation for materials that are attractive and easy to use. Not only do students get quarterly lesson books, but teachers get companion manuals of instruction and kits full of games and visual aids as well.

While David C. Cook was the most frequently mentioned nondenominational supplier of children's literature, they are surpassed in the youth market by Group Publishing. More a youth ministry resource than a curriculum, *Group* magazine and Group's Bible study books, dramas, games, and training events provide ideas and guidance for church adults who work with teenagers. Like David C. Cook, this is an evangelical publisher, but Mainline Protestant churches were as likely to cite Group as were Conservative and independent ones.

Among African American churches, the favorite nondenominational publisher is Urban Ministries. Almost as many turn to this Chicago-based supplier as use their own denominational publications. While Cook and some other evangelical publishers have been around for a century or more, Urban Ministries is relatively new, founded in 1970 to provide "Sunday School curriculum, Vacation Bible

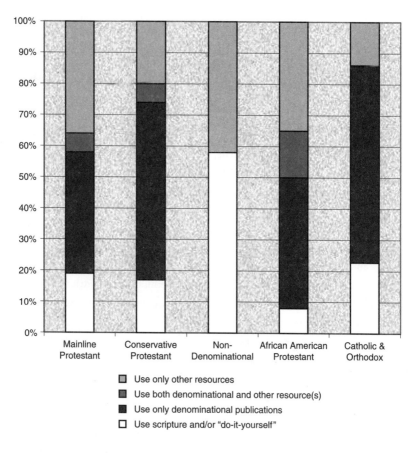

FIGURE 4

Educational Publications for Youth in Christian Congregations

School resources, books, videos, and music, all of which depict or speak to people of color in the context of their culture."[12]

Black churches are not alone in looking beyond their denominations for help with youth education (see Figure 4). In all kinds of churches, denominational offerings for youth are less likely to be used than are those for younger children; and among Mainline Protestants, the use of nondenominational materials is nearly as prevalent as the use of in-house sources. Less than half of Mainliners use any denominational youth materials, and only 39 percent stick exclusively to what their own church body provides. Some borrow across denominational lines. Others order from the nondenominational evangelical publishers like David C. Cook and

Group. But still others choose from publishers, like Youth Specialties, that are oriented to the more liberal side of Protestantism. The Canadian "Whole People of God" series, brought to the United States in 1993 by Logos Productions, claims to design their resources for "ecumenical" churches. Bible studies are based on scripture passages from the lectionary (on which many Mainline pastors base their sermons), and themes of inclusiveness and social justice are introduced as students are invited to make connections between faith and everyday life.[13]

That the teen years have been difficult for Mainline churches is reflected in the proliferation of efforts like Faith Inkubators (FINK), also begun in 1993, and now expanded into eighteen hundred congregations in thirteen denominations. Another new program, "Way to Live: Christian Practices for Teens," uses both print and a sophisticated Web site to encourage teens to explore how faith can shape everything from their play to everyday choices to grieving. This entrepreneurial ferment among liberal Protestants seems to acknowledge both their dissatisfaction with many of their own denominational publications and the need for serious attention to youth religious education.[14]

Conservative Protestants have long been known for their youth programs, and nearly three-quarters of evangelical Protestant youth report that they are active in a church youth group (C. Smith et al. 2002). Conservatives were also more likely than Mainliners to report to us that they use denominationally produced youth curricula. Sticking to tradition-specific materials is even more common among Catholic and Orthodox parishes, and it was always case for Latter-day Saints and Jehovah's Witnesses.

The Jewish synagogues in our sample, on the other hand, were drawing from a variety of resources for their youth, often using publications from across Jewish "denominational" traditions. In many synagogues primary emphasis is on day school education, preparation for bar and bat mitzvah, trips to Israel, and Hebrew school, in addition to youth groups like Conservative Judaism's United Synagogue Youth. Even more than liberal Protestants, American Jews have recently realized the need for critical attention to their youth. Not only are bar/bat mitzvah classes being taken much more seriously, but parents are also being drawn more firmly into the process (Kosmin 2000).

The typical pattern across religious traditions is to educate children and youth using weekly lessons that are aided by published curriculum packages and teaching guidelines. But in about one in eight congregations resources beyond those basics are used. Some congregations, most often from the Conservative Protestant traditions, use programs from national youth ministries such as Youth with a Mission,

Navigators, Young Life, Child Evangelism Fellowship, and Awana. These programs have been part of a major expansion of evangelical parachurch (that is, specialized and nondenominational) ministries in the last fifty years (Hamilton 2000). Awana, for instance, has clubs that meet weekly in nine thousand churches.[15] Other smaller organizations may bring together youth from several local churches; and in still other cases, connections to a national organization enable churches to provide special summer activities or mission trips. In Catholic, Mainline, and African American churches, these particular evangelical program partners are less common. Scouts, for instance, are more prevalent than Young Life or Awana. But whatever the program, national organizations can provide a congregation with a preplanned array of weekly recreational and character-building activities for their youth.

Whether a church enters the parachurch market—either for Sunday school curricula or supplemental programs—is partly a matter of its religious tradition: Catholics and Sectarians almost never choose publications that are not officially sanctioned. But among Protestants of all sorts, whether congregations look beyond their own in-house denominational suppliers is mostly a matter of social forces that have made that congregation more open to change. Using the package of curricular materials produced by a denomination is most common in the most traditional congregations. Among the newest churches (founded since 1975), fewer than half (47%) use *any* denominational materials, compared to 62 percent of congregations founded earlier. As with the use of denominational hymnals, a variety of change agents seem to be at work in loosening traditional patterns. Where the majority of members are themselves denominational switchers, only 58 percent of congregations use denominational curricula, while nearly three-quarters (72%) of congregations dominated by cradle members use tradition-specific lessons for their children.

While changes are dislodging the connection between denominations and the supply of materials for religious education, one denominational connection remains very strong. One of the most common extracurricular activities congregations provide for their children and youth is a chance to spend a week or two at a religious camp. These often-rustic hideaways are intended to create the sort of liminal, sacred space where important spiritual growth can occur. Across the Christian denominations, about a third of congregations said that camping is a routine part of their educational offerings, and the vast majority (over 90%) of the camps they use are connected to their own denomination. Camps are one of the things regional denominational units do for their churches, and churches without a denomination to provide a camp were much less likely to report that camping is something their children and youth do at all.[16]

Camping is not limited to Christian congregations. As other religions make their place in American society, camps for children and youth are already becoming a part of the educational arsenal (Warner 2002a). An extensive network of Jewish summer camps—Reform, Conservative, Orthodox, and independent—is already in place. Participation in the Conservative movement's Camp Ramah has been significant in fostering lifelong Jewish observance and increasing the likelihood of participation in synagogue activities later in life (Kosmin 2000).

Another part of the religious educational system consists of formal day schools. As we saw in Chapter 2, some churches and synagogues sponsor their own schools, but other congregations rely on the presence of religious schools in the community as resources in their own efforts to nurture the faith of their children. Evangelical churches sometimes named nearby Christian academies, and a Conservative synagogue named a local Solomon Schechter school as partners in their religious education work. Pupils at such schools are almost never confined to a single congregation's youth, but serve a larger local constituency of like-minded others.

Having a program of religious education requires both curricula and teachers, and the teachers are likely to need training, a task many denominations take to be part of their portfolio. About one in five of the congregations we studied reported that at least a few members routinely participate in educational events provided by their regional denominational body. Classes and workshops for Sunday school teachers or certification courses for catechism instruction provide church bodies the opportunity to shape the way their tradition is passed along in local congregations. Southern Baptists have excelled in this task. Even in rural Alabama, a pastor told us, "That's part of the association—courses, seminars, training. Next Monday night we'll have training for Sunday school. Seminars, training, all you want and then some." Churches (in all traditions) that told us they were especially concerned about serving families and children were also especially likely to send members to these denominational events.

So the education of children and youth involves both a wide array of Sunday school publishers and an equally wide array of other programs and institutions. Taken together, the web of agencies, publishers, camps, and schools is the organizational embrace within which the work of religious education is done. Denomination-specific publishers are the single biggest suppliers (especially for Catholics and Sectarians), but the parachurch sector is very active. Nor is that parachurch sector undifferentiated. Black churches use Urban Ministries; evangelicals use Awana; Mainline Protestants use Whole People of God. Some overlap exists, but the parachurch sector reflects—and creates—the broad religious streams that run through American religion. The divisions are neither as polarized nor as simple as predicted by Wuthnow (1988). Still, this mapping of youth religious education begins to reveal the contours of an organizational terrain that is neither strictly denominational nor flatly undifferentiated, not split between left and right but with well-worn paths that lead in distinct directions. Denominations occupy the most traditional locations in this terrain, and the parachurch agencies thrive among the newer, younger, more religiously diverse congregations, where tradition is least strong.

When we turn our attention from the nurture of children and youth to the work of sustaining adult faith, the organizational picture becomes even more complex. First of all, the work is less dominated by weekly Sunday school. One in five congregations has no educational activity for adults at all, and an additional one in five offers only ad hoc midweek studies that involve small numbers of parishioners. Of those that do have regular educational programs, 29 percent put together their own resources for at least some of their classes. They either work directly with scripture and commentaries, read inspirational books together, or piece together programs from whatever sources are at hand. This improvisational approach is more common in adult programming than for either children or youth (compare Figure 5 with Figures 3 and 4). Congregations consume fewer outside educational resources for their adults than for their children—in part because they are spending less organizational energy on the task of educating those adults.

They are also less likely to stick with denominational publications. Among Mainline and African American Protestant churches, less than half use any denominational resources. In Conservative Protestant and Catholic churches, the percentage is ten to fifteen points higher, but still not much more than half. As with children's programming, only the Sectarians (not shown in the figure) are absolutely tied to what their own organizations publish.

The array of nondenominational publishers for adults parallels the sources used for children and youth—David C. Cook, Standard Publishing, Union Gospel Press—but for adults Willow Creek Association enters the picture as well. Begun in 1992 as a spin-off from the influential Chicago megachurch (Willow Creek Community Church), this association now provides conferences, books, high-tech worship planning resources, and educational programming for children and adults.[17] Conservative Protestant churches in our sample were more likely to turn here for adult resources than to any other nondenominational publisher except David C. Cook.

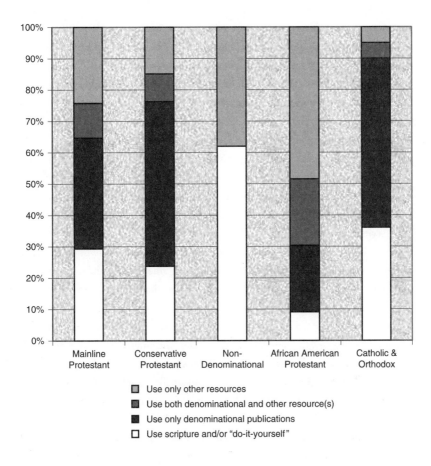

FIGURE 5

Educational Publications for Adults in Christian Congregations

Because so much adult programming is done outside the standard Sunday school format, the range of possible resources is broad and diverse. Some of the weekday spiritual programming congregations do for their adults is locally improvised, but some of it draws on national and international church and parachurch networks. About one in six congregations named at least one additional resource for their adult spiritual activities, most often ties to national and international spiritual growth movements. Some Episcopal parishes we surveyed, for instance, had groups that participate in the Cursillo movement; Methodists were part of the Walk to Emmaus; and Catholics had organized local chapters of the Legion of Mary. Each of these presents participants with opportunities to meditate, pray, share life experiences with others, explore new spiritual practices, and the like. Bible Study Fellowship organizes groups for systematic study of Christian scriptures, and we found them in both Mainline and Conservative Protestant churches.[18] A couple of Assemblies of God churches were home to groups of Women's Aglow, an international charismatic prayer and support group where women share their joys and sorrows, pray together, and listen to speakers who advise them about how to live "victoriously" in the midst of life's difficulties (Griffith 1997a).

But women are no longer alone in gathering to learn, pray, and share their lives. In the mid-1990s Promise Keepers burst on the scene in giant "stadium events" that eventually became instantiated in local "accountability groups." Founder Bill McCartney brought thousands of men to sports arenas, entertained them with rock-style music, offered them a glimpse of famous athletes, led them in rousing songs and cheers, and then challenged them to live more godly lives—especially tending to the sins that separated them from each other, their fathers, their wives and children, and people of other races. They were challenged to share their feelings, to confess their most intimate failings, to touch and hug, and to pray together.[19] At the time during which we were interviewing, Promise Keepers was frequently in the news, and it had already touched the ministries of 15 percent of all the congregations we surveyed, including a quarter of all the evangelical churches, 14 percent of the African American ones, and smaller numbers of Catholics and Mainline Protestants. Many had taken groups to nearby stadium events, while others had actually established their own accountability groups. Still others were using Promise Keeper materials to revamp their men's ministries. Promise Keepers was the single most prevalent organization providing supplemental spiritual programs and resources to the congregations we surveyed.

Beyond these programs for spiritual growth and support, congregations also draw broadly on other educational opportunities for their adult members. Nearly half (45%) of all congregations named at least one educational partner that has provided programs for their adults. Sometimes congregations call on local schools and hospitals and political organizations to make special presentations. A program on preventing depression or domestic abuse, a speech by a politician, or a talk about neighborhood crime may be included on a congregation's agenda of adult activities. Such community educational events were especially common in the adult programming of the Jewish congregations in which we interviewed.

Both Jewish and Christian congregations sometimes call on nearby religious colleges and seminaries to provide speakers as well, or they send their members to programs and workshops these schools provide. In Seattle, for instance, Fuller Seminary's local branch serves both Mainline and Conservative Protestant churches, while Seattle University serves mostly the Mainline Protestant and Catholic communities. Both schools bring well-known theologians to town for public lectures and short courses, and both offer training for teachers and other church leaders. Many schools have added this sort of short-term publicly oriented programming to their curriculum, targeting nearby churches and synagogues for potential students. Those congregations, in turn, gain access to high-level spiritual and educational enrichment for members who choose to attend.

But before they call the local seminary or link up with a parachurch organization, many congregations take a trip to the local religious bookstore. In Chicago, for instance, many local religious educators shop at the Moody Bible Institute bookstore. In Nashville, home to the giant publishing arms of the United Methodist Church (UMC), Southern Baptist Convention (SBC), and National Baptist Convention, church members can choose from the SBC's Baptist Bookstores (now called Lifeway stores) and the UMC's Cokesbury stores.[20] But in both cities, Family Christian Stores follows closely in the competition. This national chain claims to be "America's leading specialty retailer with over 340 locations and over 5,000 employees in 34 states dedicated solely to the $4.3 billion Christian retailing market."[21] Both individuals looking for inspiration and Sunday school teachers looking for ideas have created a huge industry. The Christian Booksellers Association claims twenty-five hundred member stores in the United States and provides those stores with all the marketing savvy any industry association would.

Christian Bookstores have become so big and pervasive that they tend to extend their reach outside the Conservative Protestant traditions that are their natural constituency. Still, Catholic, Orthodox, and Mainline Protestant local leaders are more likely to seek out alternative shops that carry products and books the evangelical stores might not consider "biblically accurate." Local Catholic bookstores and stores at colleges and seminaries were often named by our Catholic and Mainline respondents. And while the market is much smaller, local Jewish bookstores were almost always mentioned by synagogue leaders.

Drawing on this vast array of independent publishers and resource suppliers is a necessity for nondenominational congregations. Many of them assert a kind of radical independence by depending only on their own internal resources (see Figure 5), but the average number of outside resources named in nondenominational churches was double that in similarly conservative but denominationally aligned churches. Any increase in the nondenominational sector of congregations will likely imply an increase in the educational market base that lies outside denominational lines.

As we saw with resources for children and youth, this "open market" for adult educational resources is most often chosen by the least traditional congregations, denominational and otherwise. Using supplemental connections and materials, for instance, is most common among urban and suburban congregations, among congregations not dominated by senior adults, and among congregations founded since 1975. Nor are these differences a matter of the congregation's own wherewithal: better educated and more well-off congregations are no more nor less likely to seek outside resources when these other matters of traditionalism are taken into account. Rather, shopping the open market seems to be associated with newer cohorts of people and newer churches, no matter what their status or resources.

Entrepreneurial approaches to adult education are also more likely in churches that are less active in denominational educational events. Only about one out of two churches that has participated in a denominational training event has also used any open-market adult resource, while most churches (80%) that are nonevent-attenders use at least one outside resource. Participating in denominational events provides (and promotes) denominational resources so that a church may need fewer additional materials. Failing to attend such events seems to accompany a larger pattern in which denominational resources are absent.

Whether congregations are more or less alienated from denominational resources than in the past, we cannot say. What we can say is that the field is currently occupied by a diverse group of organizations. Denominations have not vanished from the field, but our comparisons of more and less traditional churches suggest that denominations will continue to face significant competition from other suppliers (of all sorts). Even as more adults are religiously mobile, it is not clear what they may find in the congregations they join: weekly Sunday school, a Cursillo group, a monthly Thursday night Bible study? Packaged programs from a denominational publisher, a chapter of a national women's movement, ad hoc reflections on someone's favorite book, or a carefully crafted local curriculum? While there are some variations from one religious family to another and some regularities based on just how traditional the congregation is, no single pattern predominates anywhere. Everyone seems to be experimenting with ways to meet the challenge of busy adults, some of whom have been studying all their lives, and some of whom may never before have learned a single verse of scripture or line of catechism.[22]

MANAGING CONGREGATIONS

The work of worship and religious education is at the heart of what congregations do, and a complex network of organizations provides support for those tasks. But congregations sometimes need other kinds of organizational support and guidance if they are to thrive. They need help figuring out how to raise money for big projects, help managing conflict, help maintaining their buildings and planning new ones, and help when basic organizational changes are called for. This behind-the-scenes assistance may not immediately seem important or interesting, but this is the basic organizational structure through which both material and cultural resources flow.

When we asked congregations to tell us about where they go for this sort of organizational advice and support, only about 7 percent named individual consultants or consulting organizations (such as the Alban Institute) that specialize in providing organizational development resources to churches. The world of management advisors is not the place most congregations first turn. Rather, for those who are part of a denomination, the most logical place to turn is the regional arm of their church body. Independent churches, which lack a larger organizational apparatus on which to call, use outside consulting resources at a rate four times higher than denominational churches (see Table 6). They are the only kinds of churches that use independent consultants with any regularity, and then only one in four (28%) said they had done so recently. While independent consultants make a good living advising congregations, regional denominational offices are far more likely to get the calls from their member churches. At a small Southern Baptist church, we heard, "There are a lot of things that are available. [The] Missouri Baptist Convention is known for being providers. You can call those folks and they will send someone down to help you with any need that you would have inside of the church." At an Episcopal parish in Albuquerque, a lay leader assured us that the bishop was especially helpful in the process of transition between pastors: "His staff is there to help us, help with the search process." Supporting church programming, assisting in transitions between pastors, and providing advice when problems arise are the routine tasks of local and regional associations, dioceses, synods, and the like.

Sometimes a regional church body may have difficulty meeting the needs of every congregation. In her study of regional denominational leaders, Lummis found that listening to the specific needs of congregations is a high priority, but they often find it difficult to achieve. Some regional church bodies have no paid staff at all, and others have far fewer than their large number of member congregations would make ideal. When they are able to listen, they may provide direct help

TABLE 6 Support for Congregational Development and Programming in Congregations in Different Religious Traditions

Type of Advice	Mainline Protestant (151) (%)	Conservative Protestant (239) (%)	Nondenominational (61) (%)	African American Protestant (43) (%)	Catholic & Orthodox (34) (%)	All Congregations (549) (%)
Advice from regional body*	37	26	n.a.	10	55	30[a]
Advice from national body	16	21	n.a.	14	4	17[a]
Any other advice*	6	5	28	8	0	7[b]

NOTE: Number in parentheses indicates number of congregations in that group. For type of advice marked with an asterisk at least one of the differences among the groups is statistically significant at p < .10 (Oneway ANOVA, with Scheffe post-hoc comparisons).
[a] Includes only denominationally affiliated Christian churches.
[b] Includes all congregations, including Sectarians, Jews, and Other Religions

to a church or organize a regional training event that will meet common needs they have discovered in several places. Still, regional leaders reported that "a distressing number of congregations seem to have no idea what kinds of resources their judicatory offers and they can have for the asking" (Lummis 2001). Our conversations with local church leaders would suggest that the issue is not that they are choosing other advisors instead but that they do not ask for help at all.

Still, whether congregations are tied to an official hierarchical structure (like an Episcopal diocese) or cooperating voluntarily in a "congregational" polity (like the Southern Baptists or the United Church of Christ), they are more likely to call a denominational official than to seek out an independent source of help. Nor are these two resources in competition—we found that those who seek out denominational help were *more* likely to pursue other resources as well.

Seeking both denominational and outside help is, in fact, largely a matter of organizational size. The bigger the church and the bigger its budget, the more likely it was to mention some organizational development resource it had received—both from its denominational offices and from various outside suppliers. The smallest (and ironically perhaps the neediest) churches seem to lie outside the visibility of the help-giving networks. The pastor of a small LCMS church in rural Missouri said bluntly, "They don't have a clue we exist. . . . We don't have the size; we don't have the budget; we don't have the problems; we are just doing our own little thing." Only one in five churches with attendance under fifty named any regional denominational resource they had received (compared to one in three larger churches); and fewer than one in a hundred small churches cited any other outside support for their work.

Use of national denominational resources follows a similar pattern. National resources are less commonly used than regional ones (17 percent compared to 30 percent), but it is the best-educated congregations that are most likely to draw from national departments and agencies. Perhaps educational experience gives congregational leaders the organizational savvy for navigating the national system. National assistance is not nearly so readily available as regional aid, requiring a call across the country rather than a call down the road. The person on the other end of the line is also more likely to be a stranger and the maze of offices more opaque. Without preexisting connections, local congregations are not likely to assume that someone at national headquarters can help them, while they are much more likely to know someone from their state or regional office.

The mix between regional and national connection, however, is not uniform across religious traditions. Among Mainline Protestants, regional bodies are the primary connection, with national offices playing a more minor role. The regional/national balance is more even among Conservative and African American denominations. Catholics, on the other hand, essentially have no national bureaucracy, so it is almost exclusively the local diocese that guides and assists churches. For Sectarians, by contrast, it is *only* the central body that matters. Each congregation is responsible to and dependent on a central authority that supplies whatever assistance it may need. Both religious tradition and denominational authority structures affect which cards are at the front of a congregation's Rolodex. Denominations with a stronger authority structure are more likely to be called on for local assistance, and their church officials are also more likely to take the initiative to offer resources before a congregation's leaders ask for help (Lummis 2001).

Organizational development of this sort seems largely confined to the Christian churches. Although both the United Synagogue of Conservative Judaism and the Union of American Hebrew Congregations provide ample programmatic support for local synagogues, none of the Jewish congregations we encountered talked about calling on those resources for management assistance. Nor did any of the Hindu, Muslim, or other newer religious groups talk about organizational resources they have received. Whatever equivalent "denominational" support structure may be evolving among the newer groups, it apparently does not yet parallel the routine organizational patterns found in the Christian churches.

One of the points at which congregations are most likely to ask for outside help is in planning, financing, and constructing buildings. And here polity (the official authority structure) does make a difference, something a Southern Baptist pastor in Nashville noted: "There are some services from the denomination that give help in those areas. Most of those services are for smaller churches that don't have the resources that a larger church would have. Therefore they're not real helpful to us. . . . Our polity is congregational. We use committees and so forth. . . . We voted as a church . . . to start this building process." While his perception of how helpful his Baptist state convention might be is probably not right, he is right in observing that his local congregation can make its own building choices. At a large Catholic parish in Chicago, the story was quite different: "Oh yes they provide advice—and there are regulations if you want to build. We have to go through a real process in selecting an acceptable architect, who can not only build, but knows what the church is used for. You have to get permission to begin that process—to find out if you're financially stable. So we have directives on that." The striking new building one Albuquerque Episcopal parish had built was the result of a process somewhere between those Catholic regulations and the

Baptist church's freedom. "There's an architectural consultant for the diocese, who was actually very helpful," we were told. "You are actually required to work with him in the early stages, and you have to get approval along the way." In all three cases local parish committees work with regional church offices that supply architectural and financial advice, but some churches are more obligated than others to follow that advice. The end result is that Catholic and Orthodox parishes are far more likely to have received administrative assistance of all kinds from their dioceses than are churches in any of the Protestant traditions.

The need to construct religious buildings is one of the points at which religious groups new to the United States are improvising new organizational forms.[23] None of the local groups in which we interviewed had received resources from a regional or national group for their building, but such groups are beginning to exist. The Islamic Society of North America is among the most active. It now has a Field Services office that will provide training for Islamic Centers and keep Centers in touch with each other. They have also established a fund-raising office and development funds to help Centers raise necessary money, especially for new buildings.

Just as new congregations present organizational challenges, so do old ones, congregations whose members are old, that is. Even compared to other small congregations, those with "graying" memberships are especially likely to have called on their regional denominational office for assistance (38 percent compared to 28 percent of younger congregations). Such aging congregations are not uncommon. More than a quarter of all congregations reported to us that about half or more of their members are over sixty-five years of age, and that number is dramatically higher among Mainline Protestants (44%), African American churches (43%), and Jewish synagogues (40%). Nondenominational and Sectarian groups have almost no such aging congregations (7% each). Congregations across religious traditions that have older memberships are likely to see a need for help in planning their future. Often they are located in neighborhoods or towns where population has declined or changed in demography. Older members with deep attachments remain, while younger ones have moved away and/or started going to newer, more convenient congregations (Ammerman 1997a). "Redevelopment" of these congregations is a major concern for many denominations. As Lummis discovered, such congregations pose a special challenge for regional church staff, and clearly not all of them ask for help, but in denominations that grant the regions more authority, staff sometimes seek out at-risk congregations and try to help them make needed transitions (Lummis 2001).

Congregations that are *organizationally* older (founded more than a generation ago) are a different matter. They, too, use regional denominational resources at a higher rate, but probably for different reasons. Congregations that have been around longer are not necessarily less healthy, but once they have passed at least a generation of history together, they may face important transitions for which they seek help. More established congregations may also have learned, over the course of years, where all the best resources are. New and old congregations call outside consultants at the same (relatively low) rate, but more established congregations are more likely *also* to have a routine of calling in denominational help. Older churches consume more administrative resources of all kinds.

Regional denominational offices are also sometimes called to mediate when a congregation finds itself embroiled in conflict, and how that help is received depends very much on the religious authority structure within which it is being offered. Those who are obliged to ask church officials for help seemed least happy with the results. We rarely encountered a parish that was happy with the mediation provided by a bishop. The story we heard at an Episcopal parish was typical: "The dissidents finally left and formed another congregation—with the blessing of the bishop! A lot of people here felt that should not have been permitted. The idea of being part of a larger family was that we would get some help from there, and instead what we got was grief from there." A United Methodist echoed similar sentiments: "Unfortunately I don't think it went through the process very well. It just sort of blew up. It got out of hand. The guidance wasn't very good." In churches with congregational polity, we heard few such complaints. As the pastor of a Chicago church in the Baptist General Conference noted, "They would come in if we asked them to. And they may call up, you know, if they heard there was a dispute going on, one of them may call up and say, 'How can we be of help?' and initiate that part. But they don't have the authority to come in." Providing assistance with conflict management is wading into treacherous waters. Regional denominational offices that have no direct authority over congregations may be wise in staying away. And those that do have such authority often find themselves in no-win situations.

The patterns we have been describing so far are mostly characteristic of the Mainline and Conservative Protestant denominations. Denominations in the historic African American traditions come in both hierarchical and congregational varieties, but all have patterns of interchurch assistance that are less routine, based on neither bureaucratized denominational offices nor outside consulting services (see Table 6). That does not mean that there are no networks of support. Most local associations in the National Baptist tradition are first of all networks of fellowship, and fellowship often also means advice. The president of the state convention (essentially its CEO and bishop rolled into one) is always a prominent pastor with a large church to tend and little, if any, additional personnel to help him fulfill his convention duties. But he is very likely to have extensive knowledge of and informal contact with the churches in his jurisdiction. Despite official hierarchies, the pattern of volunteer staffing is the same in the Church of God in Christ and the three black Methodist bodies. In all these denominations assistance to congregations is likely to pass through personal channels rather than professional and bureaucratic ones. Whether an official (Methodist) bishop or an unofficial (Baptist) one, the regional incumbent's duties are likely to include a regular round of preaching invitations in churches throughout the territory; and it is in the conversations surrounding these visits that advice and assistance are often exchanged.

There are also voluntary committees in local districts that organize training events for the churches, and there are elaborate opportunities for enrichment as part of state and national annual convention meetings. As we will see in Chapter 7, congregations in these traditions are much more involved in annual convention participation than are other Protestants or Catholics. Delegations of ten, twenty, or even thirty members may spend a week traveling across the country to attend the national gathering of their denomination. At those conferences, in addition to sermons and business, there are sessions for choir directors, Vacation Bible School teachers, and youth workers (as well as ushers and nurses), all providing opportunities to exchange ideas and help each other hone their skills. A similar combination of fellowship and training happens for pastors and choir directors at the annual Hampton University Ministers Conference. Educational, spiritual, and organizational resources for black churches are most often garnered in the midst of grand and inspiring events, surrounded by thousands of brothers and sisters in the faith.

Likewise, most African American churches have a variety of other congregations with which they routinely "fellowship." On a Sunday afternoon or Friday night, the pastor from one church preaches in the other, bringing along one or more of his (or occasionally her) choirs and a delegation of members. These visitors are expected to contribute generously to the offerings in their host church, knowing that their generosity will be reciprocated on another day. The pastor of a small National Baptist Church in Chicago described it this way: "We have a great fellowship program with some of the other churches. We have rallies with other churches throughout the year. . . . Our choir will fellowship with other choirs. Sort of a fund-raising movement as well as spiritual stimulant for the people." Not only do these visits facilitate a flow of monetary resources, but they also enable an exchange of ideas and encouragement. As pastors and lay leaders think and dream about what their churches might become, they have the examples of numerous sister churches at hand. These informal networks, along with the state and national conventions and the ministrations of individual bishops (official and otherwise), provide the congregational support and enrichment that many other denominations have formalized into bureaucratic offices and programs.

The assistance we have been describing is of the "advice and counsel" variety, but a few congregations (17%) also reported receiving financial support from their denominations. Other foundations, coalitions of partner churches, and grants were a source of support for a small number (5%) as well. Money from the larger Church is most common in Catholic parishes (see Table 7), where it sometimes helps to keep a parish school open, for instance. Sometimes, as at a small Chicago parish, the Church provides assistance while the parish undergoes redevelopment: "When I came here we were worried if we were going to stay open. We made some financial strides, but . . . we do get outside support from another couple of parishes to help us, through what's called the Sharing Parish program. . . . Also the diocese gives us a grant of about $30,000 a year." At a larger parish, also in Chicago, the outlook was more positive, but the help equally essential: "We've been doing a capital drive for our church, repairs and things, and we've established a matching relationship with the archdiocese on that, so that for every $2 we raise, they would give us $1 for these projects. That's another helpful thing."

Besides Roman Catholics, Mainline Protestant denominations are the only others likely to provide this sort of local assistance. The strongest factor that distinguishes churches that have received money from those that have not is not size or need or mission goals, but being otherwise well connected to regional denominational resources and participation. Strong hierarchical structures and active patterns of participation pave the way to financial assistance.

Among both Mainline and Catholic parishes, ethnic and immigrant churches are slightly more likely to get subsidies. Ethnic ministries within existing Anglo parishes sometimes get support as well. A small Seattle United Methodist Church reported, "We've got two major grants right now through the Conference. One is Church Alive, and then the other one is Ethnic Ministry, and that's the one that's funding our work with the Vietnamese groups in the area." Congregations that especially emphasized the importance of bridging ethnic differences were especially likely to have received monetary support from their regional or national

TABLE 7   Outside Financial Support Received by Congregations in Different Religious Traditions

Type of Support	Mainline Protestant (151) (%)	Conservative Protestant (239) (%)	Nondenominational (61) (%)	African American Protestant (43) (%)	Catholic & Orthodox (34) (%)	All Congregations (549) (%)
Any denominational money*	22	11	n.a.	9	45	17[a]
Any other money*	8	2	9	11	8	5[b]

NOTE: Number in parentheses indicates number of congregations in that group. For support marked with an asterisk at least one of the differences among the groups is statistically significant at p < .10 (Oneway ANOVA, with Scheffe post-hoc comparisons).

[a] Includes only denominationally affiliated Christian churches.

[b] Includes all congregations, including Sectarians, Jews, and Other Religions

denominations. Many national church groups have made racial and ethnic inclusion a high priority, and they seem to be putting their money behind their priorities.

While about 15 percent of all the congregations we surveyed reported getting denominational money (regional or national), only about 5 percent had gotten money from other outside sources. A few of those sources were actually rental income from properties the congregation owns, but the bulk were grants from foundations and other agencies to undertake programs they might not otherwise be able to launch. These grant-getters are not the smallest and poorest organizations seeking subsidies to survive; rather, they are mission-driven congregations with already-healthy budgets. Congregations that are especially concerned with serving their communities were more likely to report receiving supplemental funds, and African American churches were more likely to have received funds than churches in any other tradition (a pattern we will examine in more detail in Chapter 6).

Their more active pursuit of outside funding is another way in which black churches differ from Catholics and white Protestants. For routine organizational assistance, Catholics and white Protestants are far more likely to turn to denominational sources than to outside ones. African American churches, on the other hand, get more money and almost as much advice from independent organizations as from denominational ones. The management network that supports congregational life varies significantly from one religious tradition to another. Beyond these traditional Christian bodies, still other models are at work. Sectarians organize everything through centralized religious authorities, while non-Christian groups rarely have any regional or national offices to call. Tending to the organizational nuts and bolts of congregational life is largely the province of traditional (white) denominations, administered through their regional (and to a lesser extent national) network of offices and staff. The standard institutional template that typifies white Protestant denominations is largely absent in other religious traditions.

SUPPORTING CLERGY

Most congregations have a pastor; and about a third have more than one ordained professional on staff. The rare exceptions to this organizational rule provide an interesting contrast. First, there are religious traditions that do not ordain clergy—all of our Sectarian groups (Jehovah's Witnesses, Latter-day Saints, and Christian Scientists), plus the Society of Friends (Quakers), for example. These congregations are led by ordinary members who voluntarily provide direction for worship, education, and administration. These traditions make a theological commitment to the equal ministry of all the members.

The second set of exceptions are traditions from elsewhere in the world, in which there are roles that approximate the pastoral office and are sometimes, but not always, adapted to do so in the American context. Imams, for instance, in most of the world do not function like American clergy, but in the United States they sometimes take on a kind of full-time spiritual and administrative role for mosques that are prosperous enough to pay them (J. Smith 1999). We also found a couple of Nichiren Buddhist temples with resident monks who have taken on clergy-like roles. What they do includes much more ritual leadership and much less program planning than a typical Protestant pastor might do, but they serve as full-time spiritual leaders and exemplars for those who call that temple home. Numrich notes that the monks in the two Theravada temples he studied worked with the Sunday school children and served as a liaison with inquirers and the public, as well as being meditation instructors (Numrich 1995, 41). At a large Hindu temple where we interviewed, five priests were in residence, but our informant reminded us that finding and retaining priests is a special challenge in this country: "We want the priest to be very rigorously trained, and there are no priest-training schools in the U.S." As a result, they advertise in Indian newspapers, send delegations to India to interview candidates, and deal with the hassle of U.S. immigration requirements. Not nearly all gatherings of Hindus (or followers of other religions) have the resources or the inclination to go to such lengths to secure the services of a full-time professional religious leader.[24]

The third kind of pastorless congregation is too small to pay someone and is not part of a denomination that will supply a pastor in spite of the church's inability to pay. In the hierarchical denominations all congregations are assured some sort of professional pastoral services, although it may be a part-time or shared person or a lay worker rather than ordained clergy. The alternative is that church officials may decide that a congregation is too small to keep open at all. In contrast, small independent churches, even if they have had a pastor, may be especially vulnerable when that person leaves. They may struggle along with lay leadership and substitute preachers, but a permanent replacement may require resources they cannot muster.

These three kinds of exceptions—intentionally lay-led, resource-poor, and outside the American-style clergy pattern—were found in 7 percent of the congregations where we interviewed. Another 16 percent had a designated clergyperson but did not pay that person a salary. Some of these are volunteers leading gatherings of the newer religions. But the vast majority of the unpaid clergy are Protestant pastors who also hold secular (paying) jobs. They are sometimes referred to as "bivocational," but also sometimes call themselves "tentmakers," after the craft practiced by the New Testament apostle Paul as a means of supporting his missionary work. Churches with a hierarchical structure rarely employ this practice, guaranteeing their ordained clergy placements with a living wage. In nondenominational groups and in denominations with nonhierarchical polity, however, churches that cannot afford a salary have to improvise. Not surprisingly, this category is populated mostly by congregations with fewer attenders and smaller budgets—39 percent of the under-fifty-person groups and 46 percent of those with budgets under $50,000 have nonpaid clergy.

Having an unpaid pastor is also far more likely in black Baptist churches than in Anglo churches, even of similar size and circumstance. Black Methodist and Church of God in Christ congregations have paid clergy at the same rates as those in other hierarchical denominations, but 27 percent of all black Baptists reported no regular salary, and four out of five of the smallest black Baptist churches do not pay their pastors.[25] Black Baptist churches with attendance over three hundred sustain paid clergy at the rate other churches do when they have no more than a hundred in attendance. Culture more than resources is at work here. African American churches have a long cultural history of clergy who toil alongside their parishioners in the community, providing spiritual guidance in their off hours and delivering inspiring sermons on Sunday, but paid only whatever the congregation can muster in the way of freewill offerings.

These unpaid clergy are, nevertheless, part of the ranks of the designated leadership found in 93 percent of U.S. congregations. Whether paid or not, clergy constitute yet another sector of the religious resource market. In addition to the products and services that directly support the work of congregations, another set of suppliers is oriented to the care and feeding of congregational leaders. Priests and rabbis and pastors need the stimulation of educational events, the ideas found in specialized magazines and books, as well as the fellowship of brother and sister clergy.

Professionals of all sorts expect to engage in continuing education, and clergy are no exception; yet when we asked about what they do for their own enrichment, barely more than a quarter (28%) named any specific resource. When we added up all the resources named (including the long lists supplied by the most active), the average was about one resource for every two congregations. While most calls for *administrative* assistance go to regional church offices, fewer than one in twenty pastors named their denomination as a source for their own professional development. Indeed, no single denomination or tradition stood out. In no sector of American religion do clergy routinely seek enrichment from their own denomination.[26]

When we asked about where they go for ideas and support, pastors most often mentioned the seminars and workshops they attend, and the most common suppliers of those events are nearby (usually religious) colleges and seminaries. Missouri pastors drive to Eden Seminary in St. Louis; Seattle clergy choose among offerings from Fuller, Seattle University, and Seattle Pacific University; and Hartford pastors attend events at Yale Divinity School and Hartford Seminary. Writers and teachers such as Marcus Borg or Walter Brueggemann may draw a crowd of Mainline pastors and Catholic priests for a seminar on the Bible; and other pastors may sign up for a Saturday course at Moody Bible Institute. Pastors of independent churches are especially likely to use the resources of local educational institutions, and they by no means stick to the Moodys and Fullers of the conservative world. They were just as likely to go to a class at a nearby university, and they attend educational events of all kinds at nearly double the rate of denominational Protestant pastors.

Pastors of all sorts who are looking for professional development are also likely to look beyond their local offerings. Mainline Protestant pastors were as likely to go to a workshop across the country as to go to one at a nearby school. Princeton Seminary (in New Jersey), Claremont School of Theology (outside Los Angeles), and Pacific School of Religion (in the San Francisco Bay Area) all run extensive continuing education programs, and all were cited at least once by the Mainline clergy in our study. But the organization to which Mainline clergy most often turn is the Alban Institute. Located in Bethesda, Maryland, Alban is an "ecumenical, interfaith organization founded in 1974, which supports congregations through consulting services, research, book publishing, and educational seminars."[27] They offer short courses on starting out as a new pastor and on "staying sharp for the long haul," mobilizing volunteers, and managing conflict (among many other topics). Sometimes pastors travel to attend a seminar, but Alban also takes their courses on the road. Their books—research-based, but short and accessibly written—cover everything from closing a church to fund-raising to starting nonprofits and taking spiritual care of oneself. While Alban is also a source of consulting and administrative support, it is primarily thought of, at least by the clergy we interviewed, as a professional resource for themselves. Mainline clergy were twice as likely to tell us about something they had received from Alban as to cite an educational event sponsored by their own denomination.

Outside the Mainline, Alban was not mentioned at all. The closest to an equivalent among Conservative Protestants are the products and seminars offered by John Maxwell. Maxwell is a former pastor who is now best known as a "leadership expert" and author of the *21 Irrefutable Laws of Leadership* (Maxwell 1998). From San Jose to St. Louis to Minneapolis, Maxwell takes his "Reality Leadership" seminars around the country. For those who cannot make it "live and in person," he offers dozens of books, videos, and cassette tapes on a variety of leadership topics; and people can even sign up to be personally mentored. His "partner" organizations (whose members get discounted access to Maxwell products) run the gamut from the Assemblies of God to Primerica (a secular financial services firm). He and other popular conservative gurus are as likely to tell CEOs about the benefits of spirituality as to tell pastors about the benefits of good management. Indeed, Amazon.com indexes his books under both "business and investing" and "religion and spirituality." Maxwell follows in the footsteps of business consultants like Steven Covey and Zig Ziglar (who wrote the forward to Maxwell's first book), and energetic Conservative Protestant pastors are eager to learn his secrets and implement his advice in their local churches.

Megachurches are also a resource for pastors. These very large churches often organize programs to teach others the secrets of their success. Robert Schuller's Institute for Successful Church Leadership (at his California Crystal Cathedral), Brownsville Assembly of God (in Florida), and Seattle's Overlake Christian Church were among the places named by the pastors in our study as churches to which they have turned for ideas, inspiration, and training. The church that pioneered this model of service provision is Willow Creek Community Church, in South Barrington, outside Chicago. Famous for its own "seeker services" and its rapid growth, Willow Creek began attracting a steady stream of pastors who wanted to know more about its success. Formed in 1992, the Willow Creek Association provided a mechanism for spreading the vision and dealing with the multitudes of inquiring pastors. In 1998 the Association's president, Jim Mellado, said, "For whatever reasons, God seems to be attracting effective leaders and the churches they represent to the Association. And we realize God has called us to serve these leaders as they help establish new patterns and values for church life."[28] When we interviewed an Association staff member, he was very clear: "The association was formed to take the load off of the church . . . the calls coming in to the church for advice, help. How do you do this? How do you do that? Can we come visit you? It got too big for the church to handle."

The advice Willow Creek gives emphasizes team building, small group ministries, being culturally hip—and visionary leadership at the top. In 2002 the Association boasted "nearly 7,500 Association Member churches in more than 25 countries, representing 90 denominations,"[29] making its network about the size of the U.S. Episcopal Church and bigger than all but thirteen U.S. denominations. Across both Conservative and Mainline Protestant churches in equal numbers, Willow Creek, its association, and the materials they produce were listed by our interviewees as sources of enrichment by more pastors than named any other single church. Indeed, the association produces events and resources that are often recommended to pastors by their own denominational leaders.

Following on the heels of the Willow Creek Association, Rick Warren's Saddleback Community Church, in the foothills above Mission Viejo outside Los Angeles, has developed an even more far-flung network of churches that have adopted Warren's "Purpose Driven" model of leadership. This "PD Community" claims "over ten thousand churches in 83 countries" and offers training via conferences, DVD, satellite, and the Internet, as well as a forum through which churches share their insight with each other.[30] None of those we interviewed in 1997 and 1998 had yet joined this network, but Warren's book and conferences were often mentioned as inspirations for the pastors we talked with. Like Maxwell, Warren is much more popular among evangelicals than within the Mainline (only two of whom, in our sample, mentioned Warren's book or seminars). Pastors from the Assemblies of God, Nazarenes, Southern Baptists, and Evangelical Covenant churches are flocking to Warren's emphasis on core values, discipleship, and evangelism.

Although both Willow Creek and the PD Community use ethnically inclusive rhetoric and images, all of the participating pastors we encountered in our interviews were Anglo. Probably the closest equivalent for African American churches is T. D. Jakes, with his huge Potter's House church in Dallas and daily "Potter's Touch" television show on Trinity Broadcasting Network. Like Rick Warren and Willow Creek's Bill Hybels, Jakes has spun off major national conferences, in addition to books, tapes, and CDs. Most famous for his "Woman Thou Art Loosed" events, he has added "ManPower" conferences and annual events especially for pastors. Very few of the African American pastors we talked with were regular consumers of any resources for enrichment and professional development, but Jakes was one to whom those few turned.

Combined, the various megachurches and their pastors—along with an array of independent institutes and seminars—provide a network of classes and events to which Protestant pastors of all sorts turn. They attend conferences sponsored by these entrepreneurial leaders as often as they attend classes sponsored by colleges and seminaries. And they do both things far more often than they go to denominational pastoral enrichment programs.

Catholic and Orthodox clergy, on the other hand, stay closer to home in choosing pastoral resources. They were somewhat more likely to name their own diocese as a resource, and all but one of the colleges and seminaries where they said they had attended events were Catholic or Orthodox, respectively. Some dioceses offer programs that echo the leadership concerns one might hear at Willow Creek or Saddleback. The Center for Development in Ministry, at the University of St. Mary of the Lake in Mundelein, Illinois, offers priests the chance to "become the leader you always wanted to work with" or learn skills for "pastoring for a new millennium." In a lovely retreat setting, priests can support each other and renew their vision. Across our sample of Catholic and Orthodox priests, not many named any such events as part of a program of pastoral development, but those who did were most likely to name a supplier connected with their Church.

When pastors cannot get away to attend events and workshops, what they can do is read.[31] Specific books, journals, magazines, and the publishers and stores that supply them were named at a rate of about one for every six churches. Nondenominational churches named the most resources, and African American churches the fewest, with only small differences in the amounts reported by others. That similarity in numbers, however, masks the differences in content. Both Catholic priests and Mainline pastors were likely to read journals like *Worship* or *Homiletics*, while Conservative Protestants subscribe to *Preaching* and *Leadership* and *Christianity Today (CT)*. But then nearly everyone reads *CT*. At least a few pastors within each of the Protestant traditions named this venerable evangelical journal as a source of ideas and inspiration.

As often as they named print resources, these pastors told us that they use the Internet. Already in 1997 and 1998, the Internet was becoming a primary destination for finding sermon ideas, approaches to personal and congregational growth, liturgical resources, and networks of pastoral support. Rabbis were even more likely to use the Internet than most Protestant pastors, but nondenominational Protestants were especially enthusiastic users. At this relatively early moment in the history of the Internet, pastoral users tended to be in the higher income congregations, in cities rather than in the countryside, and in Anglo (and Protestant) rather than ethnic (or Catholic) parishes (see also Thumma 2002b). Taking these factors into account (that is, comparing congregations that are similar in income, ethnicity, and location), Conservative Protestants were more frequent consumers of this new technology than were Mainline Protestants.

These patterns of Internet usage are not unlike the overall patterns of pastoral resource use we found. Those most likely to read the books, attend the events, take the classes, as well as use the Internet, were Protestant more than Catholic, urban and suburban more than rural, and Anglo rather than African American or Hispanic. As with Internet use, size is not a determining factor. Pastors in small congregations are just as likely to look for support and enrichment as are those in bigger ones. Those that are unpaid participate as often as those on salary, those without a seminary education as often as seminary graduates, those in rich and well-educated congregations no more than those where people are less well off. The differences we see are more cultural than material. The entrepreneurial resource networks themselves are primarily white and Protestant; Catholic and African American pastors are resourced differently. And rural churches of all types are more likely to be outside this resource loop.

One group *not* outside the loop, in spite of smaller size and fewer resources, are immigrant Christian congregations. These pastors are more likely to seek out educational and professional support than are pastors with mostly native-born memberships. They go to the same events, read the same magazines, and take classes from the same schools, but they do it at higher rates than do others. Clearly these immigrant Christian pastors are making their way into the mainstream support networks for American clergy.

Much of the support clergy receive comes through routine interaction with their peers, rather than specific educational events and resources. Clergy peer groups are fairly common across most religious traditions, and we looked at three general types (see Table 8). First, for clergy in Christian denominations, were gatherings in their own regional denominational body. Depending on the denomination, this might be a relatively small and relatively local group (a "deanery," for instance) or a larger and more regional convocation. We included both in our counts. In many cases these are regular monthly or quarterly meetings that cover a variety of formal and informal functions from administrative minutiae to continuing education to emotional support to intricate maneuverings in the pecking order. Some denominations are more insistent on attendance than others, but we found no overall differences based on polity. A quarter of the clergy who belong to a denomination reported attending clergy meetings on a regular basis.

Those who do not go are disproportionately pastors of the smallest churches, whether located in cities or rural areas. Once other factors are taken into account, rural pastors attend at the same rate as urban and suburban ones. But in either location, the nonattenders are disproportionately pastors of small churches and those without a seminary degree. It is because there are more small churches and churches without seminary-trained pastors in the Conservative Protestant column

Type of Activity	Mainline Protestant (151) (%)	Conservative Protestant (239) (%)	Nondenominational (61) (%)	African American Protestant (44) (%)	Catholic & Orthodox (34) (%)	All Congregations (549) (%)
Regional denominational clergy meetings[*]	29	18	n.a.	36	23	26[a]
Formal local clergy associations[*]	28	18	33	34	23	23[b]
Informal pastor groups[*]	5	17	23	2	3	12[b]

NOTE: Number in parentheses indicates number of congregations in that group. For activity marked with an asterisk at least one of the differences among the groups is statistically significant at p < .10 (Oneway ANOVA, with Scheffe post-hoc comparisons).

[a] Includes only denominationally affiliated Christian churches.

[b] Includes all congregations, including Sectarians, Jews, and Other Religions.

that fewer of those pastors, on average, go to regional clergy meetings. Among both Mainline and Conservative churches, it is not even the polity that determines which clergy are likely to go. Those who lack key status credentials and professional socialization—a big church and a seminary degree—are more likely to avoid these meetings.

Across the churches as a whole, there was no apparent trade-off between denominational meetings and other clergy activities. Denominational participators were no more or less likely to use outside educational resources, and they were actually *more* likely to participate in the second kind of clergy group we explored—formal community-based ministerial associations. Pastors are not, in other words, spending time with coreligionists at the expense of connections with the larger community.

Local ministerial associations, often named for the neighborhood or town they encompass, are important vehicles for local networking. They usually include a broad range of clergy and undertake a variety of tasks. We will see them at work again when we look at how congregations serve the needy in their community (in Chapter 6), but here we are concerned with clergy associations as places where the clergy themselves go for mutual support, enrichment, and assistance. A Reform rabbi in Chicago reported: "I'm a member of the Downtown Clergy. That's an interfaith group that serves everybody from the Gold Coast down to the South Loop. . . . Sometimes we just have lunch. Usually, there's some kind of lecture. I spoke on resurrection a couple months ago. We've had speakers on demographics. Someone is coming up for career counseling. . . . It varies." While other forms of clergy organizing are almost exclusively Christian, these local associations are rather likely to be interfaith. Rabbis at the Reform Jewish temples in our survey, for instance, were almost all involved in local clergy groups, and some belonged to more than one. Leaders of local Hindu, Buddhist, and especially Muslim centers are likely to become a growing presence as well, especially since September 11, 2001.[32] The arithmetic of being a minority means that most people in a minority group will have cross-group ties, while majority-group members are more likely to be ethnically or religiously surrounded by people like themselves; but both arithmetic and strategy may increase the participation of non-Christian members in these local groups.

Clergy who belong to these formal community ministerial groups were most likely to be from the most educated and internally diverse congregations. Where a majority of the congregation has graduated from college and a majority are switchers from other denominations, clergy are especially likely to participate in interdenominational and interfaith community gatherings. Such groups seem to represent a particular form of networking and support that appeals to these clergy, echoing the diversity and bridge building they are doing within their own congregations.

Formal clergy associations are also especially common as a way for minority ethnic pastors to organize. Pastors of immigrant Protestant churches were more than twice as likely (53% vs. 21%) to organize as were Anglo pastors. African American pastors were also more likely to belong to at least one local clergy association (34% vs. 22% of nonimmigrant Anglos) and also more likely to belong to multiple groups (16% vs. 6%). Many of these black clergy associations have historically taken the role of mobilizing the community for action, especially in times of crisis. But they also serve the same support functions other pastor groups sometimes fill. An AME pastor talked about the interdenominational group to which he belongs: "It's mainly a support group for preachers to where, you know, if you have a young preacher—and when I say young preacher, I'm talking about one that just started pastoring a church—there are some do's and don'ts. And so we try to . . . get him aimed in the right direction, to how to pastor and what to expect, you know." In sharing the particular challenges of being minority congregations, African American and immigrant pastors often organize across denominational lines, but within their ethnic communities. Whether an Asian pastors group or a black clergy association, these gatherings provide important opportunities for networking, support and mutual mentoring.

The particular mix of spiritual activity and community concern varies from group to group and is often quite intertwined. In the south suburbs of Chicago a Reformed Church in America pastor said of his local clergy association, "They do three or four community events every year. They—it's just a great thing. We have prayer times together." A Missouri pastor found that support function especially important: "There's a lot of times that you struggle along in ministry and . . . there's no connection to any outside sources until you get together. And then you see that you're all in the same work, doing the same thing."

In more diverse communities the local clergy association may not so easily fill this desire for compatriots who understand what the pastor's life is like. There, when pastors want that kind of intimate mutual support, they may form an ad hoc group themselves. These informal pastor fellowships are the third kind of clergy group we found. A Southern Baptist in Seattle made the distinction this way: "It's not really a Ministerial Association. We don't do any business. We just meet for prayer." For many evangelical clergy, this sort of mutual sharing was not possible if the group was too religiously diverse. A Seattle Nazarene pastor was explicit about the tensions that arise when the group does not agree on basic theology: "I pray with a group of pastors. We meet on every other Thursday, but it's not a formally organized thing. It's just pastors meeting together to pray. I guess what many of us have found with ministerial associations, when it's open to everyone—often you have people who really don't believe in salvation." Evangelicals were, on average, more likely to participate in these informal groups, but they were not the only ones. A Presbyterian pastor in Seattle said, "I have some good friends who are still in the area, so I meet with a group—actually I have two groups that I meet with once a month . . . we're all pastors—and talk about what's going on in our lives." Still another Seattle pastor, this one in the RCA, said, "I have a group of pastors that I meet with in Tacoma. We study lectionary lessons for the upcoming week."

That so many of these voices come from Seattle is no accident. Pastors in our two western sites were more likely to be in informal pastor groups than were comparable pastors elsewhere. Pastors in larger churches, with relatively younger members, were more active in creating their own support as well; and controlling for all these demographic factors, it is the pastors of predominantly white congregations who are more likely to form peer groups. As we saw, immigrants and African American pastors are especially likely to create formal clergy associations that do much of the same professional support work for their members, but also take on community issues. A formal association has a public character, performing a variety of tasks and providing a public platform for its members. Informal study and prayer groups are more private and focused. The pastors who are seeking professional compatriots in this way tend to be those who otherwise have a public voice—by virtue of the size and visibility of their churches and their dominant-group ethnicity.

Pastor support group participants who are part of a denomination participate in their own area clergy meetings just as often as do their fellow denominational pastors who have no informal support group. Neither form of gathering seems either to facilitate or substitute for the other. Those who are not part of a denomination, on the other hand, are the most likely pastors to create an informal group. All of their energy is of necessity directed toward either formal community clergy groups or improvised gatherings of colleagues. Being an "independent" church does not mean being without a network of support. Independent pastors were as likely to be part of some sort of clergy group as were the denomination-based Conservatives, but Independents had to construct their own networks instead of relying on a ready-made regional denominational clergy group. Not nearly all pastors participate in any gathering of professional peers, but those who do seem to see this as part of the support necessary for doing their congregational work. Networks for exchanging ideas, information, and encouragement are another of the organizational links surrounding the local religious groups these pastors serve.

NURTURING CONGREGATIONS

The work of congregations begins with attention to the spiritual and social lives of their members. Congregations support the individuals and families who seek religious community in the midst of today's complicated world. They teach religious traditions and challenge members to pursue a life of faith, all the while also providing a welcoming space where relationships are built and enriching activities pursued. Theirs is the task of providing nourishment for individual and collective spiritual growth, but American congregations are rarely self-sufficient. They do not do this work alone. They depend on plans and products created by their denominations, as well as ideas and advice from the vast parachurch network.

The resources that sustain congregational life come from an increasingly diverse array of suppliers. Only among Sectarians and (to a lesser extent) Catholics are there anything like exclusive contracts that discourage congregations from sampling the resources offered by others. Here strict doctrine, common liturgy, strong religious authority, and sometimes ethnicity keep resource channels more closely within traditional denominational bounds. By contrast, African Americans and the newer religions have never (yet) had a comprehensive system from which to draw. Their networks have never been centralized or all-pervasive, so the notion that denominations have "declining" significance does not describe their experience.

It is the white Protestant supply systems that are most visibly undergoing significant change. Denominational systems are still the dominant suppliers of hymnals, children's educational curricula, camps, and advice for managing congregational life. But the education of youth and adults, as well as the ongoing support of clergy, are as likely to be resourced by organizations outside the denomination as by agencies in it. The religious work of congregations in white Protestant traditions—both Conservative and Mainline—is not utterly shaped by a single set of religious influences. Local congregations are choosing just how their namesake heritage will become part of the practices of their own worship, education, and fellowship. That heritage has by no means disappeared—denominations are not dead—but neither can it be taken for granted. That is a question to which we will return in Chapter 7, but first we need to look at the rest of the work congregations do.

CHAPTER FIVE · Extending the Community

Serving the Needy, Saving Souls

Building communities of fellowship and sustaining religious traditions are the foundation for everything congregations do, but for most, the tasks of spiritual nurture and human caring extend beyond their own membership. Communities of faith define their mission in terms of external impact as well as in terms of their relationships with each other and with God. The changes they seek vary enormously, from political transformations to individual ones, but congregations understand themselves to be under obligation to "serve the world" in addition to serving their own members.

This expectation is so pervasive that the exceptions are instructive. Talk about serving the community, spreading the faith, and changing the world was largely absent in the "Other Religions." The groups where we interviewed were mostly new immigrants from religious traditions outside Christianity and Judaism, groups still finding a place within American society and religion. At the Hindu temple in Nashville, for instance, they said, "Our main focus here has been to, sort of, provide a place for Hindu worship and cultural activities." The need to establish a basic religious foothold is foremost. We heard similar sentiments from Nichiren Buddhists and Sunni Muslims. The need to care for their own small and new communities is taking all their energies. They are also not yet routinely included in the religious and community service networks through which most Christian and Jewish congregations work. When a coalition is formed to deal with a local problem, churches may forget to call the Hindu temple or Muslim mosque. But as each group increasingly establishes an institutional and cultural home within the United States, participation in wider avenues of community service will likely follow.

The other distinctive pattern that stands out from typical practices of community service is the Sectarian insistence that spiritual needs are the first and foremost reason for engagement. Most American congregations do their work with any eye toward changing both material and spiritual conditions, but the leaders we interviewed in Jehovah's Witness, Latter-day Saints, and Christian Science congregations each had a distinctive way of thinking about their obligations to the world. Christian Scientists expect to make a difference in the world through prayer. The Seattle leader we spoke with said, "I think as each member reads the newspaper they do the healing work for the broader situation in the community. So that's the way we do it." Latter-day Saints, in contrast, are quite active in providing material relief for this-worldly cares, but that relief is directed almost exclusively toward their own members.[1] As we heard in Albuquerque, "We're very church minded and very aware of the needs of the people in the individual churches and help them as much as we possibly can with food, clothing, whatever is needed." For Jehovah's Witnesses, the missionary focus overwhelms all other concerns. We heard in Chicago, "We believe God's kingdom is the solution to man's problems, and that's where we direct attention to." Community soup kitchens and religious coalitions for providing material assistance are not condoned. For strictly Sectarian groups, service to the outside community is confined to the spiritual work of evangelism and prayer. Individuals are certainly not insensitive to the needs around them. Our Jehovah's Witness contact in Missouri talked extensively about the needs Witnesses often find as they visit isolated rural homes. When they encounter hunger, loneliness, and ill health, they try to help, he said, but they never forget that their primary task is delivering a spiritual message about the coming end of the world and the necessity for salvation (see also Holden 2002).

We heard similar concerns about spiritual focus from some Conservative Protestant churches. They worried that concentrating on material needs would divert important energy from the more critical task of evangelism. At an independent evangelical church in Seattle, the pastor told us, "I know Jesus loved folks, but His mission was not to eliminate poverty or all the social problems. We believe if the heart is changed, the life can be changed." It is not that they do not care about the world. Rather, they think that real this-world change will come through the spiritual transformation of individuals.

American Jews are just the opposite. Rather than putting all their energy into proselytization and none into social service, Jewish congregations reverse the

TABLE 9   Outreach Goals of Congregations in Different Religious Traditions

Goal	Mainline Protestant (193)	Conservative Protestant (226)	African American Protestant (53)	Catholic & Orthodox (45)	All Congregations (549)
	Congregations Naming This Emphasis (%)				
Serve the community*	55	32	37	45	37
Spread the faith*	12	75	57	6	50
Change the world*	6	<1	9	15	3
Defend morality*	1	5	0	3	3
Bridge differences*	7	5	0	6	6

NOTE: Number in parentheses indicates number of congregations in that group. All Congregations includes these four groups plus Sectarians, Jews, and Other Religions. For goals marked with an asterisk at least one of the differences among the groups is statistically significant at p < .10 (Oneway ANOVA, with Scheffe post-hoc comparisons).

priorities. Seeking converts is not a typical practice among Reform and Conservative Jews in the United States today.[2] More prominent today are notions of *tikkun* (repair of the world) and *mitzvot* (doing deeds of righteousness). A Reconstructionist leader told us, "The main element of being a religious person is to love our fellow human beings."

Loving fellow human beings is indeed central to the religious message that is institutionalized in American congregations, not just Jewish ones. Sectarian groups stand apart as they direct their energies almost exclusively into proselytizing. Jews are distinct for putting almost all of their energy into care for this world. The Catholics and Protestants who constitute the majority, on the other hand, serve the world *both* by caring for the needs of others *and* by sharing the spiritual resources of their traditions. As local leaders talked about how they try to make a difference in the world, those two themes were the most common (see Table 9), but there were three less common stories to be explored as well. Those five outreach concerns were heard in differing measure across the religious streams, and not everyone named any one of them as one of their congregation's top priorities. Recall that we recorded and counted the three most dominant themes in our informants' conversations about priorities. Some of those themes are not shown in Table 9 because they concern the spiritual and fellowship work we have already examined. In addition, some congregations emphasized more than one outreach theme, so the numbers in Table 9 are not intended to add up to 100 percent. They count just the outreach tasks, showing how often those themes were at the top of the list. Whether a congregational leader named any kind of outreach work and which kinds they named are, as we will see, prompted both by their particular religious tradition and by the social and material resources they can bring to the task.

SERVING THE NEEDY

Many congregations say that serving hungry, lonely, and sick people is a task to which they should devote at least some of their collective energy. Just over one-third (37%) of the congregations we surveyed named that as one of their most important goals (see Table 9). The pastor of a midsized United Methodist church in Nashville claimed, "The mission of the church *is* the community." Leaders in Mainline Protestant churches were especially likely to talk in these terms. Over half (55%) named community service as one of their congregation's highest priorities, more than in any other religious tradition. We often heard that "the church exists for mission," and what they meant by that was tending to the material needs of the world. In some cases they were explicit that their service need not be overtly religious or spiritual at all. Whenever people serve others, ministry is being done. As our informant at an Albuquerque UCC church said, "Whatever form that service can take and we can provide, it feels good to us."

The emphasis on community service was almost as common among Catholic and Orthodox parishes. On our paper-and-pencil survey, Catholic and Orthodox parishioners agreed with their Mainline Protestant counterparts that providing service to needy people is an important priority for their congregations. Their average rating was between "very important" and "essential" (3.22 on a four-point scale), an assessment that was echoed in the interviews themselves. At a very large and active Roman Catholic parish in Seattle, we heard, "They [parishioners] are so into outreach—that's such a high priority for a lot of people, and they are so generous. . . . That's a big theme, because you know Christ came to serve, and we are, as ministers, we serve." A pastor in Nashville was equally adamant: "Obviously we're meant to be community minded. That's the whole message of Vatican II. That's basic Christianity." In these parishes Catholic teachings on ministry are echoed in what leaders say about providing for service.[3] Similarly, an Antiochan Orthodox priest said simply, "Because we love God, we love all those in need."

The church's role in serving the community is central in the black church tradition as well. Throughout American history, African American churches have been the safety net for their own members and for the larger black community.[4] Both clergy and members in black churches ranked all forms of social activism higher in their survey ratings than did the clergy or laity in any other stream of religious tradition. Speaking of the church's mission in terms of caring for the downtrodden is part of the rhetoric of black church life. Just over a third (37%) specifically mentioned service activities as they talked about their church's goals. At a large National Baptist church in Albuquerque, for instance, the pastor encourages each of the auxiliaries (social and service groups within the church) to undertake at least one community service project each year, whether it is working in the church's own feeding program, linking up with a prison ministry, or something else. That intertwining of fellowship and service was typical in black churches. People gather into men's, women's, or teen groups, but they are also mobilizing their energy for people outside the church. The motto of a Progressive National Baptist Church in Chicago is "Shining like a beacon's light for mankind." The pastor's goal is "to move members from membership to discipleship," and for him discipleship means "ministries to help the community."

Leaders in predominantly white Conservative Protestant churches were considerably less unanimous in their support for community service. On the survey, some said community involvement was very important, others said it was not at all important, and others fell in between. For most Conservative Protestant congregations, service is secondary to evangelism, but in almost a third (32%) it was nevertheless named as a significant mission priority. As the pastor of an Evangelical Covenant Church in Chicago said, "I think many in this church are concerned about the poor. . . . They want to be a part of social reformation." A Nashville Seventh-Day Adventist pastor described his congregation's assistance to people who are being discharged from the local hospital: "Jesus helped people who needed help. . . . We just want to be a help to our community."

Some Conservative churches are aware, however, that their theological heritage may not encourage work in the community. An Albuquerque Assemblies of God pastor noted,

When Pentecostalism became very popular back in the early 1900s it faced the dilemma of the socialized Gospel. In other words, people were basically feeling like if they were doing good deeds they were saved. There was no confrontation of the Gospel in their life where they had to accept Christ or they had to receive the Holy Spirit. None of those things were taking place. So when the Assemblies of God came into motion, the socialized gospel—which is doing good things to help people—was a curse. I mean you didn't preach it. You didn't touch it.[5]

The challenges this pastor faces in his own ministry changed his mind: "I had to come into some personal confrontations before I saw the real need, you know. So my theology has been adjusted by just starting to work with people that are desperate." Similarly, an Assemblies pastor in Missouri noted that in his rural community, when "something happens you know about it usually, [and] . . . if there's a need we try to do what we can."

When leaders in most congregations talk about doing good in the world, they mostly had a fairly local target in mind. Providing for the needs of people in remote corners of the globe may be part of their religious mandate, but it was less often named in our interviews. Few leaders talked about hunger or war or disease in other places as something they directly address as part of their congregation's mission. Those most likely to speak globally were the evangelicals whose sense of mission includes the eternal salvation of people overseas no less than those in their own neighborhood (about which more in a moment).

But church members may harbor a greater global consciousness than their leaders perceive. Nearly three-quarters (73%) of Mainline church members (and an equal number of Catholics) who completed our survey said that "supporting mission efforts in the nation and the world" is very important or essential to what they think their congregations should be doing. That is admittedly fewer than the 85 percent of Conservative members and 89 percent of African Americans who agreed with that statement. Catholics and Mainline Protestants may define "mission efforts" differently than do evangelicals, but nearly all the individual church members we surveyed agree that congregations should extend their care to regions beyond their own backyard. Having dramatically scaled back overseas mission work, however, many denominations have fewer natural opportunities for highlighting the needs of a larger world. When they do, their members are very likely to respond generously. At a Hartford United Church of Christ (UCC) Church, the pastor reported with delight that they had "sent 44 pounds of shoes to the Ukraine. It was really gratifying to see this church respond to a simple request." For most Christian churchgoers, the task of doing good in the world is not complete when only local needs are met.

Whether a Conservative Protestant or a liberal, a Jew or a Catholic, the needs of the community often touch our hearts. We want to help, and the people who join us at church or synagogue or mosque are a likely group with which to pool our resources. Even if we have no direct involvement ourselves, knowing that our congregation does something to help is appealing. But for most congregations, the reasons to get involved go beyond philanthropic pragmatism. Most have a sense that God is in their work. A Chicago Greek Orthodox priest put it this way, "You know, we're here in this world really just to serve others and show others that love that God has for us, and that this world isn't an end in and of itself." A Missouri United Methodist pastor said, "I believe very strongly that you encounter God in the doing."

The leaders we talked with often spoke of a mandate to make the connection between what their scripture says and what is done in the world, an invitation to see God in the "least of these" and to act out of gratitude for what God has done. Each congregation has its own language, its own theology, and its own favorite stories, but in many congregations those stories compel members to be engaged in serving people who are in need, whether or not those people are fellow members. As we will see, that mandate is carried out in many ways, but it is a mandate often connected to the core of what it means to gather as a congregation.

SPREADING THE FAITH

Many U.S. congregations claim that the necessary first step on the road to taking care of people's needs is a change of heart. Among Conservative Protestants and churches in the historic African American denominations, evangelism is at the top of the list of priorities. On our surveys only the spiritual life of the congregation got higher ratings, on average, than evangelism. Leaders almost invariably said that "maintaining an active evangelism and outreach program, encouraging members to share their faith" is either "very" or "extremely" important to their congregations.[6] Similarly, the individual members who completed the Sunday morning survey ranked evangelism programs and support for world and national mission efforts nearly as highly as they ranked worship and preaching.[7]

Those survey rankings are echoed in our interviews. An emphasis on "winning souls for Christ" permeates these congregations. At a small Albuquerque Church of Christ we heard that they "want to get the word out to those that are looking for salvation." The pastor of a National Baptist Church in Chicago said his goal is to "minister to souls, save souls for Christ." And we were reminded at a large Seattle Church of God in Christ that they are "real serious about evangelism; we are missions oriented relative to our community." These are congregations that count themselves within the evangelical tradition, and that means preaching a message about the need to be saved. The most important religious work for both congregations and individuals is spreading that gospel message. Three-quarters (75%) of congregations in the Conservative Protestant tradition and over half (57%) of the African American Protestant ones named evangelism as one of the congregation's primary goals (see Table 9).

This emphasis on individual salvation is far less prevalent among the Mainline Protestant groups. Whereas nearly two-thirds (63%) of Conservative and African American Protestant leaders said on the survey that evangelism and sharing faith are extremely important to their congregation, only one in six (17%) Mainline Protestant congregations were described by their leaders that way. Several of the RCA congregations in Chicago were consciously pursuing an evangelical agenda and talked about "reaching people in America with the message of Jesus Christ." A Methodist pastor in Alabama said, "We are here as a community of Christians seeking to lead others to Christ." These particular churches, however, represent evangelical wings in denominations whose national identity tends toward a more liberal agenda. Those evangelical wings are nationally visible, however, especially through the televised presence of pastors such as John Ed Mathison of Frazer Memorial United Methodist in Montgomery and Robert Schuller of the (RCA) Crystal Cathedral in Garden Grove, California. In some denominations, both evangelical and liberal impulses are present.[8]

In the Mainline as a whole (as well as in the Catholic and Orthodox parishes we surveyed) talk about individual salvation was rare and muted. Only 12 percent of Mainline congregations named evangelism as one of their top priorities, but that is twice the proportion of Catholic and Orthodox parishes that did (see Table 9). Nearly half (45%) of the members we surveyed within the Mainline family downplayed evangelism (as did 36 percent of Catholics), saying that strong evangelism programs are only somewhat or not at all important to their congregations. Only 14 percent of the members of Conservative congregations said that. For evangelicals, conversion and proselytizing are too central to be described as not important.

Similar emphases were also present among the Sectarian groups. Two of these groups—Jehovah's Witnesses and Latter-day Saints (LDS)—are famous for their door-to-door efforts to gain converts. Much of the routine work in a Jehovah's Witness Kingdom Hall is aimed at training Witnesses for public evangelism. They study prescribed materials that prepare them to answer the questions they may be asked, and they practice making presentations in front of fellow Witnesses. The work of evangelism brings in new members, but it also reinforces the faith of existing ones. While LDS evangelism may be less scripted, it is no less pervasive. Young adults routinely give two years of their lives to full-time mission work. Their goal, as described by an Albuquerque leader, is "to invite all God's children to come unto Christ. That means that every person who has lived on this earth will have a meaningful invitation and opportunity to understand and accept the sacred covenants, ordinances, and lifestyle that are associated with discipleship." Here the work of evangelism extends even beyond this life to include "redeeming the dead," but it is the living who have flocked to local Mormon congregations (wards) in response to this message. Sectarian groups are, by definition, relatively distinct from typical American congregations, so casual "drop-in" joiners are less likely than they might be in a Baptist or Episcopal or Catholic church. Organizational success requires Sectarians to expend greater than average efforts to overcome that cultural distance. For a Sectarian group to survive, continued aggressive evangelism is essential (Stark 1987).

The habit of evangelism is often thought of as exclusively Christian, but at least a few of the other religious traditions actively seek to spread their faith as well. Although most American Jews find the notion of "sharing their faith" rather odd, Lubavitchers do want lapsed and nonobservant Jews to change their ways. The Chicago campus group we encountered has regular Friday night Shabbat dinners and sponsors talks on hot topics, all with the goal of bringing secular Jews to the point of being open and comfortable with their Jewish identity. Food also plays a role as Baha'is issue invitations to nonmembers to attend a "nineteen-day feast" in a member's home. There they will hear about the good work of the Local Spiritual Assembly (the congregation) and study the writings of Baha'u'llah. Many Baha'i groups are also active in community race relations events and hope that the publicity they receive will aid in recruiting new members into the faith (McMullen 2000). Thus some non-Christian groups share the evangelical Christian enthusiasm for introducing new practitioners to their faith. Part of the work they do as local congregations is spiritual outreach and recruitment.

For all of the groups that have conversionist goals, the scope of change lies beyond their own local community. They want to serve the world by evangelizing the people they meet, but they also want to be part of a global crusade to bring their message to the entire world. Those who are seeking the conversion of others are likely to support full-time evangelists and missionaries who travel to distant places to spread the faith, and keeping members aware of those distant efforts is part of the congregation's own sense of mission. As an LDS leader in Chicago told us, "We probably have the most active missionary ministry of any church. We have sixty thousand full time serving as missionaries. . . . Many have served on mission in every church." Such worldwide mission efforts can become a pervasive presence in the local congregation. The result, in language we often heard, is a "strong mission-minded church." The world in which they seek to make a difference is a very large one, connecting remote overseas missionaries with networks of U.S. congregations.

Taking the message of faith to the ends of the earth is the mandate many U.S. congregations understand themselves to have. They see it on posters in their class-rooms, hear it from the pulpit, and even sing about it. Their children learn the names of missionaries and are introduced to the far-flung cultures where they work. At the same time, both children and adults are surrounded by the regular rhythms of sin and salvation, redemption and enlightenment that form the spiritual world in which evangelism thrives. Their congregations offer them a spiritual mes-sage for the world, and the task of taking that message to a spiritually needy world is a primary focus of congregational life.

CHANGING THE WORLD

Some congregations try to serve the world by preaching a gospel they are con-vinced will change people's lives. Other congregations try to serve the world by making sure that hungry and hurting people are cared for. A few try to do both. But another small group (only about 3 percent of all congregations) is not content either to ameliorate social ills or trust spiritual cures. They want to see basic changes in the systems and structures that create the problems in the first place. They often speak of their mission in terms of justice. While these "activist" con-gregations are only a tiny fraction of the total, they are often the most visible. These are the pastors who are on the picket lines, the congregations providing sanctuary for illegal refugees, the delegations in the "rights" parades, the congre-gations doing "community organizing."[9]

Most of the justice-oriented activist congregations we found were either Catholic or from the historic African American denominations, plus a small con-tingent of white Mainline Protestants. Only one Conservative Protestant church placed worldly economic and political change alongside evangelism as a top con-gregational priority. This independent evangelical church in Seattle has staked out an innovative ministry in the heart of the city. Preaching the gospel is central to what they do, but it is by no means their only mission: "Our commitment is to impact a one-mile radius around the church in whatever way we can. And so things that we see that are not right we try to address or speak about." Their plans include "a job-training seminar with computers to teach skills, to have a financial seminar to learn how to buy a house and to build mortgages and stocks and these kinds of things." Talk about such economic and educational solutions to life's problems is not unknown among evangelicals—flagship groups like the Sojourners Community in Washington, D.C., are visible exemplars—but it was rare among the Conservative Protestant congregations where we interviewed to find such a conscious combination of evangelical and social action rhetoric.

Some Conservatives are involved in trying to change social structures by addressing moral issues, rather than economic and political ones. The church's mission, as they see it, includes a concern for the many ways in which U.S. society has gotten off track. Being defenders of traditional morality is part of the rhetorical world they construct, and this-worldly moral reform is their goal. About 5 percent of all Conservative Protestant churches told us that concern for the moral well-being of their communities was part of their mission (see Table 9).[10] Joining these evangelical and Pentecostal Christians were one conservative Anglican parish and an Antiochan Orthodox church (whose members had converted from evangelical Protestantism).

The Protestants who most wanted to defend a traditional way of life were in the more "traditional" locations—disproportionately from the South and from rural churches. They were most often in the Southern Baptist, Nazarene, and Missouri Synod Lutheran denominations. The pastor of a large Southern Baptist church in Nashville said that his members worry most about "the state of the nation and the future of their children." The list of concerns at a Nazarene church in town included, "the breakup of the family [and] the lack of moral teaching in our public schools."

Among the most common concerns, perhaps not surprisingly, was abortion, but most of those distressed about abortion did not really count themselves as activists in the cause. Even very conservative congregations are often not sufficiently in agreement among themselves to venture into public action.[11] Many other conservative congregations do not embrace a culture of political activism. A committed pro-life pastor in Chicago explained, "The Lutheran Church–Missouri Synod is a very pro-life denomination. We don't tend to be demonstrators and activists, but our convictions are pretty strong on that." None of these churches was likely to be on any picket line. Their concerns for the well-being of their society were more likely to take the form of individual citizen education and support for the actions of others.

Most African American and Catholic pastors, on the other hand, choose different issues. They were more likely to talk about social, economic, and political changes that would make society more equitable. When we asked the pastor of a large black Baptist church in Nashville what he thought people needed most, he replied, "I think that they need socioeconomic development." How would the church try to achieve that? we asked. "By encouraging entrepreneurship, supporting black-owned businesses and attempting to recycle the resources in the community," he said.

Many black churches were identified as community leaders during the Civil Rights struggle (and often long before that), and they have retained a place at the forefront of the search for justice.[12] No matter what else they may see as important and no matter what their resources, they still want their churches to be places that help to transform the structures of racial inequality and injustice.

In African American churches, both congregational informants and the members themselves rated community involvement more highly than did people in any other religious tradition. On our survey, nearly three-quarters (74 percent) of individual African American church members said that actively seeking social and economic justice was either very important or essential to what it means to be a good Christian. Similar numbers want their pastors to speak out on important issues and want their churches to organize groups that encourage social activism. Barely half (51%) of Mainline members said they want their pastors to speak out on public issues, and even fewer (41%) Conservative members expressed that view. Given the strong black church endorsement of activism on these survey measures, it is perhaps surprising that only 9 percent of churches in the historic African American denominations named the active pursuit of justice as central to their congregational mission. It may be that the activist heritage is so normative that it simply "went without saying." It may also be that—like all other congregations—the first priorities of black churches lie with the spiritual nurture of their members. Only a small but visible minority serve the distinctive role of mobilizing the community in pursuit of change (see also Chaves 2004, 117).

As in the African American traditions, Catholic theology provides a strong message about engagement with this world. In recent years, liberation theology has made the connection between the gospel and social change even more explicit, especially in Catholic contexts outside the United States.[13] Even though liberation theology has had less impact on American parishioners, there are other sources of Catholic teaching on issues of justice and equality. Catholic bishops here have issued public "pastoral letters" on war, the economy, and faithful citizenship, all taking a decidedly progressive stance; and more radical movements, such as the Catholic Worker and Pax Christi, have long had a presence in U.S. Catholic life. Support for these positions, however, is decidedly mixed among the faithful.[14] Half of the parishioners we surveyed said that seeking justice was a Christian virtue, while half did not. Slightly more (59%) said that it is important for their priest to speak out, and nearly two-thirds (64%) want an opportunity for social action groups in their parish. Those numbers are slightly higher in the predominantly black and Hispanic parishes, but only slightly. Of all the Catholic and Orthodox churches where we interviewed, 15 percent named social change as one of their primary parish goals.

Among those that do see worldly change as part of their mission, some set their sights on immediate neighborhood impact. Others try to get members involved in causes supported by the diocese. And still others try to find ways to expand members' concerns to a more global level. At a large mixed-ethnic parish in Hartford, the priest expressed his own concern for global issues: "There are still tremendous amounts of people who do not have the basic rights that God intended for them." He went on to describe how the parish social concerns committee has tried to increase awareness about hunger. During Lent they planned a "hunger banquet" where a few dined royally, some had a bowl of plain rice, while most had nothing at all. The meal was a dramatic consciousness raiser and challenged members to get more involved in seeking basic rights and sustenance for the world's people. At a large Hispanic parish in Albuquerque, the issues were more likely to be related to U.S. policy in Latin America. The very active priest there recalled what happened in the 1980s: "I spoke out against giving arms to people who are killing members of the clergy. I spoke about the Gospel. The Gospel is the Gospel, and the Gospel says do not kill!" The concerns we heard about in Catholic parishes spanned military policy, Third World hunger, medical care, abortion, deteriorating neighborhoods, and more. Not nearly all want these social and political issues to be at the top of the parish agenda, but there is fairly widespread support for at least some parish involvement.[15]

Catholics are joined in this concern by a small group of white Mainline Protestant churches (6%). Non-Anglo Mainline churches were twice as likely to be oriented to social change as their Anglo counterparts. In the churches where we surveyed individual members, Mainline Protestants mirrored Catholics in their attitudes toward seeking justice. Both were more sympathetic to that goal than were Conservative Protestants, but less so than African American Protestants. Justice was also tied, for many of these congregations, to their own congregational practices. A Methodist pastor in Seattle was especially eloquent in describing how his church's decision to become open to gay and lesbian persons had had ripple effects on their social consciousness. Here is how he summed up what he thought they would say to "A congregation like ours should . . .": " . . . above all things be open to all people. We should, we should always do what is right and just. Not only within our bounds, but we should try to protect and safeguard what is right and just outside of the church."

Congregational activism in behalf of economic, social, and political justice is also present in American Jewish congregations. Many have a proud history of support for civil rights and for innovative programs of economic development. In seven of the nine congregations where we interviewed, rabbis said that seeking social and economic change is very important or essential to their congregation's sense of mission. As in other traditions, Jewish congregations are very widely invested in a broad range of priorities. Education for their own members and providing a place to belong were most central, but charitable work in the community and seeking social change are a distinctive part of the Jewish tradition in this country.

Sectarians, with their emphasis on spiritual solutions and care for members, were not among the activist congregations we encountered, although Latter-day Saints have been nationally influential, especially in recent years, and especially on issues related to traditional morality and family life (Mauss 1994, 115–19; Ostling and Ostling 1999). Among the Other Religions, one of the Baha'i groups we interviewed was the exceptional activist case. Situations facing their own members had forced them to deal especially with issues of homelessness, trying to find a more lasting solution than just another service project. In the aftermath of September 11, 2001, and the U.S. "War on Terror," American mosques were similarly faced by a crisis demanding organized action. When similar situations confront others within these newer traditions, they are likely to look to existing models in U.S. congregational life, and at least a few of them are likely to take on roles as leaders in connecting religious principles with visions of this-worldly justice and morality.

We find, then, a small core of conservative moral activists and an equally small counterpart of justice-oriented activists.[16] The concerns they champion are present in many congregations but do not take center stage. Most congregations—both liberal and conservative—define their core mission in nonactivist terms, even if they are concerned about moral decay or economic injustice. Only this visible few choose to devote some of their collective energy to leading the way toward social change.

BRIDGING DIFFERENCES

One final outreach theme deserves our attention, a concern shared equally by a small vanguard of Mainline Protestant, Conservative, and Catholic churches. At least some U.S. congregations see bridging ethnic and other differences as central to their mission. Christian congregations often talk about this goal as "reconciliation," but they were joined in this concern by Baha'is, a Sunni Muslim mosque, and a Jewish synagogue, among those with whom we talked. In the South, Baha'is have often been active in seeking racial reconciliation (McMullen 2000), and at the Seattle local spiritual assembly, work with Native American groups was routine. They described their goal as trying to "foster harmonious relations between people of diverse backgrounds." As American society becomes more consciously diverse, a small group of congregations (twenty-eight of the ones we studied) provide a laboratory for bringing cultures together.

Perhaps not surprisingly, almost all of the congregations that have taken diversity as a mission have achieved some internal diversity themselves. All but three of the twenty-eight in which we interviewed reported that they have at least one secondary ethnic group that makes up a sizeable bloc (more than 10 percent) in the congregation. In just over half these cases, no single ethnic group dominates the congregation (with more than 60 percent of the membership). In a third of the cases where a dominant majority remains, the majority in question is not Anglo. In other words, two-thirds of the congregations where diversity is a priority are not predominantly Anglo, and in most of them significant ethnic diversity is a reality.

Maintaining diversity across the racial and ethnic divides that so fundamentally shape American culture requires active intention if it is to succeed. Among congregations where bridging differences was *not* named as a priority, almost none were internally diverse (see also Emerson and Smith 2000). For both Conservative and Mainline Protestants, actual ethnic diversity and an emphasis on bridging differences go hand in hand. An Episcopal parish in Hartford said of their priorities, "I think diversity would be at the top. Really committed to that and dedicated to that. We feel that's one of our major drawing cards. We brag about it purposely. And it's something that we live with every day, and it's not easy." A United Methodist church in Chicago voiced similar commitments: "This is a loving and giving—I mean, we're a reconciling congregation. We're one of the few multiracial congregations . . . we don't really care if you're Himalayan! You're part of a family." In some Mainline congregations, as in this one, being "reconciling" means both ethnic diversity and open acceptance of gays and lesbians. Attention to bridging the differences between gay and straight has sometimes been a first step into wider definitions of diversity for Mainline congregations.

The concern with racial reconciliation is by no means a monopoly of more liberal congregations. A number of Conservative churches are also multi-ethnic and have designed innovative strategies that build out of their own theological traditions.[17] Referring to a scripture that exhorts Christians to "each esteem others better than themselves," the pastor of a very diverse megachurch in Seattle talked about the challenges:

> That means that I can't get the same kind of music I want every Sunday . . . and I can't say because you like it that you are less spiritual than I am. . . . The Word crosses all barriers. But it's different worship styles, different music that we have to bring into the church so that everyone is welcome. Not only black, white, red, yellow, but also economic differences. We are to come together and forget our differences. Education-wise, socially, I mean all of these things. A person should be able to walk into the house of God and say I'm home.

James Forbes, the first African American pastor of New York's famous Riverside Church, claims that a truly integrated church is one where everyone expects to enjoy 75 percent of what is going on and be made uncomfortable by the other 25 percent (DeYoung et al. 2003).

This concern for bridging difference was not evenly spread among American congregations. It is no accident that the leaders quoted above are from Chicago and Seattle. The concern with diversity was much more common in those two cities than in any of our other sites. Both cities are known as home to especially diverse cultures, and their congregations were both more likely to *be* diverse and more likely to channel their energy toward seeking that goal.[18] By contrast, only one Alabama congregation and one in Nashville named diversity as a goal. The legacy of segregation apparently lingers. Given the ethnic uniformity of the population in rural Missouri, it is perhaps not surprising that no congregations there talked about a concern for bridging differences.

In some cases the diversity in question was more than just ethnic, however. The Seattle megachurch pastor noted that education and other social differences can keep people apart as well. The Methodist pastor talked about both cultural diversity and welcoming gays and lesbians. For a few Jewish congregations, the task of interfaith relations is a key priority. Said one rabbi, "Because this is the largest and the oldest and probably the most visible congregation in the area . . . I think people really look to us. . . . It's really important to me that we be there for the community to do those kinds of things, to participate in a variety of interfaith activities and such." Clearly, congregations outside the Christian tradition have carried the major responsibility for maintaining communication across religious lines. Only ten congregations in our sample mentioned belonging to a local interfaith coalition, and another eleven mentioned partnerships with a specific congregation from outside their faith tradition. Eight of the eleven congregation-to-congregation partnerships were between Jewish and Christian congregations. Whereas only about 3 percent of Christian congregations mentioned an interfaith tie, one-third of Jewish and other non-Christian congregations were involved.[19] The events of September 11, 2001, have given many congregations a new reason to seek interfaith engagement, and our numbers might be very different if we asked our questions today.[20] But it is also likely that those outside the United States' dominant Christian mainstream will continue to carry more than their fair share of the load.

COMMON CONCERNS AND DIVERSE GOALS

Two dominant themes run through the stories of how American congregations seek to affect the world in which they find themselves. One theme stresses reaching out through evangelism and missions to try to change the hearts of those who are lost and hurting. By offering a gospel of personal transformation (and a supportive community in which one can grow in the faith), these congregations envision a world where pain and injustice are alleviated by changing sinful habits. The other theme stresses immediate aid and comfort for a wide variety of the world's ills, hoping that spiritual transformation (if it is needed) will follow. One variation on that theme aims at more fundamental social changes that would make charitable work less necessary. And another variation has taken the reconciliation of differences as the primary change toward which it works.

These two diverging themes have been present, especially within white Protestantism, for at least a century. The theological battles of the early twentieth century often pitted "evangelism" against the "social gospel," and the legacy of that presumed division remains.[21] Only 17 percent of the congregations we surveyed named *both* evangelism and community service as primary goals (see Table 10). Roughly equal numbers choose one, but not the other—just over one-quarter (27%) of all congregations place their emphasis on some form of service or social outreach and do not include evangelism as a priority, while one-third of congregations do the reverse, emphasizing evangelism and not community service. As we will see in the pages that follow, those proportions are closely mirrored in how congregations actually spend their organizational resources.

That strain between evangelism and social outreach, however, is not the norm in African American churches. Compared to white churches, they were twice as likely to name both goals; indeed naming both was more common (32%) than either social outreach alone (28%) or evangelism alone (22%). The battles of the early

TABLE 10	Social and Evangelistic Outreach		
	Named Evangelism as Goal (%)	Did Not Name Evangelism as Goal (%)	Total (%)
Named social outreach goal[a]	17	27	44
Did not name social outreach goal	33	22	55
Total	50	49	99[b]

[a] Includes social service, activism, bridging differences, and defending traditional morality.
[b] Does not total 100% because of rounding.

twentieth century that left their imprint on white Protestants were largely irrelevant to the black churches. Feeding the body and feeding the soul have never been understood as opposing goals; the Jesus who sets a soul free from sin is just as interested in setting the body free from injustice.

Among white Protestants, the ability to hold social and evangelistic outreach together is more difficult.[22] But that should not obscure the larger point that more than three-quarters of U.S. congregations (78%) claim outreach of some sort as among their core tasks. Just as worship, religious education for children, and some form of fellowship form the internal portion of the institutional template for congregational life, some attention to social service and/or evangelism has been institutionalized as the expected outward orientation of local voluntary religious communities. Whichever form they choose, most American congregations place serving the world alongside their efforts to serve God and to provide a place to belong. Worship and religious education are foremost, but most congregations also want to ease the world's suffering. They care about providing a place for their own members to be at home, but they also think congregations should be improving the communities in which they are located and the globe to which they are inextricably connected.

HOW DO THEY DO IT?

Making a difference in the world requires more than just talk. Whether the emphasis is evangelism or social service, bridging differences or seeking political and economic change, a culture of outreach clearly permeates much of American congregational life. But what are they actually doing? How are congregational energies being channeled? The quick answers to those questions are "a lot" and "in many directions." In part, congregations inspire their members to contribute their individual time and energy to help make the world a better place. In part, congregations play the role of network hub, channeling their resources into the world by way of myriad other organizations (something we will look at in more detail in Chapter 6). But congregations also marshal their own resources to pursue the task of serving their communities and the world. They do that by providing a place where concerned members gather to educate and support one another, but also by organizing specific programs to address the needs they see in the world. We will look at each of those strategies in turn.

OUTREACH SUPPORT GROUPS

Education and support groups may at first seem like a rather passive response to the world's needs, but almost all of the local groups we heard about were a mixture of study and action. Their work involved learning about the relevant issues, goading the rest of the congregation to change specific practices, organizing fund-raising efforts, and often serving as a kind of internal conscience. The types of education and support groups we found roughly followed the kinds of mission emphases we had heard clergy describe. Indeed, specific local mission priorities are more directly reflected here than in any other aspect of a congregation's organizational life. Different religious traditions make one or another outreach goal more likely, but even within each religious tradition, the congregations that articulate those goals for themselves are more likely to organize groups of parishioners to pursue them. Size and demographics sometimes make a difference as well, but the energies of special-purpose groups in a congregation are largely channeled by a combination of local mission priorities and larger religious traditions.

Service-Provider Groups

The most common outreach support groups in U.S. congregations are gatherings of people who work together on service projects (see Table 11). These are the groups who cook and serve meals at homeless shelters, groups that tutor children after school, even groups that clean up roadsides together. They sort second-hand clothes and deliver furniture. They visit prisoners and take care of people who are sick or elderly. Sometimes this work provides an organizational home in the congregation for a network of informal caregiving. A prison ministry group, for instance, makes sure that a delegation is organized for a monthly trip to conduct a prison Bible study, but they may also take family members to visit and advocate in behalf of a prisoner seeking release. As we will see in Chapter 6, much of this service work involves organized charitable agencies (religious and secular, private and public).

TABLE 11 Outreach Support Activities of Congregations in Different Religious Traditions

Type of Program	Mainline Protestant (193)	Conservative Protestant (226)	African American Protestant (53)	Catholic & Orthodox (45)	All Congregations (549)
	Congregations with at Least One Program of Each Type (%)				
Service groups*	47	25	54	38	34
Issue groups*	18	7	27	21	13
Ethnic and/or interfaith groups*	8	6	5	32	8
Missionary support groups*	18	46	14	3	31
Local evangelism activities*	6	39	16	3	26

NOTE: Number in parentheses indicates number of congregations in that group. All Congregations includes these four groups plus Sectarians, Jews, and Other Religions. For programs marked with an asterisk at least one of the differences among the groups is statistically significant at $p < .10$ (Oneway ANOVA, with Scheffe post-hoc comparisons).

The congregational groups we are describing here thus do not themselves organize or run programs. They are the congregational mechanism for providing and mobilizing resources for the agencies that do.

Members of a "ministry group" may see each other most often in the actual doing of their work, but they may also gather for occasional educational, inspirational, and celebratory events. They work together to coordinate their activities and make sure the rest of the congregation stays informed. Their service together may also be the bond from which deep friendships form. Within these service groups members develop a culture that supports their work in the community, a set of stories and symbols, practices and shared experiences from which they can draw (Lichterman 2004). Like every other small gathering in congregational life, service groups generate social, material, and spiritual benefits all at once.

The demographics of service groups are different from those of the fellowship-oriented groups we examined in Chapter 3. Those groups were most likely to be found in urban and suburban, well-educated, well-off places; but that is not the case with service groups. The single external factor that distinguishes congregations with service groups from those without them is size. Only 18 percent of the smallest congregations (under fifty in attendance) have service groups, while half of those over three hundred do. The threshold seems to be at about one hundred attenders. In every religious tradition, congregations over that mark were about twice as likely to have a service group as were congregations under it. The more participants a congregation has—no matter how rich or poor, educated or not, rural or urban—the more likely it is that some of those participants will work and study together as a service team, directly addressing a need in the community.

That does not mean, however, that all congregations of sufficient size are equally likely to have service groups. What congregations do is very strongly shaped by the particular religious tradition of which they are a part. Conservative Protestant and Sectarian congregations spend less of their energy in this sort of community service support than do congregations in any other religious traditions. Sectarian groups, as we saw in Chapter 3, have very few internal groups of any kind; and, as we noted above, they are unlikely to say that community service is one of their goals. Conservative Protestants, on the other hand, have lots of internal social and spiritual activities and organize lots of small groups. But they are much less likely than other Christian congregations to say that community social service is part of their mission, and those priorities are reflected in the comparative rarity of social service groups in Conservative congregations (see Table 11). They are much more likely to have weekday religious education and worship and routine men's and women's groups than groups organized around a service project.

Even within a given religious tradition, the congregations that articulate service to the poor and needy as central to their own local mission are more likely to have a group dedicated to supporting that work. Whether the congregation is rich or poor, old or young, rural or urban matters less than whether the goal of serving the community is articulated as part of their identity. Over and above the difference religious tradition makes, local congregational mission helps to determine the likelihood of having a service group. Among Mainline Protestants, for instance, two-thirds (65%) of churches that say they intentionally focus on community service have a service group, compared to only a quarter of the churches that do not emphasize that goal.

Issue Groups

Congregations are also places where people organize to share their concerns about the issues that create the need to serve in the first place. Whether discussing political issues, learning about the environment, educating each other and the congregation about abortion, or providing a congregational base for supporting economic development efforts, small groups in some congregations organize to gain the knowledge and leverage they need for trying to change the world. Social issues were the focus for small groups in only 13% of congregations, but the proportion was higher among Roman Catholic parishes (21%) and even higher (27%) among African American Protestant churches. The identification of these religious traditions with social justice—and their higher propensity for naming social change as a priority—is borne out in these patterns of activity. By no means every parish is replete with activist cells, but politically concerned groups are more likely to be found in African American and Catholic parishes than anywhere else in American religion.

But differing religious traditions are not the only factor at work. Even within a given tradition, predominantly white congregations are less likely to spend energy organizing groups on political and economic issues. Only 4 percent of predominantly white congregations of any tradition had a political issue group, while 12 percent of all nonwhite congregations had one. More than a quarter of Catholic parishes that were not predominantly white had a political awareness group, as did 19 percent of ethnic Mainline congregations (more than double the proportions of their white counterparts). The realities of being a minority in U.S. culture, combined with the availability of stories, symbols, and exemplars from justice-oriented theological traditions, make many ethnic congregations especially likely to use their resources to help parishioners understand and act on political and economic issues.

Another resource matters as well. Across religious traditions and in every ethnic group, organized issue awareness groups were more likely in well-off congregations than in poorer ones. Almost one in five (19 percent) congregations with a majority of well-off families have social issue groups, while only 6 percent of low- and middle-income congregations have them. Economic power seems to be linked here with a willingness to use congregations as an organizing base. This is consonant with findings from the National Congregations Study. Chaves found that the most socially active congregations are those located in depressed communities whose *members* have better than average resources (Chaves 1999b). Religious values of altruism seem to overcome inherent economic class interests to encourage some well-off religious participants to join a congregation in a needy community and invest time and energy in behalf of the poor.

Congregations that claimed an activist, change-oriented agenda were relatively few in number, but they were far more likely (39%) to have taken the concrete step of organizing an issue group than were congregations that did not claim such goals (6%). As we have seen, different religious traditions make choosing an activist orientation more likely, but in every religious stream the particular congregations that identified themselves with the goal of this-worldly change were most likely to provide an organized issue-support group for their members. No matter what the congregation's ethnic makeup or economic resources, its own way of articulating its purpose shapes the range of activities it offers its members.

Bridging Groups

Bringing people together across ethnic, cultural, and religious traditions was the focus for groups of members within 8 percent of U.S. congregations. Some were studying the language and culture of a group other than their own. Others were offering cultural enrichment opportunities so that second and subsequent generations can value their own cultural heritage. Most commonly, congregations were offering worship services and other ministries in multiple languages. This category of activities effectively spans both internal congregational work and programs designed to reach beyond the congregation. More than with either issue or service groups, the line between member education and outreach into the larger community is almost impossible to draw with these activities. Inherent in the nature of "bridging" is a component of internal change alongside a component of external invitation. To cultivate an openness to diversity is to invite members to expand their horizons and to seek out connection with diverse others in the community.

An emphasis on the importance of diversity is roughly equally distributed across Conservative Protestant, Mainline Protestant, and Catholic congregations (see Table 9), as is the presence of *moderate* ethnic diversity (10 to 40 percent minority representation) within congregational membership. The most thorough diversity, however, is found in Catholic parishes. They are both more likely to be ethnically diverse and more likely to have substantial first-generation immigrant populations. That kind of internal diversity is strongly associated with the kinds of ethnic education and heritage groups we counted as "bridging groups." Those that have more ethnic diversity create more bridging programs, and those with more bridging programs have more ethnic diversity—it is impossible to tell which comes first. Catholics were not exceptionally likely to talk about bridging differences as a core missional task; they just respond to the difference that they find in their midst.[23]

Small minorities of Protestant churches (of all sorts) had a specific ethnic bridging group or activity, and one of the Baha'i assemblies had an active racial reconciliation group. Working on ethnic diversity is not something equally likely in all social situations. Almost no rural congregations have groups devoted to interethnic (or interfaith) concerns. Nor do the smallest congregations, which may have neither the resources nor the occasion for this sort of activity. Congregations in Seattle and Chicago were the most actively involved in forming groups, and congregations with a majority of immigrant members are more likely to have cross-cultural activities than were native-born congregations. These are not so much white versus nonwhite differences as diverse versus monochrome differences. Mixed congregations, no matter what their original or majority population, are more likely to have organized bridging groups and activities than are their single-ethnicity counterparts.

Taken together, service provider groups, issue groups, and bridging activities are found in 41 percent of congregations. Even if a congregation does not have extensive social outreach programs of its own, small groups within the congregation target issues and needs. They provide the organizational mechanism by which links are made to other service providers and store up a repository of congregational energy and knowledge. While we have used the term "bridging activity" to describe a particular kind of interethnic and interfaith work, each of these kinds of congregation-based groups is a point from which external connections are made.

They all "bridge" between the needs of a community and the passions and resources of a congregation. They help individuals to make connections between their faith and the world.

Missionary Support Groups

Almost as common as service and advocacy groups are congregational groups organized to support national and international missionary work. These groups are different in both focus and structure from the service and advocacy groups, however. Most of the latter are informal and locally initiated. Most missionary support activity, on the other hand, is done through formal national and international organizations—either denominational or parachurch. In addition, while service is an activity that is supported in at least some measure by most religious traditions, missionary activity is not. Among Christian churches, almost a third (31%) have organized at least some of their members around the task of education about and support for missionary work, but the large majority of those groups are concentrated in a single stream of religious tradition—Conservative Protestantism.

As we have already noted, support for evangelism and missions is central to the way Conservative Protestants describe themselves. A Nazarene pastor in Seattle noted that for his denomination, "one of the greatest bonds is in our missions ministry. We have over six hundred missionaries in nineteen world areas." In an adult Sunday school classroom in a Southern Baptist church in Missouri, the walls were covered with posters pertaining to missions. One was a map showing the "Status of Global Evangelization," while another explains "Where Does Cooperative Money Go?" (referring to that denomination's mission funding program). An Assembly of God pastor in Alabama noted that the church's children are "taught to give to missions through their children's church." Both children's programs and organized adult activities sustain the "mission-mindedness" of these churches.

In contrast, Catholics certainly support overseas mission work (and often have "sister" parishes elsewhere in the world), but none of the parishes where we interviewed had formed a local group to promote that activity.[24] On the Orthodox side, an emphasis on evangelization has been growing in the last twenty years, and we encountered it in one Greek Orthodox parish and in the Antiochan Orthodox parish (composed of former evangelical Protestants), both of which had local mission support groups.

As rare as missionary support groups were in Catholic and Orthodox parishes, they were numerous in Sectarian ones. Nearly every LDS ward organizes to provide regular moral and financial support to their own and other youth who are on mission. And every Jehovah's Witness is considered a missionary, so the congregation itself is a mission support group of sorts.

The Protestant pattern, on the other hand, is participation in a denominationally sponsored program, sometimes designed for children, but most often organized by adult women. From the earliest days of the American missions movement, groups of women gathered to correspond with missionaries, pray for them, and pool their resources to support their work. Those circles of women gradually consolidated into denominationally based (but often still autonomous) organizations. The tradition continues, mostly among Conservative Protestants, but in a few Mainline denominations as well.[25] United Methodist Women (UMW), for instance, accounts for more than half of all the mission support groups we found within Mainline Protestant congregations. Local UMW groups keep their congregations abreast of mission news, solicit gifts, and challenge everyone to get directly involved, both in local projects and in support for overseas needs. In 2000, for instance, United Methodist Women were working in support of the "Bishops' Appeal for Hope for the Children of Africa." A local congregation's chapter could order study books for adults and children, videos and CDs, maps and posters—all designed to help local United Methodists understand and give to the denomination's missionary work in Africa. They might then visit the organization's Web site (http://gbgmumc.org/umw) to see where and how their mission dollars were being spent. They would find information there about programs for women's health and education, assistance to street kids, AIDS awareness, and much more. The emphasis is more on service than on soul-winning, but support for national and international missionary work remains at the heart of what UMW does.

Among Mainline denominations, the Methodists are nearly alone in retaining an overseas missions force coupled with a women's organization that sustains a network of U.S. support. The nineteenth-century women's networks that were the backbone of overseas mission efforts in every denomination were, early in the twentieth century, absorbed into the centralized denominational structures of most Mainline denominations (Brereton 1991). Some sort of women's division remained, and a global ministry office was usually maintained, but links between the two were loosened. The unique organizational role of women in the foreign mission movement waned and with it any routinely organized mechanism by which local congregations were linked to denominational mission efforts. Today, fewer than one in five Mainline congregations (18%) reported any sort of missionary support group.

Although UMW is the significant exception to this pattern of decline, that organization, too, may be in danger. Many of our informants lamented that their local group just wasn't what it used to be. Methodist congregations founded since 1950 are less likely to have a mission group than are older congregations. Similarly, those with a majority of lifelong Methodists are more likely to sponsor UMW than are those with more members raised outside the denomination. Across the Mainline, it is the more established and traditional congregations, not the newer, younger, more denominationally mixed ones, that are more likely to have local mission support groups.

Both Lutherans (ELCA) and Presbyterians (PCUSA), like Methodists, retain both a global mission force and national denominational women's organizations; but unlike the Methodists, the women's and missions departments are only very loosely linked. None of the Lutheran or Presbyterian congregations we surveyed had a local missionary support group—women's or otherwise. In the Episcopal Church, Episcopal Church Women still sometimes serves as the hub for organizing local and regional church mission projects, but there is little national or international Episcopal missionary effort for the women to support. That absence was lamented in at least some of the Episcopal churches we talked with. The pastor of a large, liberal parish in Seattle said, "We used to have missionaries. . . . Now there are no missionaries of the Episcopal Church. . . . The need hasn't disappeared. . . . Some of us are saying, 'We've got to do better!'" The solution for some is to link with parachurch mission agencies, and a few others filled the gap by establishing direct partnerships between themselves and overseas parishes or dioceses in the worldwide Anglican Communion (a pattern we will explore more fully in Chapter 6).

To the extent that Mainline Protestant groups have, unlike the Episcopal church, kept their global mission efforts, their primary work is more overseas relief and development than overseas evangelism. The study materials and resources they provide to congregations are likely to be about building inclusive global communities and promoting economic justice (getting a congregation to buy "fair trade" coffee, for instance). As a United Church of Christ pastor assured us, "We are not trying to convert people, we are trying to help them." Even Mainline congregations that do see evangelism as a primary goal are hardly more likely to have a mission support group than are other Mainline churches (28% vs. 20%). The cultural package that once tied missionary support, local women's groups, and denominations together has unraveled in the Mainline.

Conservative Protestants, on the other hand, have a plethora of opportunities to help them get involved in learning about and supporting missionaries. Roughly half (46%) of Conservative congregations have a missions support organization in their local church, compared to 16 percent of other Protestant churches. If the local church sees evangelism as among its primary goals, it is even more likely to invest in mission support organizations. Fully two-thirds of white Conservative Protestant congregations where evangelism is emphasized channel some of that evangelistic energy into organized support for national and international mission work.

This is especially true where denominations provide the programs and structure. Three-quarters of Assembly of God (AG) churches, for instance, have local mission support programs and groups. Their Women's Ministries groups take on the task of raising money for world missions and sponsoring "Missionettes" for girls. Within the Missionettes program, girls can progress through a series of clubs from age three through high school, and at each level the national organization provides leaders with training, program ideas, and everything from T-shirts to posters. The preschool groups are coed, but once kids reach kindergarten, boys leave for the parallel "Royal Rangers" program. AG men participate in Light for the Lost, raising money to provide printed material for mission work in the United States and overseas. And in many congregations members provide regular support for Convoy of Hope, an independent (but AG-affiliated) organization that sends volunteers and truckloads of supplies to places with critical needs (such as the Pentagon, following the September 11 attack; Van Veen 2001). In addition, whole congregations pledge regular financial support to specific missionaries. In short, everyone has a direct stake in the denomination's mission effort. Similar strong denominational programs—with similar high levels of presence in the churches we surveyed—can be found among Missouri Synod Lutherans (Lutheran Women's Missionary League), the United Pentecostal Church (Ladies Ministries), the Southern Baptist Convention (Woman's Missionary Union), and the African Methodist Episcopal Church (the women's Missionary Society).[26]

There are some indications that forces of change may be undermining Conservative mission organizing in some of the same ways that local Mainline groups are being weakened. Rural Conservative congregations and those with the most lifelong members are most likely to have mission support groups. But there are contrary indications as well. New congregations are no less likely to have a group than are older ones founded before 1950. And congregations where most members have a college education are *more* likely to have a group than are less well-educated churches (opposite to the pattern in the Mainline). Conservative Protestant women, no less than their Mainline sisters, often find Thursday morning mission society meetings impossible to attend. But where many Mainline churches have given up, many Conservative ones have moved all their mission groups to a Wednesday evening family night, added a catered meal for busy families, and spread the task of mission education more broadly throughout the church.

Another of the ways a missionary consciousness is maintained is through visits back and forth between local congregations and mission fields. Often missionaries make specific requests for which a church raises money or collects goods (recall the shoes collected for the Ukraine), sometimes delivering things themselves. With greater U.S. affluence and ease of travel, mission trips have become far more common than they were in days of months-long voyages. Missionaries come back to the United States more often to speak in churches, but members of those churches are also likely to have visited the missionaries on their home turf. The two mission-minded Orthodox parishes we encountered were engaged in just this sort of direct missionary connection. At the Greek Orthodox church in Chicago, we heard, "Our head pastor loves missions. He's gone to Russia, Albania, and attended all the meetings. . . . They [Church headquarters in Florida] come out with the dates of when they are going where—Uganda, Mexico. That goes to local parishes. We've had at least twenty people who have served." In denominations without a strong history of congregational missions programs, these new direct efforts promise to fill an important organizational gap.

Conservative Protestants, Catholics, and others are involved in direct connections as well. The pastor of a large Seattle Seventh-Day Adventist church told us about the way his regional denominational body is facilitating short-term mission tours. Costs are shared between the denomination, the church, and the volunteer. When we asked if any of his members were interested, he replied, "Oh yes! I have more than what I need!" His members, he said, "want more hands-on evangelism." These experiences add a vivid personal dimension to the already-strong missionary consciousness in evangelical churches. Nearly every denomination is now promoting short-term volunteer service and facilitating e-mail communication between congregations and missionaries. Even when no one from the congregation is able to travel to far-off mission stations, education and fund-raising may be enhanced by links to specific overseas (and homeland) projects.

Whatever they are planning, missionary supporters need partners. Only the wealthiest congregations could afford to support a single missionary, and even they would be unlikely to support an entire hospital or school. When congregations do missionary work, they need organizational connections (and in Chapter 6 we will look in more detail at how those partnerships take shape). Denominational missions education programs have historically created that link, and organized offices for volunteer coordination have now been added to the structure, but the enduring organizational fuel is money. From the earliest "mite boxes" and "penny a week" efforts of nineteenth-century women, international mission agencies have long relied on the organizational and fund-raising skill of church women. Historian Catherine Allen estimates the capacity of the Southern Baptist WMU in the billion-dollar range (Allen 2002, 113). Organizing missionary support obviously has consequences far beyond the local church members who may gather to pray and learn. Some of the earliest "religious work" to take organizational form in the United States was overseas missionary activity,[27] and today the support of that activity remains an important part of how many congregations invest their volunteer energies.

They also invest their energies encouraging their members to share their faith close to home—sometimes through special events, but most often through training and deploying individuals who will present their religious message to others. Congregations provide classes for their members and perhaps schedule a weekly night to visit prospective converts. Some (like Mormons and Jehovah's Witnesses) go door-to-door visiting strangers, but most call on people who already have some connection with or interest in the church. Whatever the method, these congregations mobilize to seek out new members and converts.

Programs of evangelism are not something all congregations undertake. None of the Jewish congregations in our sample, for instance, had any organized program for spreading their faith. Nor did any but one of the congregations in the Other Religions. The lone exception was an African American mosque (Sunni). Nor are evangelistic programs universal across Christianity. The lone evangelistically active church in the Catholic and Orthodox category was the Antiochan Orthodox parish, exemplifying the growing number in that branch of Orthodoxy that now seek American converts. None of the Roman Catholic parishes we surveyed had such programs, although it is becoming common to see efforts to woo lapsed Catholics back into the fold and to hear Catholic theologians talk about "evangelization."

Just as some religious traditions eschew evangelistic activity, others are virtually defined by it. All of the Latter-day Saints and Jehovah's Witnesses groups were actively involved in seeking converts. Within some traditions, organizing these sorts of activities is not a matter of resources or demographics or even local priorities. Merely being part of some streams of religious tradition is enough to explain whether (or not) a congregation will have an evangelism program.

If a congregation is part of the Conservative Protestant tradition, it is very likely to have an organized evangelism program (see Table 11). Even the few congregations that do not themselves name evangelism as a specific local goal nevertheless sometimes have a program that provides opportunities for members to get involved. The vast majority (77%) of Conservative congregations do name evangelism as a priority, and nearly half of them (46%) have ensconced that priority in some regularly organized activity. These congregations are of all sizes, scattered across every region, both new and old, well-off and poor, well-educated and not, rural and urban, southern and northern, full of young people and full of older adults, predominantly white or not—demography does not determine the likelihood of a Conservative Protestant church having an evangelism program. It is just what you do, no matter who you are or what your resources.

Within the Mainline and African American traditions, on the other hand, the larger tradition does not dictate organized evangelistic activities. Few congregations named evangelism as a local priority, but those few are more likely to mobilize efforts toward achieving that goal. Evangelism is named as a goal by only 14 percent of Mainline congregations, but more than a third (37%) of those actually have programs. Forty-nine percent of churches in the traditional African American denominations name it as a goal, and 29 percent of those have programs. Congregations in Mainline and African American denominations that do *not* specifically name evangelism as a local priority almost never have evangelism programs. The inclination to focus on evangelism, in spite of the norms of the larger religious tradition, seems also to be a matter of local culture. Mainline churches that prioritize evangelism are disproportionately likely to be in the South, Southwest, or Midwest, where regional culture is more supportive of such efforts. Mainline churches outside the Bible belt rarely emphasized evangelism or organized programming to pursue it. For Conservative Protestant churches, evangelism activities are part of the institutionalized organizational template, for Mainline Protestant ones they constitute an exception to be explained.

That larger organizational template, however, does include a more general mandate to create small groups to take on projects—whether to engage in evangelizing, to educate each other and the rest of the congregation on issues, or to pray about the troubles they see. These are the primary ways congregations organize their members to make a difference in the world. The internal groups do not exist as separate nonprofit entities or dominate the congregation's energies. Almost any congregation can muster the resources to create one, and the sort of group it creates will likely reflect both the larger religious tradition of which it is a part and the particular goals the congregation sets for itself. Congregations are important sites of organized voluntarism, both for what they do collectively and for the more specialized work they enable among their members.

LOCAL COMMUNITY OUTREACH PROGRAMS

Sometimes, however, a congregation's loosely organized attempts to make a difference in the world evolve into something more elaborate and permanent—an ongoing program, rather than a group supporting the efforts of others. Much of the community service congregations undertake is organized by the support and education groups we have been examining. Gathered around service projects, social issues, and concerns about diversity, they educate their fellow congregants and work together on community projects. Only a few congregations attempt to create the more demanding programs and agencies that are nevertheless the most visible examples of congregational service to the community.

Larger, more institutionalized outreach efforts place congregations in the world of voluntary philanthropic organizations, and the shape of that world can be seen in the types of programs they create (see Table 12). Some are aimed at providing direct human services to people in need, others pursue long-term development or political advocacy, and still others enrich the educational and cultural life of the community—all categories that are familiar in the nonprofit world (Hodgkinson and Weitzman 1993). In most cases, congregationally based programs stand alongside other community agencies that do similar work, and they are often set up with separate 501(c)(3) nonprofit status. Doing this sort of work is another way some congregations embody their desire to serve the world, but institutionalized programs are shaped by a complex combination of resources, demographics, and cultural expectations. Where a congregation is located and how big it is may constrain program plans at least as much as their own traditions and priorities shape their imaginations.

Human Services

The role of "faith-based organizations" has become a recurrent subject of public debate, as new initiatives since 1996 (often referred to as Charitable Choice) have pushed congregations toward partnerships with government programs and agencies.[28] Our survey was not designed to assess the effectiveness of faith-based social service delivery, but it does allow us to assess just who is already most involved in

TABLE 12   Community Outreach Programs of Different Size Congregations

Type of Program	Congregations with Fewer than 300 Weekly Attenders (409) (%)	Congregations with 300 or More Weekly Attenders (95) (%)	All Congregations (504) (%)
Human Services			
Relief program	12[a]	30	16
Informal help	22[b]	14	21
Advocacy and Development			
Political/social activism	1[a]	8	2
Education and Enrichment			
Cultural events	11[b]	19	13
Day care	7[a]	20	9
Education & tutoring	7[a]	20	10

NOTE: Number in parentheses indicates number of congregations in that group.
[a] Differences between small and large congregations significant at p < .01 (ANOVA).
[b] Differences between small and large congregations significant at p < .10 (ANOVA).

providing the food, clothing, and shelter that form a safety net for society's neediest. As we will see in Chapter 6, a large portion of what congregations do is actually channeled through other service providers, both religious and secular. However, some congregations are themselves the primary organizational home for soup kitchens, clothes closets, homeless shelters, and food pantries. One in six U.S. congregations reported that they themselves sponsor at least one such activity (see Table 12).[29]

Creating an ongoing relief program to serve a community is not something that just any congregation can do, even if it has the inclination. The most critical single factor in making this work possible is having enough people to sustain it. More people usually means more dollars, but it is the people more than the money that makes the difference. The threshold seems to be about three hundred regular participants. Below that size, 12 percent of congregations have programs; above it 30 percent do. In addition, rural congregations are much less likely to have organized programs. Nineteen percent of urban and suburban congregations have relief programs, while only 8 percent of small town and country groups do. Among that rural 8 percent was a small Lutheran (ELCA) church in a tiny Missouri town. For many years a group of longtime friends has gathered once a week to cook, package, and deliver about forty meals to people referred to the church by a local social service agency. They get food from local grocers and from a Boy Scout food drive, but they contribute the rest themselves. This modest ministry is part of what they think their church ought to be doing to help people in need.

More typically, organized service programs are a matter of both size and location. Nearly one-third (32%) of congregations that are urban or suburban *and* large have organized relief programs. One such congregation, a United Church of Christ in Seattle, talked about a house they own and use as transitional housing for families in need. At a very large Catholic parish in Seattle, members are involved in dozens of efforts to help: "We have what we call The Friends of the Needy. . . . There's about seventy-five to a hundred volunteers that work on this program. Besides that they also give about $20,000 a year away to the poor. Besides that we have a group that—every Tuesday women use our kitchen facilities, and they will take a lot of the produce and the meat, etc., and they will make soups, casseroles, hot food and they will take it down to the shelters." All over the country, church vans and kitchens and basements—and members young and old—are mobilized in the effort to make sure that people have good food to eat and a warm place to sleep.

The likelihood that a service effort will be organized is not just a matter of numbers and location. As other studies have found, African American congregations are especially active in organizing ministries in behalf of the community. More than a quarter (27%) of African American congregations reported that they sponsor some sort of service program, and that disproportionate rate is present no matter where the churches are located or how big they are. Small African American churches are more likely to have programs than are other small churches. A small AME church in Nashville told us, "Every Thursday, we deliver over a hundred plates to the community and nursing homes and shut-ins. . . . Very tasty food." Congregations in the African American traditions are more likely to harness member energies for basic human service programs than are comparably situated white churches.

Among Conservative white Protestants, by contrast, theological rhetoric sometimes deemphasizes community service in favor of evangelism, but it is actually size and location that make more difference than theology. Almost no small rural Conservative churches have relief programs (4 percent compared to 15 percent of small rural Mainline churches which do). But when the congregation is in a different setting, with different resources, the differences between Conservative and Mainline traditions disappear. Thirty-eight percent of large urban and suburban Conservative churches have service programs, exceeding the number found in similar Mainline ones (27%). When surrounded by the needs and expectations of the city, Conservative churches are even more likely to create programs to help than are their Mainline colleagues.

Across all these differences, however, what also matters is the particular mission focus of the congregation. In every religious tradition and in every location, congregations that told us they value serving the needy were indeed more likely to create relief programs—25 percent compared to only 11 percent of congregations that did not name this as a priority. Differing streams of religious tradition may help to shape local church orientations, but local churches deploy their resources in pursuit of the particular goals they set for themselves. Serving the needy is among the goals that has a recognized presence in American congregational culture, and it is a goal that is sometimes embodied in organized programs of relief and assistance to the hungry, homeless, and desperate in our communities.

Large urban and suburban churches are likely to respond to the need around them by organizing a program, but smaller congregations and congregations in less densely populated areas see the same needs, and their response is likely to be more informal.[30] When we asked about how they try to meet the needs in their communities, smaller congregations talked about having a benevolence fund for emergency needs or vouchers they can give stranded travelers. The pastor of a small Methodist church in Missouri said, "We also help people who are passing through, that run out of gas, and they need gas, or they need a night's stay, or a couple nights. We put them up. Or they need groceries for a couple of days." Small urban churches talked about the person who walked in off the street and about those known to the congregation who need money in emergency situations. In tens and fifties and occasional hundreds, the congregation tries to help. In a large church the benevolence fund may be almost an afterthought, an addendum, but in congregations with fewer resources, it is a primary way to meet community needs.

Congregations that talked about these informal, but nonetheless intentional, responses to basic human needs were a reverse image of those who had organized programs. Forty percent of rural congregations mentioned this sort of aid, while only 15 percent of urban and suburban ones did. Over a quarter of congregations with fewer than a hundred participants claimed an informal assistance strategy, while only 7 percent of those with over five hundred participants did. The differences can even be seen in the resources of the members themselves. Nearly a quarter (23%) of middle- and lower-income parishes reported an informal assistance strategy, while only 11 percent of high-income parishes did. Informal assistance is the choice for those whose circumstances do not encourage a more elaborate programmatic response.

It is important to note that most of the more formal programs we found were not large, usually not professionally staffed, and met—at best—minimal human needs. Everyone involved recognizes that the needs are far greater than a single congregation can handle. Some of the most stellar and visible congregations have developed elaborate arrays of programs to meet nearly every need, but those congregations are extraordinarily rare. Most of the 16 percent of congregations that have invested in a formally organized social service program are struggling hard to do one fairly limited task. Theirs is such critical but draining work that volunteers sometimes have difficulty sustaining their commitment. Observers of charitable efforts to help our neediest people often note that religious volunteers have an advantage because of the faith they bring to the job. Because they see their work as a calling, they may be able to invest more deeply and for longer periods (Cress and Snow 1996). And sustained, deep investment is needed. Providing a hot meal once a week or even a bed every night is better than the alternative of cold and hungry people on the streets, but volunteers still struggle with the inadequacy of their efforts. Those who become more deeply involved sometimes recognize the larger issues at work and move into political advocacy and economic development activities (Allahyari 2001).

They also look for help. Catholic parishes, for instance, look to the whole diocese as the "church" that is ultimately responsible to the community. Catholic hospitals and Catholic Charities are not created by any single parish but by the diocese. As we will see in Chapter 6, all congregations extend their efforts by cooperating with the many other organizations, in their communities and beyond, that try to make a difference.

Advocacy and Development

Making the turn from charity to activism is not something that happens in many congregations. As we saw, only about one in fifteen congregations has a group of members who take political and economic issues as their focus. Less than half that many have organized their own regular program or activity that seeks political, economic, or social change in the larger community (see Table 12). A handful have set up economic development corporations, and another handful serve as the routine organizing and gathering point for political protests and rallies. A Seattle United Church of Christ pastor reported, "We had an initiative on the ballot last fall to make discrimination against gay and lesbian people in the workplace illegal, and it failed. But the congregation voted to support that—unanimously—and we had a big banner right outside my window here. . . . We had a big press conference; we had two TV stations show up. I'm constantly amazed at what the congregation is willing to do." The leaders we talked with in a strategically located downtown Methodist church in Chicago are similarly in the thick of things. These activities are slightly more likely to be found in Mainline and African American Protestant churches than elsewhere, and they are clearly more likely in churches with more than three hundred regular participants, but the numbers in our sample are too small to discern other clear demographic patterns.

That does not mean that congregations are not politically and economically active. As we saw, many have action groups within the congregation and educate and mobilize members on an ad hoc basis. But more importantly, almost all congregational political and economic activism is channeled through larger outside coalitions and agencies.[31] Indeed, U.S. law makes this nearly a necessity. If a congregation's political activity takes a partisan turn, it can lose tax-exempt status. And economic development activity nearly always requires a separate corporation so that money can be managed separately from congregational funds. When we turn our attention to these partner organizations in Chapter 6, the extent of congregational activism will be more apparent. Organizing congregationally based programs is not the usual way this kind of work gets done.

Education and Enrichment

Cultural events, day care centers, and a variety of other educational activities are, on the other hand, something congregations organize with fair regularity (see Table 12). Different forms of activity reflect different emphases, however, and are more prevalent in some traditions than in others.

NURSERY SCHOOLS   Nine percent of the congregations we surveyed reported that they run a day care program of some sort. Some are not full time, meeting perhaps only two or three mornings each week, but the majority are daily opportunities for preschool children to play and learn. A few are almost exclusively populated by the congregation's own members, but those are the rare exception. In most cases these programs serve both the community and the congregation.

As we will see in Chapter 6, many additional congregations provide space for independently run nursery schools, but the nearly one in ten congregations that claim childcare ministries as their own are doing more than serving as a low-rent landlord (however important that may be). The programs counted in Table 12 had their primary origin in the congregation and retain a significant congregational connection. Most have become legally separate from the congregation, but teachers and volunteers, board members and administrators, as well as space and curriculum, are provided by the congregation. Even if teachers are hired from outside, they are screened by people who have a particular congregational mission at heart. The pastor of an independent evangelical church in Seattle proudly showed us the rooms used by their preschool and talked about how important it is to the church: "Our director right now, she goes to the church here. Our staff is all out of the church here. . . . We feel as a ministry of the church, they're representing the church, and so they treat it that way, as a ministry rather than just a job." Such intentionality was not unique to Conservatives. A small urban ethnic church described their school as "a wonderful community of kids—Hispanic, white, Asian, African American. The whole rainbow is there, and I think that is just another nice witness that we can provide for the community."

The values congregations bring to this work often mean that less fortunate children have access to quality care that might not otherwise be available. While suburban tots may be taken to the local branch of a for-profit day care provider, nonprofit providers have a more diverse clientele. Like other nonprofit providers of child care, congregations are more likely to serve an ethnically and economically diverse population. They are also likely to have volunteer staff that helps maintain a higher staff-to-child ratio (Hayes, Palmer, and Zaslow 1990).

Neither the culture of the congregation's religious tradition nor its own emphasis on serving families can explain the presence or absence of a nursery school. Having enough people to create that volunteer pool does. While only 2 percent of congregations with fewer than one hundred participants can muster the resources for a day care program, 15 percent of midsized congregations (100–299 participants), and 20 percent of larger ones (over 300) have such programs. Money also matters, especially the relative affluence of a congregation's members. Preschool programs are found in nearly a third of the most well-off congregations (where a majority of members had household incomes over $65,000 in 1997). Similarly, predominantly white congregations are more likely to provide childcare programs than are any other parishes. Even comparing similarly well-off and similar-sized congregations, a predominance of Anglo members is strongly associated with having a childcare program. It is not clear whether this is another instance of well-off congregations serving a needy community or whether those well-off congregations are providing well for their own members.

OTHER EDUCATIONAL PROGRAMS   Congregations also contribute to the educational progress of their communities in a variety of activities aimed at older children and adults. One in ten congregations has organized a program to provide educational resources that may not otherwise be available. Some congregations sponsor GED or adult literacy classes, for instance; and many provide after-school and mentoring programs.[32] Some, like a large Episcopal church in Chicago, combine an extensive tutoring program with a variety of other social services. The pastor of a large National Baptist Church (NBC) in Chicago, talked about a variety of educational opportunities: "We do have courses, seminars, for the community, such as on the Internet and computer use. These are open and free for the community to come in." Another large NBC Church in Chicago has literacy and GED classes and had recently hired a new staff member "to work with job networks, and she supplies job training, interview skills, how to do resumes, and also provides placement assistance for homeless, etc." A Chicago Catholic parish, like others with after-school programs, combines recreation with educational support: "We're trying to build in recreational programs for the kids after school, to build in some educational programs for them after school (computers, a library), and again—meet their spiritual needs." Whether dealing with youth who need a combination of recreational opportunity and educational assistance or adults who need access to basic skills, congregations are a frequent source of learning in the community.

Like so many other congregational service programs, these too are mostly done by urban and suburban churches of sufficient size to sustain the effort. Only two programs we found were located in rural churches and only a handful in churches with fewer than a hundred regular participants. Again, within the population of city congregations big enough to have a program, those in the African American traditions were the most likely to have a ministry in place. These churches are particularly aware of the educational disadvantages many in their communities face, and they work hard to provide the motivation and opportunity necessary for success. Predominantly Hispanic congregations mobilize at similar levels, often helping to provide the training new immigrants need to get their start. These patterns of high engagement in non-Anglo churches are present in Catholic and Conservative Protestant churches, as well as in the traditional African American denominations themselves (see also Tsitsos 2003).

The most important factors that characterize congregations with community education programs are, again, size, ethnicity, and location. When we compare churches that are similar in those ways, differences among the various Christian traditions disappear. Differences in motivation remain, however. Among non-Anglo churches, the desire to serve families is strongly linked to providing these sorts of educational programs (32 percent versus 16 percent of congregations that did not name that as a priority). Among predominantly white churches, those that emphasize service to people in need are more likely to do so (19 percent versus 11 percent). The implication here is that for white churches, educational assistance is a service to others. In nonwhite congregations it serves the families that make up the church's own community (Gilkes 1995). Compared to nursery schools, youth and adult education occupy the energies of a different population of congregations (nonwhite rather than white) and for different reasons.

CULTURAL EVENTS   While demographics and resources help to explain who offers nursery schools and other educational programming, cultural events follow no such predictable pattern. Inviting the public into the congregation to enjoy a concert or other performance is not something every congregation does with regularity. By our count, only about one in eight does so in an organized and ongoing basis, but that minority is not distinguished by its greater resources, by its particular religious tradition, its ethnicity, or any of the differences associated with other forms of outreach programming. Even size barely makes a difference.

Various artistic activities—music, drama, dance, visual arts—are so pervasive in congregational life that the decision to extend those activities into publicly oriented performances occurs across the entire congregational spectrum.[33] One might expect a well-endowed Hartford Congregationalist (UCC) Church to organize a classical music series, but the pattern extends far beyond that. At a large African American church in Nashville, the pastor drew this analogy: "Cathedral churches generally have schools. They have enrichment. They have the arts. They have all the things that help sustain community life. And for the Nashville black community, this church runs it, and so we want to enhance that and keep that going for people to think of this as a church for the community." Back in Hartford, at a Conservative Jewish synagogue, the rabbi noted that they have a cantor who "puts together magnificent concerts. We use music as a vehicle to provide our identity." And on a smaller scale, in a small Missouri town, the whole community enjoys the high-quality performances of the Methodist Church choir.

Only two impulses seem to be associated with higher levels of involvement in public cultural events. One is predictable; the other is not. The predictable link is to a congregation's emphasis on worship. Those that place special emphasis on worship are slightly more likely to sponsor community cultural events (19 percent versus 12 percent of those for whom worship is less central). Where energy and priority is placed on what happens in worship, congregations already amass expertise in a range of arts-related activities that may spill over into public performance. The other impulse that seems to be associated with public artistic activity is an orientation toward social activism. Congregations that say they want to change the world are slightly more likely to have concerts (19 percent of them versus 13 percent of others). Congregations that open their doors for artistic performances seem also to be congregations that want to make a difference in more mundane matters as well.

Whether artistic programs or educational ones, human service delivery or organized advocacy, some congregations use their resources for the benefit of their communities. Whether legally incorporated or run as a congregational ministry, this sort of activity is common only in sectors of the congregational world that are urban and sufficiently large to muster the requisite volunteers. Which program a large urban congregation will choose depends on both its own membership and its local missional priorities. Well-off congregations are more likely to form a nursery school, for instance, and African American churches start both relief programs and tutoring. These voluntary organizational efforts are affected by the same social and resource factors that shape all nonprofit activity.

BLUEPRINTS FOR SERVING THE COMMUNITY

What we have seen here is the tremendous breadth and diversity of ways congregations in the United States attempt to have an effect on the world beyond their front doors. From soup kitchens to evangelism campaigns, from ecology groups to nursery schools, from vouchers for a tank of gas to job training programs, most congregations are concerned about more than their own members. Only a few reject this emphasis on principle, and a few restrict their efforts exclusively to evangelism (with a few more adding informal benevolence activities on the side). Another few seem not yet to have entered the mainstream where these activities are expected. Some congregations in the United States' new religious traditions, for instance, have begun to think and talk about service and evangelism, but none of the ones we interviewed had yet mustered the resources to create their own programs of outreach into the community.

The Jewish community falls somewhere between these more marginalized groups and the dominant Christian mainstream. Across the Jewish community preschool and day school programs reflect internal concerns as much as external ones, but the prevalence of issue groups and service-provider groups in synagogues is an indication of the concerns many Jews have for serving their communities. The concern for interfaith relations is especially lively within this segment of the religious world as well. Jews hear a message in their synagogues about "repair of the world" *(tikkun)* and are likely to seek ways to pursue it.

Within Christianity, each of the four families of religious tradition has a distinctive pattern of engagement. Churches in the historic African American denominations are just as likely to talk about the importance of community service as evangelism, but their activities lean toward the former more than the latter. They are more likely than any other group of churches to have an organized relief program, and substantial numbers are also involved in education and tutoring, informal assistance, and even political activism. They are also more likely to have service and issue groups in the congregation than they are to have a missions support group.

Catholic and Orthodox parishes most often emphasize providing service and relief to needy people, but a substantial minority also get involved in more activist efforts and in work that seeks to bridge the ethnic and cultural differences of our society. Mainline Protestants are very similar to Catholics in their emphasis on serving the community and in the presence of visible minorities that support political change and intercultural efforts. They are also like Catholics in largely (although not entirely) eschewing the kind of evangelism and missionary support activity that characterize most Conservative Protestant churches.

In mission priorities those Conservative Protestants are a mirror image of their Mainline counterparts. While most Mainliners emphasize community service and a few support evangelism, most Conservatives emphasize evangelism and a few support community service. Similarly, service support groups are the most prevalent type of outreach activity in Mainline churches, while missionary support groups are the most prevalent for Conservatives. Ironically, however, the two traditions are equally likely to *have* an organized relief program based in their own congregation.

The institutional template that has developed in the United States includes outreach activity as a typical expectation for congregations. We are not surprised when we see congregations harnessing volunteer energies around efforts to do some good in the world. That template creates the place on the organization chart, but it does not tell us how the place will be filled. That answer comes in large measure from the particular religious traditions and the messages they preach about how human change can and should happen.

And as with any voluntary organization, another part of the answer depends on the resources of the group—just how much human and material wherewithal can be mustered to pursue change in the world? The most important factor in making programs possible in many cases was the size of the congregation. Across all the Jewish and Christian congregations, a critical mass of members is required. Creating focused support groups inside the congregation is easier than creating an ongoing program, but both require enough people to do the work.

Neither of these forms of service and outreach tells the whole story, however. Congregations do a lot, but even more of what they do is channeled through the work of agencies and coalitions that can combine the resources of many into an effort that will have a larger impact in the community and beyond. We now turn to that network of "partner" organizations.

CHAPTER SIX · Doing Good Together

Networks of Work in the World

The typical congregation can touch the lives of many people, but its most direct impact—beyond its own members—is likely to be limited to a relatively small and local circle where emergency assistance can be rendered, the precepts of the faith shared, and support and enrichment provided. Depending on how big the congregation is, it may mount a few programs of its own, and groups of members may organize to keep issues and opportunities before the congregation as a whole. But when congregations want to reach beyond their own local community or want to do more than their own limited resources make possible, they work through other organizational channels. Which channels they choose depends in large measure on both the scope and character of work they want to do. How congregations define their mission has a major impact on how they choose partners, but the story is not merely a matter of choosing service organizations over evangelistic ones or denominational agencies over parachurch groups. The work congregations do in the world requires a wide and eclectic range of partners. Almost no one works alone. Only 3 percent of the congregations we encountered were completely without networks of partners.[1]

Denominations have been, for more than a century, the most common mode of network partnership. As the Protestant churches of Europe found their way onto American soil, they were first carried by extended families, before local congregations and councils of clergy banded together across whatever distance they could easily travel. Immigrants arrived here bearing European national and ethnic identities that were inextricably linked to religious tradition, and the European churches "back home" formed the earliest links between American congregations and religious identities beyond their own local domain. But churches of like heritage were also soon brought together by systems of correspondence and itinerancy on this side of the Atlantic, knit both by the formal movement of clergy and by the informal movement of evangelists and teachers. Both connections among scattered congregations and correspondence with distant church officials helped to promulgate and preserve theological and liturgical traditions in the new land.[2]

But as the new nation took shape and expanded, so did denominations. Over the course of the nineteenth century, agency structures began to be established to accomplish various functions in behalf of communities of believers (Mathews 1969)—most especially the work of benevolence and mission. New technologies altered the material constraints that had kept religion relatively simple and close to home. Manufacturing, marketing, and trade had their religious counterparts in publishing, evangelizing, and mission endeavors; disestablishment and a growing democracy found expression in voluntary organizations of all sorts (Hall 1998; de Tocqueville 1835). The scope of religious activity expanded ever outward and drew increasing numbers of ordinary Americans into benevolent efforts around the world. Throughout the nineteenth century these networks and special-purpose societies grew, sometimes within a single denominational sphere, but often overlapping and aggregating much of Protestantism into an evangelical empire (Hutchison 1987).

By the beginning of the twentieth century, the demands for efficiency and coordination that were creating new business forms were also affecting religious organizations. Disparate agencies began to cluster into centralized denominational structures, and missions and benevolence were brought under these same umbrellas. By the end of the 1920s many denominations had established centralized funding and budgeting mechanisms whereby money from individuals and congregations was pooled and then divided among a systematically organized array of departments and "boards."[3] These centralized agency systems allowed denominations to do everything from providing published educational materials to establishing pension boards for clergy, in addition to sustaining massive efforts at evangelism and good works around the world.

Denominations were never the only players on the field, however. From the beginning, American evangelism and benevolence, both at home and overseas, was a mix of interdenominational and single-denomination activity. And today, both nondenominational agencies and their denominational counterparts are still important mechanisms for doing good in the nation and beyond. We will return to the more global efforts and to the work of denominations at the end of this chapter, but we will begin where the majority of congregational partnerships begin—with concern for helping nearby needy people. In local communities human service is primarily the work of homegrown coalitions and nonprofit agencies.

CONGREGATIONS AND THEIR LOCAL PARTNERS

Congregational service to communities is no small matter. In recent years a number of studies have attempted to quantify what they do. A University of Pennsylvania study looked at 111 congregations that occupy historic buildings in cities around the country. They estimated that these congregations average contributing the equivalent of $145,000 per year in services to persons outside their own membership. The National Congregations Study found that 57 percent of all congregations are involved in social service activity, either through their own programs or by supporting others.[4] Our own count put the number of congregations with their own community programs at only about 39 percent, but we also found that most of what congregations do in the community is not done through the mechanism of beginning their own congregationally run programs. Much of what they do is coordinated by and channeled through outside organizations (something that may or may not have been included in the counts reported by these earlier studies).

The extent and nature of those partnerships is largely unexplored territory. By subsuming the contributions congregations make to others into assessments of their overall social service activities, other studies have missed this critical and distinct dimension of congregational work. The work of serving the needy and enriching community life links congregations with partners of many kinds, and those connections are themselves an important part of the network of voluntary religious work being done in American communities. Some connections have more substance and potential than others, but all establish potential pathways along which bridges can be built.

Congregational support to service agents takes many forms. The average congregation supports about five organizations that provide services to their community and beyond (see Table 13). This is over and above whatever they may do through a regional or national denominational body or on their own initiative. As we will see, many congregations (especially Catholics) also channel service money through regular offerings that are administered by regional and national denominational agencies, but they almost all work with other organizations as well. Across

TABLE 13 Connections between Congregations and Community Service Organizations in Different Religious Traditions

	Mainline Protestant (193)	Conservative Protestant (226)	African American Protestant (53)	Catholic & Orthodox (45)	All Congregations (549)
Average number of connections*	8.0	3.5	3.4	6.0	4.7
Percentage with at least one community connection*	93	81	77	91	82
Percentage that provide volunteers to at least one organization*	86	72	70	76	74
Average number of organizations to which volunteers are sent*	3.7	2.5	2.1	2.9	2.8
Percentage that provide space to at least one organization*	73	50	64	76	57
Average number of organizations to which space is provided*	3.1	1.3	1.2	2.3	1.8
Percentage that donate material goods to at least one organization*	50	23	26	29	30

TABLE 13 (continued)

	Mainline Protestant (193)	Conservative Protestant (226)	African American Protestant (53)	Catholic & Orthodox (45)	All Congregations (549)
Average number of organizations to which material goods are sent*	.9	.4	.3	.6	.5
Percentage that donate money to at least one organization*	91	83	82	91	84
Average number of organizations to which money is donated*	4.3	1.9	1.6	2.7	2.5
Average total contributions to service organizations*	$2,913	$2,255	$642	$3,701	$2,281

NOTE: Number in parentheses indicates number of congregations in that group. All Congregations includes these four groups plus Sectarians, Jews, and Other Religions. For items marked with an asterisk at least one of the differences among the groups is statistically significant at p < .10 (Oneway ANOVA, with Scheffe post-hoc comparisons).

traditions, nearly everyone (82%) is connected to at least one outside service organization. Only among the Sectarian groups and the newest groups (Hindus and Muslims, for instance) was it common for us to find congregations that have no connections outside their own religious world. Partnerships between congregations and other community organizations have been institutionalized as an expected pattern in most of American religion. This too is part of the organizational template that shapes how congregations do their work.

The substance of these relationships is multifaceted and varies enormously in the degree to which it is central to the congregation's sense of mission. These are not usually "partnerships" that resemble marriages, with a joint sense of mission

and equally shared resources. They are, rather, strategic alliances. They are connections that allow community organizations to mobilize needed resources and
allow congregations to extend their reach. That does not mean, however, that they
are anonymous connections buried in the treasurer's account books. Less than 10
percent of all connections involve only money, and less than 15 percent involve
only providing space. If congregations provide one kind of support, they are likely
to provide other forms as well.

As we talked with our informants in congregations throughout the country, we
asked them to tell us about as many of their connections as they could remember.
For each organization they named, we attempted to find out as much as we could
about what the group does, how long the congregation has been connected, and
what forms of support they provide. For about half the connections they named,
we were able to discern some countable measures of what is being invested. Where
our informant did not know the answers to our questions about volunteers, contributions, and the like, we have erred on the conservative side and counted as if there
are none. The numbers in Table 13 therefore clearly underestimate the size of the
contributions being made by congregations to their service partners.[5]

Still, even with incomplete information, the numbers are substantial. Over half
(57%) of all congregations, for instance, have at least one outside organization that
uses space in their buildings (either donated outright or made available at minimal
cost). This reflects the degree to which religious buildings are a valuable community resource. The vast majority of congregations (89%) own their own buildings,
and most have some sort of classroom, office, gathering, and/or kitchen space in
addition to their worship space. Some fill that space "24–7" with their own activities, but most do not, leaving a potentially valuable set of resources available for
other community organizations. Those least likely to share their space are
Sectarians (who rarely work with any outside groups) and the newer religious
groups, many of whom do not yet own buildings to share (40 percent are renters,
compared to less than 10 percent of other congregations). The average Christian or
Jewish congregation, on the other hand, provides space for two outside organizations. That means that the existence of at least three hundred thousand American
congregations helps to make possible the work of at least six hundred thousand
additional organizations that, in turn, provide a range of activities and services to
neighborhoods and cities.

Congregations are obviously more than their buildings. They are also the people
who gather there, and for every congregation, roughly three community organizations get at least some volunteers to assist in their work. Almost three-quarters

(74%) of all congregations report that they send volunteers to help in at least one group—on average five routine volunteers per group supported. Even the newer religious traditions have joined the trend, sending out volunteers at almost the rate of every other religious tradition (except the Sectarians, who are no more likely to send volunteers than to participate in any other form of outside connection). These numbers do not begin to count the number of groups in which individual members work, not as official representatives of their congregations, but at least in part because their congregations encourage such activity (something to which we will return below). It also does not count the projects taken on by intrachurch groups—such as Sunday school classes or women's groups—about which our informant perhaps did not know. The human resources gathered by congregations are clearly not hoarded inside their walls.

Nor are their monetary resources. On average, each congregation sends a monetary contribution to between two and three outside service organizations. Their contributions average roughly $900 per organization per year, and most supplement their monetary contributions with other material goods –food, clothing, furniture, Christmas gifts, and the like—collected for at least one organization.

Across all aspects of participation, the number of groups supported by Mainline Protestant congregations is roughly double that in other religious traditions.[6] They send volunteers to, provide space for, and give money and goods to roughly twice as many organizations. This is not necessarily because proportionately more Mainline churches are involved. Providing space, donating money, and sending volunteers to at least one group is an organizational pattern that is nearly as *prevalent* in other traditions. The larger *number* of partnerships formed by Mainline congregations represents a wider community network and more overall person-power, but not more money.

Across all the religious families, money does make a difference. The more money a congregation has in its budget, the more connections it is likely to form; and the more high-income parishioners it has—over and above the size of the budget—the more connections it can sustain.[7] Money, not sheer size, is what makes a difference. This stands in contrast to the pattern for forming in-house service programs, where it is people rather than dollars who make more of a difference. Big congregations that do not also have big budgets are less involved in external community partnerships; and congregations with big budgets, when located in urban and suburban areas (as most of them are), have more formal community connections than do rural congregations, even if the rural congregations have comparable budgets to spend.

But holding constant all these other factors, Mainline Protestant congregations are still distinctive for their heavier involvement in forming community partnerships. Forming alliances with groups beyond one's own doors is an organizational strategy that exists in virtually all Christian and Jewish congregations, an institutionalized cultural expectation about how to be a congregation; but this is a pattern created and still led by the congregations in the Mainline Protestant tradition.[8]

DOING GOOD IN THE COMMUNITY

When we listened to local congregational leaders describing what they hope to accomplish in their local communities, we heard themes of serving people in need, seeking basic social change, defending traditional morality, and bridging cultural and religious divisions. We saw many of those themes directly embodied in special interest groups within congregations, but less neatly parallel to the community outreach programs congregations set up for themselves. Whether forming their own outreach organization or forming partnerships with others, congregations are likely to follow the patterns that characterize the larger non-profit sector in the United States. Previous research has identified a set of categories into which this voluntary activity can be clustered; and those categories, combined with our own observations, suggest five kinds of congregational service partners:[9]

- "Human Services" connections include organizations that help congregations provide food, clothing, shelter, and other direct aid to people in need.
- "Policy Advocacy" groups are those whose primary goal is to affect legislation or to change public policies.
- "Community Benefit" organizations include the neighborhood and civic groups that seek the general betterment of their communities.
- "Health, Education, Culture, and Youth" organizations are groups that provide opportunities for individual enrichment, learning, and recreation.
- "Self-help and Growth" groups have many of the same enrichment goals as the health, education, culture, and youth groups; but they are structured as mutual support environments, rather than as formal institutions. Unlike the intracongregational small groups we saw in Chapter 3, the groups included here extend opportunities and participation into the community and do so through affiliation with a larger network or organization.

TABLE 14 Community Service Partnerships of Congregations
in Different Religious Traditions

Type of Assistance Provided	Mainline Protestant	Conservative Protestant	African American Protestant	Catholic & Orthodox	All Congregations (549)
	Congregations with at Least One Connection (%)				
Human services*	89	60	54	66	65
Policy advocacy*	20	8	9	31	13
Community benefit*	55	28	42	65	38
Health, culture, education, & youth*	81	58	54	71	73
Self-help & growth*	54	26	16	38	32

NOTE: All congregations includes these four groups plus Sectarians, Jews, and Other Religions. For assistance marked with an asterisk at least one of the differences among the groups is statistically significant at p < .10 (Oneway ANOVA, with Scheffe post-hoc comparisons).

From our long list of connections between congregations and service organizations, we created about sixty categories of activity and then grouped them under these five broad rubrics.[10]

HUMAN SERVICES

Providing direct assistance when people find themselves in need is among the most common goals of congregational outreach activity, whether it is undertaken independently or undertaken in partnership with others. Serving "the least of these" (as the Christian gospel according to Matthew exhorts) is something most congregations try to do. The individual members we surveyed also told us this was a high priority. As we saw in Chapter 5, about a third of congregations have service-oriented study and support groups, and about half that number run their own service programs, but two-thirds of all congregations have connections with at least one outside human service organization that extends what their own programs can do (see Table 14). This is the single most common kind of community connection congregations have, amounting to nearly two organizations per congregation.

Through such connections, runaway teens are housed; battered women and children find a safe place; people who are homeless find temporary shelter; and thousands and thousands of hot meals are served to people who are hungry. While many of these organizations also do advocacy and work on long-term solutions, their primary task is to relieve immediate suffering. In each community there are dozens of such agencies. In Nashville, for instance, Room in the Inn includes both shelter facilities and a "Guest House" unit for people who are too intoxicated to be admitted to the shelter. When they sober up, counseling and medical assistance are available. In Albuquerque the director of Storehouse told us they would give away that year "somewhere between thirty-eight and forty-two thousand bags of clothing. We're projecting over one hundred thousand meals. We will help 250 families with furniture." And in Seattle, Northwest Harvest is the primary distribution system for other shelters and feeding programs around the state, buying truckloads of beans and cargo containers full of rice, in addition to receiving food donations from dozens of churches and businesses. The director explained that the total "amounts to close to 15 million pounds of food a year."[11] In rural areas the organizations are smaller and sometimes less formalized, but the infrastructure is there as well.

Not surprisingly, congregations with more resources are generally more involved. Bigger budgets and better-off members mean that there are more resources of all sorts to contribute. But these patterns are not just a matter of resources. They are also a matter of religious tradition and mission. Congregations in the Mainline Protestant denominations are more broadly connected to outside service organizations than are congregations in any other religious community (89 percent have at least one connection, and the average is three). Congregations—in any of the traditions—that describe their own mission in terms of community service are also more connected to outside organizations. Beyond demographics or setting or even resources—all of which contribute to involvement—theological tradition and specific mission commitments increase congregational involvement as well.

People in congregations of all sorts want to salve some of the wounds they see every day, and most of them recognize that they cannot respond to all the need around them with only their own resources. They need to work with others, pooling money, person-power, and expertise that can go beyond a quick handout at the door. Across all traditions, if a congregation has any external connections at all, they are likely to be aimed at tending to the most vulnerable of society's members, especially those in the immediate local community. More than four out of five

TABLE 15   Organizational Scope of Outreach Partnerships

Type of Activity	Local & Regional Partner Organizations (%)	National & International Partner Organizations (%)	Total (%) (Number of Connections)
Human services	83	17	100 (1,201)
Policy advocacy	57	43	100 (144)
Community betterment	59	41	100 (390)
Health, culture, & education	78	22	100 (1,134)
Self-help & growth	18	82	100 (319)
Evangelism & missions	14	86	100 (257)

NOTE: Pearson chi-square = 911.26, p < .001.

(83%) of the human service connections we found were to local and regional organizations, rather than to national or international ones (see Table 15). Money and volunteer resources are most likely to go to nearby groups where the need is visible and the opportunity to make a difference apparent. Needs in distant places are, as we will see, more often served through denominational connections.

POLICY ADVOCACY

In addition to on-the-ground efforts to provide immediate relief, a few congregations also make connections with organizations that allow them to give voice to public policy concerns. From the environment to health care and from civil rights to animal rights, congregations sometimes pursue the cause of justice in this world through advocacy organizations. We found links that ranged from Amnesty International to the Audubon Society, from the Center for Prevention of Sexual and Domestic Violence to Children's Defense Fund, from Simple Justice (an advocacy group for gays and lesbians) to Protestants for the Common Good. While most of those groups pursue a liberal agenda, it is not just those on the political left who get involved. The March for Jesus and Right to Life activities draw some Conservative Protestants and Catholics into political action in defense of traditional moral values. Interestingly, none of the most well-known conservative political groups, like Pat Robertson's or Jerry Falwell's, were mentioned even once in the churches we talked with.[12]

In other religious traditions, congregations make connections that allow them to pursue still other issues. Classic civil rights organizations, such as the NAACP and SCLC, were supported by some African American congregations, as well as by one of the Baha'i groups we studied; and Jewish synagogues often link up with B'nai B'rith and various other pro-Israel organizations. Even the newer religious traditions are being drawn into local, national, and international coalitions (such as the American Muslim Council) aimed at protecting the rights of immigrants and expanding First Amendment rights to include new forms of religious practice. Across traditions, congregations mostly support special-interest lobbying and advocacy groups, not partisan political organizations. A few African American churches, however, reported alliances with specifically political and voter education groups, and their individual members, in turn, were also the most likely to report on our survey that they participate in political activities in the community.[13]

These ties to advocacy organizations are not nearly so numerous as the ties that facilitate direct human service (see Table 14). Less than one in seven congregations has any advocacy connection, and only one in fifteen has more than one. Where they do exist, advocacy ties are as likely to be to national and international organizations as to local ones (see Table 15). When congregations seek partners for their efforts to change policies and structures, they often realize that the issue goes beyond the local community they can see.

While Mainline Protestant, Catholic, and Jewish congregations are the most likely to establish ties to organizations that seek social change, it is not the tradition as such, but the particular orientations of congregations in those traditions that makes the difference. These are the traditions where an activist orientation is most likely, where some congregations may think of their mission in terms of changing the injustices of this world, although not nearly all do. The activist congregations are still a minority, but it is they who are most likely to seek out partners who can help them make a difference—in cleaning up the environment, achieving racial justice, saving unborn babies, protecting the state of Israel, preventing hunger, or a hundred other causes. Congregations without such an activist orientation (still the majority, even within the Mainline, Catholicism, and Judaism) are not likely to have advocacy partners, even though their larger tradition may encourage them to do so.

COMMUNITY BENEFIT

Ongoing efforts to build up the strength of a community bring together coalitions of individuals, businesses, and other organizations to form all-purpose associations such as block watch groups, neighborhood associations, civic clubs, and the like.

They take on tasks as mundane as trash pickup and as complicated as policing issues. In addition, as public gatherings of concerned citizens, they are important players in the creation of "social capital" (Putnam 2000). Whether faith communities participate as a regular member, provide space for meetings, or sign on to assist with a specific project, community groups do at least some of their work with the help of congregations.

Another common encounter between congregations and their communities comes on election day. A small contingent of the places where we interviewed serve their communities as a polling place, a practice we found most often in Chicago Catholic parishes. In this seemingly simple exercise, congregations transform themselves into public spaces in which the basic work of American democracy is done. Congregations also sometimes serve as a gathering place for a whole community in times of celebration or crisis. One pastor recalled, for instance, that his local ministerial association was called to arrange for churches to serve as shelter space when a major snowstorm wiped out all electricity in the town. After September 11, 2001, as well, hundreds of congregations all over the country opened their doors to people seeking comfort and assistance (Ammerman 2002b).

Like most other service partnerships, community betterment links are more common in Mainline and African American Protestant churches, along with Catholic and Orthodox parishes. In contrast, only about a quarter of Conservative Protestant churches (and even fewer Sectarians and Other Religions) form alliances with community betterment organizations (see Table 14).[14] Within the Mainline, this sort of community involvement seems to be normative, no matter what the congregation's own individual sense of mission or its resources. Among Catholic parishes and black churches, both the larger religious tradition and the congregation's own orientation have effects. Those that articulate community service as a particular local priority establish more community links than their less service-minded sister churches. Again, it is a combination of theology and tradition, not demographics or resources that makes the difference. This sort of community activity is not the purview only of well-educated or well-endowed congregations; rather, it is the routine of those whose tradition and/or particular theological goals make community betterment part of a religious agenda (Hall forthcoming).

Some of these community benefit activities attempt to implement long-term changes. Providing permanent affordable housing, for instance, has become a widespread concern, and the premier organization that has mobilized energies on behalf of this cause is Habitat for Humanity (Baggett 2000). Thirty-one percent of all the Mainline Protestant churches in which we interviewed have some connection to Habitat. Other traditions are involved as well, although at much lower levels. While retaining its own faith base, Habitat has reached out across traditions (and into the secular world as well). When congregations want to make a long-term difference in the lives of needy families, they can channel money and volunteer time through this rapidly growing nonprofit organization.

No other form of community economic development activity has anything like the presence of Habitat. The next most prevalent organization named by our congregations was Heifer International, an Arkansas-based ministry that provides livestock as a means toward economic self-sufficiency in communities around the world. Their Christmas opportunities to give developing-world communities gifts ranging from a flock of chicks to a portion of a llama in honor of family and friends have become especially popular holiday alternatives. Several churches also support SERRV crafts sales and the activities of Church World Service (especially its refugee settlement work). While most of the churches that named these are within the Mainline, a few African American and Conservative churches participate in Heifer Project. World Vision and Franklin Graham's Samaritan's Purse are other development organizations with a base of support among the congregations we surveyed, but their support is stronger among Conservative churches than within the Mainline.

All of these overseas agencies, even the evangelical ones, spend more of their money on humanitarian activities than on direct evangelization (Hamilton 2000, 118). World Vision is a prime example. Begun in the wake of the Second World War as an effort to care for orphans in Asia, World Vision has become one of the largest relief and development agencies in the world, drawing most of its support from individuals (and from government contracts), rather than from congregations. One of World Vision's sister relief organizations, Catholic Relief Services, similarly draws support from individuals and government contracts, but also from several of the Catholic parishes where we interviewed (and two of our non-Catholic congregations contributed to that organization as well).[15] Most of the national and international organizations to which congregations contribute have both "relief" and "development" as their goals. They can respond quickly to disasters of all sorts, but they also work with local populations to improve agricultural methods, dig wells, form marketing cooperatives, and otherwise facilitate long-term and sustainable development (Lindenberg and Bryant 2001). Roughly a third (30%) of the congregations we surveyed had links to national or international organizations that do human service, community benefit, educational, and other good work. Overseas all the various outreach goals are often linked, as when Food for the Poor says it "seeks to link the church of the First World with the church of the Third World in a manner that aids both the materially and spiritually poor."[16]

Like World Vision and Heifer International, these organizations work primarily overseas; local economic development partnerships are considerably more rare. While the idea of community development corporations (CDCs) is getting a good deal of attention, it is the rare church that has taken on this sort of local economic and political organizing.[17] Those relative few who join community organizing groups can help neighborhoods to articulate key issues and formulate solutions. Some organize to pursue grants or rehab housing or to persuade corporations to invest where it is needed most. A few even buy up property themselves or organize major housing initiatives (Freedman 1993). Some provide space for meetings and offices, while other congregations contribute volunteers and the visibility of their own pastors to the cause.

Most congregational involvement with community benefit organizations, however, simply provides a forum where community problems and crises can be addressed and where energy can be mobilized around manageable projects to make neighborhoods more livable. The local Chamber of Commerce or Kiwanis Club is a more common partner than an Alinsky-style community organizing coalition. And contributions to development agencies assisting communities around the world are as common as connections to economic development closer to home.

HEALTH, CULTURE, EDUCATION, AND YOUTH

Human service and community benefit efforts are not the only activities that bring congregations into partnerships in their communities. In at least as many cases, partnerships provide personal growth and enrichment rather than basic material needs. Around seemingly every corner, there is a congregation whose sign notes the presence of senior centers or sports leagues, music programs or self-help groups—all existing independently, but often housed and supported by churches, synagogues, mosques, and temples.

Almost three-fourths of all congregations (73%) have at least one connection to an organization that works for the health, educational, and cultural enrichment of people beyond their membership. The average congregation supports one or two such groups. Some, like the Chicago Christian Counseling Center, provide assistance with personal and family needs. Others, like Seattle's Interfaith AIDS project, provide education and support for people facing health crises. Musical groups ranging from the Albuquerque Symphony Orchestra to the Nashville Chamber Orchestra teach and rehearse and perform in spaces provided by the congregations we studied. Amateurs who enjoy everything from Irish Step Dancing to drumming gather in them as well. Other hobbies—from radio cars to quilting to pinochle—are nurtured with the help of congregations. Senior citizens gather for recreation and education in Shepherd's Centers; and nursery schools and Head Start programs are housed and supported. And congregations send their youth and adults to play in sports leagues that gather community participants for everything from soccer, basketball, and baseball to bowling. From Bach cantatas to blood pressure screening, congregations combine forces with other community organizations to make the world a little better place.

Programs for children and youth, including drug education and gang prevention efforts, are also supported by congregations. Many sponsor religious youth groups such as Young Life or Campus Crusade for Christ, but most numerous of all are the Scouts. (Counted here are the troops that were described as having a community base rather than a primarily intracongregational one.) One in five Christian churches sponsors at least one troop, with Catholic and Orthodox parishes and Mainline Protestant churches most actively involved. Scouting has long encouraged interested children to learn more about their own or other faiths. Regional and national Scout leaders help by working with various religious groups to provide appropriate materials and arrange for visits and celebrations. As a Nashville Girl Scout executive noted, "They're encouraged to work within their own denomination and go through this workbook so that they become stronger members of their family's faith." Scouts depend on the support they get from congregations, and congregations often benefit from the encouragement their children receive from Scouts.

As with many other community partnerships, these too are a distinctive Mainline Protestant practice, but better-resourced congregations of all kinds are more likely to be involved than are more struggling groups. Urban and suburban congregations that have bigger budgets and higher-income members are the most likely to partner with community enrichment organizations. Those are in part activities of noblesse oblige undertaken by the congregations that can afford them. But no matter what their resources, Mainline Protestant churches are more likely to include educational and cultural community partnerships in their ministry. All kinds of congregations participate at least to some extent, but Mainline ones more than most.[18]

SELF-HELP AND GROWTH

A closely related set of activities are those that fall into the "self-help" category. Here persons with a given concern gather to help themselves and each other deal with the problem, and people who share an interest or passion organize to teach each other more. About one in three (32%) congregations maintains a connection to at least one such group (one that encompasses more than its own members). By far the best known and most widespread are the Alcoholics Anonymous and other twelve-step groups for narcotics addicts, overeaters, and even "sex and love addicts." Congregations across the religious spectrum provide support for these groups, but Mainline churches are again especially likely to be involved (even taking demographic and resource factors into account). Over half of the Mainline churches in which we interviewed have at least one AA or twelve-step group meeting in their buildings. Conservative Protestants are about half as likely to support self-help groups, with connections to Catholic and Orthodox parishes falling between the two streams of white Protestants (see Table 14). An infrastructure of congregations is an assumed part of what makes such groups possible.

As numerous as AA groups are in the basements and parlors of American churches, there are an equal number of other support and spirituality groups as well. These include religiously focused groups like Bible study and prayer groups which (like Bible Study Fellowship) are part of national organizations. Four out of five of the support groups we documented were linked to national and international networks. When the desire for personal and spiritual growth is organized beyond a single congregation, affiliation with a national organization can provide a recognized name, program packages, and leadership training.

Support groups abound for people encountering all sorts of challenges in living. There are parenting groups for Mothers of Preschoolers (MOPS) and weight control groups, including Take Off Pounds Sensibly (TOPS) and Weight Watchers, in addition to the evangelically focused Weigh Down (Griffith 1997b). There are groups dealing with birth defects and disability, as well as groups for people who have encountered less common difficulties—Tourette Syndrome, Lyme Disease, and incest, to name a few of those we found. We also encountered groups for transvestites and for Christian motorcycle enthusiasts, for people recovering from divorce and people who are victims of violence (Nason-Clark 1997). Some are ad hoc local creations, but even the most specialized is likely to be linked to similar groups in other places. As congregations seek to help people in their communities, support groups of all kinds provide a platform for their efforts.

Wuthnow has argued that our highly fragmented and mobile society has found small groups to be an effective means for sustaining social and emotional bonds and promoting mutual aid (Wuthnow 1994b). We found support groups to be much more common in urban and suburban congregations than in rural ones.

People in small towns and in the countryside have more informal ways to help each other; it is city people who need to organize. Similarly, we found that congregations dominated by older members were unlikely to link up with self-help groups. The idea of forming groups to pursue specialized interests and needs is more common among younger generations (Roof 1993). Younger people and people in cities have fueled the growth of the support group movement, and their congregations often play a vital role.

A few very large congregations might be able to provide such specialized groups for their own members, but much more frequently, self-help and personal growth groups involve members beyond the bounds of a single congregation. When one or two people see a need, they can draw on the networks of knowledge and communication in their own congregation, link with interested others in the larger community, and often end up housing the resulting group in their building. These groups augment that congregation's efforts to provide fellowship and spiritual nurture for its own members, but they also establish bridges of communication and mutual care for the community as a whole.

When American congregations say they want to serve their communities, reaching out to make the world a better place, they often channel their energies through organizations that provide direct human services, lobby in pursuit of change, organize programs to improve community life, offer educational and cultural enrichment, and bring people together in support and growth groups of all kinds. The missional energy of congregational life spreads out into every corner of the voluntary sector. Some kinds of congregations are more involved than others, and each pursues connections consonant with its own goals, but working in partnership is how the work gets done. Congregations could not fulfill their mission without community partners, and the voluntary sector would be significantly impoverished without the money, volunteers, space, and in-kind resources provided by congregations.

WHO ARE THE PARTNERS?

The most natural organizational links between congregations and outside organizations are to religious nonprofit organizations. Both are embodiments of the voluntary religious impulses of Americans. Congregations are multipurpose communal expressions of our diverse religious traditions; religious nonprofits allow people of faith to come together around a specific common cause that is an expression of their spiritual commitments. Organizations such as Heifer International and World Vision and countless local shelters and youth programs embody religiously inspired charitable impulses throughout the country and the world.

TABLE 16   Organizational Partnerships of Congregations
in Different Religious Traditions

Type of Organization	Mainline Protestant	Conservative Protestant	African American Protestant	Catholic & Orthodox	All Congregations (549)
	Congregations with at Least One Connection (%)				
Informal coalition	72	62	61	60	62
Religious nonprofit*	80	69	42	63	66
Secular nonprofit*	83	46	50	80	58
Governmental unit	34	27	36	44	29
Any service activity through regional denominational organization*	30	22	9	56	26[a]

NOTE: All Congregations includes these four groups plus Sectarians, Jews, and Other Religions. For items marked with an asterisk at least one of the differences among the groups is statistically significant at p < .10 (Oneway ANOVA, with Scheffe post-hoc comparisons).
   [a] Average for all denomination-related congregations only.

Nearly as often, however, congregational partners are secular nonprofits such as the Audubon Society or the Red Cross (see Table 16); and still other organizations are nearly impossible to classify. They embody a mix of religious and secular, from their origins and funding to their motives and identity (Jeavons 1998). A closer look at the organizations with which congregations work reveals the ambiguity of our usual distinctions between secular and religious. Doing good in the world may begin within the community of faith, but quickly involves partnerships that transcend confessional boundaries. Almost no service organization is without a religious presence of some sort, nor is any organization—no matter how apparently religious—utterly without secular influences. Almost by definition, when charitable intentions take organizational form they are at once *both* sacred and secular.

Many of the "organizations" through which congregations do their work, however, are not formal organizations at all (see Table 16). They are often simple coalitions among two or more congregations, partnerships that have no staff of their own and often no distinct name. Many food pantries and clothes closets are run this way. A group of local congregations agrees informally that one will collect, store, and distribute furniture, while another will take care of the food, and a third will provide clothing. They may notify various social service agencies of the arrangement so that needy persons can be referred to the right place. This network of caring may never show up on anyone's annual report, but it is a critical link in the safety net in many communities. In Chicago such intercongregational sharing was the origin of what eventually became the Public Action to Deliver Shelter (PADS) system. By 1998, more than sixty-five congregations were serving as overnight shelters on a highly organized and well-supported rotating schedule. But the idea started with the same sort of informal relationships that we found among congregations in every one of our sites.

Equally informal are some of the gathered individuals who form a self-help or support group.[19] Rather than being part of a formal national network (like AA, for instance), some are just church and community folk who decide to get together. We found Alzheimer's and disability support groups and groups that gather to practice Aikido or Zen meditation, for instance. Many (although not all) of the sports leagues we encountered were similarly informal. They have an ongoing existence and a recognizable identity (an all-city church softball league, for instance), but there is little if any financial or legal infrastructure defining the group.

By far the most important of these informal groups are the clergy associations that are present in nearly every community. Some do little more than gather for an occasional lunch and schmoozing. Most, however, have a strong component of prayer and fellowship and are part of the support network for clergy that we examined in Chapter 4. But often the praying is specifically directed at needs and concerns in the community, and the concerns expressed in prayer spill over into concrete actions the group may undertake. In rural Missouri, for instance, the ministers got together to form a food pantry when they discovered that after state cutbacks more people seemed to be in need.

Not only does that county ministerial association maintain a food bank, but they also have arrangements with various local businesses to provide gasoline, medicine, groceries, and the like. Similarly, the president of a suburban Chicago Ministerial Association told us: "Instead of having Mr. and Mrs. X coming to your door and saying we need money, and then going to the next church and getting money, and the next church, we came up with a voucher system where we have a checking account and each church donates in various ways." This was a familiar refrain. Churches and synagogues are obvious stopping points for people in need, but when someone knocks on the door, it is hard for a clergyperson (or a secretary) to make a judgment about what is best. By banding together, and by enlisting the help of local merchants, congregations establish some semblance of rationality in a situation they find otherwise frustratingly ambiguous.

Ministerial associations seem to be a common vehicle for meeting ad hoc emergency needs. They raise their own money from their members, set their own agendas, and respond to needs as they choose—usually without any formal staff. They often include a wide variety of clergy, but the predominant pattern is that they encompass Christians more than others, Protestants more than Catholics, and Mainline white Protestants more than either Conservatives or African Americans. Here the legacies of privilege and exclusion live on in divisions that may now be more habitual than intentional. The group that presumes to represent "the clergy" in the community is very likely to be disproportionately Episcopal and Presbyterian, Methodist and Lutheran, rather than AME and Jewish and Baha'i.

That legacy of quasi establishment also sometimes makes local ministerial associations a sort of all-purpose civic arm for the churches. The suburban Chicago leader we heard above also noted that their group's members take turns offering prayer at the town council meetings and writing a column for the town newspaper. When crises occur, the town is likely to call on them to mobilize the resources of the churches as needed. When other celebrations or events need the blessing of a minister, the ministerial alliance is the clearinghouse that sends someone. As with other informal religious coalitions, ministerial associations are linked to wider networks by word of mouth, enabling them to respond to community needs.

RELIGIOUS NONPROFIT ORGANIZATIONS

Sometimes the work of clergy associations leads to more ongoing and formal organization. The Church Council of Greater Seattle, for instance, supports over a dozen formal programs that address everything from homelessness to care for the elderly and from urban youth to concern for the people of Iraq. It still brings official church bodies (mostly Mainline) together for mutual support, but it also now has congregational supporters that span diverse denominational and racial groups working together to address public issues.

Formal nonprofit organizations are the dominant sector through which congregations do their work in the local community (see Table 16). In the years since World War II, charitable nonprofit organizations have proliferated, with income significantly outstripping growth in the gross domestic product. In 1940 there were 12,500 such groups; by 1992 there were seven hundred thousand (Hall 1992). Nor have religious groups disappeared in favor of secular ones. In 2001 the largest nonprofit group in the United States was Lutheran Social Services, with income of $7.6 billion; and they were joined in the top ten by Catholic Charities, United Jewish Communities, and Salvation Army (Religion News Service 2003). Organizing nonprofit groups has become a primary vehicle for American charitable impulses, and congregations often provide both seedbed and infrastructure.

Religious and secular groups alike often began as informal coalitions of church and synagogue members or as the ministry of a single congregation. That early history means that founding stories and tales of early struggle are often full of spiritual meaning even today. Northwest Harvest was described to us this way: "It was strictly a religious-based ecumenical movement, pretty much designed with people power—no going after government funds or anything else. The churches to the rescue! . . . We were doing this according to St. Matthew 25:40, 'Inasmuch as you do it unto the least of these you do it unto me.'" This was not the only time we heard Matthew 25:40 cited. Jesus' admonition to care for the hungry, the thirsty, the stranger, the naked, the sick, and the imprisoned was a theological mandate for many of the nonprofit leaders we talked to.

In addition to motivation, congregations also provide connections. Loaves and Fishes is one of the primary feeding ministries in Hartford, and when it started in the mid-1980s, church connections were critical: "There were a couple of women from several different churches . . . who had a great interest in doing something about a soup kitchen on Asylum Hill. And when they realized—they all knew each other as friends—that they were representative of different churches, they decided to try to make this an ecumenical effort." The civic concerns and connections already present in many congregations make them an especially fertile seedbed for the sprouting of new religious nonprofits (Milofsky and Hunter 1995).

Once having incorporated as a separate entity, however, religious nonprofits are faced with the question of just how religious they will be. The answer to that question varied enormously among the groups where we interviewed. As is evident from the names of some of the organizations—Room in the Inn, Hesed House[20]—religious motives are often close to the surface, even if the formal charter says they are nonsectarian. Groups like the Salvation Army, Catholic Charities, and World Vision have clearly articulated religious visions and receive significant support from religious communities. Still, they also receive massive amounts of money from governmental and corporate sources, and many of their volunteers and recipients do not share the religious motives that animate the core staff.[21] On the other side of the presumed sacred-secular divide, many AA groups, food depositories, and shelters are overtly organized as secular charities but may be so filled with religious participants that faith-based goals are commonplace.

This mix of religious and secular shows up in how people talk about what they are doing. From our interviews, we can compare the ways people in different organizational contexts talk about their work. Several shelters and food pantries where we interviewed, for instance, are supported by both religious groups and secular donors. In turn, their descriptions of why people work there were a mix of secular and religious narratives as well.[22] Said one agency director, "It's people just learning to put their faith into action. People learning just how to be citizens and that they have a base out of which they can act." A few people in these mixed environments think of what they do as a specific calling from God. At a large metropolitan food depository, the person we talked with said, "I do think that most of our staff have—even if they cannot articulate it—they see this job of theirs as a form of a call." People building Habitat houses often speak of their work as "God's love in action" or as a "sermon."[23] In some cases, religious narratives of calling may help to make community action organizations more effective. As Cress and Snow noted in their study of homeless social movement organizations, "commitment to this 'calling' provided social gospelites with greater staying power, because assisting the homeless and other impoverished groups was seen as an end in itself" (Cress and Snow 1996, 1104).

In more dominantly religious settings, not surprisingly, narratives of call are much more common. In organizations like Loaves and Fishes or Catholic Charities or Hesed House, the symbols of religious traditions are overtly part of the public identity of the organization. There many people described their work as a Christian vocation. The woman we talked with at Catholic Charities in Chicago said, "Well, I'm Catholic first of all. One of the motivating things was it was a perfect fit for what I saw as my life work. . . . Knowing the work of Catholic Charities, to be able to use the skills that I have to help other people was probably one of the biggest motivating factors to come back to work." These organizations receive a variety of secular supports, but there is never any question that the mission of the group is defined in religious terms.

Sometimes the religious connections and motivations eventually fade, as an organization takes on professional staff and seeks nonreligious funding sources.[24] That was the case at Seattle's Teen Hope Shelter. Begun by a network of mostly church-based folk, it almost immediately became a secular, professionally run organization with little connection to churches, church people, or religious ideas. A similar story was told about an agency in Albuquerque: "For the first twenty or twenty-five years this was a shelter for kids, and it was funded and staffed largely by volunteers and by church people and that kind of a coordinated effort. Over the years that started to change, and we got more and more kids who got more and more kind of difficult . . . and that became more expensive. And the churches could not manage all of that, and volunteer help was not adequate when you need therapists and psychiatrists and that sort of thing." Both the scope and the nature of the work seemed to demand a secular approach.

More common, however, are religious nonprofits that retain a sense of their religious identity and mission. Both staff and volunteers are there because they have learned that living faithfully requires service. The sense of embodying God's presence in service to the poor was very strong among many of the agency staff we interviewed, even when they do not openly talk to their clients about their faith. At Hesed House in Chicago we were told, "If you don't believe that God is present in your offering of bread, in your words, in your hospitality, then God isn't going to be there because you say some prayers."[25] In some organizations talk about faith permeates the services rendered. In others, faith is in the background, but no less present.

While faith may be a central ingredient in the identity, mission, and ongoing motivation of most religious nonprofits, very few of them exist solely on money from religious sources or volunteer energy that comes only through religious channels. This description of support for St. Vincent de Paul Place in Connecticut is typical of what we heard: "The bishops' annual appeal funds us a certain amount for the salaries of the staff every year. And then the rest of the financial resources come from a few grants, a little out of donations. We have a lot of individual donations. . . . The business community and the civic organizations are very good support for us along with the churches." For a time they received state funds, but the program being funded got caught in state and city politics and was shut down. Since then, they have been cautious about government money, a caution that we heard especially strongly at Northwest Harvest. The paperwork and verifications that are necessary when state money is involved are enough to keep some religious nonprofits from seeking it. They want to be able to look a needy person in the eye and make their own assessments about whether and how to help. Other religious nonprofits, by contrast, do receive various forms of public money to assist in their work—a practice that was in place long before the current discussion about Charitable Choice and faith-based initiatives (Monsma 1996; Salamon 1995).[26]

Still, religious nonprofits have a solid base of material support that comes through religious channels, alongside the streams of volunteers mobilized by congregations. We have already noted that congregations often organize groups of workers to serve on a regular schedule, but the stories we heard in many community organizations make clear that other volunteers come on their own, because serving others is a religious virtue they embrace. When we asked individual attendees in the congregations we surveyed about their community involvement, nearly 80 percent claimed that they provide informal assistance at least occasionally, and 59 percent volunteer through organized community service organizations. In addition, nearly half gave $100 or more to secular charities in 1997.[27] Both these individual contributions and the collective involvement of congregations form a foundation that is recognized by most religious nonprofits as essential to their work.

The congregations on which they draw represent a diverse ecumenical cross section. Even a denominational agency, such as Catholic Charities or Lutheran Social Services, receives tangible support from persons and congregations outside their own tradition. We found at least fifteen non-Catholic congregations, for instance, that reported contributing to Catholic Charities, Catholic Relief Services, or another local Catholic service agency. The national umbrella organization now known as Catholic Charities since at least 1972 has acknowledged the degree to which their work encompasses both Catholics and other "people of good will" (Froehle and Gautier 2000, 96). The work of religious nonprofits doesn't just build bridges to people in need: it also builds bridges among the religious, civic, governmental, and business groups that support the work.

That does not mean, however, that congregations never work through their own denominational systems to accomplish service goals in the community. Most congregations belong to a regional denominational unit—an association, diocese, district, or "classis" (as the Reformed Church in America designates their local association of churches)—and some of those regional units pool the resources of area congregations to undertake outreach and service projects. That is especially true in the Roman Catholic parishes (see Table 16). A priest in Missouri explained to us, "The funding is managed through the Diocese. So we have . . . the Rice Bowl [a program of Catholic Relief Services to increase U.S. awareness of overseas needs]. . . . We do mission appeals, emergency appeals, if there is a disaster somewhere in the world." The hierarchical structure of the Church and the typically large size of its parishes combine to make dioceses especially potent agents for responding to needs both near and far. Catholic charitable work was historically organized at the diocese level, and even with today's large national and international networks, the bishop is the most direct face of the appeal for support (Froehle and Gautier 2000, 93–99).[28]

In most other denominations regional church bodies have few extra funds for undertaking special projects. If they manage to provide a skeletal staff to support the clergy and provide resources for local church programming, they are doing well. The traditional African American denominations have even less regional infrastructure than their white Protestant counterparts and almost never told us that they had undertaken denominationally based regional outreach programs. Still, about a quarter of all Christian churches mentioned to us that they participate with others in their denomination in an officially sponsored regional service project.

Even the giant Catholic and Lutheran social service agencies, despite their increasingly broad base of support, are at heart agencies of those religious traditions. Theologian Ronald Thiemann summarizes his study of Diakon Lutheran Social Ministries (a regional agency in the Northeast) by noting that "[t]he mission, values, and ethical principles of the new agency emphasize the distinctive Christian commitments that undergird the organization's work, and the educational and socialization efforts they have undertaken are designed to introduce their diverse employee base to Christian service in the Lutheran tradition" (Thiemann forthcoming; quoted from manuscript). Froehle and Gautier note the same process of re-visioning among Catholic agencies: "In 1998, the Campaign for Human Development changed its name to the *Catholic* Campaign for Human Development as a public reaffirmation of its origins and principles. The Catholic Healthcare Association launched a three-year initiative to formulate standards for Catholic health care providers, making room for both a Catholic identity and service to diverse communities" (Froehle and Gautier 2000, 105; emphasis in original). Denomination-based agencies have recently been reclaiming their distinctive identities, even as they employ and deliver services to a diverse population.

Religious nonprofits with a distinct denominational identity are joined by thousands of nondenominational (parachurch) religious service groups in the task of delivering multiple billions of dollars in assistance to needy Americans and people around the world. They provide space for diverse religious voices to deliberate common community concerns, and they embody diverse religious energies in behalf of those communities. And all depend on congregations and their members to supply a significant portion of the money and energy that keep them going.

When there is national and international work to do congregations are most likely to link with religious agencies; in work closer to home, secular and religious groups are about equally numerous among congregational partners. We have already noted, however, just how hard it can be to draw a line between secular and nonsecular nonprofit organizations. In spite of their secular identity and mission, some of these organizations have religious connections that are quite pervasive. The Seattle chapter of PFLAG (Parents and Friends of Lesbians and Gays) describes its mission as the support of gay, lesbian, and transgendered persons and their families. They operate as a support group and sometime lobbying organization, but they also have a volunteer who works as a liaison with churches, offering them educational programming and garnering their support. This group meets in a church building, and congregations advertise PFLAG meetings. Similarly, in Albuquerque we heard about (and witnessed) the pervasiveness of church volunteers at one food and jobs agency. It is staffed by secular professionals. The funding is from government, business, and civic groups. The programming is guided by basic social work standards, but the people who cook and serve the meals everyday are overwhelmingly groups based in churches who are quite clear that what they are doing is a ministry.[29]

In the most clearly secular settings—a couple of youth service organizations, Red Cross chapters, a Ronald McDonald house, a Hispanic Chamber of Commerce, for instance—staff members rarely used overtly religious language to describe what they do. Wuthnow's study of volunteering identified three dominant "vocabularies of motive," and in these secular contexts, we heard echoes of all three: serving as an exchange of "goods," serving as therapeutic, and serving as an opportunity for personal growth (Wuthnow 1991). In these secular settings, the people we talked with described what they were doing in simple altruistic terms, without any explicit reference to how those norms of altruism may have been developed. Individuals may internally understand doing good in religious terms, and the motives of the participants may have been shaped by religious participation, but the public narrative of the organization keeps religious connections obscured.[30]

Secular nonprofits benefit from the work of congregations in many ways. Even when resources are not directly channeled through a congregation, the virtues extolled in congregational life seem to spill into secular volunteer work. The civic orientation of many Mainline churches is evidenced in the reports their individual members gave us on their surveys. They claimed more volunteer activity in community and secular arenas than did members in other traditions. They claim to give more generously to secular charities and participate more frequently in community service organizations. What individuals do and what congregations do seem to reinforce each other. Congregational ties make volunteer and giving opportunities known to members, and members' own commitments may encourage the congregation as a whole to provide support.

Being part of the network of secular nonprofits in a local community is more common in the Protestant Mainline, but connections are also a matter of resources. Congregations with bigger budgets and well-educated, well-paid members are more heavily involved than are those with fewer resources. But taking demographic and resource differences into account, both specific local mission priorities and larger religious traditions are still important factors that can encourage or discourage work with secular nonprofits. Even within a given religious tradition, the mission orientations of individual congregations make a difference. Those that say they should be providing service to the world are indeed more likely to link up with secular organizations that do such work and, controlling for everything else, the Mainline tradition itself makes secular community cooperation more likely. For at least a century and a half, liberal Protestant churches have understood such organizations as part of their mission (Hall forthcoming).

About a third of the connections congregations make for local human service and community betterment are with secular groups, but self-help connections are thoroughly dominated by secular, rather than religious, partnerships. The large majority of the self-help groups with which congregations work are connected to secular national and international networks like AA and TOPS. Educational and cultural enrichment goals are more often accomplished through secular groups as well. The Hartford Conservatory regularly uses church space for rehearsals, performances, and lessons. Similarly, the Loyal Heights Preschool uses otherwise unoccupied space in a Seattle congregation. These institutions serve a thoroughly nonsectarian public, but draw resources of various sorts from congregations. Congregations, in turn, are able to participate in providing for the educational, cultural, and health needs of the community by assisting secular institutions in their work.

Rights and advocacy work by congregations is also likely to have a secular base, especially at the local level. At the national level, however, congregations in different religious traditions pursue different partnership strategies. Mainline Protestants, African American churches, and Jewish synagogues are most likely to partner with secular advocacy organizations, while Conservative Protestants and Catholics are most likely to partner with religious ones. This reflects both the growth of a distinctly conservative Christian political consciousness and especially the alliance between evangelicals and Catholics on the issue of abortion.[31] We encountered sixteen churches with activist national anti-abortion ties—three Catholic, twelve Conservative Protestant, and one rural Lutheran church (formerly Missouri Synod, now ELCA). A third of all the advocacy ties we found in Conservative Protestant churches were to groups working on this one issue.

In addition, many of these same churches support their local "Crisis Pregnancy Center." These Centers provide education and counseling aimed at preventing individual abortions. There are now nearly a thousand centers nationwide, with an average budget of at least $70,000 and at least twenty regular volunteers in addition to their paid staff (Hamilton 2000, 128). In Nashville, the director of volunteers told us, "About six to eight weeks before training dates are upcoming we send out notices to churches and ask them to put it in their church bulletin. . . . That is usually where our volunteers come from." Some Conservative churches do public demonstrations and lobbying, but more spend their persuasive energies on individual women who are contemplating abortions.

Another popular national event that draws Conservatives into a public demonstration of their views is the annual "March for Jesus." The idea began in England in the 1980s and has spread to 130 nations. Although not explicitly political, it is often the occasion for demonstrations of conservative political sentiment. Recently it has been combined with "Jesus Day," during which Christians offer everything from neighborhood cleanups to free car washes as a way to demonstrate their love for the community. The March for Jesus Web site describes the whole event as a chance " to praise and worship our Lord and King and to pray for our city and state governments."[32]

These Conservative efforts are the exception, however. Political advocacy is still more common in the Mainline, African American, and Jewish traditions, where it has been more at home for most of the last century. In contrast to the explicitly religious national advocacy groups with which Conservative Protestants and Catholics partner, congregations in these other traditions are much more likely to choose secular partners. Mainline congregations were more likely to provide support to groups such as Amnesty International, the Sierra Club, and Physicians for Social Responsibility than to seek out religiously based organizations, even those, such as Interfaith Alliance, that seek to mobilize liberal Christians. Bread for the World was the only faith-based justice-oriented lobbying group mentioned more than once by the Mainline congregations in which we interviewed.[33]

Secular nonprofits are the organizational vehicle of choice in education and self-help, as well as—for the Mainline—in public advocacy. These activities themselves may seem less explicitly religious, and they are not included by most congregations as part of their sense of mission, falling instead into the larger world of voluntary benevolence. Still, it would be a mistake to dismiss the theological motives that blend civic and religious virtue together for many Mainline Protestants. Having largely invented organized civic voluntarism in the wake of New England disestablishment, liberal Protestants retain a strong sense that they serve God in the work they do for their communities (Hall forthcoming).

As with any other voluntary organizational activity, size and resources play a role in what gets done through secular nonprofits, but the shape of the networks of connection comes from the religious traditions themselves and from the work to be done. The history of Mainline Protestantism has given it both a broad mandate for community betterment and an impulse for broad-based cooperation that result in widespread inclusion of secular nonprofits in the network of congregational outreach partners.

GOVERNMENT CONNECTIONS

Sometimes congregations support organizations that lobby for changes in government policy, but they also work *with* governmental institutions to improve the well-being of persons and communities. We have already noted that most nonprofit agencies—religious and secular—are themselves recipients of state funds. Congregations are therefore indirect partners with government, when both institutions support the work of community agencies. But congregations themselves also sometimes partner directly with governmental units of various sorts.

Most common of all are connections with schools, and most often those connections involve tutoring and other support programs. A Seattle Presbyterian church reported that they run a "tutoring program for kids from the local elementary school who come . . . after school. They're kind of latchkey kids, and they get tutored, and they play games. . . . The bus comes and drops them off." Another Presbyterian church, this one in Nashville, reported: "Every year we work with the teachers and administration of a rural school in Williamson County. . . . We have this offering during Christmas and buy about thirty bikes and bags of stuff. They are left at the school, and the school gives them to the parents so that the parents end up as the giver of the gifts." In both cases school staff work with church staff and volunteers to make the program work. They identify needy children and distribute information, while these churches provide money, space, and volunteers to enhance the work of the school.

Congregations are also often partners in public projects that are run by parks and police departments. Some supply chaplains to police departments, for instance, assisting both police and victims in crisis situations. In other cases the cooperation is more proactive. In Chicago a number of congregations participate in the CAPS (Chicago Alternative Policing Strategy) program. The pastor of a good-sized National Baptist church claimed, "We were able to bring the community together through this program not to solve their problems, but to show them they can't live without each other." He went on to talk about how important this is to the congregation's sense of mission and how many of his members are still involved. Does he still promote the organization? "Oh yes," he said, "whenever I meet with people. We give out flyers every month."

Congregations also get involved after cases make their way to court. In Chicago, as well as in Nashville and in Missouri, we found congregations that send volunteers to be CASAs (court-appointed special advocates). Still other congregations work with prison administrators to provide religious services and personal support to people who are incarcerated. Sometimes they work through larger religious nonprofits, like Prison Fellowship Ministries (the organization founded by Watergate figure Charles Colson), but much more often we found congregations initiating their own connections with prisons in their areas.

These connections to public agencies are much more common among the Christian churches than among any of the other groups we surveyed. One activist Reform Jewish temple in Chicago has connections to public schools and serves as a polling place. A couple of non-Christian groups work in prisons, and one LDS ward is involved in a local park project. Otherwise, Christian churches are the ones that reported being called by police and welfare departments, schools and park services. One church in Hartford even provides resources for special activities at the public library.

In both of our rural locations, churches have especially close working relationships with the county welfare office. Social workers know which churches to call when there are emergency needs. In Alabama a Christmas gift-giving operation has been set up and run by volunteers, virtually as an adjunct to the Department of Human Resources (DHR). A local Southern Baptist pastor described it this way:

> We do it through the emergency center and through DHR. . . . They list the children's list of what they want for Christmas, and we put it in a book by families. . . . We clear them through DHR to find out what their actual income really is and what they're getting. . . . We've adopted out anywhere from hundred to two hundred families a year, and every time we've adopted, we bought everything on the list—every piece of clothing they asked for and every toy they asked for. . . . All [the churches] go to Project Hope. It's a great system, you know, and there again, DHR helps us. It's our community.

Where governmental programs and services fall short, social workers, police, teachers, and even librarians, in communities all over the country, call on congregations to fill the gap. Such cooperation with governmental entities is by no means rare. Almost a third (29%) of all congregations provide space, volunteers, and other support to the efforts of city and county governments and agencies.

MAKING THE WORLD A BETTER PLACE

Congregations often understand their task to involve acts of concrete caring for their communities and the world beyond. The "parachurch" and nonprofit sectors have increasingly become the organizational vehicle through which individual compassion is channeled and social services are delivered (Wuthnow 1998b). That network of organizations does not exist on its own as a replacement for traditional institutions, however. Rather, it is connected in complex ways to existing religious organizations and their members. Our data do not suggest, for instance, that connections to these extra-denominational outreach organizations have any negative effect on a congregation's giving to their own denomination or to their sense of identification with it. The more denominationally loyal are no less active than the more independent-minded (something we will explore in more detail in the next chapter). This local service work poses no significant organizational competition for the work denominations do. The impulse to do such work through a variety of organizational channels is so embedded in American culture that complementarity more than competition seems to describe the situation. Congregations have adopted social service organizations into their organizational network.

Some of the work of caring is done by individual congregations, and much of it is done because congregations encourage their individual members to be good citizens. But a very significant portion takes the form of cooperative activity. By creating informal coalitions, providing seedbeds for and resources to religious and secular nonprofits, and serving as partners to governmental organizations, congregations enter into the network of care through which social services are delivered. Almost all congregations participate in this work to one degree or another, but Mainline Protestant ones are distinctive in both the amount and types of their participation. They are more connected than others, and they are more likely to make connections with organizations that are not explicitly religious. The practice of working across religious and secular boundaries is part of the Mainline heritage, as is the habit of tending to this-worldly material needs of those beyond their own membership. They are more involved in immediate relief efforts and in providing educational, cultural, and self-help programs for their communities. Together with

African American and Catholic churches, they exceed others in forming alliances for community benefit and policy advocacy. Again, particular religious traditions shape the way congregations respond to the larger institutional expectations for how they do their work.

Overwhelmingly, interorganizational involvement is aimed at assisting the needy and providing services that enhance the general well-being of local communities. Local means much more than immediate neighborhoods, however. Congregations are not, for the most part, "parishes" tending to those within walking distance. Their own members are likely to be scattered,[34] and congregations themselves are participants in metropolitan and countywide organizations that link them in cross-town relationships as much as in neighborhood ties. Not only do these connections get work done, but they also lay a foundation for significant bridging of diverse urban and suburban populations.

Some service-oriented ties also link congregations to organizations with a larger national and international agenda. Some congregations establish partnerships that enable them to assist in disaster relief and long-term development in far corners of the earth. Others are stretched beyond their local and regional base when they seek social change through lobbying and advocacy. There are differences across the various religious traditions in how and whether they engage this sort of outreach work, but the large majority are involved to one degree or another.

PARTNERS FOR MISSIONARY OUTREACH

When congregations support missionary outreach they employ organizational strategies that differ significantly from the strategies that shape the work of social benevolence. Missionary work is supported by a more distinct segment of American congregations and involves national and international connections more than local ones. Almost two-thirds (62%) of all national and international outreach connections are in pursuit of evangelism. When the overseas goals are relief and development, it is also disproportionately religious organizations to which congregations turn. Doing good in today's global environment takes on a very different organizational shape from the local partnerships we have just been examining.

The religious impulse to reach beyond the nearby world is by no means a novel product of twenty-first-century globalization, however. Nor was it always so distinctly confined to Conservative Protestant denominations. U.S. overseas missionary work began in 1810, in Bradford, Massachusetts, when Congregationalists (successors to the Puritans and precursors to today's United Church of Christ) formed the American Board of Commissioners for Foreign Missions. In the midst of New England's most pious and learned communities a new conviction had begun to take hold—the gospel must be preached to every soul on earth. Matthew 28:19 had commanded "Go ye therefore and teach all nations," and in those days of expanding spiritual (and technological) energy, that command suddenly took on new meaning.

The British missionary pioneer William Carey was already ministering in India; and in 1812 the first American missionaries—Adonirum and Ann Hasseltine Judson and Samuel and Harriet Newell—set sail to join him there.[35] They were but the first of thousands of American "foreign missionaries" who would follow, and the agencies that sent and supported them were among the most important players in the formation of distinctly American forms of religious organization. By the middle of the nineteenth century, perhaps two thousand American missionaries had been sent overseas, primarily to the Middle East and the Indian subcontinent (Hutchison 1987, 45).

Mission societies sprang up in an atmosphere of expanding American democracy, freedom to form voluntary associations, widespread education, and economic inventiveness, a combination contemporary evangelicals saw creating a "'fulness of time' for the world's conversion."[36] It was an era when conversion, democracy, and material well-being were as yet inseparable in American benevolence. In tracing the origins of American systems of social welfare, sociologist Theda Skocpol argues that "no one has yet found any substitute for the democratic energy unleashed historically by the best in American's tradition of Biblically inspired associationalism" (Skocpol 2000, 47). The American way of organizing—voluntary and democratic efforts to change the world—shaped and was shaped by Christian mission pioneers.

From the beginning, women were in the thick of it. As early as 1800, Mary Webb had organized the Boston Female Society for Missionary Purposes, and in the middle decades of the century women were especially active in creating new missions organizations (Robert 1997, 192–93). First the interdenominational Woman's Union Missionary Society (in 1861) and then a succession of denominational societies (in the 1870s and 1880s) harnessed the passion and piety of American Christian women in behalf of the women and girls of the rest of the world.[37] "Woman's mission to woman" was the rallying cry, as American women worked to support the education and liberation they saw as a natural consequence of Christian conversion (Robert 1997, 115–30). They collected funds and sustained networks of meetings and correspondence that were soon recognized (if sometimes grudgingly) as critical to the entire missions enterprise (Yohn 2000). It is no accident that the staunchest supporters of a Woman's Convention as part of the fledgling National Baptist Convention were the leaders of its Foreign Mission Board (Higginbotham 1993, 156–57).

That combination of Christian conversion, Western education, democratic ideals (and capitalist imperialism) remained the complicated mix that constituted American missions throughout the century. As the United States grew in military and economic power and embarked on an empire of its own, inevitably America's multifaceted incursions into foreign territory would yield tangled purposes, an entanglement between missions and imperialism that would eventually cause some liberal Protestants to disavow and even pay reparations for the cultural damage they believed they had done. But in the early twentieth century such regret was still long in the future.

In the middle of the nineteenth century the early independent mission societies had given way to agencies organized along denominational lines, but it was not long before the denominational mission societies were again joined by new nondenominational groups such as the Student Volunteer Movement and Christian Endeavor, along with a variety of new "faith missions," such as the China Inland Mission (founded 1865) and Africa Inland Mission (founded 1895).[38] The enthusiasm for missions had outstripped the ability of denominational agencies to keep up with it. As the world was slowly opening up to trade (even "inland"), and travel was becoming safer, missions advocates like A. T. Pierson proclaimed the goal of 'evangelization of the world in this generation.'

A growing number of faith mission recruits were also adherents of a premillennial theology that added new urgency to the notion of evangelization. If the Second Coming of Christ was imminent, then mission preaching was essential. As a result, evangelists began to put verbal proclamation of the Christian gospel ahead of any other humanitarian goals. Rather than expecting to see God's kingdom on earth, they worked in feverish anticipation of a Final Judgment and the end of this world. That shift in emphasis was the precursor of battles that would rage throughout the twentieth century and of the lingering split between benevolent and missionary outreach.[39]

Should missionary activity be primarily about literally preaching the gospel, or should it be about an evangelism that includes education, health, economic development, and (eventually) human rights? In 1910 the elite leaders of the Western world's mission organizations gathered in Edinburgh for a conference that would begin liberal Protestantism's movement from activist missionary preaching to the ecumenism of the later World Council of Churches (founded in 1948). On the other side of the theological fence, a fundamentalist movement in America would increasingly condemn the liberal "social gospel" (Hutchison 1987, 125). As Hutchison puts it, traditional mission enthusiasts "prided themselves on knowing the difference between an altar call and an invitation to the YMCA picnic," while a growing contingent of liberals wanted Christianity to heed its own Golden Rule and do unto other religions what we would want them to do unto us (147). The tensions were real and began to result in new evangelical mission societies not tainted with such perceived heresy.

Liberal ideas about missions reached their apex in the 1932 report *Rethinking Missions.* The result of a Rockefeller-financed research effort and dominated by Harvard philosopher William Ernest Hocking, this book signaled the demise of the nineteenth-century wedding of education, development, health, and Christian conversion, at least in the minds of the liberal Protestants who sponsored it. It was also a signal that came just as many women's missionary societies were being absorbed, often over vigorous protest, into the growing male-dominated bureaucracies of American denominations (Primer 1978). The grassroots energy of women's compassion and fund-raising was subverted at the same time that male elites proclaimed foreign missions passé (Brereton 1991).

By the 1960s and 1970s, many Mainline Protestant denominations were out of the overseas missions business entirely, and most of those that remained were working in cooperation with indigenous churches. In 1935 Presbyterians had twenty-one hundred overseas missionaries, Methodists had nearly fourteen hundred, and Episcopalians had over four hundred. In 1999 they had 772, 413, and 21, respectively (Noll 2002). But that retreat from the field by the denominations that had pioneered and dominated the nineteenth-century movement by no means signaled the demise of an American mission force scattered throughout the world (Stark 2001). The mirror image of these declining numbers can be found in denominations such as the Southern Baptists (who went from 405 to 4,562 in the same period) and the Assemblies of God (which went from 230 to 1,543). In addition, hundreds of new independent mission-sending agencies have been founded and now support personnel in numbers that rival or exceed the total of missionaries supported by all American denominations combined.

Ironically, even within Mainline Protestantism, rump mission agencies, such as the Good News movement in Methodism, continued to capture the imagination of people in the pews. Indeed, more than two-thirds (69%) of the individual Mainline members we surveyed said that it was very important or extremely important to them that their congregations support "mission efforts in the nation and the world." Supporting those efforts, however, was likely to require a Mainline congregation to look beyond its own denomination's activities.

Sending and supporting missionaries is not something any single congregation can do. This sort of global outreach has, from the beginning, required organizations that could pool the resources of American churchgoers. For some congregations missionary support remains central to how they do good in the world, and for those congregations both denominations and other agencies form the network of partners on which they depend. The organizational connections between congregations and missionary work take both monetary and personal forms that are different from the way local service work is organized. Partnerships for the sake of global evangelization entail routine budgetary contributions to denominations, special offerings for the support of that work, and direct support for specific projects. Outside the denomination, parachurch agencies garner a similar array of budgeted support, special offerings, and project support (see Table 17).

The patterns shown in Table 17 include only congregations in the Christian traditions, since (with a handful of exceptions) Jewish and other non-Christian groups rarely have missionary goals and do not pursue collectively organized missionary work. For opposite reasons the notion of partnering with missionary agencies makes no sense in the Sectarian traditions either. Jehovah's Witnesses do not have a separate corps of missionaries because every member is, by definition, a "publisher" who spends significant time each week evangelizing (Holden 2002); and Mormons have a mission corps, but it largely consists of thousands of youth who spend two years in whatever place the Church needs them. The pattern is to deputize each lay member for evangelization, rather than working through separate mission organizations.

The Catholic and Orthodox parishes we studied were among the least likely to say that missions and evangelization are important parish priorities. That does not mean, however, that there is no missions history on which to draw or larger Church support for evangelization. Long before there were Protestant mission boards, Catholic and Orthodox missionaries were taking their faiths to the far reaches of their respective nations' empires. Orthodox evangelists established the faith in Alaska, for instance, while Fransciscan friars established missions throughout what would become the American Southwest.[40] But today most ordinary lay Catholic and Orthodox members do not think they should try to convert their neighbors, and evangelism rarely ranked among top parish priorities. The consistent exception we found was the Antiochan Orthodox parish in Chicago that consists of

TABLE 17 Support for National and International Evangelistic and Missionary
Activity by Christian Congregations

Type of Support	Mainline Protestant	Conservative Protestant	Independent Protestant	African American Protestant	Catholic & Orthodox
Denominational Activity					
Average percentage of budget to denomination*	12.5	11.9	n.a.	2.5	7.2
Average amount to denomination*	$17,601	$19,030	n.a.	($6,628)[a]	$37,154
Denomination's mission activity mentioned as valuable (%)*	30	42	n.a.	29	9
Directly support at least one denominational missionary or project (%)	11	7	n.a.	0	7
Percentage of members who give >$100 to "mission offerings" at church*	41	60	n.a.	66	39
Nondenominational Activity					
Support at least one project, missionary, or organization outside the denomination (%)*	21	36	42	15	3
Average congregational donations to nondenominational missionary work*	$278	$1,687	$13,343	$42	0

TABLE 17 (continued)

Type of Support	Mainline Protestant	Conservative Protestant	Independent Protestant	African American Protestant	Catholic & Orthodox
Percentage of members who give >$100 to "other religious causes"*	30	56	40	42	34

NOTE: For items marked with an asterisk at least one of the differences among the groups is statistically significant at p < .10 (Oneway ANOVA, with Scheffe post-hoc comparisons).

[a] Data are missing for 23 of 51 congregations interviewed. This amount probably overestimates the actual average.

former evangelical Protestants. Like many others within that branch of Orthodoxy, they have a strong emphasis on missionary work, and they have adopted the Conservative Protestant habit of doing at least some of that work through independent, nondenominational mission agencies. They account for the only extra-denominational mission efforts we found in the Catholic and Orthodox traditions (see Table 17).

In spite of the absence of an evangelical emphasis among most individual members and many parishes, there are many Catholic organizations that seek to "propagate the faith," and at least a few parishes that specifically support the work of missionaries. The vast majority of Catholic missionary activity, however, is supported through the Church's various communities of women and men religious and therefore indirectly through the offerings individuals give on Sunday. About a quarter of the parishes in which we interviewed mentioned a specific missionary project or offering they promote, but in most places the round of "second offerings" (all of which are officially sanctioned Church collections) is the way people think about supporting Church missionary activity. And that activity is considerable. In 1997 over four thousand American Catholic missionaries were serving full-time overseas. That number was down from 6,782 in 1960, but a growing number of overseas personnel are lay church members who serve short-term missions. Like the members of many Protestant churches, lay Catholics are increasingly getting directly involved in their Church's mission work.

Catholics in the United States are also among the largest contributors to the worldwide Church's Society for the Propagation of the Faith (SPF), specifically mentioned by six of our forty-five Catholic parishes; and the Maryknoll Fathers and Brothers (along with the Maryknoll Sisters) have been a visible American Catholic presence throughout the world as well. Theirs has been a special concern to witness for justice and peace, proclaiming the Christian gospel in a way that honors the cultures in which they work (Froehle and Gautier 2000, 102–5). The Church's overseas work includes a broad mix of traditional evangelization, benevolent activities, and more radical work in pursuit of social change. To a certain extent parishes can choose one activity over another for special emphasis (SPF, for instance, over Catholic Relief Services). Most parishes, however, support the suggested round of collections, responding to whatever special appeals may come their way.

The various Orthodox Churches in North America have a similar mix of agendas in their efforts at national and international mission work. International Orthodox Christian Charities (IOCC) was established in March 1992 as the official international humanitarian organization of the Standing Conference of Canonical Orthodox Bishops in the Americas, a collective gathering of archbishops representing Orthodox bodies ranging from the very large Greek community to smaller groups such as Serbs and Ethiopians. The IOCC, modeling itself after Catholic Relief Services, distributes aid and fosters development activities, largely in the regions where Orthodoxy has historically been strong. But that same body of bishops has also issued a statement on missions and evangelism. They proclaimed (in part),

> It is our conviction that mission is the very nature of the Church, and is an essential expression of her apostolicity, and that the Orthodox Church is therefore commanded by the Lord Jesus Christ to teach, to preach, and to make disciples of all nations . . .
>
> We believe that our task in North America is not limited to serving the immigrant and ethnic communities, but has at its very heart the missionary task, the task of making disciples in the nations of Canada and the United States.[41]

This statement, inspired in part by the Antiochan archbishop, finds expression in the Orthodox Christian Mission Center, headquartered in St. Augustine, Florida. Since 1985, that center has been sending long-term missionaries around the world to seek converts and establish new Orthodox communities; it is enthusiastically supported by the Antiochan Orthodox parish in which we interviewed.

This stands in contrast to other Orthodox communities. Like Roman Catholics, their religious traditions have a long history of missionary activity, and there are agencies still charged with carrying on evangelization, but local parishes and individual members rarely define their faith in evangelistic terms. When local parish leaders talked about the benefits of being part of a larger tradition, they almost never mentioned cooperative missionary activity. The average parish reported sending a little over 7 percent of its operating budget to the diocese (which still amounted to a hefty $37,000; see Table 17), but that money was more likely thought of as general Church and charitable support than as a way to help convert the world.

African American Protestants have a very different mission history and a strong local and individual commitment to evangelism that contrasts sharply with the Catholic and Orthodox patterns. Black church members are as likely as white Conservatives to say that their churches should have strong evangelism programs and that individuals should try to win others to Christ. They are also as likely as other Protestants to talk about their connection to their denomination in terms of its evangelistic and missionary work (see Table 17). Indeed. the typical name for a church in the National Baptist Convention is "Missionary Baptist."

From the beginning, however, it was apparent that missionary activity would be an ambiguous enterprise for African Americans. As early as 1815, a black Baptist missionary was sent out by the African Baptist Missionary Society, headquartered in Richmond, Virginia. That missionary, Lott Carey, like his Methodist pioneer counterpart, Daniel Coker, was sent to the West African colony of Liberia, established for the repatriation of freed slaves. The interests of white Americans (both paternalistic and overtly racist) intertwined in complicated ways with the missionary zeal of black Americans. White and black church bodies often combined efforts in early missionary organizations, and women's missionary societies became meeting grounds for women on both sides of the color line (Scott 1993). Higginbotham concludes that "notwithstanding its imperfections, interracial cooperation between black and white Baptist women did find concrete ways to offer hope and opportunity" (Higginbotham 1993, 119).

In the years after the Civil War, a number of independent Home and Foreign Mission Societies were formed by African Americans to send evangelists and teachers into the South and the West as well as to Africa (S. Martin 1982). In the years surrounding the beginning of the twentieth century, those societies were largely brought under the umbrellas of the emerging national African American denominations (Lincoln and Mamiya 1990). They were not central, however, to the identity of those emerging organizations. Establishing publishing boards and fighting for justice were higher priorities than sending missionaries (Washington 1986, 136).

Today, the National Baptist Convention cooperates informally with the Lott Carey Foreign Mission Society, but it has its own internal Foreign Missionary

Society as well. Few of the black Baptist churches in our sample, however, identified any sort of cooperative effort—missionary or otherwise—as a reason for denominational participation. By contrast, about half (four of seven) of the churches in the three black Methodist traditions (AME, AMEZ, and CME) talked about valuing denominational missionary work. At a small AME church in Nashville, we heard about how the women's missionary society uses mission study books to learn about work in Africa and the Caribbean. In addition, they "take up a mission offering every Sunday. . . . some of it goes to the general church, and the general church sends it out to Africa and the third world countries and what not." The stronger organizational structures in the Methodist traditions (including a women's missionary society) are reflected in this connection between local churches and national and international missionary work.

But none of the churches in these historic African American denominations named specific mission projects they were supporting or talked about a missionary they knew. Nor do they provide significant monetary support to a denominational structure that will do the work for them. Few Baptist churches, for instance, give more than what is required for attending the annual national convention, and they are rarely mobilized by any national body in pursuit of world evangelization. In spite of a long history of missionary work, African American Protestants do not have an organizational infrastructure that can support extensive activity today.

While missionary partnerships are a significant organizational presence in many Christian congregations, they are least prevalent in African American churches and in Catholic and Orthodox parishes. The organizational pattern for missionary support is largely shaped by the white evangelical Protestants who have dominated the movement since the middle of the twentieth century.

WHITE PROTESTANTS—VARIETIES OF PARTNERS AND VARIETIES OF ACTION

Within the predominantly white Protestant traditions, the twentieth-century split between missionary and "social gospel" work is clearly present—but not as neatly as we might suppose. As we have seen, members of Mainline Protestant churches generally say they support national and international mission work, but their pastors most often (60%) said that evangelism and missions are "somewhat" or "not at all" important, with only a small minority (13%) of congregational leaders in the Mainline traditions ranking evangelism and mission among the most important parish priorities. Among Conservative Protestants, by contrast, nearly all local leaders (92%) said that evangelism was *at least* "very important," if not essential.

Eighty-four percent of the attenders we surveyed in Conservative Protestant churches agreed, saying that supporting mission efforts was "very" or "extremely important" to them.

While Conservative Protestant churches were much more likely to name evangelism as a priority, each congregation's own sense of mission, rather than the tradition itself, is the mechanism that pushes them into missionary partnerships. Mission-minded Conservative churches were no more connected to organizational partners than missions-minded Mainline ones. Where the individual congregation named evangelism as a central priority, connections with missions organizations were more extensive—whether that congregation is Presbyterian or Baptist, UCC or Nazarene. Evangelistically oriented churches are both more likely to see their denominations as a valuable mission partner *and* more likely to have established a connection to at least one parachurch mission organization.

Congregations with fewer resources seem to direct them to their denominations first. Links to parachurch agencies are less likely among the smallest congregations. Small rural congregations were especially likely to talk about how their denominations help them to be part of a much larger enterprise. In a sermon we heard in rural Missouri, the pastor reminded his small congregation that "there are Southern Baptists in 150 countries, and they are supported, in part, by us." An Alabama Assembly of God pastor talked about the concrete assistance they give to missionaries, "giving them vehicles to travel with in their work, whether it's a bicycle, if it's needed, or a moped or if it needs to be a automobile. We participate in that."

While many liberal denominations have scaled back their missionary efforts, Conservative and Pentecostal denominations make missionary support one of the primary foci of denominational investment. A comparison between the Episcopal Church and the Seventh-Day Adventists is instructive here. Both are hierarchically organized globally based churches, but with roughly half as many U.S. members, Adventists support more than ten times the overseas personnel, an equivalent mission budget, and a relief and development budget that dwarfs Episcopal efforts.[42] In 2000 the Episcopal Church made about $7 million in development grants, while the Adventist agency handed out $107 million. Both are active in redefining missions as a global enterprise, rather than solely one involving missionaries from the North Atlantic going to the developing world. While the Adventists have not yet reached their goal of having missionaries sent *from* all of the 204 countries in which there are Adventist churches, they have reached a point where there are as many non-North Americans here as there are North Americans elsewhere in the world. Anglicans spend most of their overseas mission budget in support of existing

Anglican churches in parts of the world that were formerly colonized, but there is little discussion of those churches sending missionaries to the United States.

Note that both denominations spend substantial money on relief and development as well as on direct evangelism. Michael Hamilton claims that in 1992 all categories of U.S. Protestant overseas ministry activity amounted to $2.27 billion. Over half was raised by parachurch groups, and the largest of these are now heavily committed to humanitarian work along with evangelization (World Vision being the largest). Another third of the total overseas ministry budget came from the Conservative Protestant denominations, and as the Adventist example demonstrates, a significant portion of those budgets went to humanitarian aid as well. Less than one-sixth of all overseas ministry dollars were raised by the Mainline Protestant denominations (Hamilton 2000, 119). Even if every dollar they raised went to relief and development, Mainline churches would ironically be far outstripped by the evangelical denominations and parachurch agencies in providing overseas *material* aid. Whether in a Conservative church or a liberal one, links to overseas ministry are likely to involve both spiritual and material dimensions. The religious impulses of the American people continue to be channeled into significant organizing on behalf of people around the world who are in need. The agencies and denominations that embody those impulses also establish critical bridges between large segments of the American public and ordinary citizens of the rest of the world.

The resulting connections are, indeed, increasingly likely to have a personal face. While pastors may think of denominations in terms of pension plans or seminaries or district superintendents who make periodic visits, their congregations are likely to think of denominations in terms of the missionaries who arrive each fall or spring with stories of cross-cultural adventure and spiritual triumph. Dana Robert muses, "No churchgoer born before 1960 can forget the childhood thrill of hearing a missionary speak in church. . . . In an age before round-the-clock television news, and the immigration of Asians and Latin Americans even to small towns in the Midwest, the missionary on furlough was a major link between the world of North American Christians and the rest of the globe" (Robert 2002, 59). In many congregations those born after 1960 continue building such memories; but the stories they know are now made even more vivid by missionary Web sites and e-mail correspondence that reaches the remotest mission stations. Wherever we found vibrant missionary connections, they almost always had a personal dimension.

Much as World Vision and the Christian Children's Fund have personalized overseas charity by inviting people to sponsor a specific child, some denominations have created similar sponsorship programs. Connections to missions are embodied in persons and stories, and many denominations are intent on making both widely available. An emphasis on missions is relatively unusual in the Mainline Protestant tradition, but where denominations have enabled these direct connections to missionaries and mission projects they are thriving. Connections have a similar impact for Conservative Protestants. At a large Southern Baptist church in Nashville, the pastor reported a recent upsurge in missions interest. "We had a couple of people last year to go on a mission trip, and they came back and shared it with the church, and it just ignited," he said. Some Conservative denominations have long institutionalized direct missionary connections. Rather than supporting a general fund, churches give to specific denominational missionaries. They may put pictures and recent news on a prominent bulletin board at the church, keep in touch via e-mail, and sponsor an annual mission convention or festival. A Nashville Assemblies of God church reported that they "have an international banquet and decorate the rooms like the countries." Organizing direct connections between congregations and missions projects has now become so pervasive across denominations that it is as likely in one Protestant church as in another (8 percent of all churches in white Protestant denominations).

Direct mission involvement of church members adds new stories to those supplied by denominational mission books and historic mission lore. As we saw in Chapter 5, mission support activities in local churches often begin with stories told to toddlers in their weekday Bible club, but they now extend to the stories brought home by adult volunteers who have seen the work firsthand. Short-term volunteer mission trips are increasingly popular across American Protestantism, accounting, as we noted earlier, for one sector of growth in the Catholic overseas force as well.

This is, again, not an exclusively Conservative strategy. Mainline groups are just as likely to send out teams. Only resources seem to stand in the way. Congregations with the tiniest budgets (under $50,000 per year) were much less likely to have any sort of direct connection with a denominational missionary or project (4 percent of them, compared to 11 percent of congregations with more adequate budgets). They are also less likely to support parachurch mission agencies. Basic local necessities leave little room for extra mission connections of any sort. Routine contributions to a denominational budget are the sole mission connection most of these smallest churches can afford.

In the denominational churches, small and large, many of the traditional mechanisms of connection are still in place. Nineteenth-century mission-minded women took inspiration from the New Testament story of the widow who gave her last "mite" as an offering in the Temple. In her honor, American women created "mite boxes," and some denominations still use them today. Members of the Lutheran Women's Missionary League routinely dump their spare change in a box at home. Then, as an LCMS pastor in Chicago explained, "in each church we have a box that's big. It has a slot in the top, and the ladies just drop their boxes when they're full into there, and someone counts it, and each chapter sends their money in, and it adds up real quick." Hundreds of thousands of dollars each year. These sorts of combined efforts allow even the smallest church to feel that it is part of the task of spreading the gospel throughout the world. Another Chicago LCMS pastor said, "I always bring that up—that our little congregation is all over the world, and . . . at the end of our year, our ladies have about $1,700 that we give to missionaries."

Women have been the mainstays of the connection between local churches and the overseas mission enterprise, but men have become part of the network of support as well, especially in the Conservative Protestant denominations. Like the Convoy of Hope in the Assemblies of God denomination, men's groups tend to be active and "hands-on." They channel volunteers and material support directly between local congregations and distant mission fields. After the World Trade Center disaster, American Baptist Men organized teams from around the country for the task of cleaning apartments in the affected areas.[43] Denominational organizations provide the connections that enable individuals and local congregations to extend their mission far beyond an immediate local community.

But denominations are not the only partners that congregations have for expanding their evangelistic efforts around the world. From the beginning there have been nondenominational mission agencies, and in the period since 1930 those agencies have played an increasingly important role (Carpenter 1980). It has been estimated that by sometime in the 1950s the number of evangelical missionaries sponsored by these independent agencies passed the number sponsored by the older denominations (Klay, Lunn, and Hamilton 2000, 35). That balance is not reflected, however, in the way congregations allocate their support. Parachurch agencies have achieved organizational strength that rivals the denominations, but their base is largely individual contributors. Congregations still predominantly do their mission work through denominational channels. If we were to guess that, on average, 15 percent of the money congregations give to their denominations (see Table 17) goes to the denomination's evangelism and mission programs,[44] then the average Conservative Protestant church gives more to missions through its denomination than through parachurch agencies ($2,854 vs. $1,687). Mainline denominational giving exceeds parachurch mission dollars almost ten to one ($2,640 vs. $278).

In all the denominations, individual members were more likely to report a substantial gift to a mission offering at church (over and above their regular giving) than to report a similar gift to any other religious cause. In the Mainline denominations only one church in six reported sending money to any missionary activity or organization beyond its own denomination. The proportion among Conservative Protestant churches is twice that high, but still only one in three. Links to parachurch agencies are widespread within Conservative Protestantism, but they are by no means the whole story.

Nor are parachurch connections being engaged at the expense of the denominational ones. The differences in denominational giving between parachurch givers and nonparachurch givers are not statistically significant. It appears that congregational giving beyond the denomination is increasing the overall amount of money going to missions, rather than taking dollars out of one pocket and putting them into another. Similarly, more personal and direct connections to specific projects is likely increasing overall giving to the denomination. Churches that have a direct connection to a denominational mission project are more generous in their budget allocations to the denomination. The pattern we often found in Conservative Protestant churches was a combination of denominational mission engagement alongside support for at least some parachurch mission effort. A large Chicago Reformed Church in America congregation was typical. As the pastor ran through the long list of causes they support, he said, "For example, three of these missionaries are directly out of the Reformed Church. One of them . . . is a family out of this congregation who has gone on mission with Wycliffe." The connections are personal and direct, as well as organizational, and they combine support for the denomination's own programs with support for one of the largest parachurch agencies—Wycliffe Bible Translators.

Among nondenominational churches, of course there is no denomination to which to give; but not all of these independent churches reported giving to parachurch mission agencies, either. All of them are evangelical in orientation, but less than half (42%) had established partnerships with evangelical agencies or individual missionaries. Where they do have connections, their average contributions are, not surprisingly, considerably higher than the parachurch contributions coming from Conservative churches that are part of denominational systems. Again, if we guess that 15 percent of a Conservative church's denominational contribution goes to missions, the combination of that money and what they give to parachurch mission groups ($2,854 + $1,687) is only about a third of what the average independent church spends on missions. Not all independent churches are mission-minded or mission-connected, but those that are put significant resources into the task. As a result, independent churches supply an important base of support for the para-church agencies.

Still, denominational Protestant churches outnumber nondenominational ones about seven to one. Neither nondenominational churches nor nondenominational religious agencies have yet established the kind of dominance in American religion that some commentators have seemed to imply. At least for now, the typical Christian congregation is affiliated with a denomination and gives most of its mission dollars through that denomination. Its most ambitious reach beyond its own four walls continues to be facilitated by the denominational organizations that grew out of the missionary impulse. Indeed, the newer parachurch organizations have harnessed that same missionary impulse to become significant partners to Conservative and independent churches, supplementing more than displacing traditional denominational connections.

Denominations certainly do not have a monopoly, but neither are they disappearing. Unlike local efforts at social service, the large majority of national and international congregational partners are religious, rather than secular. But the work they do is as much about feeding the hungry as about preaching the Christian gospel. "Doing missions" remains a powerful motive for connection—both with religious organizations beyond the local congregation and with causes beyond the local community.

Denominations, however, are more than mere mission agencies—even if overseas evangelism and humanitarian relief are a primary function in the minds of many of their members. Denominations are also about family ties and tradition, creeds and hymns, heroes and founders, even friends and enemies. We now turn to that more subtle form of organizing.

CHAPTER SEVEN · Nurturing Traditions

Stories and Practices for Religious Pilgrims

Congregations provide a place from which works of compassion can be organized, but also a place where communities can be formed, morality encouraged, and connections with the divine nurtured. They are places that stand within particular streams of religious tradition at the same time that what they do is both enabled and constrained by the individual and collective resources of their members, as well as by an American culture that expects congregations to encompass a predictable range of activities. Virtually nothing they do is possible without the support of outside organizations. Looked at from one angle, the web of connection we have documented here is hopelessly complex, even chaotic. It includes independent publishers and secular charities, parachurch mission agencies and local religious supply houses, an international Christian music industry and local ministerial associations—to name but a few of the connections we have encountered in our journey through American congregational life. The organizational field surrounding congregations is so vast that it is easy to see why the individual choices of local communities of faith might seem utterly idiosyncratic.

But looked at from another angle, regularities can be spotted even amid the chaos. Choices tend to be made within bounds that are defined by the broad streams of tradition that have guided our journey. Within each stream, individual denominations remain the most common markers that identify the course. Indeed, as we will see, even being "nondenominational" can be a way to identify and mark the course of a religious stream. The immense pluralism of American religion retains contours that make its variations recognizable, organizing the choices available to congregations and providing the mechanisms through which they and their members establish their place in the culture.

Throughout more than three hundred years of history, the American "denominational" experiment has allowed each of many religious traditions to seek its own truth, set up its own internal governance, and organize its own voluntary associations.[1] Over the years, the system allowed increasingly diverse ethnic and religious identities to be added to the American mix—Swedish Lutherans, Polish Catholics, Scottish Presbyterians, not to mention Chinese Buddhists, Lebanese Muslims, and Hispanic Pentecostals. It also left room for entirely new religious movements and revivals of old ones. With no prescribed official religious tradition it was possible to imagine change, renewal, and innovation. It was also possible to imagine different ways of being religious, even within a given tradition. Denominationalism allowed religious and other social identities to be combined in varying proportions and with varying degrees of intensity.[2]

So pervasive are these American cultural patterns that even groups that operate very differently elsewhere behave like denominations in the United States.[3] As we have seen, new religious groups, making their way into American society, have begun to form organizations that can serve the unique needs of practitioners. There are offices to address public issues, associations to promote religious schooling, publishers to produce religious materials in English, camps for youth, and directories of places of worship. Each is shaped by the religious precepts of its own tradition, but also shaped by the organizational and cultural imperatives of working as one religious tradition among many in the American context.

Nowhere has that been more apparent than in the post–September 11 Muslim community. Perhaps half a dozen organizations moved into high gear after the tragedies of that day, providing resources to American Muslims and interpreting the community to the American public. The American Muslim Council, based in Washington, took the lead in providing public information, but the Islamic Society of North America and dozens of smaller local groups provided speakers and educational programs.[4] American Muslims have no single central authority, and there are important differences among them, but they possess a commonly recognized and distinct (if often misinterpreted) identity. What most Muslim voices asked of the American public was to be treated as a legitimate religious community just like any other—to be treated, in other words, like a denomination.

American Buddhists had faced a similar crisis in the time following Pearl Harbor and the subsequent internment of Japanese Americans. In 1944 the Buddhist

Churches of America was formed, at least in part to establish a legitimate presence for Buddhists in this country (Mann, Numrich, and Williams 2001, 33–40). As with Muslims, a single central religious authority is unlikely to emerge. That is not the way Buddhism works, but in the United States, national resource and advocacy groups provide links for the individuals and local temples that carry the Buddhist identity.

The various Hindu traditions that have gained ground in this country since 1965 are far too numerous and diverse to fall under any single organization or authority either, but Hinduism has increasingly been recognized as one of the religious voices that must be taken into account. Hundreds of temples, large and small, house both shrines and cultural activities for a scattered but growing Hindu community, but they also have a collective voice. Dozens of Web sites create a public identity and provide religious education. The newspaper *Hinduism Today*, published by a monastery in Hawaii, claims two hundred thousand readers and boasts that when American leaders need a Hindu perspective, this paper gets the call (Melwani 2000). As a "denomination" in American society, Hinduism needs offices that can send representatives and make statements, and such institutions are emerging.

Each of these groups follows in the organizational and cultural footsteps of American Jews. Denomination is not a concept native to the Jewish tradition, although Jews have had distinct subtraditions and have lived as minorities in non-Jewish societies for nearly two thousand years. But since the middle of the nineteenth century there have been distinct "denominational" divisions within Western Judaism (Lazerwitz et al. 1998; Wertheimer 1993). Each of the modern Jewish movements—Reform, Conservative, Reconstructionist—has established its own identity, practices, and institutions within the larger whole, much as individual denominations exist within Christianity. Each has a range of supportive organizations that approximates the pattern of activity found in Protestant denominations. The religious culture they help to support is thoroughly Jewish, while the institutional form they have adopted is thoroughly American.

It is not yet clear whether the newer non-Christian groups will follow a path toward internal differentiation into distinct subgroups. What is clear is that each is establishing both the organizational infrastructure and the cultural habits that will enable it to function in a denominational society.

The unregulated religious system in the United States has allowed for this growing diversity, but it does pose serious challenges to the religious groups themselves. The state offers them no external support for their programmatic activity, and the nation offers no supportive cultural identity. Each denomination has to create and sustain its own voluntary religious citizens and maintain its own territory within the larger religious and cultural terrain. As communities that recognize their partial and limited (yet still potentially powerful) place within American society, denominations must create sufficient cultural recognition to maintain a place alongside all the others and sufficient participation to sustain whatever organizational structures they create.

Recent trends in American society have made the survival of collective denominational identities a live issue. Religious seekers who create pastiche religious identities are reported to be on the rise (Roof 1999). Traditional Mainline denominations have declined in membership, and independent nondenominational churches have become more common.[5] Even among those individuals who do choose to join a denominationally affiliated congregation, the assumption is that they are much more likely to "shop" for one that suits their tastes than to choose memberships based on denominational loyalty (Marler and Roozen 1993).

This rhetoric of religious individualism and denominational decline has become so pervasive in recent years that few have bothered to question its basis. Many students of American religion have assumed that denominational loyalty is a thing of the past and that the organizational infrastructures of the major denominations have begun a precipitous and perhaps fatal decline. In the late 1980s Robert Wuthnow (1988) wrote about a major "restructuring" in American religious life, a part of which was the "decline of denominationalism." Organizationally, he claimed, denominations, while still strong, were losing their significance in a field now crowded with religious special purpose groups.[6] Culturally, he documented the degree to which education and mobility had eroded the barriers that kept denominational identities intact. Religious work was no longer being done primarily within denominational organizations, and religious identity was no longer being ascribed by them, he argued. Following Wuthnow's lead, both scholars and religious leaders have amassed evidence and anecdotes to support the premise that denominational boundaries are vanishing (Hoge, Johnson, and Luidens 1994). By concentrating on the growth of the parachurch sector and on the increasing prevalence of "switching," a general picture of institutional erosion has become the common wisdom, the dominant conceptual narrative.[7]

Much of what we have already seen in this book calls that account into question, however. We have already seen that denominations are still critical to how their constituent congregations relate to the producers and agents vying for their attention. But why? What accounts for this organizational strength, where it exists? And why do congregations and their members still use denominational identities—if they do—to locate themselves?

Denominational identity can be thought of as a particular kind of citizenship, a claim about being related to a transcendent sacred realm, having the status of a citizen in a heavenly kingdom, perhaps. But it is a way of claiming that citizenship while also recognizing other, variously defined this-worldly allegiances. Just as national citizenship is today being transformed by the realities of global economies, communication networks, and immigration, voluntary religious citizenship may be taking new shapes at the turn of this new century as well. Nations are no less real for having more permeable boundaries (Sassen 1996), and denominations are no less real because their sovereignty is nonterritorial and nonexclusive.

Denominations can create rights and obligations, but they will exercise their sovereignty in different ways. Some may do so by erecting high cultural boundaries. Christian Smith proposes that individual evangelicals, for instance, are able to maintain a strong religious identity because they belong to groups that create a "clear distinction from and significant engagement and tension with other relevant outgroups" (C. Smith 1998). While such a subcultural identity may characterize some denominations, others may maintain a sense of distinction and place by other means. Are there other organizational mechanisms—beyond tension and exclusivism—that keep denominational identities alive today?

Margaret Somers's study of early English patterns of citizenship provides some intriguing clues about how we might understand denominational citizenship. She suggests that citizenship happens in particular "relational settings," that is, in the ways "people, power, and organizations are positioned and connected." She draws our attention to the specific things people do, to the rules they follow, to the structured organizations that shape their work, to the stories they tell about who they are, and to the "binding relationships" in which they are embedded (Somers 1993, 595). If denominations are to function as viable locations for religious citizenship, we might look for the ways in which they set out a *system of rules*, establish patterns of *structural ties* for accomplishing their work, sustain a public *narrative about their identity* and purpose, and facilitate and *nurture relationships* among fellow denominational "citizens."

DOES DENOMINATIONAL CITIZENSHIP STILL EXIST?

Citizenship of a denominational sort happens on two interrelated levels involving both individuals and organizations. For individuals citizenship involves participation and relationships and stories that link a person to a denominational tradition. Organizationally, denominations are primarily sets of functional relationships among constituent units—congregations, administrative offices, seminaries, mission societies, publishers, and the like. Under most circumstances these units are bound together into a somewhat coordinated whole, with a regulated flow of resources and authority among them. Organizational function typically coincides with individual identification in that most denominational agencies are dependent on the support of the individuals and congregations that see themselves as part of the tradition and mission represented by the denomination.

The two levels do not always coincide, however. Given a large enough set of endowments (or other funding sources), it is possible to imagine that a denominational agency might exist quite independent of any individuals or local congregations that contributed to it—a state without citizens, in effect. Indeed, some established Protestant and Catholic institutions have nearly this sort of financial and structural independence. They can carry out their own organizational agendas, sometimes to the chagrin of individuals and congregations that do not recognize the voice that is presuming to speak for their tradition. Before recent restructuring, for instance, two "Big Boards" of the United Church of Christ had just such autonomy. Barman and Chaves write, "The two recognized instrumentalities had charters that predated the denomination, and they had their own endowments and constituencies that gave them a measure of wealth and independence. . . . [L]ess than five percent of the United Church Board for Homeland Ministries' 1996 income came from congregational donations" (Barman and Chaves forthcoming; quoted from manuscript). But without the citizen participation of those local congregations, they lacked cultural legitimacy. Religious agencies without citizens are more like special purpose groups than like what we have come to recognize as denominations. Indeed, in the UCC's restructuring the "Big Boards" gave up at least some of the financial autonomy that could have made them formidable independent religious special purpose groups, in favor of the cultural clout of being a more integral part of a denomination. In the American system denominations imply individuals and congregations that recognize each other as belonging to a common tradition. National organizations may give voice and action to that tradition, but without at least some connection to local constituents they cease to fill a place in the "denominated" religious landscape.

To assess whether and how denominations are fostering effective citizenship, we can begin by asking whether and how local congregations and individual members are linking their own identity and mission with the traditions carried by denominations as a whole. As we look for the detailed patterns in denominational functioning, note that it is largely the Christian groups we will assess here. Our sample does not contain enough Jewish and other non-Christian cases to make any definitive judgments about how those congregations are connected to the networks of organization and belonging that do exist in their traditions. Some comparisons will be made where they are possible, but the details of the denominational story will have to emerge from the Christian cases.

IDENTITY AND BELONGING

No simple way exists to measure identification with a religious tradition.[8] We asked our informants a number of direct questions about the degree to which their congregation "identifies strongly with the denomination," but discussion of religious identity often came up in other contexts as well. Looking back at all of what they said, the following narrative themes can be seen:

- Thirty percent described an unequivocally strong identification with their tradition, often not really knowing how to answer our questions because they could not imagine what it would mean to be anything other than strongly identified. The pastor of a very large Seventh-Day Adventist church in Nashville said, "I mean to be a Seventh-Day Adventist, you're identifying with Seventh-Day Adventism as it is expressed by the world church." Similarly, *all* of the congregations in our Sectarian category described their identity this way. It makes no sense to them to think about being only a little bit Mormon or moderately Jehovah's Witness.

- Somewhat less strongly identified were the 34 percent who more clearly recognized why we were asking these questions. Sometimes they identified with their religious tradition, but put distance between themselves and the actions of their national denomination. A variation on that theme is the identification of Independent Baptist churches with the Baptist tradition, while refusing to belong to any organized body of Baptists. Mostly, however, the people in this category were maintaining connections while recognizing just how difficult that can be. A Presbyterian pastor in Seattle responded to our question about denominational identity this way: "There are some younger people and probably some older ones who don't care that much about it, but people join because they know that this is a Presbyterian congregation."

- In a few cases (2 percent overall), the congregation's loyalty is to a denomination that no longer exists because of an earlier organizational merger. Having been part of an older tradition, those older stories and practices are still being kept alive, often at the expense of identification with the new merged body. Only in the Mainline Protestant denominations have such denominational mergers taken place, so only there (in 6 percent of the Mainline congregations) did we find those lingering loyalties to bygone traditions.

- Another 24 percent said that the best answer to our question was "yes and no." Some in the congregation see the denominational connections and identity as important; others do not. Our informants almost always identified this as a generational divide, and most shrugged in resignation to the apparently inevitable. The pastor of a large Hartford United Church of Christ congregation described his members this way: "Their self-perception is that they are part of this church, not that they are part of a group of Congregational churches which are in association with a greater body called the UCC." An Albuquerque Presbyterian pastor said, "Our younger generation is not nearly as loyal to the denomination as our older individuals."

- Finally, 12 percent said that their congregations have little or no awareness of denominational identity or connection. A few actively downplay the congregation's connections to their denomination because they think denominational identities get in the way of their local ministry and outreach. Others actually have no denominational affiliation. A Chicago Pentecostal pastor said, "This church is a very independent church. It's a very unique church"; and a megachurch in Nashville described itself as "transdenominational with a Pentecostal flare." They may recognize larger religious traditions that shape them (e.g., Pentecostalism), but each claims the local church's prerogatives ahead of any outside tradition or authority.

Among individual members, our assessment of denominational identity comes from the survey we distributed in thirty-two diverse Christian congregations. We asked our respondents to rate various things—including denominational affiliation—that might have been important in their choice to join their present church. We also asked them to respond to various ways of describing themselves ("a very spiritual person," "independent and self-sufficient," and the like). As part of that list, they checked where their denominational identity falls, between "not me at all" (1) and "essential to who I am" (5). A third question asked them about various ways they know how they should live, including how important their "church creeds, teachings and traditions" are.[9] We also asked them about a long list of things that might be priorities for their congregation, including how important it is to "nurture a strong denominational identity." Taken together, these four questions provide us a rough measure of the intersection between denominational traditions and the individual's own priorities and choices.[10]

What we see in Tables 18 and 19 are the different ways in which denominational identification is present in different religious traditions. Most distinctive are the Catholic and Orthodox members and parishes. Their leaders were much more likely than any of the Protestants to express unquestioning identification with their religious tradition (or at least to say they are intentionally working to preserve that tradition), and none said identification was minimal. Similarly, the individual members in the Catholic parishes we surveyed claimed significantly higher attachment to the denomination than did individuals in any Protestant group. Within the Catholic and Orthodox family we encountered only four churches that fit our "yes and no" (tenuous) category, and two of those have significant populations of members who grew up in ethnic traditions (Native American in one case, and African American in the other) that are not traditionally Catholic. Those ethnic religious traditions are now being consciously mixed with traditional Catholic ritual and identity. The result, at least at this moment, is some ambivalence about just how "Catholic" they are. Their experience, however, stands in contrast to a larger tradition where denominational identity is largely assumed.

A "nondenominational" identity would seem to be the polar opposite. But that story is not nearly so straightforward as it might seem. Not surprisingly, both churches and individuals in that category are less likely to claim high levels of denominational identification. But a few of them do, and that helps to signal that there is more than one way to be nondenominational. One pattern is defined by the group of "Independent Baptists" who fill the "strong but qualified" cell in Table 18. They generally describe themselves as "fundamentalist" and have both a recognizable common identity and a set of informal networks binding them together. When we asked a Chicago pastor about his church's affiliation, he said, "We are autonomous in our church government. We have informal association with other churches of like mind, and cooperation supporting missionaries and private colleges and things like that, but as far as any formal affiliation with any identifying denomination, no." But when we asked about the mission of his church, he immediately identified it with a specific religious tradition—fundamentalism. "We are fundamentalists, Bible-believing Christians," he said. "The most important thing in our world view and our cosmology is truth—truth takes precedence over everything else." This is also a religious identity with a history this pastor knew:

TABLE 18 Denominational Identification of Congregations in Different Christian Traditions

Denominational Identification	Mainline Protestant (%)	Conservative Protestant (%)	Nondenominational Protestant (%)	African American Protestant (%)	Catholic & Orthodox (%)	All Christian Congregations (%)
Unquestioningly strong	17	32	0	26	62	29
Strong but qualified	32	34	29	51	28	33
Identify with predecessor group	6	0	0	0	0	2
Tenuous	37	25	0	21	9	24
Minimal or downplayed	7	9	71	2	0	12
Total (Number of cases)	99 (178)	100 (173)	100 (25)	100 (51)	99 (43)	100 (483)

NOTE: Pearson chi-square = 240.958, two-sided significance = .000. Some columns do not total 100% because of rounding.

TABLE 19 Individual Denominational Identification in Different Christian Traditions

Strength of Individual Denominational Identity (Scale Score)	Mainline Protestant	Conservative Protestant	Nondenominational	African-American Protestant	Catholic & Orthodox	All Christian Congregations
Low identifiers (4–9) (%)	21	17	55	19	4	15
Moderate identifiers (10–13) (%)	54	51	38	52	42	48
High identifiers (14–17) (%)	25	31	7	28	54	36
Total (number of cases)	100 (495)	99 (807)	100 (65)	99 (236)	100 (1,497)	99 (3,100)
Average score*	11.6	12.0	9.7	11.9	13.6	12.3

NOTE: Pearson chi-square = 336.188, two-sided significance = .000. Some columns do not total 100% because of rounding.

*Differences among these means were examined using Oneway ANOVA, with Scheffe post-hoc comparisons and p < .01 as the criterion. Nondenominational respondents and Catholic and Orthodox respondents are each significantly different from other categories of respondent, as well as from each other.

"J. Frank Norris, the Texas tornado, . . . he is probably the patriarch of the movement that I belong to. He was among the first Independent Baptists who split from the SBC in the 1930s." While he does not recognize any religious authority beyond his own congregation, and the church is able to freely choose its own partners in ministry, its sense of identity is clearly shaped by a tradition not utterly of its own making, a tradition others in American society recognize as well.[11]

Other churches in this nondenominational category, however, are more clearly insistent on rejecting any religious labels. They call themselves "cross-denominational" or say they are "not denominational" as a way of saying that people from many religious traditions are welcome, with none of them taking precedence. As the pastor of a megachurch in Nashville said, "There's so many people here that, if somebody else asked what denomination they are, they might still say Baptist or Lutheran or whatever, because that's where they still feel their roots are, but they attend church here, and it's just a part of the body of Christ—we're not big on the label thing." Churches like this are likely to identify themselves as "Pentecostal" or "evangelical" or "apostolic" or "fundamentalist," but they feel free to interpret those terms in their own ways. A Seattle megachurch pastor said, "We just believe that the only thing we have to do is what the Bible says. We don't have to do what any denomination or groups say." Some have chosen to be nondenominational because they believe that denominations are human constructions that stand between them and really doing God's will.

Scott Thumma, who has given close study to nondenominational churches, argues that this freedom provides the opportunity to develop strong local identities often built around distinct worship styles or even a distinctive inclusion of ethnic diversity (Thumma 1999). The very act of refusing an external label requires local "identity work" that can result in high levels of commitment. Some within this nondenominational category recognize, however, that being independent also sometimes means that they have to spend time explaining themselves. The pastor of a new evangelical church in Seattle reflected on that: "Saying you're independent makes it harder for people to understand what you represent. So then if you say 'Baptist,' there's a whole code of things that that means. If you say 'Pentecostal,' that's a whole code of things that people already know you're about, and you don't have to explain anything." Increasingly, Thumma argues, the nondenominational label itself will answer those questions. Just as claiming a Catholic or Lutheran identity provides a recognizable place on the religious map, we are now recognizing the space occupied by nondenominational churches and according it a kind of ironically "denominational" identity.

A third way of being nondenominational is to participate in a network of churches that shares a loose sense of identity and fellowship. We interviewed churches from the World Ministry Fellowship, the Victory Outreach network, the Potters House Fellowship, the International Council of Community Churches, and the Watchman Nee Association, among others. The pastor of a Potters House in Seattle talked about being part of that movement: "It's important in that it's a sense of identity that says we are of something bigger. That brings encouragement and validity to people. It does bring a sense of a broader vision or picture. But I don't preach 'We are Potters House,' although we are." Having been founded only within the last generation, a network like this may eventually take on more denomination-like characteristics.[12] As it grows, its identity may become more recognizable as another variety within the Conservative Protestant stream in American religion. Like the "Independent Baptists" and "nondenominational" churches, these networked churches are creating cultural identities, while attempting to hold the organizational structures to a minimum.

All the other groups—Protestant and Catholic and Orthodox—have the more elaborate organizational structures that go along with their denominational identity, but for some of the Protestants the structures may be stronger than the culture. In contrast to the Catholic and Orthodox parishes, all the Protestant denominations (Conservative, African American, and Mainline) exhibit significant variation in the way congregations identify with their parent body—from the most minimal sense of connection to unquestioned loyalty (see Table 18). Mainline denominations have more congregations who describe their membership as tenuous in their loyalties; and Conservative denominations have more in the "unquestioned" category (with individual Conservative Protestants having slightly higher denominational identity scores as well). Beyond that, the picture is fairly comparable across the three denominational Protestant families. Each family has congregations that describe their denominational identity in each of the typical modes we heard. No stream within Protestantism is either immune to the erosion of denominational identities or devoid of habits of loyalty.[13]

Strong denominational identities exist within Protestantism, but they are by no means universal. Some congregations are strongly linked to a denominational tradition, and some are more likely to inculcate a defiantly local way of situating themselves in the religious landscape. Denominational citizenship—in the form of strong identification with a particular religious tradition—is alive and well among almost all Catholic and Orthodox parishes and among every Sectarian congregation. But Protestants, always the most voluntary religious groups, are indeed voluntary and diverse in their willingness to claim a particular tradition that identifies them.

DENOMINATIONAL PARTICIPATION

Citizenship is more than identification: it is also participation and active contribution to the work of the whole. It is actual interaction and commitment of resources to common work—voting and paying your taxes, if you will. For denominations, that interaction happens at two different levels. While denominations are nationally and sometimes internationally based organizations, their more immediate presence is regional. In units ranging in size from a portion of a city to several contiguous states, regional jurisdictions are the face of the denomination most readily visible for most congregations. In many cases there are actually two (or more) layers between the local church and the national body—a district or association that is relatively local, and a diocese or synod or state convention that encompasses a larger area.

As we have seen, these regional organizations routinely provide educational events for both clergy and laity, sponsor camps to which churches send their youth and adults, sometimes coordinate local mission projects and help start churches, as well as helping in the placement and supervision of clergy. We spent a good deal of time during our interviews talking about the congregation's actual interaction with its regional and national denominational organizations. As we looked at what people described for us, there were five typical kinds of regional activities in which churches were involved: regional mission projects, camps, educational events, clergy gatherings, and service on governing boards, plus a catchall category of "other."[14] Sixty-nine percent of the denomination-based congregations in which we interviewed reported routine participation in at least one of those activities (see Table 20). A large majority of congregations have at least some ongoing denominational connections as they work together on a mission project, their kids go to camp together, or they see sister denominationalists at meetings and classes.

Regional participation is not uniform across all kinds of churches, however. It is highest—in every tradition—among the churches with majorities of well-educated members. Even controlling for other religious and demographic factors, education plays a role. Congregations full of college graduates are more likely to send members to denominational camps, but especially more likely to go to training events and to serve on regional committees and boards. When regional units plan training events, well-educated congregations are more likely to respond. Likewise, the best educated lay leaders get elected or appointed to regional

TABLE 20 Organizational Participation of Churches in Different
Christian Denominations

Type of Participation	Mainline Protestant (193) (%)	Conservative Protestant (188) (%)	African American Protestant (53) (%)	Catholic & Orthodox (45) (%)	All Denominational Christian Congregations (479) (%)
Participate regularly in at least one regional activity*	80	66	65	77	69
Participate at least occasionally in one or more national activities*	31	41	82	3	40
Average percentage of budget to denomination*	12.5	12.0	2.5	7.2	11.2

NOTE: Number in parentheses indicates number of congregations in that group. For types of participation marked with an asterisk at least one of the differences among the groups is statistically significant at $p < .10$ (Oneway ANOVA, with Scheffe post-hoc comparisons).

denominational committees. As Verba and associates have noted about political participation, "education enhances participation more or less directly by developing skills that are relevant to politics—the ability to speak and write, the knowledge of how to cope in an organizational setting" (Verba, Schlozman, and Brady 1995, 305). Education is also part of the explanation for how the participatory dimensions of religious citizenship work, preparing people for effective action in the events and meetings that bind congregations together into a larger whole. These same well-educated congregations also have more members and bigger budgets, and all three sets of resources increase the likelihood that a congregation will be involved in regional and national events.

Participation is also affected by the location of the church in question. For national events, rural and urban churches are equally disadvantaged, but rural congregations are often left out of regional events as well. For many in our Missouri sites, for instance, regional offices are in St. Louis or Kansas City, two or three hours away. Weeknight educational events or board meetings are not likely to draw wide participation from such churches. Even controlling for other factors, rural congregations (especially Mainline ones) participate less in their regional denominational organizations. Looking at all the factors together, those most likely to participate regionally are the well-off, well-educated, urban congregations. They are especially more likely to have members serving on boards, but the differences are not generally in kinds of participation, but in overall level of connection. Those who *can* participate are more likely to do so.

But tradition also plays a role. The Sectarian groups where we interviewed did not talk about activities that approximated the regional educational events, clergy councils, and camps we heard about in the Protestant and Catholic churches. Rather than routine regional events, they are likely to gather nationally and internationally. Three-quarters (72%) of Jehovah's Witnesses, Christian Scientists, and Mormons reported sending delegations to large national and international congresses and other events. Both Mormons and Christian Scientists have a "mother church" on U.S. soil that is both gathering place and pilgrimage destination. Since their founding in 1830, Latter-day Saints have gathered twice annually. Jan Shipps reports that in an earlier day, "conferences were occasions which brought all the church together in one place. While the growth of the church and the dispersion of its members through the world now make such a physical ingathering of the whole body of Saints impractical, the use of the electronic media carries the conference proceedings to the Saints wherever they are" (Shipps 1985, 132).

For most denominations, regional, rather than national, participation is the norm for simple, pragmatic reasons. National events are much more likely to involve significant travel, and in some denominations the number of participants at national meetings is constitutionally limited. National denominations do sponsor a variety of educational events and camps (especially for youth), but these larger events are an occasional special trip more than a routine connection. Only 40 percent of congregations reported any recent national attendance. Among both the Mainline and Conservative white congregations, the likelihood of national participation is half what we found for regional involvement. The same is even more dramatically the case for Catholic and Orthodox parishes (see Table 20). There essentially are no national organizations to which to belong, so it was little surprise that almost no parishes reported participating in national events of any kind.

The pattern of participation in the African American denominations, on the other hand, is unlike any of the others. The way citizenship is expressed in the historic black churches sets them apart from their Euro-American counterparts,

Catholic or Protestant. Black churches are far more likely to send participants to national meetings than are churches in any other tradition. A Hartford pastor told us, "The people that attend the conventions attend the convention because they love the convention. . . . They want to go and represent because of their love for their church and their love for the convention." Among African American denominations, a distinct institutional pattern is apparent. Being a citizen is being a member of the family and participating in family gatherings. "Representing" is the term we often heard, and it meant that a congregation was able to send its pastor and often several lay members, along with a monetary contribution, to the denomination's annual national gathering. The African American Protestant denominations elicit by far the smallest levels of denominational giving from their congregations because many of them have no regular pattern of monthly or quarterly check-writing. Churches do not *send* their gifts; they *take* their gifts. Being a good denominational citizen carries expectations for both attendance and giving, even though the amounts of money actually collected are comparatively quite small.

These congregational contributions to the regional and national work of the denomination are another way local congregations declare their citizenship, and the African American pattern is not the only one that is distinct. Because bigger churches can give more, we used proportional giving, rather than dollar amount, as our measure of monetary engagement.[15] The overall average, across all denominational traditions, was approximately 11 percent of the congregation's annual budget, but amounts ranged from zero to over 40 percent. These proportions were not primarily a matter of resources or demographics. Big churches may give more dollars, but they do not necessarily give a higher percentage. While polity does make a difference, as we will see, the primary differences fall along lines of religious tradition, rather than religious authority. Within some groups denominational giving is culturally expected, and in others it is not. Roman Catholics have multiple sources of funding (beyond parish contributions) to support their vast enterprises, as well as a less robust tradition of individual giving to parishes.[16] African American denominations have much smaller enterprises to support and expect relatively little money from their member congregations. White Protestants, both Mainline and Conservative, support national organizations that fall somewhere between those two traditions in size and scope but must be supported almost entirely by member contributions.

A completely different way of organizing denominational finances is found in the Sectarian groups. They don't just have high levels of identification with the denomination and very high levels of participation in national programs: most or all of their local budgets are overseen by the denomination. Among Mormons, all local offerings go to the "General Authorities" of the Church to be distributed back as needed (Ostling and Ostling 1999). Whether it is sending the group's youth on national and international missions (as Mormons do) or gathering in giant international rallies (as Jehovah's Witnesses do), citizenship for Sectarian groups is tightly linked to tangible face-to-face experiences and sacrificial contributions to joint ventures. In every sense, these groups maintain intense levels of denominational citizenship that contrast with the more mixed picture in Protestant and Catholic traditions.

Outside these Sectarian traditions, there is no such uniformity. Denominational identification and participation vary considerably. Some congregations are heavily involved and give significant portions of their budgets to denominational work. Other congregations rarely attend a meeting and give very little. Explaining those differences will take us beyond the institutional cultures of the religious traditions themselves.

SHAPING DENOMINATIONAL CITIZENSHIP

Citizenship is expressed in participation and in the identification of members with their particular religious traditions. But it is also shaped by the structures and practices of those traditions. Indeed, as Somers argues, citizenship should be understood in terms of a group's ability to set out rules, establish structures, and nurture relationships and practices. The participation and identification are in some sense the visible results of these other realities.

STRUCTURES AND RULES

To what extent are denominations able to set out a system of rules that effectively structures the behavior and relationships of their members?[17] The system of rules that binds a denomination together is often referred to as its "polity," but the lines separating one polity from another are not simple to draw (Thornton and Ocasio 1999). Depending on what the question is—property ownership, establishing new congregations, placement of clergy, or designing the worship and programming of the local congregation, for instance—the locus of authority may vary, even within the same denomination (Cantrell, Krile, and Donohue 1983). Denominations differ radically in the degree to which they claim authority over their constituent units. In some groups, common culture and shared work are entirely voluntary, while in others commonly recognized authorities structure the work.

While the distinctions are not clear-cut, we can nevertheless distinguish three broadly institutionalized ways denominational authority is practiced in American Christian traditions. (A complete chart of where we placed each of the groups we found is contained in Appendix 2.)

- Hierarchical. Where there is a hierarchy, most commonly the congregation's property is owned by an outside religious organization. That same outside body ordains and places clergy as well. Significant aspects of program and liturgy may be prescribed, and the amount of their monetary contribution to the denomination may be set by an outside authority (even if they do not necessarily meet those expectations).
- Local/Congregational. These are sometimes called the "free church" traditions to indicate the absence of outside religious authority. Here the property is owned by the congregation, there is nearly complete discretion in programming, contributions and participation are voluntary, and clergy are hired by the local body.
- Mixed. This middle position is sometimes called "presbyterian," since it often involves regional decision-making bodies similar to "presbyteries." Groups such as the Reformed Church in America, along with the Presbyterian Church, recognize regional ecclesiastical bodies that are democratic in their structure, but authoritative in their power over local church matters. Congregations owe significant accountability to this regional body, but they may still retain discretion in who they will hire, how they will contribute and participate and how they will run their church. Despite their apparent hierarchy, Episcopalians belong in this mixed category. Also included are denominations such of the Assemblies of God and the Lutheran Church–Missouri Synod, where *clergy* are significantly accountable to an outside authority, but local *churches* have wide discretion in running their affairs.

What differences do we see in denominations with different authority structures? Do they identify and participate differently? As we have already seen, patterns of denominational citizenship in the Catholic and Orthodox bodies—which have hierarchical polities—are indeed distinctive (see Tables 18–20). But it is the tradition, not the authority structure, that makes the difference. If strong authority were the key, we should expect uniformly high identification and participation, but that is not the case. In these traditions, identification *is* high, but congregational

TABLE 21   Denominational Participation and Identification of Mainline
and Conservative Protestant Churches

Type of Participation	Congregational Polity (146)	Mixed Polity (162)	Hierarchical Polity (71)	All Mainline and Conservative Protestant Congregations (379)
Participate regularly in at least one regional activity (%)	71	79	72	73
Participate at least occasionally in one or more national activities (%)*	47	31	19	37
Average percentage of budget to denomination	11	10	17	12
Strongly identify with the denomination (%)*	66	56	55	61
Member denominational identity scores* (number of individuals)	12.4 (449)	11.7 (747)	11.3 (106)	11.9 (1,302)

NOTE: Number in parentheses in column headings indicates number of congregations in that category. For items marked with an asterisk at least one of the differences among the groups is statistically significant at p < .10 (Oneway ANOVA, with Scheffe post-hoc comparisons).

contributions and regional participation are not exceptional, and attendance at national events is relatively rare. Institutional culture, rather than institutional structure, is what shapes a unique pattern of relationship and cooperation.

Differences in polity are most relevant among the predominantly white Protestant denominations, but here strong authority is equally uneven in its effects (see Table 21). Since having a "mixed" polity often means investing regional units with greater power, it is perhaps not surprising that congregations in those denominations were slightly more likely to participate in regional activities; but mostly regional participation is part of the institutional pattern in all denominations. No strong authority is necessary to compel it. Giving and national participation, on the other hand, are not uniform. Compared to churches of congregational and mixed polities, churches with hierarchies give more and attend less, and identification follows attendance more than dollars.

Participation *is* invited in denominations with congregational authority structures. The free churches tend to have democratic national assemblies at which large (if not unlimited) numbers of pastors and lay people are welcome (Farnsley 1994). Hierarchically governed denominations (and most of those in the "mixed" category) tend to have relatively small national assemblies (if at all), with elected representatives in strictly regulated numbers. The difference is between populist democracy and federalist representation (or, in some cases, monarchy).[18] And the result is that congregations in the populist denominations are more likely to have some direct participatory connection with their national body. Nearly half (47%) send members to meetings, compared to a third (31%) of those in mixed polity denominations and a fifth (19%) of those in hierarchical ones.

When it comes to producing monetary contributions, however, the hierarchical groups out-do the more locally autonomous ones. While the average congregation that does not have an official hierarchy gives 10 percent of its budget to denominational causes, the average Methodist or Seventh-Day Adventist church (where there are hierarchies) gives 17 percent. The rules under which they work require various payments (usually set by the denomination) and stipulate how salaries and budgets will be arranged, and the result is that more money goes through the denomination's account books. In at least a few instances (most commonly among the United Methodists we interviewed), this link between hierarchy and giving was not an altogether happy one. Congregations recounted a sense of alienation from a denomination that demands more than they feel they can afford to pay, but fails to respond when they seek assistance. While strong authority can extract resources, that fiscal power may diminish cultural strength. Individual members in mixed and hierarchical denominations are significantly less likely to say that their denominational tradition is shaping how they think about themselves.

Thus variations in denominational authority have at least some effects in how congregations spend their money, how and whether they participate in events beyond their region, and whether they and their members are strongly identified with the denomination. But is the strength of denominational authority also seen in how controversial issues are handled? Can strong denominational authority constrain the ability of local congregations to act independently? We know that polity can affect how clergy act. In the 1960s, for instance, Methodist pastors were much more likely to take a pro-civil-rights stand than were their Baptist neighbors (Ammerman 1980; J. Wood 1970). What accounted for the difference was not any particular demographic or even ideological difference between them, so much as the presence of a denominational hierarchy that could prevent a local congregation from firing a pastor who said unpopular things. But what about the congregations themselves?

Denominational differences of opinion have certainly not disappeared. The history of denominations in this country is a history of disagreement and schism (Liebman, Sutton, and Wuthnow 1988). We asked the leaders we interviewed about any conflicts or controversies that especially concern their congregations, and over half (53%) of those in the various Christian traditions named at least one issue. No group was immune, but each had a distinct set of issues (see Table 22). Far and away the most common was the question of homosexuality, mentioned by nearly half of the Mainline Protestant churches where we interviewed, and at least a few of the Catholic and Conservative Protestant ones as well. In the Presbyterian, Lutheran, Episcopal, and United Methodist Churches there are active and ongoing controversies over whether openly gay and lesbian members may have full ordination privileges, and/or whether churches may perform blessing ceremonies for gay couples. All but four of the twenty-one Presbyterian churches we surveyed, for instance, said they were worried about gay issues, as were two-thirds of the Episcopal ones. In Albuquerque the Episcopal divisions were especially visible. On one side of town, we heard from a church that is a member of the conservative American Anglican Council: "We would feel that the church is making a major mistake if it goes against what the scripture teaches on, you know, moral issues, and becomes trendy and reflective of a larger society." On the other side of town, a lay leader said, "I mean, we have taken a very visible stance, publicly, that has said that gay and lesbian Christians are welcome here and they don't have to change."

In most of the Mainline groups, between a quarter and a third of congregations reported being solidly on the pro-inclusion side of this issue, but more often congregational leaders reported that their members are divided—sometimes actively so, but more often still wrestling with just what they think. A Seattle Episcopal rector, reflecting on the question of "gay unions" said, "I think for us—I think most parishes—the next step is to do a rather lengthy process of education. And that will give the people a chance to talk about this." The real differences in most of the Mainline groups are not between pro- and anti-inclusion, but between undecideds and others.

TABLE 22 Denominational Issues in Congregations in Different Christian Traditions

	Mainline Protestant (191) (%)	Conservative Protestant (188) (%)	African-American Protestant (53) (%)	Catholic & Orthodox (45) (%)	All Christian Congregations (477) (%)
Named at least one issue of concern*	67	43	65	43	53
Issues Named					
Homosexuality*	49	8	0	9	20
Women's roles*	6	9	20	7	9
Other social issues	11	8	12	14	10
Worship practices*	2	11	0	6	7
Theological issues*	4	7	0	0	5
Poor management	11	7	4	2	7
Financial scandal*	1	0	36	0	4
Effects of church conflict*	2	10	2	0	6

NOTE: Number in parentheses indicates number of congregations in that group. Up to two issues were cataloged, so the totals in the bottom portion may exceed the percentage in the first row. For items marked with an asterisk at least one of the differences among the groups is statistically significant at p < .10 (Oneway ANOVA, with Scheffe post-hoc comparisons).

Among Methodists, on the other hand, the clear majority who expressed concern about this issue said that their congregations oppose inclusion of open gays and lesbians in the church. A Hartford pastor said, "This church would react very negatively if we were to do a same-sex marriage. They would be—they would go nuts." And a Nashville one said, "For this congregation the gay issue is pretty explosive." At the same time, other Methodist churches are visibly and publicly welcoming gay and lesbian people.[19] A large church in Chicago told us, "We're a reconciling congregation, which means . . . we minister with and to gay and lesbian people. And that's part of our identity as a congregation." This church is part of a distinct, if visible, minority. The high proportion of tradition-minded Methodist churches we encountered signals the difficulty gay rights advocates are likely to have in that denomination for the foreseeable future.[20]

No other issue is so widespread in American religious life. A few congregations expressed concern about their denomination's stand on other social issues—justice questions and racism and abortion, most often. No single issue dominated any one denomination, and there were congregations on all sides of each. Somewhat more contentious were the various issues surrounding the roles of women. This was especially so among the African American leaders who talked with us (see Table 22).[21] Many acknowledged that expanded roles are inevitable, but they also noted that (male) deacons and pastors in traditional black churches may be slow to give up power. At a large Chicago church the pastor reflected, "The Convention has not addressed the role of women in ministry; and this church, because it is traditional, has not addressed it—but they're going to," he chuckled. Both in local churches and in the Convention as a whole, gender will continue to be a difficult issue for black churches.

Among Conservative Protestants, the most problematic issues surround what happens in worship. For some the question is music, while others worry about the encroachment of charismatic practices in their otherwise non-Pentecostal denominations. Even within Pentecostalism, the "Brownsville revival" movement (and the Toronto blessing before that) stretched the definitions of acceptable worship practice. Pastors who have been to Brownsville are impatient with their more staid congregations, while other pastors worry that spirit-filled laughing, barking, and the like are too excessive.[22]

In the Lutheran Church–Missouri Synod, the conflict is over "close communion." Official church policy dictates that only LCMS members may partake of communion, and visitors are routinely advised that they should remain in their seats while members receive communion (which is part of each Sunday service).

LCMS members and clergy are discouraged from participating in the worship services administered by others. When Atlantic District President David Benke decided to participate in "A Prayer for America," a televised September 23, 2001, interfaith event at New York's Yankee Stadium, a firestorm ensued within the denomination's leadership (Banks 2002). Less visibly, local pastors clearly struggle with this issue as well. One pastor said simply, "If they [non-LCMS people] come up, I won't turn them away." Another explained, "If you believe in the Lord's Supper as the body and blood of Jesus Christ that gives us forgiveness of sins, we see no reason to withhold communion from you." Still another recounted the story he had heard about an elderly family member who returned for a reunion and was refused communion in her old home church because she had joined a different kind of Lutheran church in her new hometown where there were no LCMS congregations. This pastor exclaimed, "The pastor refuses to give her communion because she is no longer LCMS! Now, to me, I would like to punch out that pastor!" National policies about how to worship have very practical implications for local practice, and many of those we talked with acknowledged that this issue created a sore spot within the body as a whole (Carlson forthcoming). That all of them saw themselves on the "liberal" side of the issue may say something about the direction in which change is likely to go.

Denominational conflict was virtually a way of life for Southern Baptists in the 1980s (Ammerman 1990), but by the late 1990s this flagship Conservative denomination had completed its turn to the right, and the conflict had subsided. Still, at least a few in that denomination (as well as a few in other conflicted denominations) worried about the lingering effects of having so publicly engaged in religious infighting. These churches were not so much concerned about whether the denomination adopted a theologically correct stance as they were eager that their representatives cease making such a public spectacle of themselves.

Theological issues, interestingly, almost never came up in the congregations themselves. Some in the Assemblies of God worried about whether divorced clergy ought to be able to serve. A few in both the Mainline and Conservative Protestant traditions worried that others in their denomination are either too conservative or too liberal or that they don't know and believe what they should. But more common than these theological concerns were complaints about the more mundane realities of denominational life—bishops and bureaucrats who do not respond when needed and mismanagement of all sorts. As one Methodist pastor said of his congregation, "There is a feeling that the Conference wouldn't help us when we needed help, why should we help them." At least some church leaders fault their denominations for failing to run responsive and efficient organizations.

Occasionally, the management problems are more serious. In the mid-1990s financial scandal rocked the Episcopal Church, when the national treasurer was accused of embezzlement. The immediate result was embarrassment for the Presiding Bishop and a falloff in contributions. But by the time we interviewed local church leaders, only one Episcopal parish named this as a concern. Most scandalous at the time we were interviewing was the financial misconduct being revealed in the National Baptist Convention. Convention President Henry Lyons had been tried and convicted of mishandling several million dollars in Convention money, and many of the Baptist pastors we met reluctantly acknowledged that their denomination was facing a crisis. In both cases expectations of bureaucratic professional accountability had come up against religious systems accustomed to other rules (the personal charisma of the Presiding Bishop in one case and the patronage authority of the Convention President in the other).[23] And in both, legal requirements for fiscal management eventually superseded those traditional and charismatic claims.

The clash between traditionalist religious authorities and legal systems of accountability has nowhere been more visible than in the scandals that engulfed the American Catholic Church in 2002 and beyond. If we had been interviewing a few years later than we did, clergy sexual misconduct would surely have been a more dominant issue in our conversations. In the late 1990s the most common issues we heard about in Catholic parishes were the shortage of priests and tensions over the question of ordaining women. Issues surrounding sexual misconduct were mentioned in only three congregations, all Protestant.

As the cases of clergy abuse of children became more widely known—and as it became apparent that Church officials had covered up the problem—disaffection among Roman Catholic laity grew. The Church's authority, however, still constrained the alternatives open to them. While individual members could (and did) withhold their offerings, their collective attempts to circumvent official channels with their money were thwarted. When the lay group Voice of the Faithful sought to provide money directly to Catholic Charities in Boston, bypassing the archbishop, their contribution was refused. There are limits to the power of unauthorized Catholic organizations, limits likely to be recognized by even the most change-minded leaders in the Church.[24]

A public scandal such as this affects all the congregations in a denomination, whether they have any direct involvement or not. Most of the concerns we heard, across all the denominations, were, by contrast, relatively idiosyncratic and dispersed. A few churches here and there were worried about this or that issue.

If those concerns should coalesce around a few issues, and if parties should begin to organize to try to effect change, the outcome and process of the resulting intradenominational conflict will be significantly shaped by the structure of authority within which congregations are working. As Farnsley (1994) argues, for instance, the Southern Baptist conflict was shaped by an official structure that empowered a mass movement to seize power from bureaucratic elites—quite the opposite of the situation faced by Voice of the Faithful.

Denominations do have rules, but even the most apparently traditional hierarchies are tempered in the American context by expectations about democratic participation. The traditional hierarchy of the Roman Catholic Church is learning not to assume that local parishes will accept whatever priest is assigned to them and trust his judgment in setting parish programming and policy.[25] That the Church can refuse to accept the contributions of Voice of the Faithful illustrates the strong religious and legal authority held by the bishops; but that a discredited Cardinal Law can be forced to resign equally illustrates the power of public democratic protests by people who claim the legitimacy of the religious culture over against the power of organizational authority (Dillon 1999). That American Catholic laity can seek alternative modes of organization likewise illustrates the effects of the American voluntary context.

But Catholics are not alone in muddling through a complicated mix of ecclesiastical authority and de facto power. The power of religious authorities to constrain congregational action is not nearly so direct as their power to constrain (or enable) clergy action.[26] Church decisions about the inclusion of gay and lesbian persons, for instance, are often worked out in the breach between due ecclesiastical process and local congregational initiative. Current United Methodist Church policy prohibits the blessing of gay unions by Methodist clergy, a decision presumably binding on all clergy in the denomination and upheld in a 1999 Judicial Council decision; but groups of local clergy have publicly defied that ruling by repeatedly officiating at just such unions (J. Wood forthcoming). Strong church authority has to confront the American tradition of civil disobedience. "Mixed" polity makes the situation even more ambiguous. Among Presbyterians, Lutherans, and Episcopalians some regions are open to and affirming of gay and lesbian members and clergy, while other regions are decidedly not.[27]

Where there is no higher religious authority, congregations can either take maverick stands or, if they choose, ignore national conflicts. As the National Baptists confronted Henry Lyons's financial misconduct, few worried that it would have any effect on local congregational life. A deacon in a small Chicago church said,

"We talked about it. I think everybody was disappointed about what the allegations were." But his pastor was confident that the system would take care of itself: "By the next term, that will be the end of the road for him." A Hartford pastor hinted that his church was withholding its Convention offering, saying, "The good thing about Baptists is that we're Baptist and we are autonomous." What happens at one level has no authoritative link to what happens at another level.

The range of action available to a congregation is affected by the kind of religious authority it recognizes, but dissent of varying sorts is possible across all the Christian traditions in the United States. What effects do these tensions have on denominational citizenship? Do the congregations that are most concerned about issues give less? Yes, at least where they have the option to do so. In denominations whose official structure mandates allocations, there are no significant differences between churches that identify points of tension and those that do not. Where religious authority is strong, local discontent is less likely to be expressed financially (at least by congregations—individual contributions are another matter). But in denominations that do not have such powers, unhappy congregations can decide to give less, and they do. In the predominantly white denominations, it is the difference between average giving of 13 and 9 percent, in the African American denominations between 5 and 2 percent.

What about denominational identity? Do unhappy congregations also feel a sense of estrangement from the denomination? On average, no. Do they participate less? Again, the answer is no. Congregations that are concerned about the tensions in their denominations are the *most* active participants. At least in part, this may be a case of chickens and eggs. Those that participate more may *become* more aware of what is going on in the denomination. Across all traditions and polities, the churches that were aware of and concerned about difficulties in the denomination were also those most active, especially in regional meetings. No matter what the form of a denomination's official religious authority, discontented American participants are likely to find or create settings where their voices can be heard.

FUNCTIONAL TIES

All organizations are a complicated mix of authority and participation, but they are also systems of functional relationships. Denominations are organized ways to get work done, channeling a flow of resources into a stream of products. Especially over the last 150 years, denominations have established numerous national agencies that for many have become synonymous with the denomination itself.[28] Among the earliest agencies to be established were publishing boards that produced educational and other materials for use in member congregations. The consolidation of overseas and domestic missionary work under the umbrella of denominational agencies followed and was perhaps the single most important functional task undertaken by growing national bodies. But denominations also established systems of education, especially for their clergy, and provided those clergy with access to pension plans and insurance coverage. Many denominations added national departments that promoted various church programs, from music to children's education to men's and women's guilds. In the most fully developed of these systems, nearly everything a local congregation might want to do can be shaped and supported by an integrated system of national, state, and regional offices.[29] The church's youth choir, for instance, might be visited by a state-level Director of Youth Music and get music education resources through a multistaffed national office and a denominational publishing house. Throughout this book the products of organized denominational agencies have appeared regularly in the resources consumed by local congregations.

But do such products and the agencies that make them enhance the institutional strength of the denominations themselves? The most direct way to answer that question is to look at the groups that have avoided a fully bureaucratized model of organization. For whatever reasons, some American denominations have resisted centralizing and/or have kept national organizations to a minimum. Some have publishing houses, but no pension boards. Others have those two basic structures, but little else in the way of programmatic agencies. Among Mainline Protestants, virtually all the churches we surveyed worked within a full-fledged bureaucratic agency structure that provides a wide range of cultural products to its participating congregations. Among Conservative Protestants, however, the degree of bureaucratization varies from denomination to denomination, and we can look for the difference those organizations make (see Table 23).[30]

Congregations in denominations with more elaborate organizational structures are more likely to report attendance at regional educational events, more likely to send members to camps, more likely to have members serving on regional boards, more likely to participate in a regional mission project—in short, more likely to be involved in regional denominational activities of all sorts (an average of three kinds of participation, compared to half that many for congregations in nonbureaucratized denominations). One of the benefits of having an agency structure, after all, is the opportunity to participate in denominational education and training activities and to work together on mission projects, engagement that mostly happens at the regional level.

TABLE 23 Denominational Participation and Identification of
Conservative Protestant Congregations

	Centralized Organization (133) (%)	Networked Organization (55) (%)
Participate regularly in at least one regional activity (F = 21.56)	75	44
Participate at least occasionally in one or more national activities	41	41
Average percentage of budget to denomination (F = 13.71)	10.1	16.0
Percentage that strongly identify with the denomination	66	66

NOTE: Number in parentheses indicates number of congregations in that group. Differences of means tested using ANOVA; differences in regional participation and budgeted gifts significant at p < .001.

Ironically, the benefits of bureaucratization do not translate into other strong denominational ties. Congregations in the white Conservative denominations that have elaborate centralized agencies are no more likely to describe themselves in strongly denominational terms or to participate in national events. Most surprisingly, they also give significantly lower proportions of their budgets to denominational causes (10% vs. 16%). Churches in these "full-service" denominations give those denominations less than do the churches whose denominations provide fewer products and benefits.

Creating an efficient, centralized system for doing denominational work stands in contrast to ad hoc and personalized methods for pooling resources. In the noncentralized groups, gifts go exclusively to special causes, causes that each church is able to identify and claim as its own—and to which they are evidently willing to give more generously than to an anonymous central fund. As we saw in Chapter 6, even within centralized denominations, the most generous congregations are those with ties to specific denominational projects and missionaries. Similarly, nondenominational churches contribute more to missions through parachurch agencies they choose than do other Conservative churches to the denominations they support. These differences between bureaucratized denominations and the more loosely structured ones remain, even when demographic factors are controlled.

Without centrally funded pension boards, official publishing houses, and other denominational agencies, these groups nevertheless maintain strong connections.

The nineteen Churches of Christ in which we interviewed provide a window on how such a networked denomination works. Tracing their lineage to the nineteenth-century "restorationist" movement, local Churches of Christ vehemently denied that they were part of a denomination at all, since they have no headquarters or religious authority beyond the congregation. They sometimes even refuse to capitalize the 'c' in church, rendering their name "church of Christ." Despite the lack of an official centralized agency structure, however, they named a consistent set of publishing, broadcast, and mission ministries they support, such as *The Gospel Advocate* and *Herald of Truth,* as well as universities such as Texas Christian and Pepperdine. They also have a well-maintained Web site.[31] These multiple modes of communication and shared enterprises hold the denomination together as a voluntary network.

With neither a strong religious authority structure nor a rationally articulated bureaucratic structure, they seem to be held together by common goals and work that is shared. Their functional ties reach outward. But are there also functional ties that extend back to the congregations, offering them tangible rewards for participating? Perhaps what also holds denominations together is not the structure but the exchanges that take place within the structure. By participating in a denomination, congregations gain access to various material benefits that may affect their sense of loyalty and identification and induce more active patterns of participation.

Those rewards, however, are not widespread. Only 20 of the congregations in which we interviewed had received any recent monetary support from their denomination, and their level of attachment and participation differed not at all from those who had received no money. Another possible monetary connection—pension coverage—affects the clergy, but not necessarily the congregation. Many a clergyperson has joked that their loyalty follows their pension dollars; but even if that is true, it seems not to affect the congregation. Congregations that participate in a denominational pension plan are no more closely tied to denominational identity than are congregations that do not. Nor do they give and participate at higher levels.

Much of the support that denominations provide for local congregations is programmatic, rather than monetary. As we saw in Chapter 4, denominations help congregations do their job by supplying expertise in program development, assistance in finding clergy, and a variety of other forms of consultation. Nineteen percent of the Protestant congregations we surveyed named some form of assistance they had received from their national denomination (beyond the educational materials they may buy), while 34 percent noted help they had received from the regional office. Those congregations, however, are no more nor less likely to describe themselves as "strongly" denominational than are congregations that could name no help they had received. Nor do they participate more actively in national events or give higher proportions of their budgets to national causes.

They do participate more actively in regional events, but that appears to be more cause than effect. That is, those who participate most actively in regional events seem to gain access to everything else the denomination offers. Even controlling for demographic differences, regional participators are the most likely to be enrolled in their national denominational pension plan and are more likely to have received some sort of programmatic help from either their region or their national body. Those who participate know what is available to them. It is not so much that the resources they receive "buy" their participation as that their participation facilitates connections to resources.

Finally, what about the competition? Part of the restructuring that is presumed to be underway is the weakening of denominational organizations as a result of the presence of parachurch competitors (Wuthnow 1988). We found, however, that links to outside organizations are irrelevant to a congregation's giving, participation, or sense of identification with their denomination. When other factors are controlled, participating in extra-denominational networks neither weakens nor strengthens denominational ties. The strength of denominational institutions seems surprisingly little affected by what congregations receive and from whom. While congregations receive many benefits from outside organizations—denominational and otherwise—the ties that constitute denominational citizenship seem not well described by a model based on exchange or competition. The ability to cooperate in doing shared work is far more important than the rewards congregations might receive.

PATTERNS OF RELATIONSHIPS

The ability of American denominations to sustain themselves at this point in our history is more a matter of relationships than of organization and exchange. The stories out of which denominational identities are constructed are told among the families, friends, and communities in which people live. While there are many ways we might assess the strength of the relational bonds within a denominational system, we will look here at three measures of relational continuity—lifelong membership, higher education, and rural versus urban residence, each of which has been hypothesized to be inimical to the possibility for sustaining religious identities and practices. Each of these measures allows us to contrast relatively stable and more insular sets of relationships with those that are more diverse and changing. As people move from small town to city and gain advancing levels of education, all relationships take on a more tentative and voluntary character. Can particularistic religious identities survive in such a situation? Among Sectarian, African American, and Catholic and Orthodox religious traditions, the answer is clearly yes. Patterns of denominational citizenship are essentially determined by the religious traditions themselves, and external demographic differences have no significant impact.

Among white Protestant denominations, however, patterns of denominational loyalty and participation vary considerably. We have already seen that some of those differences can be accounted for by variations in authority and structure, but differences in relational patterns matter as well.

Previous students of denominational identity have posited that education is a major culprit in the erosion of religious loyalties (Roof and McKinney 1987; Wuthnow 1988). Higher education provides exposure to alternative narratives (and alternative relationships) that may undermine the ability of a religious group to hold its members. We found, however, that the corrosive effects of higher education are apparent only on the Conservative side of the Protestant family (see Table 24, first section). Conservative congregations that are majority college-educated are less likely to describe themselves in denominational terms (61% vs. 73%). Among Conservative Protestant individuals, the same pattern holds. Even with other factors held constant, education is negatively related to denominational identification ($b = -.09$). Better-educated Conservative members are more likely to downplay the importance of denomination in their church's identity, as well as their own. They may be the sorts of evangelicals Sikkink (1999) describes, who claim to be "just Christian," rather than identifying with a particular denomination. Within these Conservative religious groups the predicted disengagement of educated individuals from traditional denominational loyalty has at least some modest support.

But among Mainline Protestant congregations the situation is different. When other factors are controlled, it is the *more* educated congregations that are the *most* strongly attached to a denominational culture. Within this religious family 57 percent of congregations that are majority college-educated are also strongly identified with the denomination, while only 39 percent of the less-well-educated congregations are. And this positive effect remains when other cultural and structural factors are controlled. Individual Mainline college graduates are no more nor less strongly identified with their denomination than are those with less education.

TABLE 24   Effects of Education, Urban Residence, and Switching on
Denominational Identity in Conservative and Mainline Protestant Congregations

Congregational Characteristics	Percentage of Congregations with a Strong Denominational Identity	
	Mainline Protestants (157)	Conservative Protestants (161)
Education		
Majority are college graduates	57	61
Majority are not college graduates	39	73
	F = 3.31, sig = .07	F = 3.34, sig = .07
Location		
Urban congregations	42	59
Rural congregations	75	83
	F = 10.79, sig = .001	F = 12.35, sig = .001
Denominational Heritage		
Majority are switchers	45	59
Majority are cradle members	64	83
	F = 4.41, sig = .04	F = 12.52, sig < .001

Unlike their Conservative counterparts, college education has not made them less likely to see a particular denominational identity as important. In the Mainline denominations, higher education appears to reinforce (or at least not to erode) the possibility for a distinct religious culture. These denominational cultures seem to have evolved in ways that welcome higher education and make its experiences and assumptions part of church life.

But what about the mobility and diversity of urban environments? Are denominational identities a relic of older and more traditional communities? A strong pattern of denominational identification can be seen in both the Mainline and Conservative rural congregations in our study. In these rural communities, religious identity is part of communally recognized social patterns and networks. Within both Conservative and Mainline traditions, controlling for other factors, rural churches remain much more likely to describe themselves as strongly denominational (Table 24, second section).

This rural loyalty, however, creates an ironic source of potential conflict. There are often vast differences in theology and style between country churches and national offices, especially in the Mainline. As one rural Episcopal rector noted, "Some of the politics and policies of the national church sort of cross with the traditional policy and politics of this area." Among groups such as the United Church of Christ and the Episcopal Church, where rural churches constitute a small minority, this block of loyal traditionalists has little effect on internal politics. But in the United Methodist church, where rural congregations are 70 percent of the total, the struggle for policy dominance is likely to be substantial.[32] Theologically and culturally conservative rural congregations, intensely loyal to their understanding of the denomination's story, have significant resources for resisting the story promoted by a much more liberal national leadership.

One of the most important ways in which rural churches differ from urban ones is the extent to which their members have been part of a single denomination over a lifetime. Almost two-thirds of rural congregations said that "most" or "nearly all" of their members had been born into the denomination; only a quarter of urban congregations described their members that way. Throughout this book we have run into differences between congregations where most are "cradle" adherents of a tradition and congregations where most are "switchers." For individuals, being a cradle member means having a continuity of biographical narrative and a depth of denominational memory that is different from the experience of a "switcher." The switcher can learn to be a good denominational citizen, but that learning will be in the context of voluntary adult choices, rather than in the context of childhood hearth and home. For a congregation, having a majority of cradle members means that habits of language and ritual can be assumed, while congregations full of switchers have to be intentional about teaching traditions, if they are to be maintained.

We discovered that not all switchers lack a sense of identification with their current denominational home, but on average they are less inclined toward strong denominational identity (an average identification score of 11.4 compared to 12.4 for cradle members).[33] And congregations where most members are lifelong adherents are much more likely to be strongly identified with the denomination than are congregations in which most are switchers (70% vs. 48%). But when we take other factors into account, switching—like education—has its effects only in the Conservative Protestant traditions. For Mainline congregations, the differences we see in the bottom section of Table 24 turn out to be an artifact of other structural and cultural factors. Among urban Mainline congregations, the number of switchers makes no difference in the degree to which the church is identified with its denomination. Conservative congregations of all kinds, on the other hand, are affected by having a preponderance of switchers, and individual switchers in Conservative churches are less strongly identified than cradle members. Within evangelical and Pentecostal churches, continuity of tradition seems clearly linked with subjective identification. Additionally (controlling for other aspects of their relationship to the tradition), Conservative churches dominated by cradle members give more to the denomination and are more involved in regional activities. They are no more nor less likely to participate in national events, but on every other measure, Conservative Protestant churches exhibit a consistent pattern that links declines in generational continuity with declines in denominational citizenship.

Among Mainline congregations, however, once we control for other demographic and structural factors, there is no such consistent pattern. Individual cradle members are no more strongly attached than are switchers, nor are congregations dominated by cradle members significantly more (or less) likely to describe themselves in denominational terms.[34] In both the Mainline and Conservative denominations, fewer than one-third of congregations report that most or all of their members were born into the tradition. Switching is more the norm than the exception, but within the Mainline this seems much less determinative of cultural strength than it is for Conservatives. While overall strength of denominational citizenship is somewhat lower in the Mainline, that is not a result of high levels of switching. Switching is a fact of life for all Protestants, but it has greater impact in eroding denominational particularity in Conservative denominations than in Mainline ones.

Within the Mainline Protestant traditions, measures of traditionalism and continuity do not tell us much about whether and how a viable pattern of citizenship is being maintained. This is not a result modernization theories would have predicted. Those dislodged from tradition by education and mobility (both geographic and religious)—whether they are in a Conservative denomination or a more liberal one—should, according to those theories, be less predisposed to particularistic religious identities. Similarly, if we had only exchange theories at our disposal, we could not explain why congregations that receive benefits and services are no more loyal and active than those that do not. And if we had only theories of organizational authority and structure, we could not explain why different organizational patterns yield unpredictable results. Each of these aspects of denominational institutions tells us something, but the strength of the institutions themselves seems to rest elsewhere.

Strong denominational systems seem to be of three sorts, none of which is fully explained by usual organizational and cultural measures. The first set of denominations is held together by a combination of high boundaries, strong authority, and continuity of tradition. Sectarian groups have especially high boundaries and strong authorities, and the tradition is kept alive in proselytizing. Catholic and Orthodox groups have strong authorities; and both boundaries and continuity are reinforced by ties to family and ethnicity. Each has its own distinct pattern of citizenship that varies little across the congregations and individuals within it. The tradition sets the pattern, no matter what the setting or character of the particular congregation in question.

The second set of denominations is in the Conservative Protestant stream, and their strength is very much a matter of cultural change versus continuity. These are the groups best described by the "restructuring" argument about a decline in denominationalism (Wuthnow 1988). The strong Conservative Protestant denominations are indeed those most entrenched in continuity of relationship and tradition, where identities and participation have been relatively less disturbed by mobility and education. As individuals and congregations enter a more urban and diverse religious world, they are downplaying their denominational affiliation, describing themselves in more generic evangelical terms, and drawing on the resources of a burgeoning evangelical network of parachurch suppliers. They have certainly not become less "religious" or even less conservative, but they have increasingly opted for boundaries defined by the evangelical world rather than those defined by particular denominational traditions.

But Mainline Protestants fit none of these patterns. Theirs are the most precarious denominations, with high levels of switching, and highly educated constituents. If denominationalism is thriving among at least some of those well-educated and mobile individuals, we must look beyond external cultural sources for its explanation. Understanding how denominationalism functions here will require that we look beyond organizational and structural factors to the agency of the congregations themselves, to what they are doing and how they tell their own stories.

NARRATIVE PRACTICES

Across religious traditions, but especially in the Mainline, the "glue" provided by specific social practices is what allows particular denominational narratives to become part of the ongoing life of a congregation.[35] Especially when ties of cultural continuity cannot be assumed, some local congregations intentionally provide those who participate with opportunities to learn denominational lore. These local choices are a critical factor in sustaining denominational narratives and identities.

TABLE 25 Effects of Narrative Practices on Denominational Identity
in Conservative and Mainline Protestant Congregations

	Percentage of Congregations with a Strong Denominational Identity
Educational Practices	
Use denominational Sunday School curriculum	66
Use other curriculum	51
	$F = 7.77$, sig $= .006$
Worship Practices	
Use denominational hymnal	67
Use other hymnals	46
	$F = 15.61$, sig $< .001$
Mission Practices	
Talk about denominational achievements & programs	71
Mention no denominational achievements or programs	56
	$F = 6.89$, sig $= .009$

Our interviews allowed us to locate at least three key points where intentional narrative practices bring denominational identity to life.[36]

Educational Practices

The practice of using a denominational curriculum in the teaching of the congregation's children is one such identity point. Such a choice is by no means universal, especially among Protestant congregations.[37] As we have seen, churches often shop for educational resources from among the many publishing lines available from independent publishers, as well as from other denominations. Choosing to teach children through a denominational lens is not taken for granted, but it is a practice that makes a clear difference. Sixty-six percent of white Protestant congregations that report using their denomination's curriculum also report a strong denominational identity, while only 51 percent of others do. The pattern is the same for both Conservatives and Mainliners (see Table 25, top section). Whether it is a sense of loyalty that guides the choice or the choice that creates the sense of identity, how congregations teach their children is closely linked to how they define themselves. They are more likely to act as if they have a distinct story to tell.

The effect is apparent among individual adults as well. People who participate in religious education that includes denominational resources say that the denomination is more important to them. Only about a third (37%) of the adults we surveyed reported that they were in such a class, but that minority had significantly higher denominational identity scores than did those who were in no such denominationally resourced class (12.5 vs. 10.9). Paying attention to the denominational story is relatively rare in adult education, but where it happens members are more committed to their particular traditions.

Especially within Mainline Protestant groups and where the number of lifelong members is few, congregations that use denominational curricula for their children are significantly more likely to report that their connection to their denominational tradition is strong. Rural and urban, cradle member or switcher, people who are exposed to the denomination's own ways of talking about itself are more likely to describe themselves and their choices in terms of that particular religious identity.

Worship Practices

Denominational narratives are also actively sustained in ritual practices (Hadaway and Roozen 1995). Liturgical traditions, prayer books, hymnals, and the like, carry and maintain the stories of a denomination no less than does its more overt curriculum (Gill 1999). Congregations across all traditions and polities that use the hymnals and worship books of their own denomination are significantly more likely to describe themselves in strongly denominational terms (67% vs. 46%). Even among congregations that have few cradle members and otherwise have few cultural or structural supports for a distinctive religious culture, those that use denominational worship materials have a stronger sense of denominational identity.

For some denominations, particular ways of worshiping are central to who they are. Episcopalians and Lutherans, for instance, have an order of service that still bears marks of the Catholic tradition from which they came. The Book of Common Prayer and the Lutheran Book of Worship set out beautifully crafted prayers and prescribed ways of conducting everything from evening vespers to services for holidays. Learning to use these books to make one's way through a service is an acquired skill, although one easier for the highly educated members who disproportionately choose to join churches in these denominations. Those that do join and do acquire this skill have thereby invested in a tradition they may now delight in calling their own.[38] Churches that set prayer books aside as too intimidating to the hosts of switchers who populate their pews do so at a cost. Not only do congregations with more eclectic worship practices lose a strong sense of identification with their denomination, but they may also lose more adherents to future intergenerational switching (Sherkat 2001).

Emphasizing worship traditions is a critical narrative practice precisely among congregations where the structural and cultural supports for citizenship have been weakened (e.g., those in the Mainline Protestant traditions and with more than a majority of switchers as members). Rural Protestants and congregations full of cradle members, by contrast, were *less* likely to tell us that they emphasize their distinct worship traditions than were their urban and mobile counterparts. Traditions in those places need less intentional emphasis.[39] But among urban, Mainline congregations, those with a majority of switcher members were *more* likely to emphasize the distinctness of their worship than were congregations with more lifelong adherents. What for some congregations is a taken-for-granted way of life, has to be emphasized and taught in others. At a growing and diverse Episcopal parish in Albuquerque, the rector said, "We celebrate the Eucharist in a very traditional way. We really value our tradition and . . . you know, we are not trying to be all things to all people. We are saying we're going to present this wonderful rich tradition we have in a way that is open." The narratives embodied in ritual practice help to bind the story of the local congregation to the story of a larger denomination, even as these diverse mobile congregations also look for ways to be open to the newcomers who do not yet know the traditions.[40]

Mission Practices

Denominational narratives also include stories of the good work done by collective national efforts. Whether disaster relief or souls saved in a foreign land, accounts of worthy and successful denominational work are part of the repertoire of public narratives out of which denominational citizenship is made. At an exurban United Methodist church in Nashville, the pastor talked about the link between the congregation's sense of mission and the initiatives coming from the national denomination: "The bishops' initiative two years ago was on ministry with the poor and marginalized. This congregation has embraced that whole-heartedly."[41] Our informants who told such stories[42] were also more likely to describe their congregations as strongly attached to a denominational identity (see Table 25, bottom section).[43] Once again, the pattern is the same for both Conservatives and Mainliners, and again, there is reinforcing data from the individual members we surveyed. The parishioners who felt most well informed about denominational missions and programs had significantly higher denominational identity scores (12.5 vs. 11.3), as did those who ranked "supporting mission efforts in the nation and the world" as a high priority for their congregation (12.8 vs. 11.4). Even when other factors are taken into account, congregations where these stories are told are much more likely to describe themselves as strong denominational citizens; and individual members who are connected to denominational mission are more interested in sustaining a denominational identity for themselves.

It would appear, then, that denominational connection is less the result of what agencies do for congregations than the result of what those agencies allow congregations to do for others. Denominational systems allow the exchange of resources, but none of the material resources congregations *receive* made them any more likely to support or identify with their particular tradition. Denominations at their strongest represent an extension of the outreach of local congregations, not a service agency supplying consultation and grants. Our survey of individual attenders showed that the goal of providing aid and service to people in need was near the top of their list of congregational priorities, as was support for mission work beyond the local community. As we have already seen, that outreach can take myriad forms, but those who hear stories of how denominational agencies are helping them to serve the world are more likely to see themselves as citizens of a denominational system they value. Whether they are Conservative or Mainline, serving the spiritual and material needs of the world remains a primary motivation for banding together with those of like faith.

All of these narrative practices are most common in congregations that are also relatively active in their regional church bodies. Those who gather with nearby coreligionists have opportunities to develop relationships and access resources, but they also learn the stories. They are more likely to use denominational curricula and hymnals and to talk about the good work their denominations do. Regional participation facilitates a set of practices that, in turn, enhance the bonds of identification between local congregations and larger traditions. This is particularly significant since it is the better educated and urban congregations that are also more likely to get involved in regional activities. In other words, the cultural forces that might erode denominational loyalty also encourage the regional participation which can counter those forces by making the narrative resources of the denomination more available. While one path to religious identity lies within cultural continuity (lifelong membership and rural residence), another follows lines of regional organizational participation and intentional narrative engagement.

Telling denominational stories, in turn, has organizational consequences. Congregations that are more closely identified with their traditions, especially in the Mainline, also devote larger proportions of their budgets to the work of the extended organization of which they are a part. The narrative practices that build denominationally rooted identities also bode well for the organizational health of national denominations (Zech 1997). People in local congregations want to serve the larger world and seem willing to do it in concert with people and organizations they recognize as sharing a common set of religious traditions and practices.

Denominational identity thus largely results from relationships and narrative practices, not authority, organization, or patterns of exchange. Among white Protestant denominations, in spite of cultural trends that have loosened traditional bonds, local narrative practices, encouraged by strong networks of regional participation, can still sustain denominational religious identities.

INSTITUTIONAL MODELS OF DENOMINATIONAL IDENTITY AND PARTICIPATION

The picture that has emerged to this point is much more complicated than a simple story of denominational decline. There is no one answer to what creates and sustains denominational institutions, and no one answer to whether denominations remain salient points of identity for millions of American "seekers" or thousands of voluntary and independent local congregations. In spite of the cultural strains, both denominationalism as a system and particular denominations as players within that system seem to be surviving.

The health of the denominational system is perhaps best seen in the experience of the new religious traditions. Hindus, Muslims, and Buddhists, with growing numbers of adherents in the United States, are establishing local centers of worship, organizing volunteer members to carry out educational and social activities, hiring "clergy" leaders, and linking local communities together into networks and national organizations that can represent the tradition. They are inventing new organizational forms and finding new cultural patterns that will allow them to act as members of their own religious tradition in the midst of a religiously pluralist American culture.

Those existing institutional models for holding together a denomination might be thought of as bundles of practices that different traditions put together in different ways. Not only does the content of religious citizenship vary from tradition to tradition, but its form varies as well—but not in infinite and utterly idiosyncratic ways.[44]

Different institutional models, each with its own combination of rules, structural ties, relationships, and narrative practices, provide multiple templates for religious citizenship (Somers 1993).

RELIGIO-CULTURAL HOMELANDS

Among Catholic and Orthodox parishes, citizenship is based on a strong sense of narrative identity that binds local parishes to the larger Church. Reinforced by a strong hierarchical authority, ties to ethnic heritage, and vibrant and distinctive ritual traditions, it is nearly unthinkable for a Catholic or Orthodox parish to be anything other than thoroughly tied to its tradition—even though almost no one participates in national events, and very few cite any resource they receive. They are held together by ritual culture and by networks of intradenominational organizations (Holy Name societies, devotions to saints, even the Knights of Columbus or Catholic Charities), not by a centralized bureaucratic structure or exchanges of goods. There may be a good deal of worry these days about the strength of individual Catholic identities,[45] but the Catholic and Orthodox parishioners we surveyed were the most tied to their religious traditions of any people we studied.

Catholicism and Orthodoxy remain clearly identified sectors within American pluralism. Each is maintaining its own particular ways of worshiping, its patterns of educating children, its habits for organizing parish life, even distinctive patterns of involvement in local and international benevolence. Both traditions have created space for typical American expectations of voluntarism, but Catholic and Orthodox identities are recognizable as distinct variations on the American theme.

MOBILIZED MASSES

Sectarian groups, such as Jehovah's Witnesses, Latter-day Saints, and Christian Scientists, have an equally distinct denominational system. Religious authority is paradoxically both highly dispersed and strictly centralized. Latter-day Saints ordain every twelve-year-old male to the priesthood, but they also delegate to top national leadership the smallest congregational details—style of music, décor, building design, even the ward's name.[46] Jehovah's Witnesses, similarly, expect every member to be a "witness," but evangelism is highly scripted by the Watchtower Society (Beckford 1975, 72–75; Penton 1997, 237–42). In a similar pattern, Christian Scientists elect rotating "lay readers" from among their members, but their responsibilities are limited to just that—reading without comment the prescribed selections from the church's sacred texts.

High levels of lay investment and strong central authority are combined here with high boundaries that set members apart from the rest of society (Mormon dietary practices and Jehovah's Witness and Christian Science shunning of some medical practices, for instance). The costs of joining and leaving are substantial (Iannaccone 1994; C. Smith 1998), but subcultural strength is reinforced by the authority and efficiency of national organizations. The strong commitment of local congregations is apparent in the generous gifts they give, the publications they uniformly use, and the national events they attend in large numbers. Sectarian denominations are not held together by an inherited culture or familial relationships, but by a culture and relationships intentionally created by the organization (Holden 2002, 51–52).

FELLOWSHIP FOR THE MARGINALIZED

The story in the historic African American denominations could not be more different. Neither centralized religious authority nor organized denominational programs establish what it means to be a black Baptist. Even the National Baptists' headquarters building in Nashville is more a meeting house than an office building. When I arrived there at 10 o'clock on a Monday morning—when there was no meeting scheduled—the doors were locked and the building was empty. The black Methodist and Church of God in Christ denominations, with their system of bishops, have created a somewhat more elaborate structure of professional offices and services, but across both hierarchical (Methodist) and locally autonomous (Baptist) groups, it is not the use of denominational resources or any bureaucratized structure that creates attachment among African American churches.

Rather, it is a sense of camaraderie and fellowship, fostered especially by large annual gatherings to which disproportionately large church delegations are likely to go. The dominant metaphor in the National Baptist Convention is "family" more than corporation, and what the family does is have an annual reunion (Morris and Lee forthcoming). African American denominations are held together by culture, both intentional (nearly universal use of denominational hymnals) and inherited (most congregations are still dominated by cradle members). The rules that exist operate within a family-like system of patrimony, and the stories that are told come from both published sources and champion preachers (Washington 1986, 180).

The story of denominational decline is therefore not a story that makes sense within these large sectors of U.S. religion. For Sectarians, Catholics and Orthodox Christians, and African American Protestants, a combination of religious authority and a multifaceted religious culture establishes for each a distinctive place in the American denominational system and a distinct institutionalized pattern of collective activity. Each group within these religious families has the advantage of a relatively coherent cultural system that situates individuals and congregations within relationships whose boundaries and contours are clear and establishes the means for acting as part of the American religious whole.

It is Conservative and Mainline Protestants for whom the question of denominational citizenship is a challenging one. While a combination of religious doctrine and bureaucratic efficiency may have defined the institutional template of Protestantism for most of the twentieth century, there are new institutional patterns emerging.

EVANGELICAL NETWORKS

Among Conservative Protestants, a generic "just Christian" identity exists today, alongside self-designations as "evangelical," "Bible-believing," and "Spirit-filled." Each label situates its user within one of the tributaries of a broad Conservative stream. Just as theories of modernization and restructuring would predict, switching, higher education, and urbanization are associated here with lower levels of denominational identification—but certainly *not* with lower levels of religiosity or a boundary-less religious world. Urban and suburban Pentecostals and evangelicals are surrounded by the vast network of generically evangelical special purpose groups, schools, and independent churches that increasingly legitimate an identity as "Christian" (meaning evangelical) rather than denominational.[47]

These networked evangelical organizations allow maximum autonomy to local churches but still manage to create distinct identities and nurture common projects. In addition to the well-established networks like the Churches of Christ, many of the more explicitly nondenominational churches nevertheless participate in named networks as well. Even those that most vigorously claim their independence share a sense of identity (as "nondenominational" or "Independent Baptist"), use a common pool of suppliers, send their youth to an identifiable list of religious colleges, and support distinctive mission agencies and projects. In shared events, shared media, and a shared evangelical culture, a distinct Conservative religious identity is nurtured.

BOUNDARYLESS FAITH

Most of the earliest religious groups that developed the American denominational mode have become today's Mainline Protestants—Episcopalians, Congregationalists, Presbyterians, Lutherans, and the like. These are the groups that have supported the National Council of Churches, and for most of the twentieth century an ecumenical theological ideal has pushed churches and members away from denominational particularity and toward a universalized vision of Christianity. It was a theology that made sense in the modern, well-educated, and cosmopolitan world in which most leaders and members lived, its greatest virtue a tolerant openness that left aside religious particularity (Hoge, Johnson, and Luidens 1994).

While individuals and congregations in this institutional mode do need outside organizational resources, any partner of equal tolerance will do. Secular agencies can help them deliver social services to their communities, and publishers from many different traditions can provide them with resources for expanding the religious horizons of their members. Scouting programs can help them raise children who are good citizens, and international relief agencies can help them do good in the world. Their primary organizational mode is networking, but with "inclusive" rather than "evangelical" theological imperatives defining the boundaries of the networks. Denominational agencies have no special advantage in this world and must compete alongside other special-purpose groups.

PORTABLE ROOTS

Vanishing boundaries are not, however, the only institutional model among Mainline Protestants. In the Mainline, in contrast to the situation among Conservative groups, high levels of switching and equally high levels of college education have become part of nevertheless-distinct denominational cultures. Mobility and education are part of the story these congregations tell about themselves, and telling stories is the key to an institutional model that both nurtures particularity and recognizes change.

Among both Conservatives and Mainliners, denominational citizenship is strengthened by intentional congregational practices that link local life to the denomination's narratives. Telling stories about denominational mission accomplishments, singing the songs of the faith and otherwise emphasizing its distinctive worship practices, teaching children and adults from denominationally produced materials—these narrative practices are by no means universal, but where they are present, congregations are more likely to link their own identity with that of their denomination. Even (indeed, especially) where the external cultural supports have eroded, these chosen local strategies link churches to larger traditions in ways that combine the particularity and agency of the local congregation with the traditions, policies, and programs of the national body.

Local narrative practices help to explain how Mainline Protestants are sustaining distinct denominational identities without the high subcultural boundaries Conservatives construct (C. Smith 1998). While that more insular kind of identity maintenance does seem to be at work among evangelical and Pentecostal Protestants, it would be a mistake to build general theories on the Conservative pattern. Neither strict orthodoxy nor costly sacrifices are necessary to sustain commitment (as "rational choice" theories would predict; see Finke and Stark 1992; Iannaccone 1994). Some moderates and liberals are nurturing distinctive organizations by intentionally teaching new members their traditions, valorizing their denomination's work, and celebrating rituals of song and prayer that bind individual experience to a sacred drama. Mobility across religious lines persists, but life within each community remains identifiable and strong because there are stories to tell and things to do together (Ammerman 1997c).

CONCLUSIONS AND IMPLICATIONS FOR THE FUTURE

Voluntary religious citizenship remains a viable feature of the cultural landscape in the United States. It is sustained by diverse forms of relationships, structures, and narratives—in some cases nearly undisturbed, in other cases undergoing significant change. Some maintain a citizenship built on strong religious authority, relationships embedded in ethnic and traditional cultures, and sacred narratives enacted in compelling rituals or personal evangelizing.

Only among the white Protestant denominations, especially those that took the route of developing bureaucratized national agency structures, do we find the elaborate breakdown and reconstruction that has been posited by those who mourn (or celebrate) the demise of denominationalism. Especially among Conservatives, urbanization, switching, and higher education, along with the centralization and professionalization of the denominations themselves, threaten to displace denominational narratives in favor of a generalized evangelical culture.

Liberal and moderate groups, however, are full of the same sorts of educated and mobile members, but with different results. Just as immigration and transnationalism are remaking notions of nationhood and citizenship (Sassen 1996), so Mainline Protestant "switchers" are redefining denominational identity. For some, the result is a kind of homogenized religious version of "McDonaldization," a generic religiosity that allows them to find common ground in the diverse worlds in which they live.

But for others, in spite of moving easily across boundaries and forming shifting and diverse coalitions, distinct religious identities remain. Theirs is a tale of voluntary citizenship built from the everyday decisions of individuals and congregations who choose to take up the story. They take it up in how they teach their children, the way they worship, the songs they sing. Their members come, at least in part, because they want to be part of an organization that brings good into the world beyond their own communities. They choose particular religious organizations because they are recognized as legitimate contributors to that task. As denominations give them stories to tell about good work collectively done, those stories produce both stronger identification and financial support. These new denominational citizens are educated and mobile persons for whom the mission, heritage, and practices of their religious home are worth talking about. They have found stories and practices suited to religious pilgrims.

Americans will surely remain seekers, but they are also likely to establish at least temporary dwellings among the voluntary religious communities that give structure to America's plural religious landscape. What they will find in those voluntary local gatherings are traditions that are being both carried on and remade. They will find in some religious communities traditions that demand their intense devotion and full-time commitment, while others ask much less. But in each, they will find a community that knows it must take responsibility for itself, voluntarily sustaining its own tradition and communicating its own identity to the larger world.

CHAPTER EIGHT · Voluntary and Diverse
Communities of Faith

*American Congregations and
American Society*

We observed at the beginning of this book the remarkably robust character of religious life in the United States. Without state regulation—but also without state support—people in the United States regularly gather with their fellow citizens to voluntarily do religious work. Even though many Americans choose to express their religion privately, congregations and denominations persist. American law and society created a space for voluntary religious communities, and believers of all sorts have taken advantage of that free space to create congregations in which they gather to worship, learn, and serve in their own peculiar ways.

And wildly peculiar they are—from high church Episcopalians to lively Pentecostals, from Christian fundamentalists to gatherings of Wiccans and pagans, from Quakers with American roots extending to the seventeenth century to Sikhs who arrived in appreciable numbers only in the last generation. But American religious diversity is by no means new. One could argue that the diversity of eighteenth-century American religion is one of the primary reasons the constitutional framers did not seek to create an established church. There was already as much diversity on these shores as in the whole of the European continent and far more than in any one European society (Butler 1990). Sidney Mead argued that religious tolerance had already become a pragmatic necessity, that religiously diverse immigrants "learned in a relatively short time to live together in peace under the genial aegis of the Dutch and English combination of patriotic-religious fervor, toleration, cynicism, simple desire for profits, efficacious muddling through, and 'salutary neglect' that made up the colonial policy of these nations" (S. Mead 1963, 106). Congregationalists and Presbyterians and Episcopalians held a kind of privileged place in the mix, but no one religious tradition was dominant enough to be able to fight to become a state religion when the time for a constitution arrived. That, Andrew Greeley asserts, is the key to understanding the religious history that has followed (Greeley 1972).

Even in New England the established Congregationalists had to give up their privilege early in the nineteenth century, and before that century was over, this country had given birth to dozens of new religious traditions and had become the immigrant home to dozens more. Nathan Hatch describes the first third of the nineteenth century in ways that evoke our own time. Having set loose the possibility of religious liberty, what followed was "a period of religious ferment, chaos, and originality unmatched in American history. Few traditional claims to religious authority could weather such a relentless beating. There were competing claims of old denominations and a host of new ones. Wandering prophets appeared dramatically, and supremely heterodox religious movements gained followings. People veered from one church to another. Religious competitors wrangled unceasingly" (Hatch 1989, 64). Today's religious diversity stands in a long line of religious inventiveness and experimentation. And in spite of the dozens of groups who would argue that they and they alone know the true way to live, all that inventiveness has taken place with relatively little overt or violent religious conflict.[1]

The implication for religious groups themselves was that they would have to learn to be one among many. The Protestant Reformation had introduced Europeans to some modest notion of religious pluralism as the monopoly of the Roman Catholic Church was broken. There were "sects" that stood in dissent against the "Church" (Weber 1922). But most of the new Protestant movements responded by setting up their own exclusive domains—Lutherans in Germany and Scandinavia, the Church of England, Reformed (Calvinist) Protestant domains in Switzerland and the Netherlands. Only the "radical" reformers (Mennonites, Baptists, and Brethren, for instance) argued for complete separation from state power. Only these separatists ventured placing complete reliance on voluntary membership and on spiritual rather than earthly persuasion.

In the United States those radical impulses won the day. Without state authorities to enforce orthodoxy, each group's attempt to create a more nearly perfect spiritual community was free to find its own fertile soil or perish. The sectarian power of spiritual persuasion was honed in the revivals of the Great Awakenings, and in the early nineteenth century it began to find permanent expression in organized missionary and charitable societies.[2] Each group could embody its religious impulses in the pragmatic organizations that the American experiment made possible. It was a system born of the Protestant impulse, but nurtured in the pragmatic and pluralist democracy of the United States.

What of this legacy remains two centuries later? While Protestants are still, collectively, the majority in the United States, Catholics have been the largest single denomination for 150 years, and the religious diversity of the recent immigrants has introduced many new patterns of faith. Some non-Protestant traditions have complained that they have been "Protestantized" as they have accommodated to American culture. Whatever else that has meant, they are right that they have been pushed to adopt a basic commitment to live peacefully alongside religious others. The idea that a religious group could both celebrate its unique identity *and* recognize the limits of its power is a continuing legacy of the Protestants who dominated the early European settlements in North America and filled the ranks of eighteenth- and nineteenth-century political and civic leadership.

That legacy involved both the important commitment to live alongside others and the equally important willingness to invest voluntary resources in preserving and extending a religious tradition.[3] The Constitution guaranteed their right to do so, but it did not guarantee that any given group would succeed: only the group's own voluntary efforts could do that. The organizational result is the many local congregations that this book has attempted to describe and the web of denominations and other organizations that give larger expression to religious identity and mission. There are, however, strains on this system as we enter a new century. Is the U.S. system of organizing religion healthy enough to handle the increased demands of escalating diversity and mobility? To meet these demands will require a continued commitment to and extension of our norms of tolerance, as well as continued organizational investment by religious communities in their own bonds of fellowship and transcendence.

MANAGING RELIGIOUS DIVERSITY

Constitutional guarantees and basic habits of civility establish the foundation for managing the religious pluralism that we find all around us. Built on that foundation is the system of denominationalism that provides religious groups with ways to identify and organize. Denominations establish a base of legitimacy and recognition that can extend to the congregations and work that come under their aegis. To act like a denomination is both to claim a place in a recognized religious tradition and to provide a mechanism for doing good in the world—to claim a particular identity and to provide a place from which partnerships can be constructed. When we recognize a group as part of a denomination, we expect both a measure of distinctiveness and a willingness to play by American rules of tolerance.

Being part of a denomination is also, as has been argued here, to claim a place in a still larger stream of tradition, and those larger religious families provide Americans with the psychological necessity of a categorizing scheme. We enhance our sense of religious and social order by reducing the hundreds of traditions we encounter to a few broad families—more than the three (Protestant, Catholic, Jew) observed half a century ago, but still just a handful. You may not really know much about the Nazarenes, but if they tell you they are evangelicals, you may recognize that they are legitimately on the American religious map, and you may know roughly where to find them. In part we manage our diversity by identifying the larger extended families to which we belong. When people choose a new group to join, for instance, they are likely to choose from within a fairly limited selection rather than peruse the entire menu.[4] They stay within the religious family, if not within their own specific denomination. As we have seen in examining congregational life, these religious families shape common patterns that give worship and service familiar forms. Those streams of tradition have evolved over our history, dividing and multiplying, gathering new groups in, but continually establishing rough cultural categories that shape the religious landscape.

We categorize in a similar manner as we confront the vast array of organizational activity in which religious groups engage. A fairly narrow range of institutional templates gives recognizable form to the work being done. "Congregation" and "denomination" are among the most venerable. Those templates are by no means unchanging. The structure and activities we expect to find in a congregation or denomination have shifted significantly over the last 250 years,[5] but the organizational categories remain. We may not understand the nuances of Hindu philosophy, but if we imagine that the group of Hindus we encounter is like a congregation, we begin the process of incorporating that group into a predictable set of relationships and interactions. That Hindu temple may resist calling itself a congregation, but the forces of "institutional isomorphism" still push them to have a leader and a board, an ad in the Yellow Pages "churches" section, and an increasingly predictable range of worship, fellowship, and educational activities. Even if the content of those activities is strange to many Americans, the form and function are nevertheless familiar (Warner 1994). Organizational theorists point out that one of the functions of this isomorphism is to make exchanges between organizations more possible. When there are similar functions and departments, organizations know how to relate to each other (DiMaggio and Powell 1983). By establishing religious organizational templates, our culture has provided another of the mechanisms that assist in managing our diversity.

Those organizational templates have been visible frequently as we looked at American congregational life. What any local group teaches is shaped by a particular tradition, but that they have a weekly program of children's religious education is shaped by a larger organizational template. What they do when they socialize together may vary from bingo to baseball, but that they organize some sort of social activity is part of what the larger culture expects. As soon as they have sufficient resources, the culture will expect that congregation to organize some sort of outreach into the community and the world as well. U.S. culture provides us with something of a blueprint, even if the materials to make it a reality are highly variable.

Reducing the types of religions by establishing family patterns and reducing the complexity by using organizational templates are means for navigating the diverse religious terrain in modern-day America. But that does not always tell us how these diverse religions are to take their place alongside each other when matters of common public concern draw them into conversation with their neighbors. Do we really want all those different voices bombarding us with their religious visions for how we should collectively live? The possibility of several hundred religious groups sending missionaries to our doors and lobbyists to seats of government strikes terror in the minds of many. Can we really survive our religious diversity if religious opinions are not kept strictly private?

My answer is yes.[6] What we have falsely come to believe—especially in the last fifty years—is that separation of church and state means that religion must be solely a private and individual matter. Wherever two or more are gathered together, let not religion intrude. This caution about religion is born of our well-placed caution about power. The impulse to restrain the public presence of religion comes in legitimate response to the threat of either state-imposed or de facto religious authority. Our Constitution wisely prohibits any agent of the state from compelling religious belief or observance, but it also wisely protects the "free exercise" of whatever religious impulses may fall within otherwise acceptable law and practice. That constitutional regime nurtured the habits of denominationalism that have developed in the United States, enjoining each group to cultivate freely its own traditions while refraining from using state power to impose those traditions on others. But neither our religious nor our political institutions require that religious traditions remain outside everyday public life, only that they enter those public domains with a due humility.

That humility entails both a recognition that no single group is in charge and a recognition that no group can accomplish its goals alone. What we have seen in this book, for instance, is that the work congregations do as they care for their communities is largely accomplished through strategic alliances with other organizations. Congregations form informal partnerships, contribute to religious and secular nonprofit agencies, and even form alliances with businesses and governmental organizations. Is such reaching out for help a sign of religious institutional weakness, an admission that religious groups do not have the resources to do everything that needs to be done for the citizens of a community? It *is* an admission that religious groups need partners, but that is a weakness only if the comparison is to an imagined past. Religious institutions have never been the sole caretakers of the public welfare. In this country they have always been one player among several.

The complex web of partnerships documented here is critical to the American communities to which congregations contribute, as well as to the congregations themselves. Nearly every one of them has at least one link to an organization that helps them provide for the needs of people beyond their own members, and nearly every one draws on resources it did not produce. Some of those resources and partners reinforce particular traditions, and some stretch and redefine those traditions. As American congregations make their way through the marketplace of suppliers and mission partners, they attempt a delicate balance between bonding and bridging, drawing on and extending their own traditions while making common cause with diverse other organizations. The question is not *whether* congregations will work in partnership, but *what kind* of partnerships they will nurture.

Will those partnerships, for instance, be enhanced to form broader pathways for trust and communication? If so, will that erode the sense of connection and distinction congregations have within their own traditions? Most local outreach partnerships, for instance, are metropolitan or countywide in scope and extend beyond the congregation's own denomination. Does this mean that secular and parachurch agencies have replaced denominations, and that cross-tradition relationships are replacing intratradition ones? By no means. Our data do not suggest that congregations that work with community agencies are any more or less committed to and active in their denominations. Their local service work complements what they do with and through their denomination.

The result of building these cross-tradition partnerships, in turn, is that volunteers have opportunities to encounter a variety of coproviders and diverse recipients. When congregations establish links to others in the community, they not only provide necessary resources to those community groups, but also expand and redefine the nature of their own membership and citizenship in the community. As the director of Albuquerque's Storehouse said to us, "We are, in a real sense, also a ministry *to* the churches." Community agencies allow congregations to build bridges to others who share a concern and are willing to pool resources.

Locally, congregations are both working with others and working with their denominational partners. When we look at other kinds of outreach and at efforts beyond local communities, denominations are far more important as congregational partners than are parachurch organizations. In spite of the persistent parade of death notices, reports of the demise of denominations is considerably premature. Five out of six Christian congregations are affiliated with a denomination and give most of their mission dollars through that denomination. The newer parachurch organizations *are* significant partners, especially for Conservative and independent churches, but even there they appear to supplement more than displace traditional denominational connections.

Working within a tradition and reaching beyond that tradition—both patterns seem firmly in place. Each congregation is likely to put together its own functional network of denominational and parachurch partners, so if denominationalism requires having a monopoly on congregations' attention, the doomsayers are right. The networks that make it possible for congregations to work for the good of the world are not tightly contained by individual denominations. Those who work least with partners are also least likely to do charitable work at all. But if healthy congregations need multiple kinds of partnerships, this situation is good news. While maintaining the denominational ties that have shaped their history and identity, congregations are also reaching out to work with many others.

The potential of those partnerships often goes unrealized, however. The conversations that naturally occur in the midst of service activities hold great potential for knitting together diverse congregations around common concerns. The volunteers who meet at a soup kitchen and the participants who eat there share a space in which notions of the common good are being negotiated (Allahyari 2001; C. Bender 2003). Congregational members who get involved in community organizations are almost always thereby engaged with people who are different from themselves—economically disadvantaged, from different cultures and faiths, often people they might otherwise distrust. Yet congregations seldom intentionally provide them with resources from their own faith traditions for interpreting those encounters. Nor do they focus on learning from the diverse stories and experiences these volunteers might bring back (Lichterman 2004).

Often the routinization of volunteer work keeps implicit bridging partnerships from being fully realized. The same group serves the same meal on the same night of the week. Their congregation depends on them to go; they put it on their calendars; the agency gives them an identifiable and doable task (Wuthnow 1991). No one talks much about what happens and why. Only when disaster strikes are routines unsettled enough to activate the implicit links.[7] When riots struck Los Angeles in 1992, for instance, congregations became a primary organizing point for recovery. That was possible not only because they were already present in the community, but also because they were already linked to denominations and other organizations that mobilized volunteers and resources (Orr et al. 1994). A disruption activated nascent connections. After September 11, similar mobilization of nascent networks took place, opening up spaces for public conversation and connection as well as for the delivery of essential social services (Ammerman 2002b). Volunteers from the whole range of American religious communities found themselves working together to respond to the disaster.

Not content to wait for a riot or other disaster, a variety of faith-based community organizing groups (not to be confused with "faith-based initiatives") have taken their cue from models pioneered by Saul Alinsky. They work in communities around the country to create ongoing links among congregations and other civic actors. As we have seen, they reach only a small portion of congregations, but through the one-on-one conversations they sponsor across diverse community constituencies, they invite citizens to articulate their concerns and find common ground—almost always ground that is also enriched with the singing, praying, and preaching of the various faith traditions that support the effort (Pattillo-McCoy 1998; R. Wood 2002). Both these community organizing groups and the experience of responding to disaster demonstrate the bridge-building potential of faith-based partnerships.

Given the history of religiously based social movements in the United States, we should hardly be surprised to find faith and public activism in the same room.[8] Nor should we be surprised when there are diverse faith commitments that bring people together around a common cause. Cultural habits of keeping religion private and social theories that predict "secularization" have conspired to convince us that impassable walls stand between public and private, religious and secular. That has never been the case. Individual people routinely speak of God in many public arenas, religious ideas have often mobilized public action, and religious organizations routinely work in cooperation with others, for the public good. Some religious groups choose for their own reasons to remain separate and private, tending to the spiritual well-being of their own members and converts and only indirectly to the "public" good (McRoberts 2003). But as we have seen, such isolation is rare.

Congregations are not primarily political institutions, but neither are public concerns absent from the religious work they do. Nor are religious public concerns always a matter of arguments about "Truth." It is a mistake to assume that religion is inherently defined by a concern for purity and truth that will always prevent compromise and cooperation when brought to bear on public issues (see, e.g., Friedland and Alford 1991). Some religious communities do claim to be primarily concerned with preserving their particular version of sacred truth, shunning cooperation with those they consider infidels and apostates. Others enter the public arena but retain a rhetoric that claims God's exclusive blessing on their particular view of the common good. But even those convinced that God is on their side are also shaped by deep convictions that acceptable democratic civic participation requires them to win their struggle through persuasion rather than violence (Munson forthcoming). Our public arguments are often about religiously inspired moral differences, but even the most ardent believer still enters that public arena knowing that they are one voice among many. When Jerry Falwell or Pat Robertson pronounces God's blessing or curse on matters of public policy, the ironic practical effect of their pronouncements is to begin a public debate in which they implicitly acknowledge that their pronouncements are not the last word.

We can expect to hear many different religious voices in public debates. No single moral voice or religious vision guides American society—nor should it. As we attempt to debate our future and organize to care for our communities, we will hear many moral voices, both religious and secular. Our constitutional system denies any of them the ability to impose their will on us. Our denominational system encourages them to recognize their own partiality. Our organizational and cultural systems provide us with shortcuts for sorting out the arguments, and our existing systems of partnership establish potential cross-cutting bridges that can blunt the edge of division. In a variety of ways, American cultural and organizational patterns have equipped us well for the diversity we face.

Groups from within the various religious streams will engage this public conversation differently, each bringing its own strengths, but facing its own challenges in achieving more effective participation. As has been noted throughout this book, most Sectarian traditions primarily choose to work within their own communities, speaking to larger constituencies only as they seek converts or as they defend the legitimacy of their own practices. Their contribution has been that very willingness to use the American constitutional system to defend their nonmainstream place in the society, thereby helping all of us to clarify the limits of our tolerance.

Mainline Protestants, on the other hand, have been the opposite of sectarian. They have a long history and an enduring record of expecting their individual members to create and support organizations that benefit the larger community (Hall 1998). But, perhaps because people in the Mainline Protestant traditions recognize their implicit (and sometimes explicit) historic power, many have sought to exercise good citizenship by refusing to speak publicly of their faith. Rather than risk imposing Mainline Protestant ideas and practices on others, leaders and members alike have remained silent. They were actively engaged, often in partnership with a wide array of community agencies, but so humble as to be invisible.

With no dominant religious tradition in the United States today, however, this Mainline reticence is largely misplaced. The old patterns and connections that gave Protestant leaders their implicit cultural power are gone. If Mainline Protestants have a faith story to tell, they will be telling it alongside other strong religious voices. As Warner notes, "wise clergy recognize that even mainline Protestantism is today a counterculture" (Warner 1999, 236). Any religious group that seeks to exercise influence or effect change will have to do so in partnership with others.

American Catholics have their own strengths and challenges. The rich theological traditions of the Church speak clearly of public responsibility and have a publicly visible home in an official hierarchy. That visibility is a strength that can be used to great advantage.[9] As the largest and most diverse religious group in the United States, the Catholic Church can speak with considerable effect. Having resolved to take its place alongside other denominations in a voluntary and democratic system, its size and visible voices of authority provide a mechanism for effective engagement, but that same concentration of authority, when damaged by scandal, can result in devastating loss of credibility and influence.

Conservative Protestants are increasingly involved alongside Mainliners, Catholics, and others in the same volunteer organizations in their communities, but they also have a history of maintaining their own, explicitly faith-based organizations. From World Vision to Prison Fellowship Ministries, Conservatives have long struggled with the dilemmas of maintaining a distinct identity in the midst of a complicated public environment (Monsma 1996). For decades that has meant carefully identifying and administering the portions of their work that serve larger public goods (and received public funds), while pursuing their faith-based goals in

separate privately funded programs and units. That balance is now being rede-
fined, as new "faith-based initiatives" begin to channel public funding to religiously based training and to direct support of religious institutions. "Charitable
Choice" has meant that new interpretations of church-state relations are beginning
to guide public policy, explicitly inviting evangelicals into the arena of public service provision with new, more permissive, rules of engagement. The challenge for
Conservatives is to occupy that new territory in a way that enhances rather than
diminishes their ability to build bridges. They will be challenged to serve so that all
have unfettered access, while nurturing the particular gifts and styles of their own
organizations.[10]

That precarious balance between particularistic concerns and public advocacy
and service is also seen in the American Jewish community. As local partners, synagogues are often active participants in building the bridges that sustain community service and cooperation. Jewish support for civil rights and civil liberties has
built bridges as well. Having survived for more than three centuries as a small religious minority in a largely Christian society, they provide a model for an active
public engagement that has been humble by default. As the Other Religions take
their place as visible American minorities, they have a variety of models of participation, Jewish and otherwise, on which to build. Which models these various new
groups will choose—and what new models they will introduce—is not yet clear.

All these traditions, however, might learn from their African American
Protestant counterparts. In these congregations church participation is a central
component in many members' lives, but so is community service and political participation. In the historic black churches America can find its best examples of religious traditions laced through with concern for the well-being of the public, of
sacred stories that mobilize this-worldly action, and of local congregations that
care for each other and build up the civic skills of their members, while passionately
singing the praises of the God who sustains them and gives them hope.

THE FRAGILITY OF
CONGREGATIONAL LIFE

Indeed, singing may be the most important thing these churches do. In black
churches and elsewhere, congregational participants who are most deeply involved
in the worship and fellowship activities of their congregations are the people who
are most likely to be involved in service to their communities as well (Ammerman
forthcoming). Conservative white Protestants, for instance, are as involved in community activities as are their more liberal counterparts, ironically *because* they are so

involved in their churches. Participation there reinforces everyday practices of caring that spill over into community service. American Catholics have just the opposite situation. The size and understaffing of their parishes allows too many people to get lost in a crowd, and lower parish involvement means they are also less active in the community. Caring for the public and caring for each other is not a zero-sum proposition. Those most deeply involved in congregational life—Catholic or Protestant—are also most involved in their communities.[11] Maintaining effective bridges across our diverse cultures ironically requires attention to the bonds within religious communities.

Effective public partnership begins with the religious communities themselves. But there is no guarantee that today's congregations will have the resilience to build their own internal traditions and communities. In spite of the strength and pervasiveness we have observed in American congregational life, cultural forces are at work that can erode that strength. Faith communities that seek to build robust internal bonds face significant challenges. In most places today, relationships outside the congregation—families, neighborhoods, common places of work or leisure or shopping—cannot be counted on to supplement and reinforce the community-building efforts of the congregation. Congregations cannot structure their work around assumptions that members will share visible social identities or lifelong religious membership. They cannot count on a stable and integrated set of institutions and relationships to supply topics of conversation and shared lore, nor can they assume that those who see each other at a weekend service will have other connections that bring them together elsewhere during the week. They cannot greet newcomers with the assumption that they have any preexisting connections to the tradition or to other members.

The people who find their way into local congregations bring increasingly diverse life experiences out of which a community must be intentionally constructed. They are mobile and unlikely to live in the immediate neighborhood, and that means they bring to the congregation their experience of different residential communities, different school districts, different patterns of transportation, and different local politics. Building a congregation was never simple. Just as pioneers gathered strangers together into fledgling frontier congregations, today's pilgrims have to find ways to discover each other and build communities of faith. The American voluntary system has always offered individuals the challenge and the opportunity of starting over, of regrouping. Whatever vitality American religion enjoys results from voluntary communities that are continually willing and able to reinvent themselves.[12]

As they do, congregations themselves have to become sites in which diversity is negotiated. In a variety of ways the internal diversity of congregations provides opportunities for building the sorts of cultural bridges many social critics desire (e.g., Putnam 2000). In addition to the diversity engendered by a scattered and mobile membership, virtually every congregation contains generational diversity as well—at least a few children and youth, older adults, and a wide variety of ages in between. But in few congregations are the multiple generations mostly from the same families, so bonds across generational lines are not a matter of blood. Whatever links exist have to be constructed intentionally, not assumed. In a society that often defines a "generation" in terms of a few years' worth of music and clothing styles, bringing people of different ages together is not something to be taken lightly (Carroll and Roof 2002).

Social class and education have always shaped the circles in which an individual moves. While the tendency is for congregations to be identifiable in those terms, a sizeable proportion of congregations contain economic and educational diversity. Among predominantly Anglo urban congregations, one-third have a constituency of between 10 and 60 percent that is poor alongside other, middle-class, members. Comfortable professionals may be separated from poverty in their schools, neighborhoods, and shopping malls, but in their congregation they are likely to know someone who is barely getting by. In addition, two-thirds of metropolitan churches have a genuine mix of educational attainment that mirrors the mix found in the population.

Even the old truism about the racial segregation of the 11 o'clock Sunday morning service may no longer be so accurate. We found that just over 10 percent of the congregations surveyed were impossible to characterize in terms of any single ethnic group.[13] They either have two nearly equal groups among their members or several substantial minority groups so that no single one dominates. Indeed, most Anglo Americans today attend church with at least a few non-Anglo members. Most Hispanic and Asian Americans go to ethnically mixed congregations as well. As DeYoung and his associates (2003) document, experiments with multiracial congregations began in the 1940s but became much more visible after the 1960s. The large majority of American congregations remain identifiable as primarily the home of one particular ethnic group, but the high walls and racial uniformity of an earlier day have yielded to at least modest internal ethnic diversity in most places.

All of these indicators of internal congregational diversity are signs of hope for those of us who believe that faith ought to be inherently inclusive. But they are also signs that congregations cannot take the basic tasks of gathering and worshiping for granted. Members bring diverse symbols and stories, diverse life histories, even diverse languages to their congregations, and those who are most different will always tend to drift away (Emerson and Smith 2000). Congregations that wish to remain strong cannot count on homogeneous communities and cultural tradition to make their work easy. In voluntary gatherings full of temporary dwellers, internal bridges have to be built before bonds are possible, a necessity vividly described by DeYoung and his colleagues in their study of contemporary multiethnic churches. As diverse members create and sustain religious traditions, whatever common ground they have is more an achievement than a given.

BUILDING VOLUNTARY RELIGIOUS COMMUNITIES

American pluralism rests on a foundation of particularistic local gatherings, but it depends on the willingness of those local communities to nurture relationships and traditions no less than it depends on the various traditions to operate as tolerant parts of a plural whole. Both the voluntary investment and the stance of tolerance are essential to the relatively healthy diversity that has characterized American society. Making commitments to a local congregation and learning to be religious in the particular way of that congregation's tradition, far from being antidemocratic, may provide exactly the sorts of experiences, skills, and commitments that enhance the abilities of women and men, native and immigrant, small-town resident and big-city cosmopolitan to engage their fellow citizens, working together to build up our store of social capital. As Warner argues, "Subcultural religious reproduction does not require antagonism towards one's neighbor. . . . In the United States, religious difference is the most legitimate cultural difference" (Warner 1999, 236). Local congregations that sustain and express those religious differences are essential to making the system work. Demerath agrees that American congregations are a clue to our relative lack of religious violence: "In settings where a communal or congregational grouping is lacking, the faithful may be especially vulnerable to aberrant movements that offer an equivalent to the congregational experience while pursuing more secular and political agendas" (Demerath 2001, 218). The work of local congregations may have far-reaching political consequences, but only if that work is actively tended by the voluntary participants who gather there.

As we have seen in this journey through American congregational life, the bonds of fellowship and the rituals of transcendence lie at the heart of what local communities of faith do. Most also build on those activities to provide help for people in need, but none of that work can be taken for granted. If congregations are to be places where fellowship is experienced and social bonds nourished, congregations must intentionally reach out to bring people together. That is what "voluntary" has always meant. If they are also to be places where religious traditions are sustained and renewed, practices of worship and education must receive careful attention.

GATHERING THE COMMUNITY

So how do congregations build the sorts of communities that provide both strong anchors and open doors? Today people don't join a congregation because it is the closest one in their denomination, or because everyone they know goes there, or because they have gone there all their lives. They join because its ministries provide the best place for their spiritual and social needs to be met and their moral energies put to work. Many have come to call this process of choosing a congregation "shopping," but people are not necessarily just looking for the best deal. Nearly everyone will, at some point in their lives, move; and when they do, they may look for a congregation to join. Once they choose, they may not stay forever, but at any given moment they can find ways to invest in meaningful relationships and in work that serves a larger whole. Vital congregations will help them make those decisions, call them to engagement with others, and offer them work that will persist even after they leave.

I have come to understand congregational life to be fundamentally grounded in stories. Stories are the way communities situate themselves, incorporating the past into the present and dreaming together about the future.[14] Stories are about people doing things: they recount action, and they build on the relationships among their characters. No person and no congregation is ever described by any one story. There are always many to draw on, and whenever we come to a fork in the road— big or small—we sort through all our stories to imagine the next turn that the plot might take.

Strong communities of faith invite their members into the sorts of shared experiences that demand to be narrated. Whether it is a day building a Habitat house or a religious procession through the streets, actions—doing things together—are what create new stories. When we are surrounded by experiences that stretch our senses, that touch our hearts, we collectively search for the words to describe what has happened. Sometimes the people who share these emerging stories are able to hear each other easily because they already share so much else in common. But sometimes they have to work hard to communicate because their previous lives have not supplied many of the same plot lines. What congregations make possible is a meeting ground where new, shared stories evolve. We are not bound together by a common inherited culture, so we have to work hard at whatever common conversation we are able to have.

The congregations in this book highlight a nascent recognition of this task. Bigger, more urban, more mobile congregations also had more intentionally designed social activities, more places where people could meet and swap stories. Thursday morning ladies aid groups may be replaced by Thursday evening parent support groups, and potlucks may be replaced by catered dinners, but the gathering continues. In the informal, face-to-face setting of a meal or a Bible study, a support group or a missionary society, people who are otherwise strangers can tell the stories of their lives and build together the many common stories that constitute strong congregational life.

That picture of active parish social life is not always present, however. Mainline Protestant churches may be almost as likely to *have* a range of available activities, but their members are considerably less likely to participate. Members of African American and Conservative Protestant churches are nearly twice as likely to attend adult religious education, are equally likely to belong to any other congregational group, and have higher overall levels of participation in all church activities. The situation for Catholics is even more stark than for Mainline members. Only about one in five parishioners has any regular connection to the parish beyond Mass attendance. Even after controlling for other background factors, Mainline and Catholic participants are simply less active in their congregations.

The difficulty may partly lie in the kinds of groups sponsored by their churches. Mainliners in particular are more likely to have sports, scouting, reading, and other activity groups that may be little different from what members otherwise might be able to join in the community. Indeed, it is just that sort of outside civic and social engagement that Mainline pastors so often bemoan—the Sunday morning soccer games and the every-night-of-the-week lessons and clubs. Mainline congregations seem to be going head-to-head in these sorts of activities and losing. When they essentially duplicate the types of activities otherwise available in the community, they serve only a small, older, traditionalist constituency that would rather come to church for their book group.

This absence of congregational engagement is particularly worrisome since people who participate less in their church's activities are also less involved in community service. Mainline Protestants overcome this deficit by the sheer strength of their cultural and theological expectations about civic participation. Lacking the same strong cultural history, inactive Catholic parishioners are less engaged in their communities.. No evidence in our research suggests that asking congregants to invest more seriously in relationships *inside* the church deprives them of worldly attachments—quite the contrary. Congregations that encourage participation in fellowship and study groups are adding to the overall number of social bonds in their communities.

In spite of the difficulties posed by mobility and change, many people form meaningful commitments, often based in their congregations. The members of any given congregation will change over time, and they will be involved in many different relationships and loyalties even while being part of that faith community. Insular, unchanging religious loyalties are impossible, but vital congregations can provide today's pilgrims with a tabernacle, rather than a temple, with ways to locate themselves in a community of commitment in the midst of their complex lives.

SEEKING TRANSCENDENCE

The strength of congregations extends beyond these social ties. Building a strong congregation means creating opportunities to find and share stories, but it also means cultivating the particular habits required for encountering and telling stories of transcendence. Congregations are where people hear the stories of divine action in the world, experience a sacred presence as part of their own unfolding life narrative, and build the relationships that allow new shared faith stories to be added to the collective lore. This implies that strong communities of faith will be intentional about telling their sacred stories—both those unique to their particular local history and those that come from the larger heritage of their faith tradition.

Telling and enacting sacred stories is what congregations do as they gather for worship. In hymns, scripture, sermon, sacrament, prayer, chant, bowing, kneeling, lighting candles and incense, wearing vestments, displaying art—the words, signs, and symbols tell the story of the gods and the creation and the direction of history. As people listen and move and see and smell, they are asked to encounter a reality beyond themselves, and in song and movement together they may find experiences that allow them to build bridges with strangers (Warner 1997). The practices carried on by organized local communities of faith are the carriers of the transcendence that many modern seekers find absent elsewhere. The most important work congregations do is to provide a place where worship and spiritual enrichment can occur.

Again, there are signs of both strength and caution in the data we have examined. Some congregations invest much more heavily than others in the work of worship and spiritual nurture. Christian congregations in the sacramental traditions—both Catholic and Protestant—often offer multiple opportunities for worship each week and organize groups of members to tend to the ritual tasks surrounding those events. Resources are expended on special clothing and ritual objects, as well as on prayer books and hymnals. Leaders are trained in the arts of liturgical performance, and new members are offered mentoring in the skills of worship. Similarly, although the traditions themselves are vastly different, members and leaders in Buddhist, Hindu, Muslim, and other newer American traditions often spend much of their organizational energy in assembling the material necessities for proper worship and gathering to honor their Holy One. No matter what else they may do, they begin with time and space for prayers and offerings.

The centrality of gathering for worship is also seen in this country's African American churches. Services last longer than in most other traditions, multiple choirs are likely to contribute their time and talent, ushers and pastor's aid groups and others support and guide the church's experience. Many churches invite worshipers back for Sunday, midweek, or Friday evening services that are filled with prayers, testimonies, and songs contributed by all the participants. These churches are also likely to expect both children and adults to attend Sunday school classes, with a cadre of adult teachers who spend a significant amount of time training and preparing. Black churches are critical to African American communities in all sorts of ways, not least their role in supporting and nourishing the spiritual lives of their members.

For Conservative white Protestants, worship and spiritual nurture receive significant attention as well, oriented toward individual conversion and education in the faith. In most evangelical and Pentecostal groups more emphasis is placed on *hearing* the Word than on the sights and smells that might evoke God's presence for someone in another tradition. Still, those who preach the Word are eager to gather listeners into sacred space as often as possible. Having an additional church service, beyond the Sunday morning event, is typical for Conservatives. Sunday nights and Wednesday nights often find these church buildings abuzz with activity that blends fellowship and learning. While nearly all congregations, of all traditions, have at least some minimal offering of religious education for their children and adults, Conservative Protestant churches are likely to schedule classes for adults that meet at the same time children are in Sunday school (when the most adult members are also at the church). They are also likely to have weekday educational programs for their children, and at least some have classes for new adult members. Some even send their children to Conservative Christian day schools. Learning about scripture and about how one is supposed to live occupies a good deal of energy in these churches, as well as in the Sectarian communities of Jehovah's Witnesses, Christian Scientists, and Latter-day Saints.

Religious education is also important in Catholic and Jewish congregations. Youth are given special attention with CCD classes in Catholic parishes and week-day Hebrew schools in Jewish synagogues, in addition to the parish elementary and high schools and the Solomon Schechter schools. New adult members receive intensive RCIA classes in Catholic parishes and comprehensive introductions to Judaism in synagogue classes for aspiring converts. What neither Catholic nor Jewish groups do as well, however, is tend to the adults who have grown up in the faith. Once having passed through confirmation or bar/bat mitzvah, the opportunities for continued spiritual learning and growth diminish, unless one is a convert.

Others outside the Protestant traditions are beginning to build a programmatic infrastructure for educating their youth and adults as well. Hindus, Buddhists, and Muslims have all established camping programs that invite American adherents into an immersion in religious practice and tradition. After-school programs are joining Sunday school in the effort to provide youth with religious tools for living as religious outsiders. Adults who took their religious tradition for granted in a home country where it was all around them are forming study circles and importing religious leaders who can teach them the things they need to know.

The religious groups that spend the least organizational energy on worship and religious education are the Mainline Protestant ones. Beyond the sacramental traditions of the Episcopal and Lutheran churches, they are unlikely to have a worship service at any other time than Sunday morning or to have any group of members that spends time planning and supporting their worship activities. Most do have some form of adult religious education, but it is less likely to be scheduled in prime time alongside children's Sunday school and more likely to be a small group that meets during the week. Mainline Protestants rarely offer religious education for children during the week, and almost none of them sponsor or support a religious school. While all the other traditions have some particular organizational effort that supports the spiritual nurture of their members, white Mainline Protestants seem to be putting all their eggs in the basket of Sunday morning worship and children's Sunday school.

Whether this minimalist organizational structure can support robust spiritual lives is questionable. Other traditions, each in their own ways, recognize their outsiderness in American culture. Their ethnic heritage or theological traditions, if not both, have not historically been reinforced by other institutions in American society, and they have built organizational structures to compensate for that absence. Indeed, many of these other groups have explicitly sought to equip their members for cultural resistance and survival in an otherwise unfriendly environment. Mainline Protestants have either never made such assumptions or have seen them diminish as their immigrant and revivalist constituencies have made their peace with American society. For Presbyterians and Episcopalians, American culture has always been a friendly place. For Lutherans and Methodists, it has become so.[15]

For much of American history, Mainline Protestants taught all the children in the public schools, ran the government, and owned the businesses. Protestant symbols were what hung on the walls, and Protestant holidays were the ones observed. Protestant churches did not have to bear the full weight of religious enculturation because their stories, symbols, and practices were available in a variety of everyday contexts. Today, even if the stories and symbols are still there, they are harder to find. Soccer games are scheduled on Sunday morning, and the civic clubs to which their members belong may or may not open with a Protestant prayer. If Mainline Protestants wish to engender a lively engagement with transcendence or to perpetuate distinct spiritual traditions, they cannot depend on institutions in the larger culture to help them. Individual congregations will need to relearn the organizational habits of voluntarism if this stream of American religious tradition is to maintain its vitality. They need not become an oppositional counterculture with high boundaries, but they will have to focus their energies on building their own religious traditions.

Strong communities of faith, of whatever sort, will have to encourage their members to talk with each other in terms that acknowledge and celebrate the particular spiritual presence they come together to celebrate. While such talk may come more naturally to a Conservative or Sectarian group, these conversations are not impossible for liberals. A pastor in a northeastern city recently challenged members of her liberal UCC church to share their testimonies each Sunday during Lent. The only rule, she said, was that God had to be part of the story. The result was a powerful experience for both speakers and listeners. The testifiers explicitly recognized God's presence in the stories of their lives. The listeners were challenged to think of their own lives differently. The congregation ended up having a Lenten experience that is now the stuff of congregational lore. Creating and telling stories of faith is at the heart of how congregations tend to their spiritual work.

As congregations face the task of religious education and spiritual nurture, they are confronted by significant dilemmas—not only how distinctive they want to be, but where that distinctiveness will come from as well. As we have seen throughout this book, congregations do not invent their way of doing things from scratch. They situate themselves more or less clearly within larger traditions. For most, the larger tradition that situates them is a denominational identity, and even congregations that pride themselves on being independent and nondenominational work hard to signal to the world that they are "biblical" or "full gospel," or some other identity they share with a larger category of churches.

Stories of distinctly denominational cultures are still prevalent enough in American culture to make us laugh in recognition when we hear them. Public radio storyteller Garrison Keillor regularly reminds "Prairie Home Companion" listeners of the peculiar ways of Lake Wobegon Lutherans (and their cross-town Catholic counterparts at Our Lady of Perpetual Responsibility). When the national Lutheran church (the ELCA) announced an agreement on exchanging various liturgical functions with the Episcopal Church, Keillor was moved to extol his beloved Lutheran traditions in song:

> We sit in the pew where we always sit,
> And we do not shout Amen.
> And if anyone yells or waves their hands,
> They're not invited back again.
> . . .
> We've got chow mein noodles on tuna hotdish
> And Jello with cottage cheese,
> And chocolate bars and banana cream pie,
> No wonder we're on our knees.
> . . .
> I'm a Lutheran, a Lutheran, it is my belief,
> I am a Lutheran guy.
> We may have merged with another church
> But I'm a Lutheran til I die.[16]

Not long ago, most observers would have argued that Lake Wobegon Lutherans would not be long for this world. Isolated European ethnic enclaves had seen their cultural boundaries opened, and without those intact cultures, the assumption was that the denominational distinctions would disappear as well.[17] Do Lake Wobegon Lutherans still exist? That sort of deep denominational culture is strongest in precisely the Lake Wobegon sorts of places—rural locations more than urban ones, southern and midwestern regions more than in the rest of the country, and among

Catholics and Sectarian groups more than in any sector of Protestantism. Lake Wobegon Lutherans also thrive best in places where they are surrounded by a contingent of others who share their lifelong attachments to a single denomination—that is, where most people in their church are "cradle" members. But those kinds of places are few and far between. Only one in four white Protestant congregations reported that most of their members were cradle members of the denomination. Even in Lake Wobegon, being Lutheran (or Catholic) is not something people can take for granted.

If most churches face the reality that half or more of their members did not grow up with the programs, heroes, liturgies, and lore of the denomination at their fingertips, denominational cultures are indeed fragile. Many faced with this situation throw up their hands and change the name of the church. But as we have seen, not every congregation that is full of modern, urban, mobile switchers has chosen to deemphasize denominational identity. Even among congregations where denomination is not a matter to be taken for granted out of a shared heritage, nearly half report that they consider themselves strongly in the denominational camp.

How do they manage it? In part they are intentional about teaching the tradition. As new members from other traditions join, they are taught the distinctive beliefs and practices of their new fellowship. But these congregations are also intentional about the way they undertake worship and education. In the face of multiple curricular choices, they opt for their own denomination's educational materials. In the face of vast changes and blending of worship styles, they emphasize the distinctiveness of their own tradition. Alongside all the other partnerships they forge, they celebrate the work they do together with denominational compatriots around the world.

The range of religious practices, resources, and potential mission partners on which congregational leaders can draw is mind-boggling. Nearly half of the Protestant churches in which we interviewed had created a local patchwork with few distinctly denominational motifs. While pieces of denominational connection and influence remain (often far more than the descriptions would lead one to believe), no conscious strategy gives denominational connections pride of place.

But for the other half of Protestant churches, an intentional retrieval and construction of tradition is replacing the Lake Wobegon Lutherans with New York and St. Paul Lutherans (like Keillor himself). Tradition is for them no longer taken for granted, but chosen, no longer a matter of enclave and birth, but a matter of faith and practice. In spite of the mobility that has brought more switchers than lifelong members into most pews, in spite of the diversity of families and communities in which we live, in spite of the ways in which old traditions have been dislodged, some congregations are putting down roots into the deep and broad traditions of their faith. These congregations see their theological heritage as a gift, intentionally teach newcomers about the faith, and celebrate their own unique worship practices. As denominational identity disengages itself from inherited cultures, it need not disappear, but it does have to be intentionally sustained to survive. As people teach each other what it means to be Baptist or Presbyterian or Lutheran or Nazarene—or Catholic or Jewish or Muslim—they collectively reclaim and redefine that tradition. They develop stories of faith that are both rooted and portable.

In doing this work, they tap deep resources from within their faith community, but in the act of learning to communicate the stories to newcomers, they develop accessible ways of defining their own traditions and practice, creating a language that bridges between inside and out. At the same time that each particular local community of believers creates and tells stories that are theirs alone, their conscious acknowledgement of their debt to larger traditions reminds them that no single community's story is sufficient to encompass us all.

Robust religious traditions are kept alive, then, in the work of thousands of local congregations. They are kept alive because those congregations spend most of their energy on worship, religious education, and building a place where modern wanderers can find a meaningful, even if temporary, home. This basic congregational work requires constant voluntary investment if any local community of faith is to thrive. And, I am suggesting, it is work that is not wasted. Not only does it sustain the individuals who find a spiritual home there, but it also provides resources and models for our larger life together. We learn everyday skills for being together and working together with diverse others in part because we have learned to be together and to work together in congregations. We learn to speak with both confidence and humility as we root ourselves in a tradition that recognizes itself as one among many.

We also learn to care for the world because congregations have tended to their work as spiritual and social institutions. Our society needs congregations to mobilize resources to care for needy people and enrich community life, but busy citizens may never even see the needs without the moral and spiritual perspective provided by faith. Worship is where their eyes are opened, religious education is where they get their focus, caring communities of faith are where people practice the arts of compassionate response. The most important thing congregations can do for the world, then, is to tend first to the spiritual well-being of the pilgrims who find their way to their doors. The most important thing they can do for the unity of that world is, ironically, to find ways to teach their own distinct traditions to those pilgrims.

The American religious experiment continues as a wider and wider array of the world's religions try their hand at engendering voluntary religious commitment that is both rooted and tolerant. Local congregations, like those we have visited in this book, form the base on which America's religious work is organized and a primary site where deeply held distinctions are nurtured alongside habits of partnership. They have survived because ever-changing groups of people have found in this way of gathering something to which they are willing to devote themselves. Perhaps they have also survived because they have provided individuals, communities, and society a set of resources and practices too essential to lose.

APPENDIX ONE · Sampling and Measurement

The sampling frame with which we worked began with lists generated by the American Yellow Pages on CD-ROM. If a congregation had a phone, it was on that list—still not all congregations, but probably about 85 percent.[1] This was supplemented by official lists from eight denominations that were the focus of simultaneous related research projects. In each case we drew our sample of interviewees using random methods (drawing every n-th case, with a random start), replacing ineligible or duplicate or nonresponding congregations with the next eligible name on the list. When a congregation from one of the eight focus denominations appeared in the sample from the master list, it was treated as ineligible (since it had been eligible from the other list) and replaced.

Some congregations were easy to reach and readily agreed to an interview; others were much more difficult. Our interviewers averaged two to four attempts at contacting the nonresponding congregations. In roughly two-thirds of the cases, they never reached a person, either because no one answered the phone or was present at the address we had or because the phone had been disconnected. In the other third of cases, researchers left repeated messages on the (home) answering machines of pastors who never returned their calls.

Two significant differences have been noted between our sample and the National Congregations Study. Our sample contains more new congregations (founded since 1950) and fewer old ones (founded before 1900), by about

10 percentage points in each case. Our Nashville and Seattle locations have probably biased our sample in this slightly "younger" direction. Second, the ethnic distribution of our sample seems to be tilted slightly in the direction of more ethnically mixed congregations. Our percentages of African American (15.2%), Hispanic (0.9%), and Asian (1.4%) congregations match the NCS almost perfectly, but NCS reports that 62.1 percent are 90 percent or more white in participation, while we found 51.7 percent (Chaves 2000). This may represent a social desirability effect (informants who thought they should report to us more diversity than was warranted), but it may also represent the relatively more mixed ethnic picture in newer congregations and in our Albuquerque and Seattle locations.

VARIABLES AND MEASUREMENT

Our measures of the organizational dimensions of congregational life are of two primary sorts. For a good deal of basic information—attendance, budget, and the like—we can draw on the written survey our informants completed, but for less obvious dimensions we rely on the interviews themselves. All the data-gathering instruments for this study can be accessed at http://hirr.hartsem.edu/about/about_orw.html. The more open-ended questions we asked face-to-face allowed congregational leaders to describe their situations in their own words. As we read the transcripts of their responses, we grouped their ways of describing things into categories.[2] Once those categories were created and the interviews coded, that information, along with the survey information, was entered into a numeric database and analyzed using the Statistical Package for the Social Sciences (SPSS-PC).

Multiple factors were tested as predictors of the many dimensions of congregational activity we examined. Depending on the nature of the dependent variable, multiple regression, logistical regression, or analysis of variance was used to identify the significant effects. Limitations of space meant that most equations are not discussed in detail in the text, but the control factors routinely tested included the following:

- Size. We took typical weekly attendance as our primary measure of size. We also recorded membership size, but it is attendance that tells us how many people are routinely available for doing the congregation's work.[3]
- Budget. We asked leaders about "the size of your total annual operating budget—excluding capital campaigns (such as building funds) and affiliated

organizations (such as schools)." We also asked about how much, if any, of this came from endowments or outside subsidies, but it is the actual operating budget size that is most important.[4]

- Founding Era. We asked when the congregation was founded and recorded the year (ranging from 1731 to 1998). While there were occasional differences among the older congregations, the most significant dividing lines tended to be between pre-1945 and post-1945 and between pre-1975 and post-1975.[5]
- Region. Our sites span the Northeast, Southeast, Midwest, and West, but we found the regions themselves rarely to be helpful in explaining the differences we found. While the regions are very different, it is the particular mix of religious traditions that accounts for those differences, rather than the region as such.
- Rural vs. Urban. Where context does make a difference is in the size of the community. Within regions, congregations in rural locations were systematically different from those in urban locales. By also taking size into account, we can note where rural differences are actually the effect of the *setting*, not just of the disproportionately small size of the congregations located there.[6]
- Membership Demographics. We asked our informants to estimate the proportion of their congregation that could be described by a variety of demographic categories. They marked ranges that we labeled "hardly any (< 10%)," "some (10–39%)," "about half (40–60%)," "most (61–90%)," and "nearly all (> 90%)."[7]

How accurate are such estimates? In the case of thirty of our congregations we have both the estimate of the informant and the results of our Sunday morning survey of attenders. When we compare the two, we find that two-thirds of the estimates place the congregation in exactly the same category the survey results indicate, and 90 percent of the estimates are close enough that the congregation would have been placed in the correct group of categories (e.g., high vs. low). In some cases the informant may also be more accurate than the survey results, since older or less educated members may disproportionately have failed to complete the survey. All in all, there are good reasons to trust these estimates as a fair assessment of the characteristics of the congregations they are describing.[8] The demographic factors we routinely tested included the following:

- Education. The critical differences consistently proved to be between congregations where college is the norm and those where it is not. In most cases we compare those that say more than half of their members have a high school diploma or less with those that say the majority have at least some college.

- Income. Here the critical differences are between those where more than half have household incomes above $65,000 and those where the average household has less income than that.[9]

- Age. The dividing line we found to be most critical identifies "graying" congregations (where 'almost half' or more of the congregation was estimated to be over 65), compared to those where the majority is younger and middle-aged adults.[10]

- Ethnicity. We specifically asked for estimates of the number who are white (non-Hispanic), Hispanic, Asian American, and African American, as well as how many were born outside the United States. We then grouped congregations into those with a dominant majority of one of those groups, those predominantly of one group (usually white), but with a greater than 10 percent minority, and those that were more thoroughly mixed (either with something close to a 50–50 distribution or with multiple sizeable contingents). We classified as "immigrant" those where most or nearly all the members were estimated to have been born outside the United States.

Denominations Classified by
Religious Tradition, Polity,
and Denominational Structure

Religious Family	Local/ Congregational Polity	Mixed Polity	Hierarchical Polity
Mainline Protestants	American Baptist Churches Disciples of Christ Mennonite Church Metropolitan Community Churches* Unitarian Universalist United Church of Christ	Episcopal Church Evangelical Lutheran Church in America Presbyterian Church, USA Reformed Church in America	United Methodist Church

Religious Family	Local/ Congregational Polity	Mixed Polity	Hierarchical Polity
Conservative Protestants	American Baptist Association	Advent Christian Church*	Cherubim & Seraphim*
	Association of Vineyard Churches*	Assemblies of God	Church of God, Cleveland
		Christian & Missionary Alliance	Four Square Churches
	Baptist General Conference		International Church of Christ*
	Baptist Missionary Association	Christian Reformed Church	Pillar & Ground of Truth*
		Lutheran Church–Missouri Synod	
	Beachy Amish*		Seventh-Day Adventist
	Brethren		
	Calvary Chapel	Nazarenes	
	Christian Churches*	Orthodox Presbyterian Church in America	
	Churches of Christ*		
	Evangelical Covenant	Presbyterian Church in America	
	Evangelical Free Church		
	Free Will Baptists	United Pentecostal Church*	
	General Association of Regular Baptists		
	Messianic Jews*		
	Plymouth Brethren*		
	Primitive Baptists*		
	Southern Baptist Convention		
	Wesleyans		
	Wisconsin Evangelical Lutheran Synod		

TABLE (continued)

Religious Family	Local/ Congregational Polity	Mixed Polity	Hierarchical Polity
African American Protestant	National Baptist Convention of America*	Church of God in Christ	African Methodist Episcopal
	National Baptist Convention, USA, Inc.*		African Methodist Episcopal, Zion
	National Free Will Baptist*		Christian Methodist Episcopal
	Progressive National Baptist Convention*		
	Dually Affiliated: National & Southern or National & American Baptist		
Catholic & Orthodox			Antiochan Orthodox
			Assyrian Catholic*
			Byzantine Catholic*
			Greek Orthodox
			Roman Catholic
			Ukrainian Catholic*
Sectarian Groups	Christian Science	Jehovah's Witnesses	Latter-day Saints
	Unity		Reformed Latter-day Saints
Jews	Conservative		Lubavitcher*
	Reconstructionist*		
	Reform		
Other Religions	Hindu*	Nichiren Buddhist*	Baha'i
	Spiritualist*	Zen Buddhist*	Church Universal and Triumphant*
	Sunni Muslim*		Gnostic*

* Denominations with "networked" agencies rather than centralized bureaucracies.

NOTES

CHAPTER 1

1. Details on rates of American religious affiliation and belief can be found in polls conducted by the Gallup Organization (Gallup and Lindsay 1999). A more conservative estimate of church attendance is advocated by Hadaway and associates (Hadaway, Marler, and Chaves 1993).

2. The expectation that modern religion would be found primarily in individual consciousness goes back at least to Durkheim (1898 [1975]) and Simmel (1908 [1971]). More recent research in that tradition has included work by Bellah and associates (1985), Marler and Roozen (1993), Roof (1993; 1999), Roof and Gesch (1995), and Hammond (1992). Roof and McKinney (1987, 57) report that 81 percent of the American public agreed with the statement that one should arrive at one's own religious beliefs independent of a church or synagogue. However, there is considerable reason to doubt that "spiritual" and "religious" have become separate categories (Marler and Hadaway 2002).

3. The importance of religious institutions and rituals in times of transition and crisis is discussed by Davie (2000) and Ammerman (2002b).

4. This is an argument made persuasively by Warner (1993; 1994; 1999), building on historical accounts, such as those by Hatch (1989) and Butler (1990). The key role of regulation (or the absence thereof) is argued by Chaves and Cann (1992).

5. American Church Lists, a marketing firm, has roughly 320,000 entries in its list. The Yearbook of American and Canadian Churches includes listings that total about the same number (National Council of Churches 1998). Both inadvertently include

defunct congregations and other overcounts. On the other side of the equation, however, they are likely to miss non-Christian and non-Jewish bodies, as well as the small, independent congregations that have no denominational affiliation and often no phone. While those two sources of error may cancel each other out, no one knows exactly how many congregations there are.

6. The classic statement of this theoretical approach to organizations is given by DiMaggio and Powell (1983). Penny Edgell Becker (1999) uses this insight to delineate four cultural models that shape expectations for how congregations do their work.

7. Among the voluminous studies of the Mainline, see Roof and McKinney (1987), Wuthnow (2002), Bendroth (2002), Roozen (1995), and Wellman (1999).

8. To this day, Episcopalians and Presbyterians are represented in far more than their proportional numbers in the governing bodies of the United States (Davidson, Pyle, and Reyes 1995).

9. We will have occasion to note along the way that a significant portion of those Methodists, however, retain their more conservative leanings.

10. A full accounting of how we classified each denomination can be found in Appendix 2.

11. This style is called "lay liberalism" by Hoge et al. (1994). I have described it as "Golden Rule Christianity" (Ammerman 1997b).

12. Sources on the history of the black churches include Baer and Singer (1992), Gilkes (2001), Lincoln and Mamiya (1990), Genovese (1974), and Sobel (1988).

13. On the history of the Pentecostal movement, see Blumhofer, Spittler and Wacker (1999), Martin (2002), Blumhofer (1993), and Wacker (2001). On the Church of God in Christ see Lincoln and Mamiya (1990, 80–84). Like Lincoln and Mamiya (1990, 1), we have categorized the African American churches that belong to predominantly white denominations with those other denominations. We found that a black Lutheran or United Methodist church had more in common in *organizational form* with its white counterparts than with a National Baptist or African Methodist Episcopal congregation. However, we will have numerous occasions to examine the difference ethnicity makes within the predominantly white Protestant (and Catholic) traditions.

14. On the history and culture of evangelicalism, see Hunter (1983), Ammerman (1987), Warner (1988), Hutchison (1987), Balmer (1989), Carpenter (1997), Wagner (1997), and C. Smith (1998).

15. Christian Smith provides a vivid illustration of the disdain intellectuals have for evangelicals, as well as evidence for evangelicals' own sense of alienation (C. Smith 1998).

16. Krindatch (2001) provides an excellent accounting of Orthodox groups in the United States, enumerating a total of twenty-four hundred congregations.

17. The two traditions come together, however, in the so-called Uniate churches— parishes that exist under Roman Catholic jurisdiction but worship in Eastern fashion.

18. The tug of war between American bishops and the Roman curia over accused priests is but one example of the continuing tension; see Steinfels (2002).

19. On Roman Catholic patterns of governance, see Dolan (1994). For one account of Greek Orthodox experience, see Papaioannou (1994).

20. This sketch of Catholic and Orthodox histories and traditions is drawn from Albanese (1992), P. Williams (1990), and Ahlstrom (1975). Recent Catholic life is analyzed in Burns (1992), Castelli and Gremillion (1987), and McGreevy (1996).

21. Both our sample and the National Congregations Study arrive at this percentage. American Church Lists includes about thirty-five hundred synagogues, and the Glenmary study lists about thirty-seven hundred (Association of Statisticians of American Religious Bodies 2002).

22. On this new pluralism, see especially Warner (1998) and Eck (2001).

23. On the diversity of both current and historic Native American religious experience, see Albanese (1992) and P. Williams (1990). Treat (1996) documents the emergence of a more explicit Native voice within Christian traditions as well.

24. Tension with society is the best way to define "sectarianness," according to Johnson (1963). The role of minority religions in testing legal definitions is explored in Handy (1998).

25. McDannell (1995) provides a fascinating description of Mormon "garments," received in a secret Temple ceremony and always worn under the member's clothing.

26. On the history of Christian Science, see Albanese (1992), P. Williams (1990, 312–16), and Gottschalk (1973). The role of healing in this crucial period is analyzed by Baer (2002). See also Bednarowski (1999).

27. On Jehovah's Witnesses, see Holden (2002) and Beckford (1975).

28. The latest count for Christian Science (probably high) was about eighteen hundred congregations. Jehovah's Witnesses reported 11,582 U.S. congregations in 2001, and Latter-day Saints reported 11,515. For Mormons and Christian Scientists, see the Glenmary study (Association of Statisticians of American Religious Bodies 2002). For Jehovah's Witnesses, see their Web site at http://www.watchtower.org/statistics/worldwide_report.htm.

29. "Nones" amount to about 16 percent of people in the Pacific region, as compared with about 8 percent in the rest of the country (GSSDIRS 2001).

30. Borrowing from theologian Virgilio Elizando, Warner uses this term to talk about the creative religious syntheses that develop from new immigrant populations (Warner 1997).

31. An excellent introduction to Chicago and its religious traditions can be found in the collection of studies edited by Livezey (2000).

32. The 549 includes three additional Reformed Church in America congregations in central New York, added to balance the RCA distribution for the parallel national denominational project.

33. The completion rate ranged from a low of 61 percent in Chicago to a high of 88 percent in Missouri. Appendix 1 gives a more complete description of our sampling method and response rate.

34. For instance, we report 5.8 percent with a parish school, while NCS reports 5.9 percent. We report that 17 percent have 90 percent or more of their participants within a ten-minute drive, while the NCS reports 18.7 percent. We report 10.7 percent with female clergy, and NCS reports 9.2 percent. We report that 89.3 percent own their buildings, while NCS reports 86.4 percent.

35. James Gustafson describes this intersection using the biblical metaphor of "treasure in earthen vessels" (1961).

36. Appendix 1 includes a detailed discussion of measurement and statistical strategies.

37. There were no ready-made categories to guide this exploration. Other recent studies of congregational social service delivery, for instance, have been hampered by failure to distinguish clearly between services for which the congregation is the primary sponsor and services offered in cooperation with others, and they have gathered little specific data on the forms of support congregations provide (e.g., Chaves 1999a; Dudley and Roozen 2001; Woolever and Bruce 2002). As a result their arguments about "how much" congregations do are very much "apples and oranges" conversations.

38. Theorists who understand the organization of society around an array of inherent "functions" often hypothesize that there will always be some sort of organized social attention to "meaning" or "moral order," for instance (Bellah 1963; Durkheim 1915 [1964]; Luckmann 1967).

CHAPTER 2

1. They were present in the other congregations, as well (as we will note below), even though we do not have enough cases to venture reliable estimates of the numbers.

2. The congregations studied by Penny Edgell Becker (1999) all reported that worship was an essential part of their mission, but those that shape their organizational culture primarily around ritual she called "Houses of Worship." While our measures are somewhat different from hers, we too will note the effects of designating worship as a specific local mission priority.

3. Gillespie (1995) and D. B. Bass (2002) provide interesting accounts of the importance of the liturgy in Episcopal parishes.

4. The history and practices of Pentecostalism are examined in a number of sources (Blumhofer 1993; Sanders 1996; Wacker 2001). On its expansion into non-Pentecostal denominations, see Blumhofer (1999). Miller (1997) provides an account of the worship and appeal of the Vineyard and similar churches.

5. Ritterband (2000) provides an account of Conservative synagogue members' beliefs. Kosmin (2000) writes about Conservative Jewish youth, and Prell (2000) is an excellent source on celebrating rituals.

6. The long history of spiritual healing in Christian Science and other American traditions is explored by Baer (2002).

7. There are many good descriptions of evangelical church culture (Ammerman 1987; Balmer 1989; Harding 2000; Warner 1988).

8. This emphasis on education is echoed in the survey findings reported by Fishman (1999), as well as in the ethnographic study reported by Prell (2000).

9. On the role of the Bible in evangelical churches, see Ammerman (1987) and Boone (1989).

10. Mark Noll (1998) offers a fascinating study of the way African slaves took the Protestant Bible and made it their own.

11. Here I am describing congregations in a way informed by the "new institution-alists" in organizational theory (DiMaggio 1998; Powell and DiMaggio 1991).

12. Two of the key statements on the positive effects of religious pluralism are offered by Iannaccone (1991) and Stark and Iannaccone (1994). For an overview of the arguments for why plural alternatives should lead to higher participation, see Jelen (2002). A concise summary of the U.S. case viewed through this lens is provided by Finke and Stark (1992). On the methodological flaws in this literature, however, see Voas, Olson, and Crockett (2002).

13. Pentecostal worship practices are detailed by Poloma and Hoelter (1998) and Wacker (2001). There are several excellent descriptions of worship in African American churches (Nelson 1996; Raboteau 2001; Williams 1974). Sobel (1988) and Chireau (1997) are among the sources that trace the interconnections between African practice and African American Christianity. Both Heilman (1973) and Wilkes (1994) provide vivid descriptions of synagogue services. Descriptions of American Muslim worship are provided by Abusharaf (1998) and Jane Smith (1999). Warner (1997) points to the importance of chanting, singing, and bodily movement in various reli-gious traditions.

14. The addition of organs and choirs was one of the most visible American adap-tations of late-nineteenth-century Reform Judaism (Sarna and Goldman 1994), and one of the Reform temples where we interviewed did have a choir.

15. Ross (2003) describes the opposite end of this spectrum, where some Conservative churches have sufficient resources to mount Broadway-style productions.

16. Lincoln and Mamiya say that "singing is second only to preaching as the magnet of attraction" in black churches (1990, 346). Costen (1999) provides a helpful historical overview of the development of black church music traditions.

17. The role of singing and choirs is an underresearched topic (Clark 1991).

18. For a variety of reasons our data gathering in these congregations left gaps that were difficult to fill once they were discovered. One researcher in particular often did not follow our research protocol.

19. Gladys-Marrie Sypher, posted to class discussion board, March 2, 2003.

20. M. Williams (1974) provides vivid descriptions of how missionaries and deacons perform their roles. Glimpses of these activities are also found in Gilkes's work (Gilkes 2001).

21. On American Hindu religious education, see Kurien (1998).

22. This is at least partly a legacy of the days when public schools included Bible reading and prayer in ways that explicitly supported a Protestant worldview. Catholics and Jews were well aware that teaching their own traditions would require extracurricular time (Brereton 1998; Moore 1986).

23. The acronym stands for "Approved Workers are not Ashamed," taken from II Timothy 2:15: "Study to shew thyself approved unto God, a workman that needeth not to be ashamed, rightly dividing the word of truth" (King James Version).

24. Orthodox parishes were less likely to have schools, hence the average for Catholic and Orthodox together was the 44 percent shown in Table 2.

25. On Catholic schools, see Greeley and associates (1976).

26. Brown (1993) reports that there are over sixty Schechter schools in the United States, almost all of them K–8. The positive religious effects of day school participation are reported by Cohen (1997).

27. Lutheran day schools have been ignored by researchers, with but a few exceptions (Diefenthaler 1984; Lueking 1995; Schmidt 1979). The figures reported here are taken from Lutheran Church–Missouri Synod (2002) and Evangelical Lutheran Church in America (2002).

28. North American Division of Seventh-Day Adventists (1998).

29. See Wagner (1997). Conservative Christian schools have been widely examined (Ammerman 1987; Peshkin 1986; Rose 1988).

30. Goldstein and Goldstein (2000, 72) report that 37 percent of Reform Jews are in a mixed marriage, compared to 21 percent of Conservative Jews and 7 percent of Orthodox. Heilman (2000) notes that intermarriage is a fact of life and that both converts and non-Jewish spouses are now part of Jewish congregational life. In some cases these converts spur greater involvement by the Jewish spouse as well.

CHAPTER 3

1. Marler (1995) shows that the tie between family formation and religious participation has remained strong, but it has the ironic effect of making "nonfamily" persons (who are a growing segment of the population) less "at home" in congregational life.

2. *Gemeinschaft* is a way of describing relatively small, traditional, face-to-face communities where relationships are often tied to family and land (Tönnies 1887 [2001]).

3. A number of recent studies have given attention to immigrant congregations (Ebaugh and Chafetz 1999; 2000; Kim 1996; Kwon, Kim, and Warner 2001; Warner and Wittner 1998; Yang 1999).

4. Recall that our sample likely overrepresents mixed congregations (see Appendix 1), but that should not affect the patterns we note *within* that group. Several studies have outlined the challenges of interethnic congregations (Becker 1998; Day 2001; DeYoung et al. 2003; Foster and Brelsford 1996).

5. The most common Muslim youth groups are the Muslim Student Associations found on college campuses, rather than groups based in a local masjid. Attention to all the ways immigrants (and others) are providing space for their youth is the task of the Youth and Religion Project at the University of Illinois at Chicago (Warner 2002a; R. Williams 2002).

6. Edgell (forthcoming).

7. This desire for children to become good citizens coincides with the sort of inclusive and tolerant model of familism Wilcox (2002) describes as typical of Mainline churches. The other place where scouting is common is among Latter-day Saints. Mormons are among the largest sponsors of scouting in the United States. Each ward is encouraged to establish a troop to help enhance the character of young men as they assume their roles as priests (something all young Mormon men who are in good standing do), so we counted these groups as weekday religious education. While these troops are part of the Boy Scouts of America organization, they are also integral to the Latter-day Saints' religious mission.

8. Chaves (2004) has emphasized the importance of congregations as a site for musical and artistic production. Wuthnow (2001) argues that artistic practices often have a spiritual dimension.

9. As I first wrote these words, my own extended church family, Oakhurst Baptist in Decatur, Georgia, was surrounding one of its families with care and support through the agonizing death from cancer of their sixteen-year-old daughter. Even those of us scattered from the community were drawn into that circle through the "OBC" e-list. Internet communication is becoming a powerful community builder for many congregations (Thumma 2002b).

CHAPTER 4

1. Wuthnow (1994a) takes up the theme of religion as a culture that is produced and consumed in *Producing the Sacred*.

2. Note that every Liturgical congregation that is counted as *not* using an official worship book is in that column because of missing data. They may be experimenting with other ways of structuring their worship, but more likely they just did not provide the information we requested. It is a safe guess that every Catholic and Orthodox parish uses an officially prescribed liturgy, even if they do not put published prayer books in their pews.

3. Note that the nondenominational churches are analyzed separately from other Conservative Protestants, since by definition these independent churches draw exclusively on resources not defined by denominational traditions and suppliers.

4. Abbington (2001, 2–3) notes that classically trained musicians and singing from a hymnal were more prevalent in black churches before the 1960s, before the rise of neo-Pentecostal and Afrocentric emphases in worship.

5. Biersdorfer (2002) describes the emergence of high-tech enhancements being introduced in many congregations.

6. The worship styles of "Gen-X" have been widely discussed (Gubkin 2000; Hayward 2000). The role of music in mixed-generational churches is discussed by Carroll and Roof (2002).

7. *CCLI in the United States* (2002).

8. See especially McDannell (1995). Inspired by McDannell's work, the "Material History of American Religion" project gathered an impressive archive of photos and essays, accessible from http://www.materialreligion.org/index.html. Ironically, in focusing on the religious significance of everyday material objects, they have paid comparatively little attention to liturgical objects themselves. An exception is the attention paid by Winston (1999) to the material settings and costumes of the evangelistic performances of the Salvation Army.

9. Eck describes one Hindu community's experience of using make-do space and then constructing new sacred spaces (Eck 2001, 88–93).

10. P. Williams (1997) provides an excellent discussion of architects and styles, but relatively little attention to the more mundane aspects of creating a religious building. The evolution of American church architecture is more thoroughly explored by Loveland and Wheeler (2003).

11. Cook Communications Ministries (2002).

12. Urban Ministries, Inc. (2002).

13. Wood Lake Books & Logos Productions (2002).

14. On FINK, see Faith Inkubators Project (2002). For information on "Way to Live: Christian Practices for Teens," see Popular Front Interactive Communications (2002). The ineffectiveness of many Mainline youth programs is illustrated in a story told by Warner (2002b). The long-term effects can be seen in the high exit rate of the youth who came through Presbyterian confirmation programs during the Baby Boom (Hoge, Johnson, and Luidens 1994).

15. Awana Clubs International (2002).

16. It is also apparent that camps are an important part of the local denominational infrastructure. They are the single most commonly cited connection between churches and regional bodies. Without their camps, local and regional church structures would lose an important reason for their existence.

17. *Willow Creek Association* (2002a).

18. Bible Study Fellowship International (2001).

19. On the culture and appeal of Promise Keepers, see R. Williams (2001) and Bartkowski (2003).

20. Nashville is also home to the National Baptists' publishing board, but their single small store was (in 1998) open only limited hours and seemed to get less customer traffic. I was the only one there on a Saturday afternoon and the clerk had to unlock the door to let me in. It has since been closed.

21. Family Christian Stores (2002).

22. Hoge, Johnson, and Luidens (1994) describe the wide range of adult religious trajectories to be found among a group who all shared the experience of having been confirmed in the Presbyterian church as teens.

23. This is a point made by both R. B. Williams (1988, 228–29) and Eck (2000).

24. These leadership challenges are underscored by R. B. Williams (1988, 286).

25. Our numbers may overestimate the number of paid black clergy. Based on data collected a decade earlier, Lincoln and Mamiya reported that 58 percent of rural black clergy and 45 percent of urban black clergy had employment other than their pastoral duties (1990, 134). This pattern of leadership helps to account for the difficulty we experienced in completing interviews in small African American churches. The people we were trying to reach were often working nine-to-five jobs and tending to their parishioners in the evenings. They had little time or energy—even if they got our messages—for meetings with researchers. We probably failed to interview more of those who are unpaid than those who are full-time pastors.

26. This may not accurately reflect the situation among Catholic pastors, for whom the relevant term is "ongoing formation." It is likely that our questions did not elicit reports from them about activities that should have been included in this category. It is also possible that they did not think of these required formation events as "something they do for their own growth and development" (as our question asked).

27. Alban Institute (2002).

28. "Vision of a Movement" (1998, 2).

29. *Willow Creek Association* (2002b).

30. Purpose Driven (2002).

31. We did not investigate television and video consumption and so are unable to add that resource use to this picture. It is undoubtedly considerable.

32. The Faith Communities Today survey reported that fewer than 10 percent of congregations had either worship or ministry-based ties that crossed interfaith lines (Thumma 2002a).

CHAPTER 5

1. May (1990) provides a theological and historical discussion of this Mormon emphasis on caring for their own. He notes that "the Saints were enjoined to express their deepest love for humankind by converting all to the gospel; the converts would then enter a community where social, spiritual, and material needs could be effectively nourished" (213–14).

2. The exception, as we will explore below, was the Lubavitcher group in which we interviewed, and they were not so much seeking converts as "evangelizing" nonobservant Jews (see also Davidman 1991). For a discussion of earlier periods in which Jewish proselytizing was more prevalent, see Stark (2001).

3. The emphasis on activism is, however, stronger among the clergy than among the laity. As much as they may say they want their parishes to be involved in service, individual Catholics are themselves less engaged in volunteer work than their church's teachings and clergy rhetoric would predict. On this "Catholic puzzle," see Bane (forthcoming) and Ammerman (forthcoming).

4. There are a number of good sources on the critical role of black churches in the Civil Rights movement (Billingsley 2000; Franklin 1997; Lincoln and Mamiya 1990).

5. Dayton (1976) has described this historic split between evangelicalism and the "social gospel."

6. African American and Conservative Protestants averaged 3.53, compared to the Mainline and Catholic average of 2.46.

7. Ratings for the importance of both preaching and worship averaged 3.27 across all the religious traditions. Ratings of the importance of evangelism programs averaged 3.24 among African American and Conservative Protestant churchgoers, compared to 2.69 among Mainline and Catholic churchgoers.

8. On the tensions between evangelical and liberal wings in Mainline denominations, see J. Wood (forthcoming), Wellman (1999a), and Weston (1997).

9. Accounts include Cavendish (2000), Harris (1994), and R. Wood (2002).

10. The relative lack of political involvement by white Conservative Protestant churches flies in the face of the presumed strength of the New Christian Right, but our finding is consistent with research by Chaves (1999b; 2004) and C. Smith (2000). The rhetorical world of those who *are* politically mobilized is captured by Harding (2000).

11. On this see especially Munson (forthcoming).

12. On the role of African American churches in the civil rights movements see among others Morris (1984) and Lincoln and Mamiya (1990).

13. The role of liberation theology in Latin America is also hotly debated (Levine 1992; Smith and Prokopy 1999).

14. This is the "puzzle" explored by Bane (forthcoming). McMullen (1994) looked at parishioner awareness of the bishops' letters, and Cavendish (2000) provides an overview of factors affecting Catholic parish activism.

15. D'Antonio et al. (2001, ch. 6) provide a thorough examination of Catholic attitudes on Church social teachings.

16. As we will see, activity does not necessarily follow rhetoric. While there is rough equality in the small numbers of Mainline and Conservative congregations that adopt an activist identity and sense of mission, Conservatives are less involved in actual political organization and practice.

17. One such church (dubbed "City Baptist") is described by Ammerman (1997a).

18. In 2000, King County, Washington, was 73 percent Anglo, 6 percent Hispanic, 11 percent Asian, 5 percent African American, and 5 percent other groups. Cook County, Illinois, was 48 percent Anglo, 26 percent African American, 20 percent Hispanic, 5 percent Asian, and 1 percent other groups (United States Census Bureau 2002). On Chicago congregations, see Livezey (2000).

19. Emerson and Smith (2000) point out that this is at least in part a mathematical reality. Minority members simply encounter more majority members than vice versa. It is also, as they point out, a cultural reality that the burden for bridging falls on the minority.

20. Hartford Institute for Religion Research (2001).

21. Dayton (1976) takes up this period of division and its legacy among evangelicals.

22. The visible exceptions to this generalization are evangelicals such as Jim Wallis of the Sojourners Community and Ron Sider, editor of *The Other Side* magazine.

23. Organizational response to ethnic diversity is not always ideal in the Catholic Church, however. See, for instance, the case of "St. Catherine's" (Ammerman 1997a, 65–73). The checkered history of race relations in the American Catholic Church is documented by McGreevy (1996), and Gamm (1999) examines the ethnic consequences of the Church's geographical parishes.

24. Although we did not find any such groups, Catholic women, like Protestant ones, have a history of forming "circles" to raise money and otherwise support missionary activity (Dries 2002).

25. On the history and impact of women's missionary societies, see especially the work of Robert (1997; 2002), along with numerous others (Epstein 1981; Scott 1993; Welter 1976).

26. On SBC mission education, see Hoyle (2002). Higginbotham (1993) shows how the fund-raising and organizing efforts of women's missionary societies were vital to the early growth of the National Baptist Convention. By the early twentieth century, the Women's Convention was raising money for a variety of social reform and missionary activities. None of the NBC churches where we interviewed, however, reported an ongoing local mission fund-raising group.

27. Walls argues that missionary societies are among the first examples of voluntary organizations and are significant models for the other efforts that followed (Walls 1996, 241–27).

28. There are many important sources on Charitable Choice (Bartkowski and Regis 1999; Chaves 1999b; Farnsley 2003; Pipes and Ebaugh 2002; Sherman 2000).

29. Chaves (1999a) reports that 57 percent of congregations support social service activity. His count includes, however, both activities that we classify as political action or cultural enrichment and activities that are supported by giving to other organizations.

30. This contrast corresponds to the historical transitions from small town to big city that took place in the early twentieth century. During this period, when the majority

of the American population shifted to urban areas for the first time, the dominant model of congregational life shifted from what Holifield (1994) calls the "devotional" (focused on worship and fellowship) to the "social" (focused on programs and service). The great early-twentieth-century student of congregations H. Paul Douglass clearly thought the more programmatic model was the future of the church (Douglass 1927).

31. Among the most common and visible modes for mobilizing coalitions of congregations for political and economic activism are Faith-Based Community Organizations, modeled on the community organizing pioneered by Saul Alinsky (Warren 2001; R. Wood 2002).

32. Hayes, Palmer, and Zaslow (1990) point out that nonprofit organizations are critical in providing after-school care, since schools themselves are often resistant for a variety of reasons to organizing such programs themselves.

33. On the pervasiveness of the arts in congregational life, see Chaves (2004, ch. 6).

CHAPTER 6

1. Half of these congregations were African American, and two-thirds were very small (fewer than fifty regular participants). None was more than fifty years old, and half were less than fifteen years old. As noted in Chapter 1, there is reason to believe that this type of congregation is more prevalent than any of the current surveys has been able to determine, since these are the cases most likely to be nonrespondents.

2. On the early history of American religious organizations, see Richey (1994) and Butler (1990).

3. Historical transformations in forms of denominational organization are documented by Weeks (1992), Primer (1978), and Richey (1994).

4. See Chaves, Giesel, and Tsitsos (2002), as well as Hodgkinson and Weitzman (1993, 22–51). Cnaan (2002) reports that the historic congregations they surveyed provided services through an average of four programs, including those independently run.

5. Our undercount is probably less serious in the Mainline Protestant congregations than in others. They were much more likely to give us copies of annual reports and other written documents from which precise information could often be gleaned. It was our impression that the generation of such written reports, and the willingness to share them with researchers, was more common among Mainline Protestants than among other groups.

6. The patterns of Mainline connection are explored more fully in Ammerman (2002a), in which portions of this chapter first appeared.

7. African American pastors reported that their churches place fairly high emphasis on promoting social change and working together in the community, but that emphasis does not translate into higher levels of partnership activity. These results suggest that the primary explanation for that fact is resources—both the number of well-off people in the congregation and the overall size of the church's budget.

8. On the history of Mainline involvement in voluntary organizations, see Hall (forthcoming).

9. Virginia A. Hodgkinson, Heather A. Gorski, Stephen M. Noga, and E. B. Knauft in *Giving and Volunteering in the United States, 1994*, vol. 2: *Trends in Giving and Volunteering by Type of Charity* (Washington, D.C.: Independent Sector, 1995), as cited in Wuthnow (1999). Our "human services" category almost exactly conforms to theirs. We have separated out "Policy Advocacy" from their larger category of "Public Benefit" (which we call "Community Benefit"). And we have combined their four Health, Education, Culture, and Youth organizations categories into one. We have put recovery and self-help groups into a separate category, however.

10. It should be noted that a given organization may engage in multiple kinds of activities, so our categorization is dependent on the particular activity the congregation supports, not necessarily on an overall characterization of the organization itself. For instance, a congregation may cooperate with the local Red Cross in conducting a blood drive (something we classified as a health enhancement activity) or channel disaster relief contributions through the national Red Cross office (something we classified as a human service activity).

11. These are the actual names of the service organizations. Direct quotations are used by permission.

12. Hamilton is adamant that these political organizations do not have the support of the evangelical community (2000, 129–31). Chaves also found that few churches were involved in Christian Right political activity (1999b).

13. Chaves (2004, 112–18) also found African American churches to be most politically active. There is an extensive literature on the involvement of African American Churches in political and civil rights activity. Pattillo-McCoy (1998) provides a fascinating analysis of the role of church culture in political organizing. R. Wood (1999) finds similar cultural processes at work in other activist congregations.

14. Our results are generally parallel to those offered by Wuthnow (1999). He notes that people in Mainline churches are more likely than those in Evangelical ones to be members of and volunteer for nonreligious civic organizations.

15. Where a congregation mentioned supporting the work of an agency based in another denomination, we coded that connection as a "religious nonprofit." That same agency, when supported by a congregation in its own denomination was coded as a "denominational" connection. On Catholic Relief Services, see Froehle and Gautier (2000, 100–102).

16. Taken from the Food for the Poor Web site (Food for the Poor 2002).

17. Links between churches and economic development are explored by R. Wood (1994). See also Hart (2001) and Warren (2001).

18. This is consistent with the "Golden Rule" patterns of religiosity described by Ammerman (1997b).

19. See Wuthnow (1994b, ch. 5) for a discussion of organizational structure in small groups. He notes that religious organizations have been a primary resource for meeting space and a primary seedbed for the formation of groups (90–93).

20. Referring to a word for "mercy" from the Hebrew scriptures.

21. Even among explicitly religious activist organizations, very different forms of discourse can prevail (Hart 2001). Interesting accounts of the differing narratives that shape charitable action are provided by Allahyari (2001), C. Bender (2003), and Lichterman (forthcoming).

22. Nason-Clark (2000) notes that both needs and strategies cross sacred/secular lines in serving abused women.

23. The delicate balance between faith and efficiency struck by Habitat is analyzed by Baggett (2000).

24. Zald's 1970 study of the YMCA is the classic examination of this process. For a discussion of the implications of institutional differentiation for the religious organizations themselves, see Wittberg (2000).

25. The complex ways in which action is perceived to be religious are explored by C. Bender (2003).

26. The 1996 Welfare Reform Act introduced provisions intended to encourage religious organizations to compete for government contracts, thereby increasing the choices available in the provision of services to poor people. The administration of George W. Bush significantly increased funding for and attention to these initiatives. On the relationship between religious charities and state funding, see Monsma (1996) and Salamon (1995).

27. The levels of community involvement we are reporting appear to be quite comparable to those being reported by a massive study of American churchgoers. They found that 38 percent had donated to secular charities, for instance, while our overall figure is 41 percent (Silverstein 2002). The mechanisms for mobilizing this individual voluntarism are explored more thoroughly in Ammerman (forthcoming).

28. It is not surprising that when the confidence of members is shaken by church scandal, a "bishop's appeal" for charitable funds would go wanting.

29. Our liberal Protestant and Catholic respondents were more explicit about the religious bases for their service work than were the respondents in Becker and Dhingra's study (2001). The different ways faith is deployed by evangelicals doing social service are explored by Unruh (2002).

30. Within the nonprofit sector, altruistic values can be eclipsed by instrumental concerns (Allahyari 2001). Gardner (1998) issues a call to reclaim these public values.

31. The growth of the Right to Life movement has been the subject of an enormous body of research (Bendyna et al. 2001; Dillon 1995; Ginsburg 1989; McVeigh and Sikkink 2001; Munson forthcoming).

32. Jesus Day/March for Jesus USA (2002).

33. Congregational support for denomination-based advocacy activities is even less common than support for parachurch advocacy groups. There are both regional and national denominational groups across a variety of religious traditions that educate and lobby on social policy issues; but only three congregations—two Mainline and one Conservative—mentioned such efforts as a denominational benefit they knew about and valued. More commonly, social policy activities were mentioned as a point of tension between the congregation and its national denomination.

34. Less than half claim that most or all of their members live within a ten-minute drive, while a quarter claim that at least some of their members drive more than thirty minutes.

35. My primary sources for this sketch of the history of the American missions movement are Hutchison (1987) and Robert (1997).

36. "The Time for the World's Conversion Come" by Rufus Anderson, quoted in Walls (1996, 223).

37. Women's missionary work was often tied to a variety of charitable and reform movements in the nineteenth century (Epstein 1981; Ryan 1979; Scott 1993).

38. On this period, see Hutchison (1987) and Hamilton (2000).

39. On the fundamentalist-modernist battles, see Marsden (1980) and Ammerman (1991).

40. See Ahlstrom (1975, 74–88, vol. 1) and Albanese (1992, 286–88).

41. Standing Conference of Canonical Orthodox Bishops of the Americas (1994).

42. These comparative accounts were compiled from information accessed September 3, 2002, from www.episcopalchurch.org, www.adventist.org, and http://anglican.org/domain/admin/countries.html, accessed September 4, 2002.

43. American Baptist News Service (2001).

44. Global mission allocations vary between about 20 and 50 percent of national denominational budgets (excluding special offerings). However, congregational giving generally goes first to the state or region, which typically keeps more than half, leaving perhaps 10 to 20 percent of the original dollars going to national missions budgets. Patterns vary not only from one denomination to the next, however, but also from one region to the next within each denomination. Fifteen percent is therefore a reasonable ballpark figure.

CHAPTER 7

1. The nature of American religious pluralism and of the denomination as a peculiar form of religious organization has been examined by a number of sociologists and historians (Greeley 1972; Hatch 1989; D. Martin 1962; S. Mead 1963; Weber 1946).

2. "Denominational" is often taken to describe a mode of religiosity that presumes (by virtue of pluralism) that religious identities are less central or serious than the identities of "sectarians" and have less force than when religion is a monopoly "church" (Niebuhr 1929). That is not the way I am using the concept here.

3. This is a thesis first advanced by Warner (1993). It was given further development by Yang and Ebaugh (2001).

4. Hartford Seminary, as one of the leading centers for the study of Islam and Christian-Muslim relations, exemplified such educational efforts. In addition to public forums, the Seminary also cooperated with Beliefnet to offer an online educational experience and produced a book of essays (Markham and Abu Rabi 2002).

5. Roof and McKinney (1987) have documented Mainline decline. Thumma (2000) and Miller (1997) have written about the rise of megachurches.

6. The notion that recent restructuring constitutes "decline" is a peculiarly ahistorical assertion, ignoring the many different organizational configurations that have constituted American denominationalism (Butler 1990; Richey 1994). It misses both the longer history of change and the more diverse experience of traditions with other organizational patterns.

7. Perhaps the most widely read examples of the "decline" literature are from L. Mead (1991; 1998). Major collections have addressed the issues (e.g., Coalter, Mulder, and Weeks 1990; Roozen and Hadaway 1993), but most of this work has been concerned with general organizational decline, especially among the liberal and moderate Protestant denominations. For an excellent overview and critique of the notion that denominational identities are declining, see Bibby (1999).

8. Previous studies that have attempted to measure congregational and individual denominational identity include Carroll and Roozen (1990) and Luidens and Nemeth (1999).

9. This question does not tell us how much our respondents actually *know* about those creeds, only about whether they subjectively see church teachings as important to them.

10. The internal consistency of answers to these questions is measured by a scale alpha = .67. Scores ranged between 4 and 17 (m = 12.43, s.d. = 2.67).

11. His words could easily have come from the pastor of the "Independent Baptist" church that is the setting for *Bible Believers* (Ammerman 1987).

12. The Cooperative Baptist Fellowship is another example of a quasi-denominational network (Ammerman 1993).

13. That evangelicals would not be immune to declines in denominational identity is in line with findings discussed in Sikkink (1999) and Wagner (1997).

14. If no involvement in an activity was mentioned, a score of 0 was recorded; if one activity in the category was mentioned, a score of 1 was recorded; and if more than one activity was mentioned, a score of 2 was recorded. The scale, therefore, varies between 0 and 12.

15. Congregations were asked the size of their "total annual operating budget—excluding capital campaigns (such as building funds) and affiliated organizations (such as schools)." They were also asked how much, if any, they gave "last year to denominational mission work and programs." This variable is a ratio of those two amounts.

16. Hoge et al. (1996) discuss the distinctive character of individual giving in Catholic parishes. Tithing and pledging have been less common practices, and average giving is significantly lower than in Protestant churches, even controlling for many of the organizational factors that have been assumed to account for the differences.

17. The effects of polity have been widely examined (e.g., Farnsley 1994; Harrison 1959; McMullen 1994; Monahan 1999; Takayama and Cannon 1979; J. Wood 1970).

18. Both the Presbyterians and the Episcopalians claim that their system of government served as the model for the U.S. Constitution. Given the dominance of both groups in colonial life, either claim is plausible.

19. Finke and Stark (2001) claim that pro-inclusion represents moral laxness and giving in to cultural pressures. Given dominant cultural attitudes against homosexuality, especially in the rural South where Methodists still have much of their strength, to be pro-inclusion, quite to the contrary, would be distinctly countercultural.

20. Moon (2004) provides an insightful account of these grassroots-level differences among Methodists.

21. This was also a key issue in the Southern Baptist controversies (Ammerman 1990). The question of ordaining women remains an issue in many denominations, especially those that identify themselves with biblical inerrancy (Chaves 1997). A thorough examination of the contested roles of women in black churches is provided by Gilkes (2001). The deeply gendered nature of the National Baptist Convention is discussed by Morris and Lee (forthcoming).

22. On this tension between revival and more staid habits of worship and organization in the Assemblies of God, see Poloma (forthcoming). For an account of a congregation shaped by the Toronto blessing, see Hayward (2000).

23. On the Episcopal case, see Swatos (forthcoming), and on the National Baptist issues, see Morris and Lee (forthcoming). On the tension between religious and bureaucratic authority in American denominations, see Chaves (1993a).

24. This account is based on reporting by Michael Paulson (2003a; 2003b). The *Boston Globe* won a Pulitzer Prize in 2003 for its coverage of the scandal in the Church. An archive of their extensive reporting and other background material is found at http://www.boston.com/globe/spotlight/abuse/. On Catholic dissent, see Dillon (1999). On women in the Church, see Winter, Lummis, and Stokes (1994).

25. On Catholic laity, see the works of D'Antonio and various associates (D'Antonio, Davidson, and Hoge 1996; D'Antonio et al. 1989; 2001).

26. Dykstra and Hudnut-Buemler (1992) propose that denominations have moved from being "corporations" to being "regulatory agencies." Similarly, Wuthnow (1994a) places emphasis on denominational policy pronouncements as one of few viable functions for national offices. Our findings make both those assertions doubtful.

27. These differences among Episcopalians were vivid in the controversy surrounding the installation of an openly gay bishop in one diocese (New Hampshire), which caused a furor in others (see Massing 2004).

28. This organizational history has been examined by Coalter, Mulder, and Weeks (1992), Primer (1978), Chaves (1993b), and Ammerman (1994).

29. One such highly developed agency structure could be found in the Southern Baptist Convention (Ammerman 1990). On the growth of Protestant denominational organizations in the twentieth century, see Winter (1968).

30. The African American churches are the other places to look for differences based on organizational structure, but here structure and polity coincide in ways that make it impossible to know which is the more important factor. In the black Methodist denominations and the Church of God in Christ, the combination of stronger authority and more robust organization produces consistently stronger participation. Still, these organizational effects are miniscule compared to the way denominational citizenship (lower giving and higher national participation) is shaped by being part of the organizational culture of the historic African American churches.

31. Internet Ministries (2001). On the history of the movement, see Hughes and Roberts (2001).

32. This figure courtesy of Faith Communities Today, Carl Dudley and David A. Roozen, codirectors (Hartford Institute for Religion Research, March 2001), with permission from the General Council on Ministry, United Methodist Church.

33. Just how complicated the issue of switching is can be seen in the extensive "switching" literature (e.g., Hadaway and Marler 1993; Kalmijn 1991; Sherkat 2001; Sullins 1993). Movement tends to be between relatively similar groups and does not always seem to lead to declines in denominational identification.

34. Mainline congregations with a majority of cradle members do give more to the denomination, but this is the only measure of connection on which having a majority of switchers seems to affect the denominational commitment of Mainline congregations.

35. My use of the term "practice" builds on ideas traceable to Bourdieu (1979) in social theory, and to MacIntyre (1984) in ethics. The term has been appropriated recently to describe religious action by D. Bass (1997) and Wuthnow (1998a). I have written elsewhere about practices as a base for understanding religion (Ammerman 1997b; 1997c).

36. I have expanded elsewhere on the idea of narrative practices as a way to understand the formation of religious identities (Ammerman 2003).

37. We asked each congregational informant to name the publisher(s) of the material they "use in your children's religious education program," as well as naming what they use in their youth and adult programs. If they named an officially sanctioned denominational publisher, this variable is coded 1. If not, it is coded 0. If they have no classes, the variable is coded 0. Individual respondents were asked, if they participate in

any religious education activity, whether it primarily uses publications produced by the denomination. Those that do are coded 1. Those that do not are coded 0.

38. To use Iannaccone's terms, they bring "human capital" to the task, and their investment in it redounds to the overall store of such capital available for producing the congregation's collective goods (Iannaccone 1990).

39. This parallels the differences between settled and unsettled cultural contexts as described by Swidler (1986).

40. Kennedy's interviews with "exemplars" of Christian virtue from a variety of traditions revealed the power of music as a point of contact with transcendence that also reinforced religious identity and connection with one's religious community (Kennedy 2002).

41. J. Wood (forthcoming) argues that this sense of common mission—and the structures with which to accomplish it—are critical challenges currently facing the United Methodist Church. Forty years ago Gibson Winter assumed that Protestant denominations had lost their missionary orientation, and he too suspected that regaining some appropriate substitute was necessary if denominational organizations were to do anything other than perpetuate themselves (Winter 1968, 42–43).

42. If the informant mentioned any denominational program or activity that is emphasized in the congregation, this variable is coded 1. If nothing is mentioned, it is coded 0.

43. The stories favored by many liberal national denominational staffs are, ironically, especially out of tune with the sense of mission expressed at the local level, thereby often encouraging local clergy to *avoid* talking about what the national offices do (Hadden 1969; Roozen, Carroll, and Roof 1995, 70). The result, documented by Zech (1997), is alienation from denominational mission efforts, failures in communication about those efforts, and a resulting loss of revenue by denominations.

44. Here I follow Penny Edgell Becker's way of talking about institutional models (Becker 1999).

45. Among the studies that explore these dimensions of Catholic cultural and organizational life are Castelli and Gremillion (1987), McGreevy (1996), and Orsi (1996). Literature on the changing character of individual Catholic identity is numerous (D'Antonio, Davidson, and Hoge 1996; Dillon 1999; Hoge 2000; McNamara 1992).

46. On Church financial authority, see Ostling and Ostling (1999, 149–57), but on the decline in the authority of the local Mormon bishop, see Mauss (1994, 15–17).

47. Sikkink (1999), Thumma (1999), and Wagner (1997) have written on this "generic" evangelical identity.

CHAPTER 8

1. Demerath (2001) has compared the United States to fourteen other societies where the mix of religion and politics has sometimes been violent. He concludes that religious liberty is not what distinguishes the United States, but that disestablishment

(unlinking state power from religious privilege) is a key to our relatively less violent history.

2. Here I follow the logic of Sydney Mead's argument (1963).

3. Markham claims that this discovery is also an important contribution to Christian theology. The American experiment was the "first cultural attempt to marry commitment and plurality" (Markham 1999, 79).

4. This shows up in the literature on "switching" (Hadaway and Marler 1993; Sherkat and Wilson 1995).

5. On historic shifts in congregational patterns see Holifield (1994). On changes in denominational form, see Richey (1994).

6. I follow here the conclusions reached by a diverse group of American religious and political leaders brought together in the "American Assembly." They asserted that even in an increasingly diverse society, "religious voices are a vital component of our national conversation, and should be heard in the public square" (Marty et al. 2000, 11).

7. I thank Penny Edgell (Becker) for this insight.

8. The following discussion draws on arguments developed in *Taking Faith Seriously*, and some of the language is borrowed from my contributions to the conclusion of that volume (Bane, Coffin, and Higgins forthcoming).

9. Demerath and Williams (1992) write of the way religion exercises "cultural power" in the public arena, and one of their most telling examples is of a nun, in her habit, who publicly shamed a mayor into paying attention to the needs of homeless people.

10. On this policy evolution see Denniston (2003). The irony of evangelical political support for these initiatives is that as of the late 1990s, Conservative Protestant churches were the least likely churches to say they would be open to seeking government funding (Chaves 1999b). On the dilemmas of the faith-based initiatives, see, among many others Farnsley (1998) and Sherman (2000).

11. These Catholic patterns are traced by Bane (forthcoming). Lower levels of Catholic civic skills are documented by Verba et al. (1995), and the mechanisms by which official Catholic pronouncements reach ordinary laity are analyzed by McMullen (1994). On the generally prosocial effects of church attendance, see Gill (1999).

12. The contrasting network patterns to be found in cosmopolitan communities, as compared to traditional ones, are explored by Eiesland (2000). The nature of metropolitan community networks is also the subject of Fischer's work (e.g., 1991). The tendency to see current strains as the "demise of community" runs deep in American history. Thomas Bender (1978) documents recurring "end of community" rhetoric that goes all the way back to the seventeenth century.

13. Even with our relatively stringent criterion of a 60 percent majority, this number is higher than the number found in the National Congregations Study and reported in DeYoung et al. (2003). They report that 7.5 percent of all congregations have no racial

group over 80 percent of the total membership, with only 5.5 percent of Christian congregations being that mixed.

14. I have written elsewhere about uses of narrative as an analytical tool (Ammerman 2003). My work builds especially on Somers (1994).

15. The story of ethnic assimilation is especially true of Lutherans who, for instance, once maintained a thriving day school system. Methodists, on the other hand, were always part of the ethnic mainstream but in the nineteenth century maintained a much stronger sense of religious difference. They sustained religious fervor in a vibrant system of "class meetings" that demanded much more than Sunday-morning commitment from adult members (Finke and Stark 1992).

16. Keillor (1999).

17. The ties to ethnicity were one of the things that most distressed H. Richard Niebuhr (1929).

APPENDIX ONE

1. Chaves et al. (1999) estimate that the regular Yellow Pages accounts for 80 percent of congregations. Since American Yellow Pages on CD includes all listings, not just those who have paid a fee, the coverage should be somewhat higher.

2. Our analysis was guided by principles such as those outlined in Jorgensen (1989) and Lofland and Lofland (1984).

3. On the effects of size, see Benson and Hassinger (1972), Routhage (n.d.), and Wilken (1971).

4. On the role of monetary resources, see Chaves and Miller (1998), Hoge et al. (1996), and McKinney (1998).

5. Postwar expansion is examined by Hoge and Roozen (1979), Hudnut-Beumler (1994), Roozen, Carroll, and Roof (1995), and Warner (1990). The dynamics of newly established congregations are discussed in Ammerman (1997a, ch. 7).

6. Sources on rural churches include Brewer et al. (1967) and Chalfant and Heller (1991). Lischer (2001) provides a fascinating first-person depiction of rural church life, and the transition between small town and urban region is examined by Eiesland (2000).

7. These categories reflect structures that are dominant/token, majority/minority, and mixed (Kanter 1977).

8. Chaves et al. (1999) make a similar argument about the reliability of key informants for these observable characteristics. See also McPherson and Rotolo (1995).

9. One of the few recent writers to take social class seriously as a dimension of congregational life is Sample (1990).

10. Generational differences have been studied by Carroll and Roof (2002).

REFERENCES

Abbington, James. 2001. *Let Mt. Zion Rejoice! Music in the African American Church.* Valley Forge, Penn.: Judson Press.

Abusharaf, Rogaia Mustafa. 1998. "Structural Adaptations in an Immigrant Muslim Congregation in New York." In *Gatherings in Diaspora: Religious Communities and the New Immigrants,* edited by R. Stephen Warner and Judith Wittner, 235–61. Philadelphia: Temple University Press.

Ahlstrom, Sydney E. 1975. *A Religious History of the American People.* 2 vols. Garden City, N.Y.: Doubleday.

Ahmed, Gutbi Mahdi. 1991. "Muslim Organizations in the United States." In *The Muslims of America,* edited by Yvonne Y. Haddad, 11–24. New York: Oxford University Press.

Alban Institute. 2002. *About Us.* http://www.alban.org (accessed June 12, 2002).

Albanese, Catherine L. 1992. *America, Religions and Religion.* 2nd ed. Belmont, Calif.: Wadsworth.

Allahyari, Rebecca Anne. 2001. *Visions of Charity: Volunteer Workers and Moral Community.* Berkeley: University of California Press.

Allen, Catherine B. 2002. "Shifting Sands for Southern Baptist Women in Missions." In *Gospel Bearers, Gender Barriers: Missionary Women in the Twentieth Century,* edited by Dana L. Robert, 113–26. Maryknoll, N.Y.: Orbis Books.

American Baptist News Service. 2001. *American Baptist Men Disaster Relief Teams Participate in New York City Clean-up.* http://www.abc-usa.org/news/102201.htm (accessed November 26, 2001).

Ammerman, Nancy T. 1980. "The Civil Rights Movement and the Clergy in a Southern Community." *Sociological Analysis* 41: 339–50.

———. 1987. *Bible Believers: Fundamentalists in the Modern World.* New Brunswick, N.J.: Rutgers University Press.

———. 1990. *Baptist Battles: Social Change and Religious Conflict in the Southern Baptist Convention.* New Brunswick, N.J.: Rutgers University Press.

———. 1991. "North American Protestant Fundamentalism." In *Fundamentalisms Observed,* edited by Martin E. Marty and R. Scott Appleby, 1–65. Chicago: University of Chicago Press.

———. 1993. "SBC Moderates and the Making of a Post-modern Denomination." *Christian Century* 110, no. 26: 896–99.

———. 1994. "Denominations: Who and What Are We Studying?" In *Re-imagining Denominationalism,* edited by R. Bruce Mullin and Russell E. Richey, 111–33. New York: Oxford University Press.

———. 1997a. *Congregation and Community.* New Brunswick, N.J.: Rutgers University Press.

———. 1997b. "Golden Rule Christianity: Lived Religion in the American Mainstream." In *Lived Religion in America: Toward a History of Practice,* edited by David Hall, 196–216. Princeton: Princeton University Press.

———. 1997c. "Organized Religion in a Voluntaristic Society." *Sociology of Religion* 58, no. 3: 203–15.

———. 2002a. "Connecting Mainline Protestant Congregations with Public Life." In *Quietly Influential: The Public Role of Mainline Protestantism,* edited by Robert Wuthnow and John Evans, 129–58. Berkeley: University of California Press.

———. 2002b. "Grieving Together: September 11 as a Measure of Social Capital in the U.S." In *September 11: Religious Perspectives on the Causes and Consequences,* edited by Ian Markham and Ibrahim Abu Rabi, 53–73. London: Oneworld Publications.

———. 2003. "Religious Identities and Religious Institutions." In *Handbook of the Sociology of Religion,* edited by Michele Dillon, 204–24. Cambridge: Cambridge University Press.

———. Forthcoming. "Porous Boundaries and Busy Intersections: Religious Narratives, Community Service, and Everyday Public Life." In *Taking Faith Seriously,* edited by Mary Jo Bane, Brent Coffin, and Richard Higgins. Cambridge, Mass.: Harvard University Press.

Association of Statisticians of American Religious Bodies. 2002. *Religious Congregations & Membership in the United States.* Glenmary Research Center. http://www.thearda.com/arda.asp?Show = Home (accessed October 15, 2002).

Awana Clubs International. 2002. *The World of Awana*. http://www.awana.org/background.asp (accessed November 22, 2002).

Baer, Hans A., and Merrill Singer. 1992. *African-American Religion in the Twentieth Century*. Knoxville: University of Tennessee Press.

Baer, Jonathan R. 2002. "Empowered Bodies: Divine Healing and American Culture, 1870–1930." Ph.D. dissertation, Yale University.

Baggett, Jerome P. 2000. *Habitat for Humanity: Building Private Homes, Building Public Religion*. Philadelphia: Temple University Press.

Balmer, Randall. 1989. *Mine Eyes Have Seen the Glory*. New York: Oxford.

Bane, Mary Jo. Forthcoming. "The Catholic Puzzle: Parishes and Civic Lives." In *Taking Faith Seriously*, edited by Mary Jo Bane, Brent Coffin, and Richard Higgins. Cambridge, Mass.: Harvard University Press.

Bane, Mary Jo, Brent Coffin, and Richard Higgins, eds. Forthcoming. *Taking Faith Seriously*. Cambridge, Mass.: Harvard University Press.

Banks, Adele. 2002. *Missouri President Faces Charges from Synod*. http://www.thelutheran.org/0201/page52a.html (accessed December 23, 2002).

Barman, Emily, and Mark Chaves. Forthcoming. "Strategy and Restructure in the United Church of Christ." In *Adaptive Change in National Denominational Structures: Practiced Theology*, edited by David Roozen and James Nieman. Grand Rapids, Mich.: Eerdmans.

Bartkowski, John P. 2003. *The Promise Keepers: Servants, Soldiers, and Godly Men*. New Brunswick, N.J.: Rutgers University Press.

Bartkowski, John P., and Helen A. Regis. 1999. "Religious Organizations, Anti-poverty Relief, and Charitable Choice: A Feasibility Study of Faith-Based Welfare Reform in Mississippi." Arlington, Va.: PricewaterhouseCoopers Endowment.

Bass, Diana Butler. 2002. *Strength for the Journey: A Pilgrimage of Faith in Community*. San Francisco: Jossey-Bass.

Bass, Dorothy. 1997. *Practicing Our Faith: A Way of Life for Searching People*. San Francisco: Jossey-Bass.

Becker, Penny Edgell. 1998. "Making Inclusive Communities: Congregations and the 'Problem' of Race." *Social Problems* 45, no. 4: 451–72.

———. 1999. *Congregations in Conflict: Cultural Models of Local Religious Life*. Cambridge: Cambridge University Press.

Becker, Penny Edgell, and Pawan H. Dhingra. 2001. "Religious Involvement and Volunteering: Implications for Civil Society." *Sociology of Religion* 62, no. 3: 315–35.

Beckford, James A. 1975. *The Trumpet of Prophecy*. New York: John Wiley & Sons.

Bednarowski, Mary Farrell. 1999. *The Religious Imagination of American Women*. Bloomington: Indiana University Press.

Bellah, Robert N. 1963. "Religious Evolution." In Bellah, *Beyond Belief*, 20–50. Boston: Beacon.

Bellah, Robert N., Richard Madsen, William M. Sullivan, Ann Swidler, and Steven M. Tipton. 1985. *Habits of the Heart*. Berkeley: University of California Press.

Bender, Courtney. 2003. *Heaven's Kitchen: Living Religion at God's Love We Deliver*. Chicago: University of Chicago Press.

Bender, Thomas. 1978. *Community and Social Change in America*. New Brunswick, N.J.: Rutgers University Press.

Bendroth, Margaret. 2002. *Growing Up Protestant: Parents, Children, and Mainline Churches*. New Brunswick, N.J.: Rutgers University Press.

Bendyna, Mary E., RSM, John C. Green, Mark J. Rozell, and Clyde Wilcox. 2001. "Uneasy Alliance: Conservative Catholics and the Christian Right." *Sociology of Religion* 62, no. 1: 51–64.

Benson, J. Kenneth, and Edward Hassinger. 1972. "Organization Set and Resources as Determinants of Formalization in Religious Organizations." *Review of Religious Research* 14: 30–36.

Bibby, Reginald. 1999. "On Boundaries, Gates, and Circulating Saints: A Longitudinal Look at Loyalty and Loss." *Review of Religious Research* 41: 149–64.

Bible Study Fellowship International. 2001. *Welcome to BSF International*. http://www.bsfinternational.org (accessed May 23, 2002).

Biersdorfer, J. D. 2002. "When Worship Gets Wired." *New York Times*, May 16, G1, G5.

Billingsley, Andrew. 2000. *Mighty like a River: The Black Church and Social Reform*. New York: Oxford University Press.

Blumhofer, Edith. 1993. *Restoring the Faith: The Assemblies of God, Pentecostalism, and American Culture*. Urbana: University of Illinois Press.

Blumhofer, Edith, Russell P. Spittler, and Grant Wacker, eds. 1999. *Pentecostal Currents in American Protestantism*. Urbana: University of Illinois Press.

Boone, Kathleen. 1989. *The Bible Tells Them So: The Discourse of Protestant Fundamentalists*. Albany: State University of New York Press.

Bourdieu, Pierre. 1979. *Outline of a Theory of Practice*. New York: Cambridge University Press.

Boylan, Anne M. 1988. *Sunday School: The Formation of an American Institution, 1790–1880*. New Haven: Yale University Press.

Brereton, Virginia Lieson. 1991. "United and Slighted: Women as Subordinated Insiders." In *Between the Times: The Travail of the Protestant Establishment in America, 1900–1960*, edited by William Hutchison, 143–67. Cambridge: Cambridge University Press.

———. 1998. "Education and Minority Religions." In *Minority Faiths and the American Protestant Mainstream*, edited by Jonathan D. Sarna, 279–304. Urbana: University of Illinois Press.

Brewer, Earl D. C., Jr., Theodore H. Runyon, Barbara B. Pittard, and Harold McSwain. 1967. *Protestant Parish: A Case Study of Rural and Urban Parish Patterns.* Atlanta: Communicative Arts Press.

Brown, Steven M. 1993. *The Choice for Jewish Day Schools.* Solomon Schechter Day School Association. http://uscj.org/item20_108.html (accessed November 22, 2002).

Burns, Gene. 1992. *The Frontiers of Catholicism: The Politics of Ideology in a Liberal World.* Berkeley: University of California Press.

Butler, Jon. 1990. *Awash in a Sea of Faith.* Cambridge, Mass.: Harvard University Press.

Cantrell, R. L., J. F. Krile, and G. A. Donohue. 1983. "Parish Autonomy: Measuring Denominational Differences." *Journal for the Scientific Study of Religion* 22: 276–87.

Carlson, David. Forthcoming. "Fellowship and Communion in the Post-modern Era: The Case of the Lutheran Church–Missouri Synod." In *Adaptive Change in National Denominational Structures: Practiced Theology*, edited by David Roozen and James Nieman. Grand Rapids: Eerdmans.

Carpenter, Joel A. 1980. "Fundamentalist Institutions and the Rise of Evangelical Protestantism, 1929–1940." *Church History* 49: 62–75.

———. 1997. *Revive Us Again: The Reawakening of American Fundamentalism.* New York: Oxford University Press.

Carroll, Jackson W., and Wade Clark Roof. 2002. *Bridging Divided Worlds.* San Francisco: Jossey Bass.

Carroll, Jackson W., and David A. Roozen. 1990. "Congregational Identities in the Presbyterian Church." *Review of Religious Research* 31: 351–69.

Castelli, Jim, and Joseph Gremillion. 1987. *The Emerging Parish: The Notre Dame Study of Catholic Life since Vatican II.* San Francisco: Harper & Row.

Cavendish, James C. 2000. "Church-Based Community Activism: A Comparison of Black and White Catholic Congregations." *Journal for the Scientific Study of Religion* 39, no. 1: 64–77.

CCLI in the United States. 2002. http://www.ccli.com/ccli/CompanyProfile.cfm (accessed May 10, 2002).

Chalfant, H. Paul, and Peter L. Heller. 1991. "Rural/Urban Versus Regional Differences in Religiosity." *Review of Religious Research* 33, no. 1: 76–86.

Chaves, Mark. 1993a. "Denominations as Dual Structures: An Organizational Analysis." *Sociology of Religion* 54, no. 2: 147–69.

———. 1993b. "Intraorganizational Power and Internal Secularization in Protestant Denominations." *American Journal of Sociology* 99, no. 1: 1–48.

———. 1997. *Ordaining Women: Culture and Conflict in Religious Organizations.* Cambridge, Mass.: Harvard University Press.

———. 1999a. "Congregations' Social Service Activities." Washington: Urban Institute.

———. 1999b. "Religious Congregations and Welfare Reform: Who Will Take Advantage of 'Charitable Choice'?" *American Sociological Review* 64: 836–46.

———. 2000. *National Congregations Study.* St. Denis Library at University of Arizona. http://saint-denis.library.arizona.edu/natcong/ (accessed October 15, 2002).

———. 2004. *Congregations in America.* Cambridge, Mass.: Harvard University Press.

Chaves, Mark, and David E. Cann. 1992. "Regulation, Pluralism, and Religious Market Structure: Explaining Religion's Vitality." *Rationality and Society* 4, no. 3: 272–90.

Chaves, Mark, Helen Giesel, and William Tsitsos. 2002. "Religious Variations in Public Presence: Evidence from the National Congregations Study." In *Quietly Influential: The Public Role of Mainline Protestantism,* edited by Robert Wuthnow and John Evans, 108–28. Berkeley: University of California Press.

Chaves, Mark, Mary Ellen Koneiczny, Kraig Beyerlein, and Emily Barman. 1999. "The National Congregational Study; Background, Methods, and Selected Results." *Journal for the Scientific Study of Religion* 38, no. 4: 458–76.

Chaves, Mark, and Sharon Miller. 1998. *Financing American Religion.* Thousand Oaks, Calif.: Altamira Press.

Chireau, Yvonne. 1997. "Conjure and Christianity in the Nineteenth Century: Religious Elements in African American Magic." *Religion and American Culture* 7, no. 2: 225–46.

Clark, Linda J. 1991. "Hymn-Singing: The Congregation Making Faith." In *Carriers of Faith,* edited by Carl S. Dudley, Jackson W. Carroll, and James P. Wind, 49–64. Louisville: Westminster/John Knox.

Cnaan, Ram A. 2002. *The Invisible Caring Hand: American Congregations and the Provision of Welfare.* New York: New York University Press.

Coalter, Milton J., John M. Mulder, and Louis B. Weeks. 1990. *The Mainstream Protestant "Decline": The Presbyterian Pattern.* Louisville: Westminster/John Knox.

————. 1992. *The Organizational Revolution: Presbyterians and American Denominationalism.* Louisville: Westminster/John Knox.

Cohen, Steven M. 1997. "Day School Parents in Conservative Synagogues," 18–23. New York: Ratner Center for the Study of Conservative Judaism, Jewish Theological Seminary of America.

————. 2000. "Assessing the Vitality of Conservative Judaism in North America." In *Jews in the Center: Conservative Congregations and Their Members,* edited by Jack Wertheimer, 13–65. New Brunswick, N.J.: Rutgers University Press.

Cook Communications Ministries. 2002. *Cookministries.Com.* http://www.cookministries.com/index.cfm (accessed May 22, 2002).

Costen, Melva Wilson. 1999. "African-American Liturgical Music in a Global Context." *Journal of the Interdenominational Theological Center* 27: 63–110.

Cress, Daniel M., and David A. Snow. 1996. "Mobilization at the Margins: Resources, Benefactors, and the Viability of Homeless Social Movement Organizations." *American Sociological Review* 61, no. 6: 1089–1109.

D'Antonio, William V., James D. Davidson, and Dean R. Hoge. 1996. *Laity American and Catholic: Transforming the Church.* Kansas City: Sheed & Ward.

D'Antonio, William V., James D. Davidson, Dean R. Hoge, and Catherine Meyer. 2001. *American Catholics: Gender, Generation, and Commitment.* Walnut Creek, Calif.: Altamira.

D'Antonio, William V., James D. Davidson, Dean R. Hoge, and Ruth Wallace. 1989. *American Catholic Laity.* Kansas City: Sheed & Ward.

Davidman, Lynn. 1991. *Tradition in a Rootless World.* Berkeley: University of California Press.

Davidson, James D., Ralph E. Pyle, and David V. Reyes. 1995. "Persistence and Change in the Protestant Establishment, 1930–1992." *Social Forces* 74, no. 1: 157–75.

Davie, Grace. 2000. *Religion in Modern Europe: A Memory Mutates.* Oxford: Oxford University Press.

Day, Katie. 2001. *Difficult Conversations: Taking Risks, Acting with Integrity.* Silver Spring, Md.: Alban Institute.

Dayton, Donald W. 1976. *Discovering an Evangelical Heritage.* New York: Harper & Row.

Demerath, N. J., III. 2001. *Crossing the Gods: World Religions and Worldly Politics.* New Brunswick, N.J.: Rutgers University Press.

Demerath, N. J., III, and Rhys H. Williams. 1992. *A Bridging of Faiths: Religion and Politics in a New England City.* Princeton: Princeton University Press.

Denniston, Lyle. 2003. "A Theory Evolves on Church, State." *Boston Sunday Globe,* June 1, A17.

DeYoung, Curtiss, Michael O. Emerson, George Yancey, and Karen J. Chai. 2003. *United by Faith: Multiracial Congregations as a Response to the Racial Divide*. New York: Oxford University Press.

Diefenthaler, Jon. 1984. "Lutheran Schools in America." In *Religious Schooling in America*, edited by James C. Carper and Thomas C. Hunt, 35–57. Birmingham: Religious Education Press.

Dillon, Michele. 1995. "Religion and Culture in Tension: The Abortion Discourses of the U.S. Catholic Bishops and the Southern Baptist Convention." *Religion and American Culture* 5, no. 2: 159–80.

———. 1999. *Catholic Identity: Balancing Reason, Faith and Power*. New York: Cambridge University Press.

DiMaggio, Paul J. 1998. "The Relevance of Organization Theory to the Study of Religion." In *Sacred Companies*, edited by N. J. Demerath et al., 7–23. New York: Oxford University Press.

DiMaggio, Paul, and John Mohr. 1985. "Cultural Capital, Educational Attainment, and Marital Selection." *American Journal of Sociology* 90, no. 6: 1231–57.

DiMaggio, Paul J., and Walter W. Powell. 1983. "The Iron Cage Revisited: Institutional Isomorphism and Collective Rationality in Organizational Fields." *American Sociological Review* 48: 147–60.

Dodson, Jualynne E., and Cheryl Townsend Gilkes. 1995. "There's Nothing like Church Food." *Journal of the American Academy of Religion* 63: 519–38.

Dolan, Jay P. 1994. "Patterns of Leadership in the Congregation." In *American Congregations: Portraits of Twelve Religious Communities*, edited by James P. Wind and James W. Lewis, 225–56. Chicago: University of Chicago Press.

Douglass, H. Paul. 1927. *The Church in the Changing City*. New York: Doran.

Dries, Angelyn, O.S.F. 2002. "American Catholic 'Woman's Work for Woman' in the Twentieth Century." In *Gospel Bearers, Gender Barriers: Missionary Women in the Twentieth Century*, edited by Dana L. Robert, 127–42. Maryknoll, N.Y.: Orbis Books.

Dudley, Carl S., and David Roozen. 2001. *Faith Communities Today: A Report on Religion in the United States Today*. Hartford: Hartford Institute for Religion Research.

Durkheim, Émile. 1898 [1975]. "Individualism and the Intellectuals." In *Durkheim on Religion*, edited by W. S. F. Pickering, 59–73. London: Routledge & Kegan Paul.

———. 1915 [1964]. *The Elementary Forms of the Religious Life*. Translated by Joseph Ward Swain. New York: Free Press.

Dykstra, Craig, and James Hudnut-Beumler. 1992. "The National Organizational Structures of Protestant Denominations: An Invitation to a Conversation." In *The Organizational Revolution: Presbyterians and American Denominationalism*, edited by

Milton J. Coalter, John M. Mulder, and Louis B. Weeks, 307–31. Louisville: Westminster/John Knox.

Ebaugh, Helen Rose, and Janet Saltzman Chafetz. 1999. "Agents for Cultural Reproduction and Structural Change: The Ironic Role of Women in Immigrant Religious Institutions." *Social Forces* 78, no. 2: 585–613.

———. 2000. *Religion and the New Immigrants: Continuities and Adaptations in Immigrant Congregations*. Walnut Creek, Calif.: Altamira Press.

Eck, Diana L. 2000. "Negotiating Hindu Identities in America." In *The South Asian Religious Diaspora in Britain, Canada, and the United States*, edited by Harold Coward, John R. Hinnells, and Raymond B. Williams, 219–38. Albany: State University of New York Press.

———. 2001. *A New Religious America*. New York: HarperSanFrancisco.

Edgell, Penny. Forthcoming. *Religion and Family in a Changing Society*. Princeton: Princeton University Press.

Eiesland, Nancy. 2000. *A Particular Place: Urban Restructuring and Religious Ecology*. New Brunswick, N.J.: Rutgers University Press.

Emerson, Michael O., and Christian Smith. 2000. *Divided by Faith: Evangelical Religion and the Problem of Race in America*. New York: Oxford University Press.

Epstein, Barbara L. 1981. *The Politics of Domesticity: Women, Evangelism, and Temperance in Nineteenth-Century America*. Middletown: Wesleyan University Press.

Evangelical Lutheran Church in America. 2002. *Department for Schools: Frequently Asked Questions*. http://www.elca.org/dhes/schools/questions.html (accessed November 27, 2002).

Faith Inkubators Project. 2002. *About Faith Inkubators*. http://www.faithink.com/html/about.htm (accessed May 22, 2002).

Family Christian Stores. 2002. *Family Christian Stores: Corporate Information*. http://www.familychristian.com/corporate/ (accessed June 6, 2002).

Farnsley, Arthur Emery, II. 1994. *Southern Baptist Politics: Authority and Power in the Restructuring of an American Denomination*. University Park: Pennsylvania State University Press.

———. 1998. "Can Churches Save the City? A Look at Resources." *Christian Century* 115, no. 34: 1182–84.

———. 2003. *Rising Expectations: Urban Congregations, Welfare Reform, and Civic Life*. Bloomington: Indiana University Press.

Finke, Roger. 1992. "An Unsecular America." In *Religion and Modernization: Sociologists and Historians Debate the Secularization Thesis*, edited by Steve Bruce, 145–69. New York: Oxford University Press.

Finke, Roger, and Rodney Stark. 1992. *The Churching of America*. New Brunswick, N.J.: Rutgers University Press.

———. 2001. "The New Holy Clubs: Testing Church-to-Sect Propositions." *Sociology of Religion* 62, no. 2: 175–89.

Fischer, Claude S. 1991. "Ambivalent Communities: How Americans Understand Their Localities." In *America at Century's End*, edited by Alan Wolfe, 79–90. Berkeley: University of California Press.

Fishman, Sylvia Barack. 1999. *Jewish Life and American Culture*. Albany, N.Y.: State University New York Press.

Food for the Poor. 2002. *About Us: History*. http://www.foodforthepoor.com (accessed December 16).

Foster, Charles R., and Theodore Brelsford. 1996. *We Are the Church Together: Cultural Diversity in Congregational Life*. Valley Forge, Penn.: Trinity Press International.

Franklin, Robert M. 1994. "The Safest Place on Earth: The Culture of Black Congregations." In *American Congregations: New Perspectives in the Study of Congregations*, edited by James P. Wind and James W. Lewis, 257–84. Chicago: University of Chicago Press.

———. 1997. *Another Day's Journey: Black Churches Confronting the American Crisis*. Minneapolis: Augsburg Fortress.

Freedman, Samuel G. 1993. *Upon This Rock: The Miracles of a Black Church*. New York: HarperCollins.

Friedland, Roger, and Robert R. Alford. 1991. "Bringing Society Back In: Symbols, Practices, and Institutional Contradictions." In *The New Institutionalism in Organizational Analysis*, edited by Walter Powell and Paul DiMaggio, 232–63. Chicago: University of Chicago Press.

Froehle, Bryan T., and Mary Gautier. 2000. *Catholicism USA: A Portrait of the Catholic Church in the United States*. New York: Orbis.

Gallup, George, Jr., and D. Michael Lindsay. 1999. *Surveying the Religious Landscape*. Harrisburg, Penn.: Morehouse.

Gamm, Gerald. 1999. *Urban Exodus: Why the Jews Left Boston and the Catholics Stayed*. Cambridge, Mass.: Harvard University Press.

Gardner, Deborah S. 1998. "Vision and Values: Rethinking the Nonprofit Sector in America." New York: Nathan Cummings Foundation and the Program on Nonprofit Organizations.

Genovese, Eugene. 1974. *Roll, Jordan, Roll: The World the Slaves Made*. New York: Pantheon.

Gilkes, Cheryl Townsend. 1995. "The Storm and the Light: Church, Family, Work, and Social Crisis in the African-American Experience." In *Work, Family, and Religion in Contemporary Society*, edited by Nancy Tatom Ammerman and Wade Clark Roof, 177–98. New York: Routledge.

———. 2001. *"If It Wasn't for the Women . . . ": Black Women's Experience and Womanist Culture in Church and Community.* Maryknoll, N.Y.: Orbis Books.

Gill, Robin. 1999. *Churchgoing and Christian Ethics.* Cambridge: Cambridge University Press.

Gillespie, Joanna B. 1993. "Gender and Generations in Congregations." In *Episcopal Women*, edited by Catherine Prelinger, 167–221. New York: Oxford University Press.

———. 1995. *Women Speak: Of God, Congregations and Change.* Valley Forge, Penn.: Trinity Press.

Ginsburg, Faye D. 1989. *Contested Lives: The Abortion Debate in an American Community.* Berkeley: University of California Press.

Goldstein, Sidney, and Alice Goldstein. 2000. "Conservative Jewry: A Socio-demographic Overview." In *Jews in the Center: Conservative Congregations and Their Members*, edited by Jack Wertheimer, 66–94. New Brunswick, N.J.: Rutgers University Press.

Gottschalk, Stephen. 1973. *The Emergence of Christian Science in American Religious Life.* Berkeley, Calif.: University of California Press.

Greeley, Andrew M. 1972. *The Denominational Society.* Glenview, Ill.: Scott-Forsman.

Greeley, Andrew M., William C. McCready, and Kathleen McCourt. 1976. *Catholic Schools in a Declining Church.* Kansas City: Sheed and Ward.

Griffith, R. Marie. 1997a. *God's Daughters: Evangelical Women and the Power of Submission.* Berkeley: University of California Press.

———. 1997b. "The Promised Land of Weight Loss: Law and Gospel in Christian Dieting." *Christian Century* 114, no. 15: 448–54.

GSSDIRS. 2001. *General Social Survey: 1972—2000 Cumulative Codebook.* National Opinion Research Center at the University of Chicago. http://www.icpsr.umich.edu/GSS/ (accessed February 2, 2002).

Gubkin, J. Liora. 2000. "Friday Night Live: It's Not Your Parents' Shabbat." In *GenX Religion*, edited by Richard W. Flory and Donald E. Miller, 199–210. New York: Routledge.

Gustafson, James M. 1961. *Treasure in Earthen Vessels.* Chicago: University of Chicago Press.

Hadaway, C. Kirk, and Penny Long Marler. 1993. "All in the Family: Religious Mobility in America." *Review of Religious Research* 35, no. 2: 97–116.

Hadaway, C. Kirk, Penny Long Marler, and Mark Chaves. 1993. "What the Polls Don't Show: A Closer Look at U.S. Church Attendance." *American Sociological Review* 58, no. 6: 741–52.

Hadaway, C. Kirk, and David Roozen. 1995. *Rerouting the Protestant Mainstream.* Nashville: Abingdon.

Hadden, Jeffrey. 1969. *The Gathering Storm in the Churches.* Garden City, N.Y.: Doubleday.

Hall, Peter Dobkin. 1992. *Inventing the Nonprofit Sector and Other Essays on Philanthropy, Voluntarism, and Nonprofit Organizations.* Baltimore: Johns Hopkins University Press.

——. 1998. "Religion and the Organizational Revolution in the United States." In *Sacred Companies,* edited by N. Jay Demerath III et al., 99–115. New York: Oxford University Press.

——. Forthcoming. "The Word Made Flesh: Theology, Polity, and Civic Engagement in America." In *Taking Faith Seriously,* edited by Mary Jo Bane, Brent Coffin, and Richard Higgins. Cambridge, Mass.: Harvard University Press.

Hamilton, Michael S. 2000. "More Money, More Ministry: The Financing of American Evangelicalism since 1945." In *More Money, More Ministry: Money and Evangelicals in Recent North American History,* edited by Larry Eskridge and Mark Noll, 104–38. Grand Rapids: Eerdmans.

Hammond, Phillip E. 1992. *Religion and Personal Autonomy: The Third Disestablishment in America.* Columbia: University of South Carolina Press.

Handy, Robert T. 1998. "Minority-Majority Confrontations, Church-State Patterns, and the U.S. Supreme Court." In *Minority Faiths and the American Protestant Mainstream,* edited by Jonathan D. Sarna, 305–34. Urbana: University of Illinois Press.

Harding, Susan Friend. 2000. *The Book of Jerry Falwell: Fundamentalist Language and Politics.* Princeton: Princeton University Press.

Harris, Fredrick. 1994. "Something Within: Religion as a Mobilizer of African American Political Action." *Journal of Politics* 56: 42–68.

Harrison, Paul M. 1959. *Authority and Power in the Free Church Tradition.* Princeton: Princeton University Press.

Hart, Stephen. 2001. *Cultural Dilemmas of Progressive Politics : Styles of Engagement among Grassroots Activists.* Chicago: University of Chicago Press.

Hartford Institute for Religion Research. 2001. *How Common Are Interfaith Ties among U.S. Congregations?* http://www.hirr.hartsem.edu/research/quick_question14.html (accessed November 29, 2001).

Hatch, Nathan G. 1989. *The Democratization of American Christianity.* New Haven: Yale University Press.

Hayes, Cheryl D., John L. Palmer, and Martha J. Zaslow. 1990. "Who Cares for America's Children? Child Care Policy for the 1990s." Washington, D.C.: Panel on Child Care Policy, Committee on Child Development Research and Public Policy, Commission on Behavioral and Social Sciences and Education, National Research Council.

Hayward, Douglas. 2000. "Saturday Night in Pasadena: Wholeness, Healing, and Holiness at Harvest Rock Church." In *GenX Religion,* edited by Richard W. Flory and Donald E. Miller, 163–84. New York: Routledge.

Heilman, Samuel C. 1973. *Synagogue Life: A Study in Symbolic Interaction.* Chicago: University of Chicago Press.

———. 2000. "Holding Firmly with an Open Hand: Life in Two Conservative Synagogues." In *Jews in the Center: Conservative Synagogues and Their Members,* edited by Jack Wertheimer, 95–195. New Brunswick, N.J.: Rutgers University Press.

Herberg, Will. 1960. *Protestant-Catholic-Jew.* Garden City, N.Y.: Anchor Doubleday.

Higginbotham, Evelyn Brooks. 1993. *Righteous Discontent: The Women's Movement in the Black Baptist Church, 1890–1920.* Cambridge, Mass.: Harvard University Press.

Hodgkinson, Virginia A., and Murray S. Weitzman. 1993. "From Belief to Commitment: The Community Service Activities and Finances of Religious Congregations in the United States: 1993 Edition." Washington, D.C.: Independent Sector.

Hodgkinson, Virginia A., Murray S. Weitzman, and Arthur D. Kirsch. 1990. "From Commitment to Action: How Religious Involvement Affects Giving and Volunteering." In *Faith and Philanthropy in America: Exploring the Role of Religion in America's Voluntary Sector,* edited by Robert Wuthnow and Virginia A. Hodgkinson, 93–114. San Francisco: Jossey-Bass.

Hoge, Dean R. 2000. "Jewish Identity and Catholic Identity: Findings and Analogies." Paper presented at the Religious Research Association, Houston, October.

Hoge, Dean R., Benton Johnson, and Donald A. Luidens. 1994. *Vanishing Boundaries: The Religion of Mainline Protestant Baby Boomers.* Louisville: Westminster/John Knox.

Hoge, Dean R., and David A. Roozen, eds. 1979. *Understanding Church Growth and Decline.* New York: Pilgrim Press.

Hoge, Dean R., Charles Zech, Patrick McNamara, and Michael J. Donahue. 1996. *Money Matters: Personal Giving in American Churches.* Louisville: Westminster/John Knox Press.

Holden, Andrew. 2002. *Jehovah's Witnesses: Portrait of a Contemporary Religious Movement.* London: Routledge.

Holifield, E. Brooks. 1994. "Toward a History of American Congregations." In *American Congregations: New Perspectives in the Study of Congregations*, edited by James P. Wind and James W. Lewis, 23–53. Chicago: University of Chicago Press.

Hoyle, Lydia Huffman. 2002. "Queens in the Kingdom: Southern Baptist Mission Education for Girls, 1953–1970." In *Gospel Bearers, Gender Barriers: Missionary Women in the Twentieth Century*, edited by Dana L. Robert, 101–12. Maryknoll, N.Y.: Orbis Books.

Hudnut-Beumler, James. 1994. *Looking for God in the Suburbs*. New Brunswick, N.Y.: Rutgers University Press.

Hughes, Richard T., and R. L. Roberts. 2001. *The Churches of Christ*. Edited by Henry Warner Bowden. Vol. 10, *Denominations in America*. Westport, Conn.: Greenwood Press.

Hunter, James Davison. 1983. *American Evangelicalism: Conservative Religion and the Quandary of Modernity*. New Brunswick, N.J.: Rutgers University Press.

Hutchison, William R. 1987. *Errand to the World: American Protestant Thought and Foreign Missions*. Chicago: University of Chicago Press.

Iannaccone, Laurence R. 1990. "Religious Practice: A Human Capital Approach." *Journal for the Scientific Study of Religion* 29, no. 3: 297–314.

———. 1991. "The Consequences of Religious Market Structure: Adam Smith and the Economics of Religion." *Rationality and Society* 3, no. 2: 156–77.

———. 1994. "Why Strict Churches Are Strong." *American Journal of Sociology* 99, no. 5: 1180–1211.

Internet Ministries. 2001. *The Church of Christ Welcomes You*. http://www.church-of-christ.org (accessed March 20, 2001).

Jeavons, Thomas H. 1998. "Identifying Characteristics of 'Religious' Organizations: An Exploratory Proposal." In *Sacred Companies: Organizational Aspects of Religion and Religious Aspects of Organizations*, edited by N. J. Demerath III et al., 79–96. New York: Oxford University Press.

Jelen, Ted, ed. 2002. *Sacred Markets, Sacred Canopies: Essays on Religious Markets and Religious Pluralism*. New York: Rowman and Littlefield.

Jesus Day/March for Jesus USA. 2002. *What Is Jesus Day?* http://www.mfj.org/page2.shtml (accessed December 16, 2002).

Johnson, Benton. 1963. "On Church and Sect." *American Sociological Review* 29: 539–49.

Jorgensen, Danny L. 1989. *Participant Observation: A Methodology for Human Studies*. Vol. 15, *Applied Social Research Methods Series*. Newbury Park, Calif.: Sage Publications.

Kalmijn, Matthijs. 1991. "Shifting Boundaries: Trends in Religious and Educational Homogamy." *American Sociological Review* 56: 786–800.

Kanter, Rosabeth Moss. 1977. *Men and Women of the Corporation*. New York: Basic Books.

Keillor, Garrison. 1999. *I'm a Lutheran*. Prairie Home Companion Performance Archive, October 2. http://phc.mpr.org/programs/19991002/lutheran.htm.

Kennedy, Paul. 2002. "The Power of Religious Experience through Music and Miracles in the Lives of Exemplars of Christian Virtue." Paper presented at the Society for the Scientific Study of Religion, Salt Lake City, November 1.

Kim, Ai Ra. 1996. *Women Struggling for a New Life: The Role of Religion in the Cultural Passage from Korea to America*. Albany: State University of New York Press.

Klay, Robin, John Lunn, and Michael S. Hamilton. 2000. "American Evangelicalism and the National Economy, 1870–1997." In *More Money, More Ministry: Money and Evangelicals in Recent North American History*, edited by Larry Eskridge and Mark Noll, 15–38. Grand Rapids: Eerdmans.

Knight, George R. 1984. "Seventh-Day Adventist Education: A Historical Sketch and Profile." In *Religious Schooling in America*, edited by James C. Carper and Thomas C. Hunt, 85–109. Birmingham: Religious Education Press.

Kosmin, Barry A. 2000. "Coming of Age in the Conservative Synagogue: The Bar/Bat Mitzvah Class of 5755." In *Jews in the Center: Conservative Synagogues and Their Members*, edited by Jack Wertheimer, 232–68. New Brunswick, N.J.: Rutgers University Press.

Kosmin, Barry A., and Seymour P. Lachman. 1993. *One Nation under God: Religion in Contemporary American Society*. New York: Harmony.

Krindatch, Alexei D. 2001. *Research on Orthodox Religious Groups in the United States*. Hartford Institute for Religion Research. http://hirr.hartsem.edu/research/research_orthodoxsummary.html (accessed October 22, 2002).

Kurien, Prema. 1998. "Becoming American by Becoming Hindu: Indian Americans Take Their Place at the Multicultural Table." In *Gatherings in Diaspora*, edited by R. Stephen Warner and Judith G. Wittner, 37–70. Philadelphia: Temple University Press.

Kwon, Ho-Youn, Kwang Chung Kim, and R. Stephen Warner, eds. 2001. *Korean Americans and Their Religions: Pilgrims and Missionaries from a Different Shore*. University Park, Penn.: Pennsylvania State University Press.

Lazerwitz, Bernard, J. Alan Winter, Arnold Dashefsky, and Ephraim Tabory. 1998. *Jewish Choices: American Jewish Denominationalism*. Albany: State University of New York Press.

Levine, Daniel H. 1992. *Popular Voices in Latin American Catholicism*. Princeton: Princeton University Press.

Lichterman, Paul. 2004. *Elusive Togetherness: Religion in the Quest for Civic Renewal*. Princeton: Princeton University Press.

Liebman, Robert C., John R. Sutton, and Robert Wuthnow. 1988. "Exploring the Social Sources of Denominationalism: Schisms in American Denominations, 1890–1980." *American Sociological Review* 53: 343–52.

Lincoln, C. Eric, and Lawrence H. Mamiya. 1990. *The Black Church in the African American Experience*. Durham: Duke University Press.

Lindenberg, Marc, and Coralie Bryant. 2001. *Going Global: Transforming Relief and Development NGOs*. Bloomfield, Conn.: Kumarian Press.

Lischer, Richard. 2001. *Open Secrets: A Spiritual Journey through a Country Church*. New York: Doubleday.

Livezey, Lowell W. 2000. *Public Religion and Urban Transformation: Faith in the City*. New York: New York University Press.

Lofland, John, and Lyn H. Lofland. 1984. *Analyzing Social Settings: A Guide to Qualitative Observation and Analysis*. Belmont, Calif.: Wadsworth.

Loveland, Anne C., and Otis B. Wheeler. 2003. *From Meetinghouse to Megachurch: A Material and Cultural History*. Columbia: University of Missouri Press.

Luckmann, Thomas. 1967. *The Invisible Religion*. New York: Macmillan.

Lueking, F. Dean. 1995. "Parochial Education: For the Sake of the Children." *Word and World* 15: 99–101.

Luidens, Donald A., and Roger J. Nemeth. 1999. "Refining the Center: Two Kinds of Reformed Church Loyalists." In *Re-forming the Center: American Protestantism 1960 to the Present*, edited by Douglas Jacobsen and William Vance Trollinger Jr., 252–70. Grand Rapids: Eerdmans.

Lummis, Adair. 2001. *The Art and Science of Subtle Proactivity: Regional Leaders and Their Congregations*. Hartford Institute for Religion Research. http://hirr.hartsem.edu/org/faith_judicatories_Lummis2.html (accessed November 24, 2002).

Lutheran Church–Missouri Synod. 2002. *School Ministry Information: Statistical Summary for 2001*. http://dcs.lcms.org/?s = school (accessed November 27, 2002).

MacIntyre, Alasdair. 1984. *After Virtue: A Study in Moral Theory*. Notre Dame, Indiana: University of Notre Dame Press.

Mann, Gurinder Singh, Paul David Numrich, and Raymond B. Williams. 2001. *Buddhists Hindus and Sikhs in America*. New York: Oxford University Press.

Markham, Ian S. 1999. *Plurality and Christian Ethics*. Rev. ed. New York: Seven Bridges Press.

Markham, Ian, and Ibrahim Abu Rabi, eds. 2002. *September 11: Religious Perspectives on the Causes and Consequences.* London: Oneworld Publications.

Marler, Penny Long. 1995. "Lost in the Fifties: The Changing Family and the Nostalgic Church." In *Work, Family, and Religion in Contemporary Society,* edited by Nancy Tatom Ammerman and Wade Clark Roof, 23–60. New York: Routledge.

Marler, Penny Long, and C. Kirk Hadaway. 2002. "'Being Religious' or 'Being Spiritual' in America: A Zero-Sum Proposition?" *Journal for the Scientific Study of Religion* 41, no. 2: 289–300.

Marler, Penny Long, and David A. Roozen. 1993. "From Church Tradition to Consumer Choice: The Gallup Surveys of the Unchurched American." In *Church and Denominational Growth,* edited by David A. Roozen and C. Kirk Hadaway, 253–77. Nashville: Abingdon.

Marsden, George M. 1980. *Fundamentalism and American Culture.* New York: Oxford University Press.

Martin, David. 1962. "The Denomination." *British Journal of Sociology* 13: 1–14.

————. 2002. *Pentecostalism: The World Their Parish.* Malden, Mass.: Blackwell Publishers.

Martin, Sandy Dwayne. 1982. "Black Baptists, Foreign Missions, and African Colonization, 1814–1882." In *Black Americans and the Missionary Movement in Africa,* edited by Sylvia M. Jacobs, 63–76. Westport, Conn.: Greenwood.

Marty, Martin E., Azizah Y. al-Hibri, Jean Bethke Elshtain, and Charles Haynes. 2000. "Matters of Faith: Religion in American Public Life." New York: American Assembly, Columbia University.

Massing, Michael. 2004. "Bishop Lee's Choice." *New York Times,* January 4.

Material History of American Religion Project. 2001. Vanderbilt University Divinity School. http://www.materialreligion.org/index.html (accessed November 22, 2002).

Mathews, Donald G. 1969. "The Second Great Awakening as an Organizing Process, 1780–1830." *American Quarterly* 21: 23–43.

Mauss, Armand L. 1994. *The Angel and the Beehive: The Mormon Struggle with Assimilation.* Chicago: University of Illinois Press.

Maxwell, John C. 1998. *The 21 Irrefutable Laws of Leadership:* Nashville: Thomas Nelson.

May, Dean L. 1990. "The Philanthropy Dilemma: The Mormon Church Experience." In *Faith and Philanthropy in America: Exploring the Role of Religion in America's Voluntary Sector,* edited by Robert Wuthnow and Virginia Hodgkinson, 211–31. San Francisco: Jossey-Bass.

McBeth, Leon. 1987. *The Baptist Heritage*. Nashville: Broadman Press.

McDannell, Colleen. 1995. *Material Christianity*. New Haven: Yale University Press.

McGreevy, John T. 1996. *Parish Boundaries: The Catholic Encounter with Race in the Twentieth-Century Urban North*. Chicago: University of Chicago Press.

McKinney, William. 1998. "Resources." In *Studying Congregations: A New Handbook*, edited by Nancy T. Ammerman, Jackson W. Carroll, Carl S. Dudley, and William McKinney, 132–166. Nashville: Abingdon.

McMullen, Michael. 1994. "Religious Polities as Institutions." *Social Forces* 73, no. 2: 709–28.

———. 2000. *The Baha'i: The Religious Construction of a Global Identity*. New Brunswick, N.J.: Rutgers University Press.

McNamara, Patrick H. 1992. *Conscience First, Tradition Second: A Study of Young American Catholics*. Albany: State University of New York Press.

McPherson, J. Miller, and Thomas Rotolo. 1995. "Measuring the Composition of Voluntary Groups: A Multitrait-Multimethod Analysis." *Social Forces* 73, no. 3: 1097–1115.

McRoberts, Omar Maurice. 2003. *Streets of Glory: Church and Community in a Black Urban Neighborhood*. Chicago: University of Chicago Press.

McVeigh, Rory, and David Sikkink. 2001. "God, Politics, and Protest: Religious Beliefs and the Legitimation of Contentious Tactics." *Social Forces* 79, no. 4: 1425–58.

Mead, Loren. 1991. *The Once and Future Church: Reinventing the Congregation for a New Mission Frontier*. Bethesda, Md.: Alban Institute.

———. 1998. *Financial Meltdown in the Mainline Churches*. Bethesda, Md.: Alban Institute.

Mead, Sidney E. 1963. *The Lively Experiment*. New York: Harper & Row.

Melwani, Lavina. 2000. *Hey, Just Who Are You Guys Anyway?* Himalayan Academy. http://www.hinduismtoday.com/History/about_us.html (accessed December 20, 2002).

Miller, Donald E. 1997. *Reinventing American Protestantism*. Berkeley: University of California Press.

Milofsky, Carl, and Albert Hunter. 1995. "Where Nonprofits Come From: A Theory of Organizational Emergence." Paper presented at the Southern Sociological Society, Atlanta, April.

Monahan, Susanne C. 1999. "Who Controls Church Work? Organizational Effects on Jurisdictional Boundaries and Disputes in Churches." *Journal for the Scientific Study of Religion* 38, no. 3: 370–85.

Monsma, Stephen V. 1996. *When Sacred & Secular Mix: Religious Nonprofit Organizations and Public Money.* Lanham, Md.: Rowman & Littlefield.

Moon, Dawne. 2004. *God, Sex, and Politics: Homosexuality and Everyday Theologies.* Chicago: University of Chicago Press.

Moore, R. Laurence. 1986. *Religious Outsiders and the Making of Americans.* New York: Oxford University Press.

Morris, Aldon D. 1984. *The Origins of the Civil Rights Movement: Black Communities Organizing for Change.* New York: Free Press.

Morris, Aldon D., and Shayne Lee. Forthcoming. "The National Baptist Convention: Traditions and Contemporary Challenges." In *Adaptive Change in National Denominational Structures: Practiced Theology,* edited by David Roozen and James Nieman. Grand Rapids: Eerdmans.

Munson, Ziad. Forthcoming. "Fighting for the Sanctity of Life: Juggling God, Democracy, and Abortion in the American Pro-life Movement." In *Taking Faith Seriously,* edited by Mary Jo Bane, Brent Coffin, and Richard Higgins. Cambridge, Mass.: Harvard University Press.

Nason-Clark, Nancy. 1997. *The Battered Wife: How Christians Confront Family Violence.* Louisville: Westminster/John Knox.

———. 2000. "A Marriage of Convenience: The Sacred, the Secular and the State." Paper presented to the Society for the Scientific Study of Religion, Houston.

National Council of Churches, Office of Research, Evaluation and Planning. 1998. *Yearbook of American and Canadian Churches.* Nashville: Abingdon Press.

Nelson, Timothy J. 1996. "Sacrifice of Praise: Emotion and Collective Participation in an African-American Worship Service." *Sociology of Religion* 57, no. 4: 379–96.

Niebuhr, H. Richard. 1929. *The Social Sources of Denominationalism.* New York: World Publishing.

Noll, Mark. 1998. "The Bible, Minority Faiths, and the American Protestant Mainstream, 1860–1925." In *Minority Faiths and the American Protestant Mainstream,* edited by Jonathan D. Sarna, 191–231. Urbana: University of Illinois Press.

———. 2002. "The American Contribution to World-Wide Evangelical Christianity in the Twentieth Century." Paper presented at the International Conference on Evangelical Protestantism, Groupe de Sociologie des Religions et de la Laïcité, Paris.

North American Division of Seventh-Day Adventists, Office of Education. 1998. *News and General Statistics.* http://nadeducation.adventist.org (accessed November 26, 2002).

Numrich, Paul David. 1995. *Old Wisdom in the New World: Americanization in Immigrant Theravada Buddhist Temples.* Knoxville: University of Tennessee Press.

Orr, John B., Donald E. Miller, Wade Clark Roof, and J. Gordon Melton. 1994. *Politics of the Spirit: Religion and Multiethnicity in Los Angeles.* Los Angeles: University of Southern California.

Orsi, Robert A. 1996. *Thank You, St. Jude.* New Haven: Yale University Press.

Ostling, Richard N., and Joan K. Ostling. 1999. *Mormon America: The Power and the Promise.* New York: HarperCollins.

Papaioannou, George. 1994. "The History of the Greek Orthodox Cathedral of the Annunciation." In *American Congregations: Portraits of Twelve Religious Communities,* edited by James P. Wind and James W. Lewis, 520–71. Chicago: University of Chicago Press.

Paris, Peter. 1985. *The Social Teachings of the Black Churches.* Philadelphia: Fortress Press.

Pattillo-McCoy, Mary. 1998. "Church Culture as a Strategy of Action in the Black Community." *American Sociological Review* 63: 767–84.

Paulson, Michael. 2003a. *Church Refuses Group's Money.* http://www.boston.com/globe/spotlight/abuse/stories4/040103_money.htm (accessed May 22, 2003).

———. 2003b. "One Year Later, Voice of the Faithful Faces New Tests." *Boston Sunday Globe,* April 13, A1, A22.

Penton, M. James. 1997. *Apocalypse Delayed: The Story of Jehovah's Witnesses.* 2nd ed. Toronto: University of Toronto Press.

Peshkin, Alan. 1986. *God's Choice: The Total World of a Fundamentalist Christian School.* Chicago: University of Chicago Press.

Pestana, Carla Gardina. 1991. *Quakers and Baptists in Colonial Massachusetts.* New York: Cambridge University Press.

Pipes, Paula F., and Helen Rose Ebaugh. 2002. "Faith-Based Coalitions, Social Services, and Government Funding." *Sociology of Religion* 63, no. 1: 49–68.

Poloma, Margaret M. Forthcoming. "Charisma and Structure in the Assemblies of God: Revisiting O'Dea's Five Dilemmas." In *Adaptive Change in National Denominational Structures: Practiced Theology,* edited by David Roozen and James Nieman. Grand Rapids: Eerdmans.

Poloma, Margaret M., and Lynette F. Hoelter. 1998. "The 'Toronto Blessing': A Holistic Model of Healing." *Journal for the Scientific Study of Religion* 37, no. 2: 257–72.

Popular Front Interactive Communications. 2002. *Way to Live: Christian Practices for Teens.* http://www.waytolive.org (accessed November 22, 2002).

Powell, Walter W., and Paul J. DiMaggio, eds. 1991. *The New Institutionalism in Organizational Analysis.* Chicago: University of Chicago Press.

Prell, Riv Ellen. 2000. "Communities of Choice and Memory: Conservative Synagogues in the Late Twentieth Century." In *Jews in the Center: Conservative Synagogues and Their Members,* edited by Jack Wertheimer, 269–358. New Brunswick, N.J.: Rutgers University Press.

Primer, Ben. 1978. *Protestants and American Business Methods.* Ann Arbor: UMI Research Press.

Purpose Driven. 2002. *PD Community.* http://www.purposedriven.com/community/ (accessed June 13, 2002).

Putnam, Robert D. 2000. *Bowling Alone: The Collapse and Revival of American Community.* New York: Simon & Schuster.

Raboteau, Albert J. 2001. *Canaan Land: A Religious History of African Americans.* New York: Oxford University Press.

Religion News Service. 2003. "Lutheran Services Tops Largest Nonprofits List." *Christian Century* 120, no. 2: 15.

Richey, Russell E. 1994. "Denominations and Denominationalism: An American Morphology." In *Re-imagining Denominationalism,* edited by R. Bruce Mullin and Russell E. Richey, 74–98. New York: Oxford University Press.

Ritterband, Paul. 2000. "Public Worship: The Partnership between Families and Synagogues." In *Jews in the Center: Conservative Synagogues and Their Members,* edited by Jack Wertheimer, 199–231. New Brunswick, N.J.: Rutgers University Press.

Robert, Dana L. 1997. *Women in Mission: A Social History of Their Thought and Practice.* Macon, Georgia: Mercer University Press.

———. 2002. "The Influence of American Missionary Women on the World Back Home." *Religion and American Culture* 12, no. 1: 59–89.

Roof, Wade Clark. 1993. *A Generation of Seekers.* San Francisco: Harper San Francisco.

———. 1999. *Spiritual Marketplace: Baby Boomers and the Remaking of American Religion.* Princeton: Princeton University Press.

Roof, Wade Clark, and Lyn Gesch. 1995. "Boomers and the Culture of Choice." In *Work, Family, and Religion in Contemporary Society,* edited by Nancy T. Ammerman and Wade Clark Roof, 61–80. New York: Routledge.

Roof, Wade Clark, and William McKinney. 1987. *American Mainline Religion.* New Brunswick, N.J.: Rutgers University Press.

Roozen, David A., Jackson W. Carroll, and Wade Clark Roof. 1995. "Fifty Years of Religious Change in the United States." In *The Post-war Generation and Establishment Religion,* edited by Wade Clark Roof, Jackson W. Carroll, and David A. Roozen, 59–85. Boulder: Westview.

Roozen, David A., and C. Kirk Hadaway, eds. 1993. *Church and Denominational Growth.* Nashville: Abingdon.

Rose, Susan D. 1988. *Keeping Them Out of the Hands of Satan: Evangelical Schooling in America.* New York: Routledge.

Ross, Bobby. 2003. "Pageants a Big Hit in Megachurches." *Boston Globe,* December 22, A3.

Routhage, Arlin J. n.d. *Sizing up a Congregation for New Member Ministry.* New York: Episcopal Church Center.

Ryan, Mary. 1979. "The Power of Women's Networks: A Case Study of Female Moral Reform in Antebellum America." *Feminist Studies* 5: 66–86.

Sack, Daniel. 2000. *Whitebread Protestants: Food and Religion in American Culture.* New York: St. Martin's Press.

Salamon, Lester M. 1995. *Partners in Public Service: Government-Nonprofit Relations in the Modern Welfare State.* Baltimore: Johns Hopkins University Press.

Sample, Tex. 1990. *U.S. Lifestyles and Mainline Churches.* Louisville: Westminster/ John Knox.

Sanders, Cheryl. 1996. *Saints in Exile: The Holiness-Pentecostal Experience in African American Religion and Culture.* New York: Oxford.

Sarna, Jonathan D., and Karla Goldman. 1994. "From Synagogue-Community to Citadel of Reform: The History of K.K. Bene Israel (Rockdale Temple) in Cincinnati, Ohio." In *American Congregations: Portraits of Twelve Religious Communities,* edited by James P. Wind and James W. Lewis, 159–220. Chicago: University of Chicago Press.

Sassen, Saskia. 1996. *Losing Control? Sovereignty in an Age of Globalization.* New York: Columbia University Press.

Schmidt, Stephen A. 1979. "American Education: A Lutheran Footnote." In *The Lutheran Church in North American Life,* edited by John E. Groh and Robert H. Smith, 168–93. St. Louis: Clayton Publishing.

Scott, Ann Firor. 1993. *Natural Allies: Women's Associations in American History.* Urbana: University of Illinois Press.

Sherkat, Darren. 2001. "Tracking the Restructuring of American Religion." *Social Forces* 79, no. 4: 1459–93.

Sherkat, Darren, and John Wilson. 1995. "Preferences, Constraints, and Choices in Religious Markets: An Examination of Religious Switching and Apostasy." *Social Forces* 73, no. 3: 993–1026.

Sherman, Amy. 2000. "Churches as Government Partners: Navigating 'Charitable Choice.'" *Christian Century* 117, no. 20: 716–21.

Shibley, Mark. 1991. "The Southernization of American Religion." *Sociological Analysis* 52, no. 2: 159–74.

Shipps, Jan. 1985. *Mormonism: The Story of a New Religious Tradition*. Urbana: University of Illinois Press.

Sikkink, David. 1999. "'I Just Say I'm a Christian:' Symbolic Boundaries and Identity Formation among Church-Going Protestants." In *Re-forming the Center: American Protestantism 1960 to the Present*, edited by Douglas Jacobsen and William Vance Trollinger Jr., 49–71. Grand Rapids: Eerdmans.

Silverstein, Evan. 2002. *Survey Finds High Rate of Turnover in the Pews*. E-mail, PCUSANEWS. presbynews.topic@ecunet.org (accessed January 17, 2002).

Simmel, Georg. 1908 (1971). "Group Expansion and the Development of Individuality." In *Georg Simmel on Individuality and Social Forms*, edited by Donald N. Levine, 251–93. Chicago: University of Chicago Press.

Skocpol, Theda. 2000. "Religion, Civil Society, and Social Provision in the U.S." In *Who Will Provide? The Changing Role of Religion in American Social Welfare*, edited by Mary Jo Bane, Brent Coffin, and Ronald F. Thiemann, 21–50. Boulder: Westview Press.

Smith, Christian. 1998. *American Evangelicalism: Embattled and Thriving*. Chicago: University of Chicago Press.

———. 2000. *Christian America? What Evangelicals Really Want*. Berkeley: University of California Press.

Smith, Christian, Melinda Lundquist Denton, Robert Faris, and Mark D. Regnerus. 2002. "Mapping American Adolescent Religious Participation." *Journal for the Scientific Study of Religion* 41, no. 4: 597–612.

Smith, Christian, and Joshua Prokopy, eds. 1999. *Latin American Religion in Motion*. New York: Routledge.

Smith, Jane I. 1999. *Islam in America*. New York: Columbia University Press.

Sobel, Mechal. 1988. *Trabelin' On: The Slave Journey to an Afro-Baptist Faith*. Princeton: Princeton University Press.

Somers, Margaret R. 1993. "Citizenship and the Place of the Public Sphere: Law, Community, and Political Culture in the Transition to Democracy." *American Sociological Review*: 587–620.

———. 1994. "The Narrative Constitution of Identity: A Relational and Network Approach." *Theory and Society* 23: 605–49.

Standing Conference of Canonical Orthodox Bishops of the Americas. 1994. *Statement on Church Mission and Evangelism*. Orthodox Research Institute. http://www.orthodoxresearchinstitute.org/encyclicals/scoba/scoba_mission_evangelism.htm (accessed December 16, 2002).

Stark, Rodney. 1987. "How New Religious Succeed." In *The Future of New Religions*, edited by David Bromley and Phillip Hammond, 11–29. Macon, Georgia: Mercer University Press.

———. 2001. *One True God: Historical Consequences of Monotheism*. Princeton: Princeton University Press.

Stark, Rodney, and Laurence R. Iannaccone. 1994. "A Supply-Side Reinterpretation of the 'Secularization' of Europe." *Journal for the Scientific Study of Religion* 33, no. 3: 230–52.

———. 1997. "Why the Jehovah's Witnesses Grow So Rapidly: A Theoretical Application." *Journal of Contemporary Religion* 12: 133–57.

Steinfels, Margaret O'Brien. 2002. "Rejecting the Bishops." *New York Times*, October 22, A31.

Sullins, D. Paul. 1993. "Switching Close to Home: Volatility or Coherence in Protestant Affiliation Patterns?" *Social Forces* 72, no. 2: 399–419.

Swatos, William H., Jr. Forthcoming. "A Primacy of Systems: Confederation, Corporation, and Communion." In *Adaptive Change in National Denominational Structures: Practiced Theology*, edited by David Roozen and James Nieman. Grand Rapids: Eerdmans.

Swidler, Ann. 1986. "Culture in Action: Symbols and Strategies." *American Sociological Review* 51: 273–86.

Takayama, K. Peter, and L. W. Cannon. 1979. "Formal Polity and Power Distribution in American Protestant Denominations." *Sociological Quarterly* 20: 321–32.

Thiemann, Ronald F. Forthcoming. "What's Faith Got to Do with It? Lutheran Social Ministry in Transition." In *Taking Faith Seriously*, edited by Mary Jo Bane, Brent Coffin, and Richard Higgins. Cambridge, Mass.: Harvard University Press.

Thornton, Patricia H., and William Ocasio. 1999. "Institutional Logics and the Historical Contingency of Power in Organizations: Executive Succession in the Higher Education Publishing Industry, 1958–1990." *American Journal of Sociology* 105, no. 3: 801–43.

Thumma, Scott. 1999. *What God Makes Free Is Free Indeed: Nondenominational Church Identity and Its Networks of Support*. http://www.hirr.hartsem.edu/bookshelf/thumma_article5.html (accessed January 4, 2002).

———. 2000. *Exploring the Megachurch Phenomena: Their Characteristics and Cultural Context*. hirr.hartsem.edu/bookshelf/thumma_article2 (December 19, 2000).

———. 2002a. *After 9–11: The Ecumenical and Interfaith Fallout*. Faith Communities Today/Hartford Institute for Religion Research. http://fact.hartsem.edu/topfindings/topicalfindings_article7.htm (accessed November 25, 2002).

———. 2002b. *Religion and the Internet*. Hartford Institute for Religion Research. http://hirr.hartsem.edu/bookshelf/thumma_article6.html (accessed November 20, 2002).

Tocqueville, Alexis de. 1835 [2000]. *Democracy in America*. Translated by George Lawrence. New York: Harper Perennial.

Tönnies, Ferdinand. 1887 [2001]. *Community and Civil Society (Gemeinschaft und Gesellschaft)*. Translated by Jose Harris and Margaret Hollis. New York: Cambridge University Press.

Treat, James, ed. 1996. *Native and Christian : Indigenous Voices on Religious Identity in the United States and Canada*. New York: Routledge.

Troeltsch, Ernst. 1931. *The Social Teaching of the Christian Churches*. London: George Allen.

Tsitsos, William. 2003. "Race Differences in Congregational Social Service Activity." *Journal for the Scientific Study of Religion* 42, no. 2: 205–15.

United States Census Bureau. 2002. *State and County QuickFacts*. Updated September 24. http://quickfacts.census.gov (accessed December 14, 2002).

Unruh, Heidi Rolland. 2002. *Perceptions of Religious Meaning in Faith-Based Social Services*. www.hirr.hartsem.edu/research (accessed January 23, 2002).

Urban Ministries, Inc. 2002. *Urban Ministries: The African American Christian Publishing & Communications Co*. http://www.urbanministries.com/umihistory.cfm (accessed May 22, 2002).

Van Veen, Dan. 2001. *"How Can I Help?" Christ in Action Ministry Explains What Is Needed*. Assemblies of God News Service, September 21. http://ag.org/top/news (accessed November 26, 2001).

Verba, Sidney, Kay Lehman Schlozman, and Henry E. Brady. 1995. *Voice and Equality: Civic Voluntarism in American Politics*. Cambridge, Mass.: Harvard University Press.

"Vision of a Movement." 1998. *WCA News*, January/February, 1–6.

Voas, David, Daniel V. A. Olson, and Alasdair Crockett. 2002. "Religious Pluralism and Participation: Why Previous Research Is Wrong." *American Sociological Review* 67, no. 2: 212–30.

Wacker, Grant. 2001. *Heaven Below: Early Pentecostals and American Culture*. Cambridge, Mass.: Harvard University Press.

Wagner, Melinda Bollar. 1997. "Generic Conservative Christianity: The Demise of Denominationalism in Christian Schools." *Journal for the Scientific Study of Religion* 36, no. 1: 13–24.

Wah, Carolyn R. 2001. "An Introduction to Research and Analysis of Jehovah's Witnesses: A View from the Watchtower." *Review of Religious Research* 43, no. 2: 161–74.

Walls, Andrew F. 1996. *The Missionary Movement in Christian History: Studies in the Transmission of Faith*. Maryknoll, N.Y.: Orbis Books.

Warner, R. Stephen. 1988. *New Wine in Old Wineskins*. Berkeley: University of California Press.

———. 1990. "Mirror for American Protestantism: Mendocino Presbyterian Church in the Sixties and Seventies." In *The Mainstream Protestant "Decline": The Presbyterian Pattern*, edited by Milton J. Coalter, John M. Mulder, and Louis B. Weeks, 198–223. Louisville: Westminster/John Knox.

———. 1993. "Work in Progress toward a New Paradigm for the Sociological Study of Religion in the United States." *American Journal of Sociology* 98, no. 5: 1044–93.

———. 1994. "The Place of the Congregation in the Contemporary American Religious Configuration." In *American Congregations: New Perspectives in the Study of Congregations*, edited by James P. Wind and James W. Lewis, 54–99. Chicago: University of Chicago Press.

———. 1997. "Religion, Boundaries, and Bridges." *Sociology of Religion* 58, no. 3: 217–38.

———. 1998. "Approaching Religious Diversity: Barriers, Byways, and Beginnings." *Sociology of Religion* 59, no. 3: 193–215.

———. 1999. "Changes in the Civic Role of Religion." In *Diversity and Its Discontents: Cultural Conflict and Common Ground in Contemporary American Society*, edited by Neil J. Smelser and Jeffrey C. Alexander, 229–43. Princeton: Princeton University Press.

———. 2002a. "Growing Up Hindu in America: A Surprising Success Story." Chicago: Youth and Religion Project, University of Illinois at Chicago.

———. 2002b. "Two Young United Methodists Speak about Their Religion and Their Parents." Chicago: Youth and Religion Project, University of Illinois at Chicago.

Warner, R. Stephen, and Judith G. Wittner. 1998. *Gatherings in Diaspora: Religious Communities and the New Immigration*. Philadelphia: Temple University Press.

Warren, Mark R. 2001. *Dry Bones Rattling: Community Building to Revitalize American Democracy*. Princeton: Princeton University Press.

Washington, James Melvin. 1986. *Frustrated Fellowship: The Black Baptist Quest for Social Power*. Macon, Ga.: Mercer University Press.

Watchtower Bible and Tract Society of New York. 2002. *Statistics: 2001 Report of Jehovah's Witnesses Worldwide*. http://www.watchtower.org/statistics/worldwide_report.htm (accessed October 22, 2002).

Weber, Max. 1922 [1963]. *The Sociology of Religion*. Boston: Beacon.

———. 1946. "The Protestant Sects and the Spirit of Capitalism." In *From Max Weber*, edited by H. H. Gerth and C. Wright Mills, 302–22. New York: Oxford University Press.

Weeks, Louis B. 1992. "The Incorporation of the Presbyterians." In *The Organizational Revolution: Presbyterians and American Denominationalism*, edited by Milton J. Coalter, John M. Mulder, and Louis B. Weeks, 37–54. Louisville: Westminster/John Knox.

Wellman, James K., Jr. 1999a. "The Debate over Homosexual Ordination: Subcultural Identity Theory in American Religious Organizations." *Review of Religious Research* 41: 184–206.

———. 1999b. *The Gold Coast Church and the Ghetto: Christ and Culture in Mainline Protestantism*. Urbana: University of Illinois Press.

Welter, Barbara. 1976. "She Hath Done What She Could: Protestant Women's Missionary Careers in Nineteenth-Century America." In *Women in American Religion*, edited by Janet Wilson James, 111–26. Philadelphia: University of Pennsylvania Press.

Wertheimer, Jack. 1993. *A People Divided: Judaism in Contemporary America*. New York: Basic Books.

Westermeyer, Paul. 1993. "Twentieth-Century American Hymnody and Church Music." In *New Dimensions in American Religious History*, edited by Jay P. Dolan and James P. Wind, 175–208. Grand Rapids: Eerdmans.

Weston, William J. 1997. *Presbyterian Pluralism: Competition in a Protestant House*. Knoxville: University of Tennessee Press.

Wilcox, W. Bradford. 2002. "For the Sake of the Children? Mainline Protestant Family-Related Discourse and Practice." In *Quietly Influential: The Public Role of Mainline Protestantism*, edited by Robert Wuthnow and John Evans, 287–316. Berkeley: University of California Press.

Wilken, Paul H. 1971. "Size of Organizations and Member Participation in Church Congregations." *Administrative Science Quarterly* 16: 173–79.

Wilkes, Paul. 1994. *And They Shall Be My People: An American Rabbi and His Congregation*. New York: Atlantic Monthly Press.

Williams, Melvin D. 1974. *Community in a Black Pentecostal Church*. Pittsburgh: University of Pittsburgh Press.

Williams, Peter W. 1990. *America's Religions: Traditions and Cultures*. Urbana: University of Illinois Press.

———. 1997. *Houses of God: Region, Religion, and Architecture in the United States*. Urbana: University of Illinois Press.

Williams, Raymond Brady. 1988. *Religions of Immigrants from India and Pakistan: New Threads in the American Tapestry*. Cambridge: Cambridge University Press.

———. 1994. "Swaminarayan Hindu Temple of Glen Ellyn, Illinois." In *American Congregations: Portraits of Twelve Religious Communities*, edited by James P. Wind and James W. Lewis, 612–62. Chicago: University of Chicago Press.

Williams, Rhys, ed. 2001. *Promise Keepers and the New Masculinity*. Lanham, Md.: Rowman & Littlefield.

Williams, Rhys. 2002. "The Second Generation: Americans Who Happen to Be Muslims." Chicago: Youth and Religion Project, University of Illinois at Chicago.

Willow Creek Association. 2002a. http://www.willowcreek.com/index.asp (accessed May 23, 2002).

Willow Creek Association. 2002b. http://www.willowcreek.org/chapter2/wca.asp (accessed June 13, 2002).

Winston, Diane. 1999. *Red Hot and Righteous: The Urban Religion of the Salvation Army*. Cambridge, Mass.: Harvard University Press.

Winter, Gibson. 1968. *Religious Identity: The Formal Organization and Informal Power Structure of the Major Faiths in the United States Today*. New York: Macmillan.

Winter, Miriam Therese, Adair Lummis, and Allison Stokes. 1994. *Defecting in Place: Women Claiming Responsibility for Their Own Spiritual Lives*. New York: Crossroad.

Wittberg, Patricia. 2000. "Declining Institutional Sponsorship and Religious Orders: A Study of Reverse Impacts." *Sociology of Religion* 61, no. 3: 315–24.

Wood, James R. 1970. "Authority and Controversial Policy: The Church and Civil Rights." *American Sociological Review* 35: 1057–69.

———. Forthcoming. "Leadership, Identity, and Mission in a Changing United Methodist Church." In *Adaptive Change in National Denominational Structures: Practiced Theology*, edited by David Roozen and James Nieman. Grand Rapids: Eerdmans.

Wood, Richard L. 1994. "Faith in Action: Religious Resources for Political Success in Three Congregations." *Sociology of Religion* 55: 397–417.

———. 1999. "Religious Culture and Political Action." *Sociological Theory* 17, no. 3: 307–32.

———. 2002. *Faith in Action: Religion, Race, and Democratic Organizing in America*. Chicago: University of Chicago Press.

Wood Lake Books and Logos Productions. 2002. *Join Hands: An Online Community of Faith*. http://www.joinhands.com/mainmenu_1.taf (accessed May 22, 2002).

Woolever, Cynthia, and Deborah Bruce. 2002. *Field Guide to U.S. Congregations: Who's Going Where and Why*. Louisville: Westminster/John Knox.

Wuthnow, Robert. 1988. *The Restructuring of American Religion*. Princeton: Princeton University Press.

———. 1991. *Acts of Compassion: Caring for Others and Helping Ourselves*. Princeton: Princeton University Press.

———. 1994a. *Producing the Sacred*. Urbana: University of Illinois Press.

———. 1994b. *Sharing the Journey.* New York: Free Press.

———. 1998a. *After Heaven: Spirituality in America since the 1950s.* Berkeley: University of California Press.

———. 1998b. *Loose Connections: Joining Together in America's Fragmented Communities.* Cambridge, Mass.: Harvard University Press.

———. 1999. "Mobilizing Civic Engagement: The Changing Impact of Religious Involvement." In *Civic Engagement in American Democracy,* edited by Theda Skocpol and Morris P. Fiorina, 331–63. Washington, D.C.: Brookings Institution Press.

———. 2001. *Creative Spirituality: The Way of the Artist.* Berkeley: University of California Press.

Wuthnow, Robert, and John H. Evans, eds. 2002. *The Quiet Hand of God: Faith-Based Activism and the Public Role of Mainline Protestantism.* Berkeley: University of California Press.

Yang, Fenggang. 1999. *Chinese Christians in America: Conversion, Assimilation, and Adhesive Identities.* University Park: Pennsylvania State University Press.

Yang, Fenggang, and Helen Rose Ebaugh. 2001. "Transformations in New Immigrant Religions and Their Global Implications." *American Sociological Review* 66, no. 2: 269–88.

Yohn, Susan M. 2000. "'Let the Christian Women Set the Example in Their Own Gifts': The 'Business' of Protestant Women's Organizations." In *More Money, More Ministry: Money and Evangelicals in Recent North American History,* edited by Larry Eskridge and Mark Noll, 180–206. Grand Rapids: Eerdmans.

Zald, Mayer N. 1970. *Organizational Change: The Political Economy of the YMCA.* Chicago: University of Chicago Press.

Zech, Charles E. 1997. "Determinants of the Mission Funding Crisis." In *Connectionalism: Ecclesiology, Mission, and Identity,* edited by Dennis Campbell and Russell Richey, 245–66. Nashville: Abingdon.

INDEX

activism, 124, 136–37, 151, 168–69, 185–86, 261

African American Protestants, 5–6, 30, 98–99, 112, 121–22, 126, 198–99, 221–22, 249, 264. *See also* black church tradition

age: of congregations, 98, 281; of members 97, 282. *See also* graying congregations

Alban Institute, 105

altar guilds, 40–41

American religious history, 4–12, 80–81, 158–59, 190–93, 254–55, 302n6

architecture, 96–97 .

arts, 65, 155, 172–73. *See also* music

authority, religious, 231–33. *See also* polity

Baha'i, 123, 129

belonging, 51–56, 265–70

benevolence (informal), 150, 177–78

black church tradition, 6, 39–41, 74, 98–99, 104, 119, 149, 153–54

book stores (religious), 91

bridging differences, 128–31, 137–38, 259–61

Buddhism, 26, 208–9. *See also* immigrant congregations; Other Religions

budget (size of), 102–4, 164, 202, 280–81, 298n7

buildings, use of, 163

bureaucracy (denominational), 140–41, 159, 211, 233–36, 283–85

camping, 86–87, 219, 221

Catholic parishes, 7–9, 30, 37, 42, 44, 48, 96, 100, 108, 118, 126–27, 138–39, 148, 151, 156, 170, 182–83, 194–97, 214, 222, 231–32, 247, 263, 269, 295n26

CCLI (Christian Copyright Licensing International), 76–77

Charitable Choice, 146, 181–82, 264

choice (of congregations), 33–34, 268, 291n12

choirs, 38–40

Christian Science: history, 11. *See also* Sectarian Religions

Churches of Christ, 236

339

Habitat for Humanity, 170–71
Hartford Institute for Religion Research,
    ix, 5, 19, 280
Hartford Seminary, 302n4
Heifer International, 171
Hinduism, 74, 208. *See also* immigrant
    congregations; Other Religions
history (American religion), 4–12, 80–81,
    158–59, 190–93, 254–55, 302n6
homosexuality, 62, 127–28, 151, 227–29
hymnals, 72–76

identity (denominational), 183, 209–16,
    243–47, 274–76
immigrant congregations, 42, 55–56,
    79–80, 100, 103, 109, 115, 207–8, 282
individualism, 1–2, 209, 253
interfaith ties, 111, 130–31
internet, 80, 108–9, 201
institutional isomorphism, 3, 36, 42,
    49–50, 57–58, 68, 115, 156–57, 162,
    207, 247, 257–58
Islam, 10, 97, 128, 207. *See also*
    immigrant congregations; Other
    Religions

Jakes, T. D., 107
Jehovah's Witnesses, 11–12, 49, 140, 194.
    See also Sectarian Religions
Judaism, 9, 31, 44, 48, 116–17, 208, 264

Keillor, Garrison, 274–75

Lake Wobegon, 274–75
Latter-day Saints (Mormons), 11, 53,
    139–40, 194, 293n7. *See also* Sectarian
    Religions
Lilly Endowment, ix
liturgical traditions, 26–27, 37, 71–72,
    244–45. *See also* worship
Lubavitchers, 123
Lutherans, 44–45, 274–75; Missouri
    Synod, 229–30

Mainline Protestants, 4–5, 38–39, 64–65,
    77, 85, 97, 105, 118, 122, 141, 164–65,
    170–74, 184–85, 193, 212–13, 227–29,
    238–42, 242–46, 251–52, 263, 269,
    272–74
management (of congregations), 93–102
Maxwell, John, 105–6
meals, 59, 123. *See also* fellowship
megachurches, 76, 106–7
men, 61, 203
Methodists (United Methodist Church),
    140, 229, 240, 288n9
methodology: interviews, 16–18, 24, 34,
    70–71, 163, 212, 280–81; partner
    organizations, 19; sample, 16, 279–80,
    295n25; survey of attenders, 18,
    213–14, 281
ministerial associations, 111–12, 177–78
misconduct: financial, 231; sexual,
    231–32, 289n18
mission trips, 143, 202
missionaries, 123–24, 143, 200–201; in
    black churches, 67
missions: history, 140, 190–99; support
    for, 139–44, 245–46
modernization, 238, 250, 287n2
Mormons (Latter-day Saints), 11, 53,
    139–40, 194, 293n7. *See also* Sectarian
    Religions
multiethnic congregations, 46, 56,
    129–30, 267, 280
music, 37, 72–78, 155, 172–73, 264
Muslims, 10, 97, 128, 207. *See also*
    immigrant congregations; Other
    Religions
mutual care (in congregations), 54–55,
    66–67, 264–65

narratives, 180–81, 242–47, 251–52,
    260–61, 268, 273–76
National Baptist Convention, 231
National Congregations Study, x, 17, 37,
    160, 279–80, 289n21, 290n34

Compositor:	International Typesetting and Composition
Text:	10.25/14 Fournier
Display:	Fournier
Printer and Binder:	Maple-Vail Manufacturing Group